CLIO'S CONSCIOUSNESS RAISED

the text of this book is printed
on 100% recycled paper

Clio's Consciousness Raised

New Perspectives on the History of Women

EDITED BY
Mary S. Hartman
AND
Lois Banner

HARPER COLOPHON BOOKS
Harper & Row, Publishers
New York, Hagerstown, San Francisco, London

First HARPER TORCHBOOK edition published 1974

LIBRARY OF CONGRESS CATALOG CARD NUMBER: 74–12001

STANDARD BOOK NUMBER: 06–090506–9

For further information contact Feminist Studies, Inc., 417 Riverside Drive, New York, New York 10025.

78 79 80 81 82 10 9 8 7 6 5

CONTENTS

PREFACE

Women's history is developing into a new research area at a particularly exciting time. It has been stimulated by two related but essentially independent developments: the maturation of social history and the appearance of a renewed women's movement. However, a lively debate is under way about the status of women's history.

Some social historians, perhaps jealous of the "property" of their discipline, have been reluctant to accord independent recognition to the history of women. Most feminists, on the other hand, have been eager to recognize it; but they have on occasion been guilty of either a simple-minded search for heroines or a narrow and uncritical use of the "male oppression model" in explaining women's roles. The best new work, however, shows the value of combining the methods and insights of social history with a heightened awareness of and concern about women. Clio is indeed having her consciousness raised.

The fourteen papers in this collection represent a sampling of recent research in the history of women. All were presented at a conference entitled "New Perspectives on the History of Women," sponsored by the Berkshire Conference of Women Historians, and held in March, 1973, at Douglass College, Rutgers University. Most of the papers are reprinted here from a recent special issue of *Feminist Studies* devoted to women's history. Although they range quite widely in the times, places, and subject matter covered, they relate to one another in ways that indicate the directions that the new research is taking.

First, each paper deals with a group of women who for the most part were not figures of outstanding public prominence or achievement, but who shared a set of common experiences. This approach reflects the general urge of social historians to explore the life experiences of ordinary people; but more specifically it reflects a special desire to demonstrate what most historians, despite the new social history, have ignored: that women have a past that is worth knowing.

Second, all the papers are concerned not to "extract" women from history but rather to place them within their social context. Success in this endeavor has until recently been limited to a few biographies and a handful of studies on reform movements and on working-class women, an outcome that is hardly surprising. The problems of entering into the lives of large numbers of women, most of whom left behind no records of their existence, are immense. Still, the challenges of finding sources and developing methodologies are being met in imaginative ways.

In recreating the social worlds of their subjects, the authors have consulted such sources as medical treatises, women's magazines, household manuals, novels, hymnals, court records and sermons, in addition to the more traditional materials such as diaries, census reports, parliamentary papers, and various institutional records. They have also made extensive use of recent findings in areas including demographic and family history, histories of diet and drink, studies of income patterns, and work on sexual attitudes and behavior. Many of the conclusions are still tentative, but all the papers bring us closer to real women coping—or failing to cope—with the problems of their lives.

A third quality that unites these essays is a curiosity about myths and received opinions concerning women's nature and roles. In some cases, authors have chosen to explore the effects of dominant myths as they influenced the behavior of women and men in different settings. For example, three of the essays deal with the ways in which assumptions about women's sexual nature were reflected in medical attitudes and practice in Victorian America. The study by Ann Wood describes various disturbing and primitive clinical treatments administered to women as unconscious expressions of male animosity. Wood argues that some doctors assumed the role of sadistic godlike avengers, a stance that revealed both their deep fear of women and their desire to punish them for what they suspected was a revolt against their "wifely duties" and the "natural" function of motherhood. Although agreeing with some of this analysis, Carroll Smith-Rosenberg concentrates more on the ambiguous situation of women at a time when rapid social changes were calling into question the functions of the nuclear family and sex role differentiation. She sees the doctor as the defender of women's role in the home, providing both biological and medical rationales for that role. Regina Morantz acknowledges that doctors were no doubt "products of their cultural milieu," and admits that they did uphold the wife-mother role, but she cautions against hasty recourse to male oppression models. Morantz stresses both the appalling laxness of nineteenth-century medical training and the fact that doctors' treatment of men was often as "sadistic" as their treatment of women.

In a related study, Linda Gordon traces the growth of the early feminist movement for "voluntary motherhood," whose proponents expressed openly the resentment over involuntary motherhood only intimated by many of the women treated by Wood's physicians. Gordon shows that despite their hostility to unwanted pregnancies and their championing of woman's rights over her body, early feminists nevertheless refused to accept contraception, which they regarded as "unnatural." Instead, they recommended temporary abstinence from sexual intercourse. Although they did endorse female sexuality in a limited way, they still refused to divorce sexual enjoyment from reproduction. Gordon argues that in large part it was the still-debated belief in a 'maternal instinct" that limited further development of birth-control ideas.

In her analysis of the entrance of women into the professions in modern France, Catharine Bodard Silver examines the sources of the special tenacity in that country to the notion that "women's place is in the home." Silver stresses the higher social esteem accorded to married in contrast to single women, and suggests that a greater reinforcement of their status in the home has made French women less likely to be attracted to feminist goals and movements. Indeed, she shows that despite the fact that there are currently impressive numbers of women in the professions in France, French professional women are deeply ambivalent about their careers. Most of them, as she indicates, are working in public service, the most conservative and least change-oriented sector of professional life, a situation that both reflects and reinforces their traditionalism.

The study by Elizabeth Fee shows how nineteenth-century anthropologists used their discipline in the defense of another cultural myth that they saw as threatened: male supremacy. Fee demonstrates how the anthropologists reinvigorated older patriarchal theory by creating an evolutionary success story, in which human progress was linked with the triumph of male superiority and patriarchal monogamy over "primitive" licentiousness and female independence. The so-called "degraded" women of the Victorian period were viewed, she argues, as the leftovers of a previous anthropological era; and the new domesticated angel was the product and achievement of masculine civilization, which had conquered brutish lust.

Other contributors have treated received opinions about women in a different manner, showing a healthy skepticism concerning some less myth-laden assumptions about women's historical roles. One of these is the generally accepted view that, with the rare exception of a few heads of state, women have infrequently exercised genuine direct power in societies. An examination of the roles of women in early medieval Europe by JoAnn McNamara and Suzanne Wemple demonstrates that, contrary to beliefs about ancient suppression of women and their restriction to wife-mother roles, some women in the tribal and feudal hierarchies in this period exercised considerable political authority.

Some other studies propose that assumptions about women's power have been wrongly confined to male norms and require drastic revision. Analyzing the situation of women in Victorian America, Daniel Smith challenges current notions of a dichotomy between the supposedly powerless, static role of woman-in-the-home, and that of the public woman who engages in activist movements for reform and liberation. He provides evidence that married women in the late Victorian period moved toward greater autonomy and improvement of their condition in the home in a development which can fairly be labeled "domestic feminism."

Barbara Welter's discussion of the "feminization of religion" in nineteenth-century America provides another argument for revising notions about women's power. Although she acknowledges that women may well have moved into a "power vacuum" in the traditional sense and that ministerial functions remained with men, she nonetheless shows that feminine influence became pervasive in organized religion, affecting all aspects of public worship. She suggests, moreover, that the experience which women gained from participation in religious organizations helped them to carve out identities and promoted a new feeling of social equality and self-confidence that prompted their involvement in other reform movements outside the church.

However, the limitations of the sorts of power that American women were gaining is suggested in the study by Dee Garrison of the feminization of librarianship in the United States in the last decades of the nineteenth century. Garrison shows that, in contrast to their limited entrance into all other professions except teaching, women made such rapid gains in librarianship that by 1910 they constituted more than seventy-five per cent of library workers. She argues that, in consequence, library work, much like church work, was soon conceived as a properly feminine domain, where women were encouraged to act out traditional domestic non-assertive roles, to the detriment of their personal development and professional status and to the detriment of library services in general.

Two of the most persistent received opinions about women are called into question in the essays by Patricia Branca and Judith and Daniel Walkowitz. Branca questions the pervasive image of middle-class Victorian women in England as essentially idle, pampered creatures leading self-indulgent parasitic lives, surrounded by servants. By investigating the economic realities of middle-class existence, she gives a radically different picture which suggests that the most typical women in this group led extremely demanding lives. They were required to fulfill a whole set of new roles in a rapidly changing society with which, as Uttrachi points out, they were both psychologically and educationally ill-equipped to deal.

In their study of prostitution in Victorian England the Walkowitzes challenge the view that women who became prostitutes formed a class—or indeed a caste—apart, who remained in their trade as long as age and health would permit. The Walkowitzes' research suggests that the majority of prostitutes were poor working women whose economic situations made prostitution an active "choice" for part-time or temporary employment, and that, contrary to accepted opinion, most did not remain prostitutes for more than a few years. By using court records and statistical data on the communities where prostitutes lived, this study breaks new ground in its historical reconstruction of the harsh social realities for poor young working women. It also shows that despite tremendous odds, some of these women who were labeled "common prostitutes" were capable of organizing resistance to the measures used against them, and that they did so with the sympathy and support of others in their communities.

Finally, two analyses by Laura Oren and Ruth Cowan question some apparently incontrovertible "received truths." In her study of the family economy of the poor in Victorian England, Oren disputes the plausible view that all individuals in a given family had the same standard of living. Following impoverished young women into marriage, she demonstrates that in fact, by tradition and choice, wives—and to a lesser extent children—received a disproportionately small share of the meager family income. As a consequence, they had poorer nutrition, poorer health care, less adequate clothing, and even fewer opportunities for entertainment than the men. Remarkably, this differential, which was known to Victorian observers, has been virtually ignored by such prominent social historians as Eric Hobsbawm and E. P. Thompson, who have done extensive work on the laboring poor.

Ruth Cowan takes on a more firmly established commonplace: the view that "labor-saving devices" freed women for more rewarding occupations. Aware that her study is still speculative, she collects some intriguing evidence to suggest that the "technological revolution," rather than liberating women, may actually have added to their work, albeit changing the nature of that work considerably. Cowan suggests that both inside and outside the home, technological advance operated in many ways to reinforce women's passive, service-oriented roles.

A final aspect of all of these essays is that they reflect current concerns about women and women's roles. Such a preoccupation is "presentist" in the best sense, since it involves a rigorous and empathetic effort to understand the historical roots of issues that especially touch women today. It is natural that many of the authors have turned to the nineteenth century, when so many changes affected sexual relationships and roles, to find perspectives on their contemporary concerns. Their achievement is impressive, and it points the way to much further study.

Focusing as it does on women in European and American societies, this collection provides new evidence and hypotheses that will aid in cross-cultural and comparative research on women. Moreover, by giving special attention to the less dramatic private and public roles of women, these articles offer useful "intra-cultural" comparisons with existing studies of the more familiar and publicized reformist and revolutionary movements. This discovery of typical or representative women in different groups will, it is hoped, not only dispel clichés and caricatures but also prompt re-evaluations of those women already singled out as "extraordinary." Indeed, the writing of biography stands to benefit greatly from the enriched understanding of the social context, which will provide more realistic criteria by which to define and interpret "exceptional" women.

More immediately, all the articles have the value of raising questions as provocative as their conclusions. The treatment of women by physicians, for example, prompts investigation of how women have fared at the hands of other male-dominated professions, such as the law. The discovery that feminist birth-control movements initially forbade the use of known contraceptive devices suggests further inquiry into the attitudes and material circumstances that conditioned women's receptivity to technological change. Evidence that some groups of women inside the home were staking out larger spheres of autonomy encourages further examination of how their new roles affected the nature and quality of familial relationships. The analyses of "feminization" in religion and librarianship suggest other inquiries into areas where willingly or by force women performed similar peculiar marriages of old and new roles. Exploration of the lives of three groups of women in Victorian society—working and middle-class wives, and prostitutes—raises the important question of whether women perhaps bore a disproportionate share of the burdens in the transition to industrial society. Finally, the possibility is worth pursuing that women are still being more hindered than helped by the technological wonders of industrialization.

Many other issues present themselves, but perhaps the most important question that most of these articles provoke concerns the effects on the lives of women of the changes broadly associated with modernization. There can as yet be no definitive verdict, but the record so far suggests that women in all groups of society were obliged initially to juggle new and more traditional functions, and that they normally did so in a position of disadvantage relative to that of the men in their social groups. More comparative work is needed, both within and between societies, on such topics as education, family structure, and patterns of employment and authority, as well as on more elusive qualities, such as relative happiness or discontent. While investigating the agents of change, we also need more study of the persistence of traditional attitudes and institutions that particularly touched women. It is worth knowing to what extent older habits and roles, as opposed to new ones, actually reinforced women's power. Certainly, the traditional identification of the woman as the special repository of religious values in the family, especially in Roman Catholic countries, gave her enhanced status. On the other hand, as working-class families increasingly adopted new middle-class values, including the prohibition of employment for married women, the power of wives was reduced in significant ways. If in the end the result of modernization has been greater personal autonomy for most groups of women, the story of this achievement is still imperfectly known. But hope is in order. Women's history is a field that is coming of age.

Mary S. Hartman
Douglass College, 1974

"THE FASHIONABLE DISEASES": WOMEN'S COMPLAINTS AND THEIR TREATMENT IN NINETEENTH-CENTURY AMERICA

Ann Douglas Wood

Historians of nineteenth-century American culture and society have become increasingly aware that many of the medical theories and practices of the period fall within their province rather than within that of the scientist. Furthermore, the consensus of historical opinion seems to be that nineteenth-century treatments of mental illness, "nervous" conditions, and sexual difficulties, although telling little about scientific advancement, are particularly sensitive indicators of cultural attitudes. Historians Huber and Meyer, for example, have considered the "mind cure" movement of the late nineteenth and early twentieth centuries not as incipient psychoanalysis, but as an expression of contemporary conflict-laden ideas of success and achievement. Rothman has based his recent study of development of the asylum in the Jacksonian period on the stated assumption that "the march of science cannot by itself explain the transformation in the American treatment of the insane." He proceeds to analyze the asylum and the methods it adopted as the result of the tensions and ideas of Jacksonian society.[1]

Such an approach is clearly dictated in the consideration of nineteenth-century diagnosis and treatment of American women's nervous and sexual diseases.[2] The historian reading through the health books and medical manuals of the day dealing with the topic is confronted at once with a combination of scientific imprecision and emotionally charged conviction which demands interpretation.

Books written in the period between 1840 and 1900 consistently, if questionably, assert that a large number, even the majority of middle-class American women,

This article is reprinted from *The Journal of Interdisciplinary History* 4, no. 1 (Summer 1973): 25-52, with the permission of the publisher.

were in some sense ill. Catharine Esther Beecher, daughter of the famous minister Lyman Beecher and a pioneer in women's education and hygiene, took as her chief concern in later life "the *health of women and children*" which, she wrote in 1866, had become "a matter of alarming interest" to all. In *Physiology and Calisthenics* she had already warned her readers that "there is a delicacy of constitution and an increase of disease, both among mature women and young girls, that is most alarming, and such as was never known in any former period." In *Letters to the People on Health and Happiness* she attempted to back up her apocalyptic rumblings with statistics. She had asked all of the numerous women she knew in cities and towns across the United States to make a list of the ten women each knew best, and rate their health as "perfectly healthy," "well," "delicate," "sick," "invalid," and so on. Her report, which covered hundreds of middle-class women, was as "alarming" as Beecher could have desired. Milwaukee, Wisconsin provides a typical example:

> Milwaukee, Wisc. Mrs. A. frequent sick headaches. Mrs. B. very feeble. Mrs. S. well, except chills. Mrs. L. poor health constantly. Mrs. D. subject to frequent headaches. Mrs. B. very poor health. Mrs. C. consumption. Mrs. A. pelvic displacements and weaknesses. Mrs. H. pelvic disorders and a cough. Mrs. B. always sick. Do not know one healthy woman in the place.[3]

The accuracy of Beecher's findings is clearly open to question. How representative of other American women were her friends? How bad did a headache have to be to qualify a woman for ill health? And what woman in 1855 wanted to admit to so crude a state as robust vitality? Heroines of the sentimental fiction so popular with the women in the middle ranks of society whose health concerned Beecher were more often than not bearing up under a burden of sickness that would have incapacitated any less noble being. Indeed, as commentators on American society at the time emphasized, ill health in women had become positively fashionable and was exploited by its victims and practitioners as an advertisement of genteel sensibility and an escape from the too pressing demands of bedroom and kitchen.[4]

If the reliability of Beecher's statistics is shaky, their significance, on which this essay will focus, is not. Although American women of the eighteenth century may have been more sickly than their supposedly frail nineteenth-century descendants, they did not talk of themselves as sick; they did not define themselves through sickness, and their society apparently minimized rather than maximized their ill health, whatever its actual extent. As Meyer has argued, "attention" to a problem in a given period is as telling to the cultural historian as its actual "incidence," which may be almost impossible to determine.[5] Beecher's statistics at least reveal that a sizable number of American women wanted or needed to consider themselves ill.

Equally important, the self-diagnosis of these women was confirmed, even encouraged, by their society. Literary observers of the American scene like Cooper and Hawthorne were appalled at the delicate health of American women.[6] The doctors who specialized in women's diseases were equally gloomy and a good deal more verbose on the subject. Alcott, a noted Boston physician and author of several books on women's health, had estimated that one half of American women suf-

2

fered from the "real disease" of nervousness. When Clarke of the Harvard Medical School published his controversial *Sex in Education*, he saw the ill health of middle- and upper-class American women as so pervasive that he pessimistically concluded they would soon be unable to reproduce at all. "It requires no prophet to foretell that the wives who are to be mothers in our republic must be drawn from trans-atlantic homes," he announced.[7]

Beecher not only emphasized that many American women in the middle and upper ranks of society were sick, but she also implied that they were ill precisely *because they were women*. Most of the ailments that she records—pelvic disorders, sick headaches, general nervousness—were regarded as symptoms of "female complaints," nervous disorders thought to be linked with the malfunctioning of the feminine sexual organs.

This is not to imply that men could not and did not display similar symptons, Napheys, for example, in 1878, noted peevishness, listlessness, pallor, and headaches in men and boys who practiced the "secret vice" of masturbation. Beard found men and women suffering from what he termed "American nervousness."[8] No doctor implied that signs of nervous disorder were apparent only in women in nineteenth-century America, and the historian should not overlook this evidence. The fact remains, nonetheless, that to some extent the *diagnosis*, and to a greater extent the *treatment* by doctors of these symptoms in women, was different from their interpretation of the same signs in men. This difference was inevitable, because medical analysis of a woman began and ended with consideration of an organ unique to her, namely her uterus. Here, supposedly, lay the cause and the cure of many of her physical ailments. As a result of this special focus, medical reactions to female nervous complaints are indicative of nineteenth-century American attitudes not only toward disease and sexuality in general but, more significantly, toward feminine sexual identity in particular.

Doctors in America throughout the nineteenth century directed their attention to the womb in a way that seems decidedly unscientific and even obsessive to a modern observer. Popular manuals on women's health neglected discussion of widespread and fatal diseases like breast cancer and consumption and concentrated on every type of menstrual and uterine disorder conceivable.[9] Hubbard, a professor from New Haven, addressing a medical society in 1870, explained that it seemed "as if the Almighty, in creating the female sex, *had take the uterus and built up a woman around it.*"[10] And the uterus, so essential to womankind, was apparently a highly perilous possession. Dewees, professor of midwifery at the University of Pennsylvania in the early part of the nineteenth century, stated in his standard work on the diseases of females that woman was subject to twice the sicknesses that affected man just because she has a womb. Her uterus exercises a "paramount power" over her physical and moral system, and its sway is "no less whimsical than potent." Furthermore, "she is constantly liable to irregularities in her menstrua, and menaced severely by their consequences."[11] It was these highly contagious irregularities in her womb's workings which were thought to produce the headaches, nervousness, and feebleness detailed by Beecher. Byford, professor of gynecology in the 1860s at The University of Chicago, was moved to exclaim in his monograph on the uterus, "It is almost a pity that a woman has a womb."

Rather complacently viewing the havoc that their natural biological disadvantages wreaked on women, these doctors detailed the symptoms of a typical case of (uterine-caused) nervous prostration. Its victims, like the women on whose health Beecher reported, according to Byford, would usually lose weight: They would frequently show a peevish irritability and suffer every kind of nervous disorder ranging from hysterical fits of crying and insomnia to constipation, indigestion, headaches, and backaches.[12] Since many of the practitioners of the first half of the nineteenth century traced all of these problems to disorders of the uterus, they consequently tried to cure them through what came to be called "local treatment," remedies specifically directed at the womb. This meant that not only the women suffering from *prolapsus uteri* as the result of childbearing or the lady with cancer of the uterus or any menstrual difficulty, but also the girl suffering from backache and an irritable disposition with no discernible problem in her uterus might well be subjected to local treatment in the period 1830-1860.

"Local treatment" could mean manual adjustment by a doctor of a slipped uterus, a problem all too current in an age of poor midwifery, and the insertion of various pessaries for its support. It was more frequently used to designate a course of local medication for everything from cancer to cantankerousness. This treatment had four stages, although not every case went through all four: a manual investigation, "leeching," "injections," and "cauterization." Dewees and Bennet, a famous English gynecologist widely read in America, both advocated placing the leeches right on the vulva or the neck of the uterus, although Bennet cautioned the doctor to count them as they dropped off when satiated, lest he "lose" some. Bennet had known adventurous leeches to advance into the cervical cavity of the uterus itself, and he noted: "I think I have scarcely ever seen more acute pain than that experienced by several of my patients under these circumstances."[13] Less distressing to a twentieth-century mind, but perhaps even more senseless, were the "injections" into the uterus advocated by these doctors. The uterus became a kind of catch-all, or what one exasperated doctor referred to as a "Chinese toy shop": Water, milk and water, linseed tea, and "decoction of marshmellow . . . tepid or cold" found their way inside nervous women patients.[14] The final step, performed at this time, one must remember, with no anesthetic but a little opium or alcohol, was cauterization, either through the application of nitrate of silver, or in cases of more severe infection, through the use of the much stronger hydrate of potassa, or even the "actual cautery," a "white-hot iron" instrument.[15] The principle here is medically understandable and even sound: to drive out one infection by creating a greater inflammation, and thus provoking the blood cells to activity great enough to heal both irritations. But the treatment was used, it must be remembered, even when there was no uterine infection, and it was subject to great abuses in itself as its best practitioners realized. "It is an easy matter," Byford noted, "to do violence to the mucous membrane by a very little rudeness of management." In a successful case, the uterus was left "raw and bleeding" and the patient in severe pain for several days; in an unsuccessful one, severe hemorrhage and terrible pain might result.[16] It should be noted that the cauterization process, whether by chemicals or by the iron, had to be repeated several times at intervals of a few days.[17]

In the 1870s and 1880s, this form of treatment was largely dropped. Austin, in his book *Perils of American Women*, came out against local treatment and dismissed cauterization as a relic of the barbaric past of a decade ago:

> Thus it happened that thousands of women have been doomed to undergo the nitrate-of-silver treatment—their mental agony and physical torture were accounted nothing—in cases where soap and water and a gentle placebo would have been amply sufficient.[18]

Austin had his own panacea for women's nervous diseases, however. He was a devoted believer in the Philadelphia doctor S. Weir Mitchell and his famous "rest cure."

Firmly opposed to the cauterization school, Mitchell evolved a method of his own, which, in his own words, was "a combination of entire rest and of excessive feeding, made possible by passive exercise obtained through steady use of massage and electricity."[19] When he said "entire rest," he meant it. For some six weeks, the patient was removed from her home, and allowed to see no one except the doctor and a hired nurse. Confined to her bed flat on her back, she was permitted neither to read, nor, in some cases even to rise to urinate. The massage treatment which covered the whole body lasted an hour daily. Becoming progressively more vigorous, it was destined to counteract the debilitating effects of such a prolonged stay in bed. Meanwhile the patient was expected to eat steadily, and gain weight daily. Mitchell's claims to have cured menstrual disorders and every kind of "nervous" ailment met with widespread acceptance. He was the best known and most successful woman's doctor of his generation.

Both the local treatment and the rest cure look to a modern viewer at best like very imperfect forms of medical treatment for complex problems. The first was always painful and often fruitless; the second was frequently tedious and occasionally irrelevant. Both, as we will see, could exacerbate rather than diminish the nervous state they were designed to cure. One's first temptation is to dismiss them as the products of an unscientific age, and there is ample evidence to support such an attitude.

Before the Civil War the American doctor was quite simply ignorant, and even his post-Civil War successor did not receive the training expected of a doctor today. Few medical schools before 1860 required more than two years of attendance; almost none provided clinical experience for their fledgling physicians.[20] Furthermore, gynecology at this period was perhaps the weakest link in the already weak armor of the nineteenth-century doctor's medical knowledge. Lectures on "midwifery" and the sexual organs, as Elizabeth Blackwell was to learn, usually provided a professor more opportunity for dirty jokes than for the dissemination of knowledge.[21] J. Marion Sims, a pioneer in gynecological surgery, frequently lamented the frightening ignorance which seemed especially to attend doctors on the subject of women's ailments. He wrote feelingly about one lady who had long suffered from internal problems and from the cures designed to relieve them:

> The leeching, the physicking, the blistering, the anodynes, the baths, the mountain excursions, the sea-bathing and sea voyages that this poor patient suffered and endured for years are almost incredible![22]

5

He restored her to health by a simple operation.

Doctors had some excuse for their ignorance of woman's internal organs, although little for their pretended knowledge. Ladies were expected, even by their doctors, to object to "local examination," to prefer modesty to health, and many of them did.23 The French physician, Médéric Louis Elie Moreau de St. Méry, had commented on the unwillingness of Philadelphia women in the late eighteenth century to undergo even crucially necessary medical scrutiny, and Dewees, in the same city at the start of the next century, recounted several tales of women who put themselves in the hands of quacks rather than endure this ordeal. Bennet, the London authority, crusaded against the "absolutely criminal" delicacy of doctors who respected such fears in female patients.24 He rightly attributed the birth of gynecology as a science to the increased possibility of uterine examination because of the use of the speculum and gradually changing attitudes.

Yet the ignorance of American doctors and the difficulties in the way of over-coming it certainly cannot explain the *forms* of the treatments they devised for nervous women. To understand these, one must cease to regard these fledgling gynecological techniques as part of a developing science and scrutinize them as part and parcel of a fully formed culture, and, as such, sharing in all the biases and assumptions about women which the culture possessed. This in no way suggests a failure of concern or good will on the part of nineteenth-century American doctors. Undeniably, the majority of these physicians were anxious to aid their female patients. J. Marion Sims, who devoted his life to the intelligent relief of woman's diseases is only an illustrious example of what was surely a numerous class. Yet it seems equally undeniable that a complicated if unacknowledged psychological warfare was being waged between the doctors and their patients. Even the best-intentioned practitioner was forced into a role in part hostile to his woman patients simply by the misconceptions he was trained to hold. Until well after the Civil War, for example, physicians in America, as in Europe, arguing by analogy with the animal world, maintained that woman's fertile period was right before and after menstruation.25 Hence the nineteenth-century American woman, perhaps in ill health and eager to practice a semi-respectable form of birth control, conscientiously slept with her spouse squarely in the middle of her menstrual cycle.

Given the presumably disastrous results action on this belief must have produced, one must turn from the world of science to the realm of culture to explain its surprising tenacity, and the equal persistence with which treatments like cauterization and the rest cure kept their hold in the medical world. Physicians both of the cauterist school and of the rest-cure school brought certain unexplored but pervasive presuppositions to their work. They assumed, as already mentioned, that women were physically dominated by their wombs. They held, moreover, even less carefully scrutinized beliefs about the social and psychological nature of femininity and its role and responsibilities in their society, beliefs which colored their attitude toward the illness of their female patients.

The first point to be noted is the element of distrust, even of condemnation lurking behind their diagnoses. Physicians tended to stress a certain moral depravity inherent in feminine nervous disorders and to waver significantly between labeling it a result and analyzing it as the cause of the physical symptoms involved. The patient, according to Byford's experience, may become "a changed woman"—irritable, indecisive, lacking in will power, morose, jealous. She is likely to show "a guarded cunning, a deceitful and perverted consciousness"; indeed, she may commit "acts of a depraved and indecent nature," and neglect her "duty in all the relations of life."[26]

In part, Byford was indirectly expressing his doubts as to whether or not his patients were truly sick. Such doubts were widely shared. Dixon, in *Woman and Her Diseases*, cautioned the physician always to pay "profound attention" to what he delicately called "moral circumstances." These moral causes were often, he warned, not of a nature "calculated to move our sympathy," and he was all too aware that women were cunning enough to "pretend hysteric attacks, in order to excite sympathy and obtain some desired end."[27] Even more important, of course, was the doctor's unspoken guess at the reason behind this calculated exploitation of illness. Who can doubt that, in an age when sex and childbirth involved very real threats to the health and life of women, some women would use the pretext of being "delicate" as a way not only of escaping household labor but also of closing the bedroom door while avoiding the guilt consequent upon a more flagrant defiance of their "duties"? Harriet Beecher Stowe understood the process and dramatized it at its worst in her portrait of Mrs. St. Clair (in *Uncle Tom's Cabin*) lying on her sofa, shirking responsibility and demanding attention. And Stowe herself, who suffered the burden of relative poverty and of a weak and dependent but potent husband, took periodic refuge from him and their numerous offspring in those havens of escape, the health establishments.[28]

Clearly, in the case of a woman like Stowe, however, we do not have the simple problem of a woman failing to live up to her sexual and domestic responsibilities as we do in the case of her own fictional creation, Mrs. St. Clair. It is rather that her responsibilities, despite all her histrionic and martyred posturings about them, were genuinely more than she could handle: They were almost killing her. Doctors of the period were intermittently and partially aware of the frustrations inherent in the middle-class woman's lot. Alexander Combe, the Scottish phrenologist so influential in America, attributed the high level of insanity in women of this class to the monotony of their lives.[29] In 1834, Dr. Alcott of Boston advocated that ladies be trained as nurses because "these are individuals who need some employment, for the sake even of the emolument; but more especially to save them from ennui, and disgust, and misery—sometimes from speedy or more protracted suicide."[30] Professional work, however, was hardly a socially acceptable escape from a lady's situation, but sickness, that very nervous condition brought on by the frustrations of her life, was.

Yet, many doctors, despite the apparent conscious understanding shown in the analysis of Combe and Alcott, in practice tended unconsciously to see the neuralgic ailments of their female patients as a threatening and culpable shirking of their duties as wives and mothers, and to look upon those duties as the cure, not the cause, of the illness. Self-sacrifice and altruism on a spiritual level, and child-bearing and housework on a more practical one, constituted healthy femininity in the eyes of most nineteenth-century Americans. Dr. Clarke of Harvard, who believed that girls of the 1870s were ill because they were quite literally destroying their wombs and their childbearing potential by presuming to pursue a course of higher education intended by nature only for the male sex, was very much a spokesman for the doctors of his generation.

One finds an underlying logic running through popular books by physicians on women's diseases to the effect that ladies get sick *because* they are unfeminine—in other words, sexually aggressive, intellectually ambitious, and defective in proper womanly submission and selflessness. Bad health habits were often put forth by doctors and others as causes of nervous complaints. But these, consisting as they did of improper diet, light reading, late hours, tight lacing, and inadequate clothing. were in themselves a badge of the "fashionable" and flirtatious female, only a step removed in popular imagination from the infamous one. Byford believed that "the influence of lascivious books" and frequent "indulgence" in intercourse would precipitate neuralgia.[31] Significantly, in Mitchell's fiction, the sick woman is almost invariably the closest thing he has to a villainess, and she is often intelligent and usually predatory to an extreme. In *Roland Blake*, published in 1886, Octapia Darnell, an invalid, is branded by her name. Octapuslike, she uses her sickness like tentacles to try to squeeze the life out of her innocent young cousin, Olivia Wynne. Although we see her in genuine nervous spasms, Mitchell never shows her seized by a convulsion where it would be inconvenient to her purposes, nor does he let us forget that when she needs physical strength to accomplish her will, she always summons it. Again, the heroine of *Constance Trescott* (1905), his last and best novel, is driven by a demonic will to possess utterly where she loves and to revenge totally where she hates. Rather predictably she turns to invalidism at the book's close to gain her ends.

It is not that Mitchell totally condemns these women. Instead, he understands them, and adopts a tone of pitying patronage toward them. He thinks they are genuinely sick, but he believes, as did Clarke, that the root of their sickness was their failure to be women, to sacrifice themselves for others, and to perform their feminine duties. Typically, Octapia Darnell has a brief period of improvement when a "recent need to think of others had beneficently taken her outside of the slowly narrowing circle of self-care and self-contemplation, and, by relieving her of some of the morbid habits of disease, had greatly bettered her physical condition."[32] The truth is that Mitchell does not even need to blame or punish her: In his view, nature has conveniently done that job for him.

Mitchell's analysis, then, one standard with doctors in the nineteenth century, served an important psychological purpose, whatever its medical validity. The doctor, on some unacknowledged level, feared his female patient. Could he so emphasize the diseased potency of woman's unique and mysterious organ, the womb, if he did not worry that his sex, the contant companion of hers, was in some way menaced? How comfortable Mitchell must have felt, when, addressing a graduating Radcliffe class, he expressed his clearly faint hope "that no wreck from these shores will be drifted into my dockyard."[33] They might begin as his competitors, but, despite it—in fact, because of it—they would end as his patients.

Mitchell and his peers could indeed afford to pity the fair sex, even perhaps to "cure" them. Yet the consequent "cures" bore unmistakable signs of their culturally determined origin, for they made a woman's womb very much of a liability. Since her disease was unconsciously viewed as a symptom of a failure in femininity, its remedy was designed both as a punishment and an agent of regeneration, for it forced her to acknowledge her womanhood and made her totally dependent on the professional prowess of her male doctor. The cauterizer, with his injections, leeches, and hot irons seems suggestive of a veiled but aggressively hostile male sexuality and superiority, and the rest-cure expert carried this spirit to a sophisticated culmination.

Mitchell's treatment depended in actuality not so much on the techniques of rest and overfeeding, as on the commanding personality and charismatic will of the physician. "A slight, pale lad of no physical strength" by his own description, he moved as a young man in the shadow of his dominating, joyous, strong doctor-father.[34] To be the strong, healing male in a world of ailing, dependent women had obvious charms for him. "Electric with fascination" for women as his grand-daughter saw him, he acknowledged that he played the "despot" in the sickroom, and boasted of reducing patients to the docility of children.[35] Doctors had always preferred to keep women in ignorance, and Mitchell was no exception. In a characteristically urbane and aphoristic remark, he said, "Wise women choose their doctors and trust them. The wisest ask the fewest questions."[36] But he wanted to be more than trusted: He wished to be revered, even adored, and he succeeded. The totality of the power he could acquire is revealed in a letter he received from a sick woman who positively grovels before him as she rhapsodizes on his potency:

> Whilst laid by the heels in a country-house with an attack of grippe, also an invalid from gastric affection, the weary eyes of a sick women fall upon your face in the *Century* of this month—a thrill passed through me—at last I saw the true physician![37]

It is clear, moreover, that Mitchell encouraged this worshiping attitude as an important element in his "cure." A doctor, in his view, if he had the proper mesmeric powers of will, could become almost god-like.[38] Women doctors would always be inferior to male physicians, he believed, precisely because they could not exercise such tyranny: They were unable to "obtain the needed control over those of their own sex."[39] Mitchell here skated on the edge of a theory of primitive healing through mesmeric sexual powers.[40] Furthermore, his treatment was designed to make his female patients take his view of the doctor's role. They were allowed to see no one but him, and to talk of their ills and problems to no one else. As doctor he became the only spot of energy, the only source of *life*, during the enforced repose of a cure process.

Undoubtedly, if Mitchell were aware of what he was doing, he would have felt it justifiable and even merciful. He was curing his patients—by restoring them to their femininity or, in other words, by subordinating them to an enlightened but dictatorial male will. His admirers delighted to tell how, when a strangely recalcitrant patient refused to rise from bed after Mitchell had decreed that the rest cure was over, Mitchell threatened to move into bed with her if she did not get up, and even started to undress. When he got to his pants, she got up. Although the story may well be apocryphal, its spirit is not. Not surprisingly, the lady in question was fleeing the fact where she embraced the shadow, for symbolically, Mitchell, like his cauterizing predecessor, played the role of possessor, even impregnator, in the cure process. Dominated, overfed often to the point of obesity, caressed and (quite literally) vibrating, were not his patients being returned to health—to womanhood?[41] The only other time that the Victorian lady took to her bed and got fat was, in fact, before delivery. J. Marion Sims had noted that his colleagues were erroneously wont to lament about a sick woman: "If she could only have a child, it would cure her."[42] Although he was a generation later, Mitchell was not so different from the doctors Sims opposed who looked to pregnancy for the cure of all feminine ills.

Here one senses a clue to the pertinacity with which doctors told women anxious to avoid pregnancy that they should sleep with their husbands only during what we now know as their most fertile period. In a sense, the practices and writings of the medical profession provide the other half of the picture of ideal womanhood presented in the sentimental literature of the day. Woman was at her holiest, according to the genteel novels and poetry of Victorian America, as a mother. Pregnancy itself, however, was avoided by the authors of such works as completely as the act of impregnation. The medical manual took on the role of frankness disowned by its more discreet companion. All the logic of contemporary medical lore adds up to the lesson that women were at their most feminine when they were pregnant. Pregnant, they were visible emblems of masculine potency.

It is impossible to determine how many nineteenth-century middle-class American women went to doctors, just as it is difficult to tell how real their much-advertised ailments were. Reluctant as American women apparently were to undergo local examination, many of them presumably stayed home and suffered with no medical aid except that provided by earlier versions of Lydia Pinkham's patent medicine. Others trusted to the hydropathic remedies provided at numerous water-cures or used homeopathic drugs, both of which represented forms of protest against current medical practices.[43] Furthermore, the majority of women suffering from uterine and/or nervous disorders who underwent a form of local treatment or, later, the rest cure, were presumably in real distress and glad of whatever help their physician could offer.[44] Some, however, were undoubtedly using prescribed treatments for their own purposes. According to numerous masculine and feminine observers, many women grew positively addicted to local treatment as others did later to the rest cure, but, not surprisingly, these women have not left any direct confessions to posterity.[45]

What we do have record of is a masked but almost hysterical paranoia among a small group of feminist hygiene experts and female doctors, a paranoia stemming from their exaggerated but astute perception of the unconscious purposes underlying the attitudes and practices of doctors with women patients. In their excited view, current medical treatment was patently not science, for which they professed respect, but a part of their male-dominated culture, for which they had both fear and contempt. They saw it as a form of rape, designed to keep woman prostrate, a perpetual patient dependent on a doctor's supposed professional expertise.

No one expressed this attitude better than did two Beecher women, Catherine Esther Beecher, who crusaded against local treatment, and her grandniece Charlotte Perkins Gilman, who protested against Mitchell's rest cure a generation later. Each of them wrote a work dedicated to exposing what they felt were the unstated motives of physicians treating women patients. In *Letters to the People on Health and Happiness,* Beecher described with heavy-handed irony the ineffectuality of the string of "talented, highly-educated and celebrated" doctors who had tried to cure her own severe nervous ailments (115).[46] She consumed sulphur and iron, she let one doctor sever the "wounded nerves from their centres," she let another cover her spine with "tartar emetic pustules," she subjected herself to "animal magnetism" and the water cure, but all to no purpose.

Beecher does not admit to having personally undergone local treatment, but when she discusses it, her tone changes from the condescending playfulness she uses to devastate such methods as the "tartar emetic pustules" to one of outraged horror. Doctors playing professional games with pustules had kept her sick perhaps, but they had left her with her honor. Local treatment, roughly equivalent to rape according to Beecher, seldom allowed a lady to retain that valuable possession. It is "performed," she explains, "with bolted doors and curtained windows, and with no one present but patient and operator," by doctors who have all too often "freely advocated the doctrine that there was no true marriage but the union of persons who were in love." Predictably, these immoral practitioners were said to have "lost all reverence for the Bible." With his "interesting" female patients, such a physician "naturally," in Beecher's gloomy view, tries "to lead them to adopt *his views of truth and right*" on moral matters. "Then he daily has all the opportunities indicated [through local examination]. Does anyone need more than to hear these facts to know what the not unfrequent results must be?" omniously concludes (136). By the time she is through with this subject, she is calling the female patients "victims" and lamenting their "entire helplessness" (137). She refers the reader to an appended letter from a woman doctor, Mrs. R. B Gleason of the Elmira Water Cure in New York, who solemnly testifies that manual replacement for *prolapsus uteri* was "in most cases totally needless, and in many decidedly injurious" (6*). After such evidence, Beecher can hardly avoid "the painful inquiry": "how can a woman *ever know* to whom she may safely entrust herself . . . in such painful and peculiar circumstances?" (138).

Gilman, a brilliant theorist and critic on women's role in American society, went through periods of nervous prostration strikingly similar to those of her aged relative's.[47] She sampled the fruits of medical wisdom a few decades later, undergoing Mitchell's rest cure. She expressed the result in a story entitled "The Yellow Wall Paper," published in 1890, and designed to convince Mitchell "of the error of his ways."[48]

The story concerns a married woman, the mother of a young child, suffering from "nervous" disorders, and clearly laboring under disguised but immense (and justifiable) hostility for both her spouse and her offspring. Her husband, John, who is a doctor, is ostensibly overseeing her cure, but is in reality intent with sadistic ignorance on destroying her body and soul. John, apparently modeled on Mitchell himself, confines his wife to a country house, which to her seems "haunted," remote from friends or neighbors. Presumably hoping to force her back to her feminine and maternal functions, he symbolically makes her sleep in an old nursery. With its barred windows, rings attached to the wall, bed nailed to the floor, and disturbing and torn yellow wallpaper, this nursery all too significantly and frighteningly resembles a cell for the insane. Treating her like a pet, the doctor alternates condescending tenderness ("Then he took me in his arms and called me a blessed little goose" [323]) with threats of punishment ("John says if I don't pick up faster he shall send me to Weir Mitchell in the fall" [326]). Since John "never was nervous in his life" (323), and is a doctor "of high standing" (320) to boot, he can "laugh" at her fears because he "knows there is no *reason* to suffer, and that satisfies him" (323). Complacently smug in his masculine insensitivity and his professional superiority, he is totally obtuse about the nature of her suffering and its possible cure. An early-day "mad housewife," she has been so browbeaten by his calm assumption of superiority that she can only timidly air the frightening truth:

> John is a physician, and *perhaps*—(I would not say it to a living soul, of course, but this is dead paper and a great relief to my mind)—*perhaps* that is one reason I do not get well faster (320).

He has left her with only one recourse, and she takes it. Slowly but steadily, she goes mad, thus dramatically pointing up the results of his "cure." At the story's close, she is creeping on hands and knees with insane persistence around the walls of her chamber. In a symbolic moment, her husband, suspicious about her behavior, breaks down the door she has finally locked against him. His act is the essence of his "cure" and her "problem"; like Catharine Beecher, Gilman sees the doctor "treating" his patient as violating her. But this patient is finally beyond feeling. When John faints away in shock at her state, their roles have been reversed: *He* has become the woman, the nervous, susceptible, sickly patient, and she wonders with a kind of calm, self-centered vindictiveness fully equal to his former arrogance: "Now why should that man have fainted? But he did, and right across my path by the wall, so that I had to creep over him every time!" (337). She has won, because she can ignore him now as completely as he ignored her, but she has won at the cost of becoming what he subconsciously sought to make her—a creeping creature, an animal and an automaton.

Beecher's *Letters* and Gilman's story are both intended to convey a nightmare vision of sick women dependent on male doctors who use their professional superiority as a method to prolong their patients' sickness and, consequently, the supremacy of their own sex. Both writers also hint, however, at a possible escape for such feminine victims. Beecher, according to her account, was finally cured by a timely tip from a *woman* physician, Dr. Elizabeth Blackwell. Gilman's heroine knows what her cure should be—work and intellectual stimulation—although she is too cowed and powerless to insist on it. Both Gilman and Beecher simply in writing their works are implying that the untutored common sense of two women can outdo the professionally trained brains of those male doctors who labored in vain to cure them. Both are thus in essence urging that a woman should be independent, that *she be her own physician,* so that the real business of healing can get under way.[49]

After all, Beecher and Gilman realized, there might be two possible ways of looking at the much-advertised problem of the increasingly bad health of middle-class American women. Doctors like Clarke and Mitchell liked to think that the fault lay with the women themselves, who were neglecting their homes and pursuing such an unfeminine goal as higher education. Women like Beecher and Gilman, shrewdly reversing the charge, queried whether the blame might not belong to the men who were supposed to cure them and to the professional training which was supposed to enable them to do it. Harriot Hunt, one of the most impressive of the early women doctors in America, put the challenge succinctly: "Man, man alone has had the care of *us* [women] and I would ask how *our health stands now.* Does it do credit to *his* skill?[50] Hunt is clearly aware that what had been a condemnation of women (the charge of ill health) could be used as a powerful weapon in their defense. The women doctors who began to appear on the American scene in the 1850s saw women's diseases as a *result* of submission, and promoted independence from masculine domination, whether professional or sexual, as their cure for feminine ailments.[51]

In dealing with these pioneer women doctors and their theories, one is at once aware that here, too, the issues are inevitably cultural rather than scientific. Their primary aim, often an unconscious one, was to free ailing women from male control. On the one hand, this desire could and did further scientific advancement, for their distrust of the male doctor made them eager to reject aspects of medical practice that were in fact unscientific, if not harmful. Their paranoid fear that the male doctor was degrading his female patient paradoxically led them to some sound conclusions about the worthlessness of many drugs and the necessity of sanitation and preventive medicine. On the other hand, the same fear also made them, on occasion, throw out the baby with the bath water. Their hostility to the male doctor too often became a hostility to any scientific practice which appeared to their oversensitive consciousness as an invasion of the patient's privacy. Gynecological surgery, for example, which, despite undoubted abuse, represented a significant step in medical treatment of women, was often rejected by these early pioneers. Yet one must keep in mind that what is unwitting stupidity from a scientific point of view can be (albeit equally unwitting) shrewdness from a social or political point of view. These women bypassed science in large part because they had a goal quite distinct from its advancement: namely, the advancement of their sex.

Nowhere is this aim clearer than in the work of Hunt, a well-known, if home-trained, Boston practitioner and the most outspoken of the first generation of women doctors. Her autobiography, *Glances and Glimpses* (1856), published when she was forty-one, is clearly over-simplified, one-sided, and sentimentalized, but one must keep in mind that she was writing not a scientific report, nor even a history, but rather a special kind of mythologized propaganda, a scenario for a sexual revolution.

The ritualized drama begins with Hunt's explanation of why she chose medicine as a career—her stunned realization of the profound ignorance of the male doctors treating feminine diseases (81).[52] Her ailing sister was put through a course of remedies somewhat similar to the one Beecher tried, and she, and Harriot, came away having "lost all confidence in medicine" (85). The male practitioner here emerges as one of the villains of Hunt's piece. According to her testimony, he usually made his living by creating false dependencies in his female patients, by keeping them ignorant and totally reliant on his short-sighted or even harmful remedies (32, 89). Indeed, Hunt insinuates, his professional training led him actually to want his patients to be sick so that he would have something to do with all the games he had learned.

Professional exploitation by the doctor of his female patient was a mask, in Hunt's opinion, for a deeper and more humiliating sexual exploitation. Like Catharine Beecher, Hunt was publicly and loudly aghast at local examinations. They were "*too often unnecessary*" (271) and their moral effects were terrible. Many medical men, in her view, were skeptics, who lived "sensually" (177), and contaminated their patients. At this point, Hunt's scenario grows both alarmist and lurid. A woman once forced to submit to local examination, Hunt reveals, was well on the road to ruin: She felt "disgraced, and a don't careativeness [*sic*] and sort of sullen desperation" settled on her (184). Yet this fantasized sexual violation was dreadful, according to Hunt, not so much because of the moral degradation involved as because of the patient's loss of control and her consequent dependence on the doctor's will. In describing a physician who took advantage of a patient and left her with an illegitimate child, she explains significantly: His "will overmastered the weaker will of his patient" (376).

The doctor's was not the only malevolent will pitted against his woman patient's will in Hunt's story. The villainous physicians who kept women sick were only collaborating with the villainous husbands who had caused their illness in the first place. In her favorite role as minister-doctor, she collected many of what she called the "heart-histories" of her women patients, and publicized them as evidence that women's "physical maladies" stemmed from "concealed sorrows" (139), often at the "sins" of their spouses (159).[53] Hunt never married, but she was always ready with sympathy for those who had. One married patient after another apparently confided to her: "I thank heaven, my dear doctor, that you are a woman; for now I can tell you the truth about my health. It is not my body that is sick but my heart" (120).

Hunt's vision, so filled with villains and victims, has a savior to offer as well. This heroine is of course Hunt herself, as a woman doctor and simply as a woman. As a doctor, she dramatically renounced "medical science" as "full of unnecessary details," but without "a soul . . . a huge, unwieldy body—distorted, deformed, inconsistent and complicated" (121). Medicine was generally "worse than useless" (371), she remarked; moreover, it did not meet her "perception of the dignity of the human body." She did not enter "the medical life through physics, but through metaphysics" (127). She was only too eager to announce her disavowal of "science," because she considered her disrespect precisely her strongest claim to respect. Flaunting her anti-professionalism like a medal of honor, she loved to proclaim herself an eclectic, as indeed she was, the "disciple of no medical sect" (171), but the sworn servant of her sex.[54]

Hunt's treatment consisted of telling her patients to throw away their medicines, begin a diary, and think of their mothers (401). The last item of this prescription is not simply the pure sentimentalism that it might appear. Hunt was symbolically turning her patients' thoughts to an acceptable but potent emblem of *female strength*.[55] It was from this source that she expected her patients to find their cure—not in the arms of their husbands, nor under the hands of the male doctor. The medicine that she gave her patients as a sure antidote to the wares peddled by her masculine colleagues was the example of her own ample and self-sufficient womanhood. Could they forget their mothers with Hunt before them?

It was from this source that she expected her patients to find their cure—not in the arms of their husbands, nor under the hands of the male doctor. The medicine that she gave her patients as a sure antidote to the wares peddled by her masculine colleagues was the example of her own ample and self-sufficient womanhood. Could they forget their mothers with Hunt before them?

Hunt was an ardent and proclaimed feminist and suffragist, but other women pioneers in medicine who did not share, or did not avow such sympathies, were almost without exception part of her crusade.[56] The most famous of these was Elizabeth Blackwell, usually considered the first woman doctor in America. In her girlhood an avowed admirer of the fiercely virginal goddess Diana, Blackwell always loved to project an almost monstrous force as woman's natural dowry.[57] Yet she was clearly drawn to such fantasies precisely because of her deep-seated perception and fear of the dependent role women usually played. With paradoxical logic, she explained that precisely *because* she was very "susceptible" to men and perpetually in love, she had determined never to marry. Not initially attracted to medicine, she deliberately chose it as a potentially "strong barrier between me and all ordinary marriage. I must have something to engross my thoughts, some object in life which will fulfill this vacuum and prevent this sad wearing away of the heart."[58]

Professionally, despite her soft-spoken, conciliating manner, she fought the code of the male medical establishment which in her view victimized women as surely as did matrimony. During medical school, she was shocked at the "horrible exposure" of women to male physicians, finding it "indecent for any poor woman to be subjected to such a torture."[59] In her later years, when local treatment was less common, Blackwell crusaded against its medical descendant, ovariotomy, or as she called it with characteristic dramatic flair, "the castration of women." Estimating that 1 of every 250 women in Europe had been "castrated," she collected newspaper clippings which supported her belief that young doctors were performing this operation needlessly on unsuspecting women just to obtain professional practice.[60]

The validity of Blackwell's fears is hard to estimate. Many reputable people shared them. Yet Dr. Maria Zakrewska lamented the fact that women had come to her Boston hospital insisting that their ovaries be removed as a birth control device.[61] Nonetheless, in Blackwell's eyes, male doctors were performing a kind of "vivisection"—a practice that she violently opposed in any form—on their female patients.[62] Ovariotomies for her simply dramatized the anti-woman bias of much of modern science. If man were going to dedicate himself to cold-blooded experimentation, would not woman be his ultimate subject? Consequently, despite her fine mind and excellent training, Blackwell, an incipient Christian Scientist, obstinately opposed not just the usual run of drugs and medication, but vaccination and "all medical methods which introduce any degree of morbid matter into the blood of the human system."[63] All such practices were "especially antagonistic to women."[64] Blackwell's medical shortsightedness seems ludicrous, perhaps culpable, but it furthered her underlying and non-medical goals.

To distrust science was to distrust masculinity, and to create an apparent immediate and desperate need for women doctors. She saw these projected new physicians, moreover, as undercover agents in enemy territory. Her advice to them reads a bit like a lesson in subversion. Proud that she had determined early in her career to "*commit heresy* with intelligence" to escape the perils of professionalized medicine, she declared that women doctors should not countenance practices like ovariotomies, vaccination, and vivisection.[65] In a crucial essay entitled "The Influence of Women in the Profession of Medicine" (1889), she urged women medical students, unfortunately, like all of their sex, trained to "accept the government and instruction of men as final" (20), to exercise a "mild skepticism" (21).[66] Their task was quite simply to revamp the whole medical profession, for, as she explained, "methods and conclusions formed by one half the race only must necessarily require revision as the other half of humanity rises into conscious responsibility" (20). They had a sure guide in this apparently momentous undertaking: Nothing that revolted their "moral sense as earnest women" could be scientifically true, and no "logical sophistry" (30) could make it so. In a letter to a medical colleague, she echoes Emerson as she anticipates a day when women will plant themselves firmly "on the God-given force of their maternal nature" and oppose the male intellect in its too restless search for scientific truth.[67]

Blackwell was very clever. Male doctors had indirectly told their women patients that their procreative femininity was their dearest treasure. Coining that treasure into current cash, Blackwell pointed to her sacred maternal nature as justification for a revolt against the ways of the male doctor. For the woman physician of Blackwell's vision, womanhood was hardly a liability, and very much a weapon. She was no subordinate, but an aggressive censor of the masculine world.[68] Blackwell herself was only too ready. Calling herself a "Christian psysiologist," she fought prostitution, masturbation, and obscene literature in addition to various medical abuses. It was in these crusades that her underlying anti-male bias most dramatically expressed itself. With so many of her feminine peers, she liked to see male sexuality, like male science, as one more method used by man to debase women to their own level by seducing them, and to keep them dependent by forcing them into parasitism. Blackwell's target in the anti-prostitution campaign organized by the Purity Alliance was not the prostitute, but her exploiter.[69] "Male lust must be restrained in order to check female obscenity"[70] was the telling slogan Blackwell issued in one of her many essays on the subject. It is not too much to say that the paid whore whom Blackwell wished to regenerate was simply another version of the female patient corrupted by immoral medical practices whom Beecher and Hunt had sought to redeem.

It is telling that Blackwell, like most of the first generation of women doctors, chose hygiene, or preventive medicine, as her chosen field, and she made great contributions there, despite her distrust of vaccination. There can be no doubt, furthermore, that she and her feminine colleagues contributed significantly to improve treatment of women's and children's diseases.[71] But they also answered a different and more subtle need strongly felt by some members of their sex. If the woman patient dependent on the male doctor had seemed to feminists like Beecher and Gilman emblematic of the most degrading elements in woman's relation to man in nineteenth-century America, the woman doctor, able to take care of herself and cure the world's ills, appeared to them not only as a beacon of hope but as an avenger of the wrongs of all those prostrate women, whether victimized in an office or in their own homes.

Elizabeth Stuart Phelps, an immensely popular post-Civil War authoress who knew personally every variety of nervous disorder in its most acute form, celebrated this revengeful angel in *Dr. Zay* (1882), a novel about a woman doctor.[72] Dr. Zay's first name rather appropriately is Atalanta. Totally self-confident, direct, brilliant, and rather unpoetic although womanly, she exudes the independence and the self-sufficiency that Elizabeth Blackwell and Harriot Hunt had so longed to see in their sex. Like them, she has devoted herself to relieving the sufferings of women and, a Christian physiologist of the first order, she even brings off shotgun weddings as part of her healing mission. The novel centers around her relationship with her only male patient—a young man named Waldo Yorke, poetic and unmotivated, although attractive and personally charming. He falls deeply in love with her, and Phelps devotes most of the plot to the resulting role-reversal which apparently fascinates her. Convalescent and ironically suffering from "nervous strain" (69), Yorke needs Dr. Zay, but she, in splendid health, "leaned against her own physical strength, as another woman might lean upon a man's" (110).[73]

By a further twist of irony, a twist clearly delightful to Phelps herself, Dr. Zay, out of her superfluous strength and in her off-hours, can provide salvation for man in the shape of Yorke, but he has nothing to offer her except the so-called feminine gifts of devotion and sexual attractiveness. The circle of revenge is complete, for Phelps is implying through Atalanta that the truly diseased sex is not woman, woman with her radiant maternal strength, but man, man with his barren professional pretenses and sexual excess. And so the last act of mercy Phelps' rather sadistic angel performs is to consent to enter the marriage relation with a sex she has demonstrated so clearly to be the inferior of her own.

Phelps' superwoman Dr. Zay is clearly the exaggerated product of wish-fulfillment fantasies on the part of a lifelong invalid and feminist, but she forcefully symbolizes what some women wanted women doctors to prove to them.

With this novel, the drama of women and medicine in nineteenth-century America has in a sense reached its extreme dénouement. Unlike the male and female physicians who preceded (and succeeded) her, Phelps makes no pretense of interest in medicine as science. Her only concern is with medicine as a weapon in a social and political struggle for power between the sexes. In *Dr. Zay,* Phelps has seized upon the cultural assumptions underlying contemporary male doctors' treatments of women's diseases in order triumphantly to reverse them. Dr. Zay's example is meant to testify that, far from being the constitutionally diseased and dependent creature that Dewees and Byford saw, woman could be self-reliant. In Phelps' vision, woman need not be a prisoner in her own sick body, awaiting the coming of her deliverer, man, but a healer herself, the support of her sex, and by caring for its members, the donor to them of a new kind of self-esteem.

NOTES

1 See Richard Huber, *The American Idea of Success* (New York: McGraw-Hill, 1971), pp. 124-186; Donald Meyer, *The Positive Thinkers: A Study of the American Quest for Health, Wealth, and Personal Power* (New York: Doubleday, 1965); David Rothman, *The Discovery of the Asylum: Social Order and Disorder in the New Republic* (Boston: Little, Brown, 1971), xvi. For another treatment of insanity in the same period, see Norman Dain, *Concepts of Insanity in the United States 1789-1865* (New Brunswick, N.J.: Rutgers University Press, 1964).

2 G.J. Barker-Benfield has given consideration to these medical practices from a cultural point of view in "The Spermatic Economy: A Nineteenth-Century View of Sexuality" *Feminist Studies* 1, no. 1:45-74. His primary focus is on masculine sexuality, however, while mine is on feminine sexuality. For a more general, and somewhat superficial survey of American sex mores and roles in the nineteenth century, see Milton Rugoff, *Prudery and Passion* (New York: G.P. Putnam's Sons, 1971).

3 Catherine E. Beecher, "The American People Starved and Poisoned," *Harper's New Monthly Magazine,* 32 (1866): 771; *Physiology and Calisthenics for Schools and Families* (New York: Harper & Brothers, 1856), p. 164; *Letters to the People on Health And Happiness* (New York: Harper & Brothers, 1855), p. 124. Her findings were still being referred to in 1870. See the popular manual Edward B. Foote, *Plain Home Talk* (New York: Murray Hill, 1880), p. 451.

4 For a popular satire on the subject see Augustus Hopper, *A Fashionable Sufferer: or Chapters from Life's Comedy* (Boston: Houghton Mifflin, 1883). There is an interesting chapter on the subject in Page Smith, *Daughters of the Promised Land: Women in American History* (Boston: Little, Brown, 1970), pp. 131-140. Wendell Phillips' wife was a typical example of a long-suffering but equally long-lived victim of nervous complaints. See Irving H. Bartlett, *Wendell Phillips: Brahmin Radical* (Boston: Beacon, 1961), p. 79. One could multiply examples almost endlessly of women of this period who never expected to live through the next year and survived into their eighties and nineties. Still this evidence, like all the evidence in this area, is ambiguous. There are many diseases and ailments which, in the absence of sufficient medical knowledge, can become chronic and make their victim's life a torment without ending it.

5 Meyer, *The Positive Thinkers,* p. 30.

6 See James Fenimore Cooper (ed. Robert E. Spiller), *Gleanings in Europe* (New York: Oxford University Press, 1930), 2:92-97, and Nathaniel Hawthorne, *Our Old Home,* in *The Complete Works of Nathaniel Hawthorne* (Boston: Houghton Mifflin, 1898), 7: 66-68, 390-391.

7 William A. Alcott, *The Young Woman's Book of Health* (Boston: Tappan, Whittemore and Mason, 1850), p. 17, Edward H. Clarke, *Sex in Education: or a Fair Chance for Girls* (Boston: Houghton, Osgood, 1878), p. 63. For the history of similar arguments, see Willystine Goodsell, *The Education of Women: Its Social Background and Problems* (New York: Macmillan, 1923). In 1868, Dr. F. Saunders wrote a book quite frankly pleading with middle-class American woman to have more children. See *About Women, Love, and Marriage* (New York: G. W. Carleton, 1868).

8 See George H. Napheys, *The Transmission of Life: Counsels on the Nature and Hygiene of the*

Masculine Function (Philadelphia: David McKay, 1889), pp. 71 ff. This was a standard analysis and countless supporting sources could be cited. One of particular interest is *Satan and Society by a Physician* (Cincinnati: C. F. Vent, 1872). See also George Beard, *American Nervousness* (New York: G. P. Putnam's Sons, 1881).

9 See, for example, Alcott, *The Young Woman's Book of Health;* Frederick Hollick, *The Marriage Guide or Natural History of Generation* (New York: T. W. Strong, 1860); George H. Napheys, *The Physical Life of Woman: Advice to the Maiden, Wife and Mother* (Philadelphia: H. C. Watts, 1880).

10 Quoted in M. L. Holbrook, *Parturition Without Pain: A Code of Directions for Escaping from the Primal Curse* (New York: Wood & Holbrook, 1875), p. 15.

11 William P. Dewees, *A Treatise on the Diseases of Females* (Philadelphia: Lea & Blanchard, 1843), pp. 17, 14. For a discussion of attitudes toward menstruation in the period, see Elaine and English Showalter, "Victorian Women and Menstruation," *Victorian Studies* 14 (1970): 83-89.

12 William H. Byford, *A Treatise on the Chronic Inflammation and Displacements of the Unimpregnated Uterus* (Philadelphia: Lindsay & Blakiston, 1864), pp. 22-41. For a similar discussion of symptoms, see S. Weir Mitchell, *Doctor and Patient* (Philadelphia: J. B. Lippincott, 1888), pp. 25-27, and *Fat and Blood and How to Make Them* (Philadelphia: J. B. Lippincott, 1877), p. 35.

13 James Henry Bennet, *A Practical Treatise on Inflammation of the Uterus, Its Cervix and Appendages and on Its Connection with Other Uterine Diseases* (Philadelphia: Blanchard & Lea, 1864), p. 237.

14 Ibid., p. 224.

15 Ibid., p. 255; Byford, *A Treatise on the Chronic Inflammation,* p. 152.

16 Ibid., pp. 103, 117, 158, 164.

17 Bennett, *A Practical Treatise on the Inflammation of the Uterus,* p. 244.

18 G. L. Austin, *Perils of American Women: or, A Doctor's Talk with Maiden, Wife, and Mother* (Boston: Lee & Shepard, 1883), pp. 198, 158-160. See also Monfort B. Allen and Amelia C. McGregor, *The Glory of Woman, or Love, Marriage, and Maternity* (Philadelphia: J. H. Moore, 1896), p. 241.

19 Mitchell, *Fat and Blood,* p. 7. This cure, since it did not focus directly on the uterus, could be used on men as well as women, but it rarely was. Significantly, in twenty-four case histories described by Mitchell in an account of his method, only one involved was a male. Furthermore, this man was suffering from consumption rather than a nervous complaint. See *Fat and Blood,* p. 93.

20 See J. Marion Sims, *The Story of My Life* (New York: Appleton, 1884).

21 Elizabeth Blackwell, *Pioneer Work in Opening the Medical Profession to Women* (New York: Longmans, Green, 1895), pp. 257-259.

22 Quoted in Seale Harris, *Woman's Surgeon: The Life Story of J. Marion Sims* (New York: Macmillan, 1950), p. 181.

23 Charles D. Meigs, a conservative gynecologist of Philadelphia, wrote in 1848 that he "rejoiced" at the difficulty of making local examinations since it was "an evidence of a high and worthy grade of moral feeling" in American women (quoted in Harvey Graham, *Eternal Eve: The History of Gynecology and Obstetrics* [New York: Doubleday, 1951]), p. 495.

24 Dewees, *A Treatise on the Diseases of Females,* pp. 224-225, 242-243; Bennet, *A Practical Treatise on the Inflammation of the Uterus,* p. 19. Another widely used foreign authority made the same point. J. W. von Scanzoni, (trans. Augustus K. Gardner) *A Practical Treatise on the Diseases of the Sexual Organs of Women* (New York: Robert M. DeWitt, 1861), pp. 37-38. See also Byford, *A Treatise on the Chronic Inflammation,* p. 98.

25 Graham, *Eternal Eve,* p. 451. For an example, see Napheys, *The Transmission of Life,* pp. 190-191.

26 Byford, *A Treatise on the Chronic Inflammation,* pp. 22-41. Mitchell also testified to this pattern of moral degradation, *Fat and Blood,* pp. 27, 28. One should add here that condemnation disguised as diagnosis and punishment offered as cure were hardly unique to medical treatment of women in this period. Napheys hints at "surgical operations" to curb masturbation in men and advocated blisterings and "infibulation" (*Transmission of Life,* pp. 80-83). Rugoff discusses various painful contraptions used to prevent nocturnal emission (*Prudery and Passion,* p. 53). I am simply trying to show how two particular courses of punitive medicine reflected and supported culturally induced ideas about female sexual identity.

27 Edward H. Dixon, *Woman and Her Diseases from the Cradle to the Grave* (New York: A. Ranney, 1857), pp. 134, 140.

28 For a discussion of Stowe's marital problems and responsibilities, see the following biographies: Joanna Johnston, *Runaway to Heaven: The Story of Harriet Beecher Stowe* (New York:

Doubleday, 1963), and Forrest Wilson, *Crusader in Crinoline: The Life of Harriet Beecher Stowe* (Philadelphia: J. B. Lippincott, 1941). Also of value is Edmund Wilson, *Patriotic Gore: Studies in the Literature of the American Civil War* (New York: Oxford University Press, 1966), pp. 3-58.

29 '"Insanity: From Combe's Work on Mental Derangement," *Ladies' Magazine* 8 (1835): 461-463.

30 W. A. Alcott, "Female Attendance on the Sick," *Ladies' Magazine* 7 (1834): 302.

31 Byford, *A Treatise on the Chronic Inflammation*, p. 15.

32 S. Weir Mitchell, *Roland Blake* (Boston: Houghton Mifflin, 1886), p. 254.

33 Anna Robeson Burr (ed.), *Weir Mitchell: His Life and Letters* (New York: Duffield, 1929), p. 374. Mitchell makes the same point in *Doctor and Patient*, p. 13.

34 Burr, *Weir Mitchell*, p. 37. The best recent biography is Ernest Earnest, *S. Weir Mitchell: Novelist and Physician* (Philadelphia: University of Pennsylvania Press, 1950).

35 Mitchell, *Fat and Blood*, p. 48.

36 Mitchell, *Doctor and Patient*, p. 48.

37 Quoted in Burr, *Weir Mitchell*, p. 290.

38 There are striking similarities between Mitchell's conception of his role, and that of Freudian psychiatrists. See Earnest, *Weir Mitchell*, p. 250.

39 Mitchell, *Fat and Blood*, p. 39.

40 He tried hypnosis in his practice, though with little success. See Earnest, *Weir Mitchell*, p. 229. Robert Herrick was to dramatize this aspect of the physician's role in *The Healer* (New York: Macmillan, 1911) and in *Together* (New York: Macmillan, 1909).

41 For examples of these weight gains, see Mitchell, *Fat and Blood*, pp. 80-94. One 5'8" woman went from 118 lbs. to 169 lbs.

42 Quoted in Harris, *Woman's Surgeon*, p. 181.

43 Both the homeopathic school, with its distrust of drugs and violent remedies, and the hydropathic school, with its reliance on the efficacy of water, advocates relatively mild treatments for women's ailments. For examples, see John A. Tarbell, *Homeopathy Simplified: or Domestic Practice Made Easy* (Boston: Otis Clapp, 1859), pp. 214-218; R. T. Trall, *The Hydropathic Encyclopedia: A System of Hydropathy and Hygiene* (New York: Fouters and Wells, 1852), II, pp. 285-296. It must also be added, however, that such doctors were outside the higher echelons of American medicine. Furthermore, it is striking how many women turned to such doctors as a result of bad experiences at the hands of more orthodox doctors. In other words, it seems likely that the lady at the water-cure had also sampled other forms of treatment.

44 Angelina Grimké, for instance, a famous abolitionist and speaker for women's rights, suffered terribly from *prolapsus uteri*. See Gerda Lerner, *The Grimké Sisters from South Carolina* (Boston: Houghton Mifflin, 1967), pp.288-292.

45 See Austin, *Perils of American Women*, pp. 94-95.

46 All page references will be to the edition already cited.

47 See her own account in her autobiography, *The Living of Charlotte Perkins Gilman* (New York: D. Appleton-Century, 1935), pp. 90 ff. She may have felt her similarities to Beecher since she named her daughter after her.

48 All page references will be to Charlotte Perkins Gilman, "The Yellow Wall Paper," in *The Great Modern American Short Stories*, ed., William Dean Howells (New York: Boni and Liveright, 1920), pp. 320-337. Gilman, *Living of Charlotte Perkins Gilman*, p. 121.

49 The demand for women doctors could be quite explicit. See Julia Ward Howe (ed.), *A Reply to Dr. E. H. Clarke's 'Sex in Education'* (Boston: Roberts Brothers, 1874), p. 158.

50 Harriot K. Hunt, *Glances and Glimpses: or Fifty Years Social, Including Twenty Years Professional Life* (Boston: John P. Jewett, 1856), p. 414.

51 For the history of women doctors in America, see Kate Campbell-Hurd, *Medical Women in America: A Short History of the Pioneer Medical Women of America and of a Few of Their Colleagues in England* (Fort Pierce Beach, Fla.: Froben Press, 1933); Esther Pohl Lovejoy, *Women Doctors of the World* (New York: Macmillan, 1957).

52 All page references will be to Hunt, *Glances and Glimpses*. For similar motivation in another woman doctor see Helen McKnight Doyle, *A Child Went Forth* (New York: Gotham House, 1934), pp. 15-18.

53 There was some medical truth underlying this apparently sentimental declaration. Aside from subjecting women to the perils of childbirth, men not infrequently unwittingly gave them syphillis. See Elizabeth Blackwell, *Essays in Medical Sociology* (London: Ernest Bell, 1902): I, 90-91.

54 Anti-professionalism in women doctors had another complex side which mainly lies outside the scope of this article. Women had been active medical practitioners in America as midwives until the time of the Revolution. Then licenses, obtainable only in the newly opened medical schools,

which did not take women, began to be required. So, in effect, professional requirements had spelled the demise of the woman physician in the late eighteenth century. Hence, the mistrust felt for such training by her nineteenth-century feminine successor was not surprising. Unquestionably, late eighteenth-century and early nineteenth-century American doctors had welcomed and even pushed for this change (see Victor Robinson, *White-Caps: The Story of Nursing* [Philadelphia: J. B. Lippincott, 1946], p. 137), although a few regretted it (see A. Curtis, *Lectures on Midwifery and the forms of Disease Peculiar to Women and Children* [Columbus, Ohio: Jonathan Philips, 1841], p. 9.). On the whole question of women and the professions in this period, see Gerda Lerner, "The Lady and the Mill-Girl: Changes in the Status of Women in the Age of Jackson," *Mid-Continent American Studies Journal* 10 (1969): 5-15.

55 American society throughout this period agreed on the importance and potency of motherhood. In part this was a simple rationale of the fact that, since the American father was at work, the American mother was raising the children. See Anne L. Kuhn, *The Mother's Role in Childhood Education* (New Haven: Yale University Press, 1947); Bernard Wishy, *The Child and the Republic: The Dawn of Modern American Child Nurture* (Philadelphia: University of Pennsylvania Press, 1968), pp. 24-29. Contemporary paens to motherhood are legion, but see Jabez Burns, *Mothers of the Wise and Good* (Boston: Gould, Kendall and Lincoln, 1850), and Margaret C. Conklin, *Memoirs of the Mother and Wife of Washington* (Auburn, N.Y.: Derby, Miller, 1851).

56 I have picked the two most famous of the early women doctors in America, but most of the others fall into similar patterns. All of them devoted themselves professionally almost exclusively to women, few of them married, and most of them met determined opposition from the majority of their male colleagues, in some cases amounting to what Elizabeth Blackwell called "medical starvation" (unpublished letter of January 23, 1855, to Emily Blackwell in Blackwell Collection, Radcliffe Archives, Cambridge, Mass.). For works on and by the other three most famous women doctors of the period, Emily Blackwell, Mary Putnam Jacobi, and Marie Zakrewska, see the Blackwell Collection; Ruth Truax (ed.), *Life and Letters of Mary Putnam Jacobi* (New York: G. P. Putnam's Sons, 1925); *Mary Putnam Jacobi, M.D.: A Pathfinder in Medicine: With Selections from Her Writings* (New York: G. P. Putnam's Sons, 1925); Rhoda Truax, *The Doctors Jacobi* (Boston: Little, Brown, 1952); and the Jacobi papers, also at Radcliffe.

Jacobi was one of the most brilliant doctors of her day, and her monograph, *The Question of Rest for Women During Menstruation* (New York: G. P. Putnam's Sons, 1877), an answer to Clarke, won the Harvard Boylston Medical Prize. For Zakrewska's autobiography, see Caroline H. Dall, (ed.), *A Practical Illustration of Woman's Right to Labor: or A Letter from Marie E. Zakrewska, M.D.* (Boston: Walker, Wise, 1860); Agnes C. Victor, (ed.), *A Woman's Quest: The Life of Marie E. Zakrewska, M.D.* (New York: D. Appleton, 1924). Also of great interest, although falling outside of official professional ranks, were Lydia Fowler and Mary Gove Nichols. See Frederick C. Waite, "Dr. Lydia Folger Fowler: The Second Woman to Receive the Degree of Doctor in the United States," *Annals of Medical History* 4 (1932): 290-297; T. L. Nichols and Mary S. Gove Nichols, *Marriage: Its History, Character and Results* (New York: T. L. Nichols, 1854); Mary S. Gove Nichols, *Mary Lyndon, or Revelations of a Life: An Autobiography* (New York: Stringer and Townsend, 1855); Helen Beal Woodward, *The Bold Women* (New York: Farrar, Straus and Young, 1953), pp. 149-180.

57 Ishbel Ross, *Child of Destiny: The First Life Story of the First Woman Doctor* (New York: Harper & Brothers, 1949), p. 43.

58 Blackwell, *Pioneer Work*, pp. 28, 32. She consistently opposed the marriages of the male members of her large family; the women all stayed single. See Elinor Rice Hays, *Those Extraordinary Blackwells: The Story of a Journey to a Better World* (New York: Harcourt, Brace, & World, 1967), p. 155. Zakrewska felt the same way. See *A Woman's Quest*, p. 193.

59 Blackwell, *Pioneer Work*, p. 72.

60 "Increase of Operations," undated paper in the Blackwell Collection. See also Elizabeth Blackwell, *Essays in Medical Sociology* (London: Ernest Bell, 1902), 2: 120.

61 Letter of March 21, 1891 in the Blackwell Collection.

62 See Blackwell, *Essays*, 2, pp. 119 ff. Anti-vivisection had many passionate feminine adherents, medical and lay. Elizabeth Stuart Phelps, a popular writer and feminist of Blackwell's era, devoted much of her work to the cause. See especially *Though Life Do Us Part* (Boston: Houghton Mifflin, 1908), pp. 54-55, where she explicitly links male cruelty in vivisection with male cruelty in marriage, and *Trixy* (Boston and New York: Houghton Mifflin, 1904) in which a girl refuses to marry a vivisectionist.

63 See Blackwell, *Pioneer Work*, pp. 178, 157, 240. See also Blackwell, *Essays*, 2: 69ff.

64 Blackwell, *Essays*, 2: 26. Jacobi seems to be making a similar point about the male intellect in "The Mad Scientist," in *Stories and Sketches* (New York: G. P. Putnam's Sons, 1907).

[65] Blackwell, *Pioneer Work*, p. 173.

[66] All page references for this essay are to Blackwell, *Essays*, 2.

[67] Undated letter to Dr. McNutt in the Blackwell Collection.

[68] Blackwell nowhere makes this more clear than in *The Human Element in Sex: Being a Medical Enquiry Into the Relation of Sexual Physiology to Christian Morality* (London: J. & A. Churchill, 1884).

[69] A good introduction to the spirit and work of the Purity Alliance is Aaron M. Powell, (ed.), *The National Purity Congress: Its Papers, Addresses, Portraits* (New York: The United Purity Alliance, 1896).

[70] *Wrong and Right Methods of Dealing with Social Evil as Shown by English Parliamentary Evidence* (New York: A. Bretano & Co., n.d.) p. 41. See also "The Purchase of Women: The Great Economic Blunder" in Blackwell, *Essays*, 1: 133-174.

[71] See Campbell-Hurd, *Medical Women in America*, and Robinson, *White-Caps*

[72] For her own account, see *Chapters from a Life* (Boston: Houghton Mifflin, 1897), pp. 228-242. Her most important fictional accounts of illness are "Shut In" in *Fourteen to One* (Boston: Houghton Mifflin, 1891), pp. 66-99, about an invalid's recovery, and *Walled In* (New York: Harper & Brothers, 1907), about the relationship between a nurse and a male patient.

[73] All page references are to Elizabeth Stuart Phelps, *Dr. Zay* (Boston: Houghton Mifflin, 1886). I owe much of my thinking on Phelps to Christine Stansell's "Elizabeth Stuart Phelps: A Study in Female Rebellion," *Massachusetts Review* 13 (1972): 239-256. For other contemporary fictional works on women doctors, see William Dean Howells, *Dr. Breen's Practice* (Boston: J. R. Osgood, 1881), and Sarah Orne Jewett, *A Country Doctor* (Boston: Houghton Mifflin, 1884).

PUBERTY TO MENOPAUSE: THE CYCLE OF FEMININITY IN NINETEENTH-CENTURY AMERICA

Carroll Smith-Rosenberg

Adolescence and the coming of old age are pivotal processes in human experience. On one level, they are socially defined crises, points of entrance into new social roles and responsibilities. More primitively, they are physiological processes that each individual and each culture must incorporate into basic patterns of social structure and ideology. They are marked by hormonal and emotional flux, maladjustment and depression—in the case of old age, by disease and fears of disease. The coming and fading of sexual maturity, moreover, force cultures and individuals to deal with the question of human sexuality. The menstrual blood and wet dreams of puberty, the hot flashes of menopause are physical signposts that even the most sexually repressed and denying culture must acknowledge and rationalize in terms consistent with its social values generally (as must each individual within that culture, in terms appropriate to his or her particular psychic needs). Few values are more central to this process than those relating to women and women's role.

This article[1] proposes to examine Victorian-American attitudes toward puberty and menopause in women. It will do so from one specific perspective— the perspective of the medical profession as expressed in both its professional and its popular writings. Since puberty and menopause are both physiological processes and possible triggers of disease, every nineteenth-century gynecology textbook and most popular medical guides devoted sections to them, as, of course, did the professional journals. In non-medical Victorian literature, on the other hand, these subjects remained veiled.[2]

Puberty, menstruation and menopause could be specifically medical problems as well. The depressions and irritability of adolescence, the breast and uterine cancer of the aging woman were conditions physicians had to face—and if not cure, at least explain, and in explaining hope to mitigate. The physician's hypothetical explanation of these disorders thus served to express and rationalize the often intractable realities of puberty and menopause—and, at the same time, helped the physician act out his own role as healer. Inevitably, as well, the physician's would-be scientific views reflected and helped shape social definitions of the appropriate bounds of woman's role and identity. In exploring these medical arguments then, I want to stress not their internal consistency and even less their scientific significance, but rather the ways in which they represent a particular nineteenth-century attempt to resolve the perplexing interplay of socially defined sex roles and the ambivalence surrounding puberty and menopause.

Woman, Victorian society dictated, was to be chaste, delicate and loving. Yet her Victorian contemporaries assumed that behind this modest exterior lay a complex network of reproductive organs that controlled her physiology, determined her emotions and dictated her social role. She was seen, that is, as being both higher and lower, both innocent and animal, pure yet quintessentially sexual. The central metaphor in these formulations, central both emotionally and in content, pictures the female as driven by the tidal currents of her cyclical reproductive system, a cycle bounded by the pivotal crises of puberty and menopause and reinforced each month by her recurrent menstrual flow.[3]

The extent to which the reproductive organs held sway over woman's body had no parallel in the male. Male sexual impulses, nineteenth-century physicians and laymen alike maintained, were subject to a man's will; they were impulses that particular men could at particular times choose to indulge or to repress.[4] Not so with woman's sexuality. Woman's sexual and generative organs were hidden within her body, subject not to her will but to a biological clock of which women were only dimly aware and which they were clearly unable to control. Each month, for over thirty years, these organs caused cyclical periods of pain, weakness, embarrassment, irritability and, in some cases, even insanity. "Woman's reproductive organs are pre-eminent," one mid-century physician explained in typical phrases. "They exercise a controlling influence upon her entire system, and entail upon her many painful and dangerous diseases. They are the source of her peculiarities, the centre of her sympathies, and the seat of her diseases. Everything that is peculiar to her, springs from her sexual organization."[5]

Such views had been familiar since classical antiquity. Between 1840 and 1890, however, physicians, reflecting a growing physiological sophistication generally, and, more specifically, increasingly circumstantial knowledge of the female reproductive system, were able to present a far more elaborate explanation of woman's peculiar femininity—and hence a rationale for her role as wife and mother.[6] Woman became not only a prisoner of her reproductive functions but quite explicitly of two tiny and hitherto ignored parts of that system—the ovaries. "Ovulation fixes woman's place in the animal economy," one doctor explained in 1880. "With the act of menstruation is wound up the whole essential character of her system." "A woman's system is affected," health reformer J. H. Kellogg commented as late as 1895, "we may almost say dominated, by the influence of these two little glands. . . . Either an excess or a deficiency of the proper influence of these organs over the other parts of the system may be productive of disease."[7]

The ovaries began their dictatorship of woman's life at puberty. They released her, often exhausted and debilitated, at menopause. Puberty and menopause were thus seen as peculiarly sensitive physiological turning points in a woman's life—stages at which new physical and emotional equilibria had to be established.[8] Both men and women, of course, experienced such crises of developmental readjustment. For women, however, such periods of crisis and resolution occurred more frequently, and seemed both more dangerous and more sexual. Puberty was, for example, more precipitate and difficult for women—and was followed immediately by the monthly crisis of menstruation, by pregnancy, childbirth, lactation and finally menopause. As late as 1900, a physician could picture the dangers in these melodramatic terms:

> Many a young life is battered and forever crippled in the breakers of puberty; if it crosses these unharmed and is not dashed to pieces on the rock of childbirth, it may still ground on the ever-recurring shadows of menstruation, and lastly, upon the final bar of the menopause ere protection is found in the unruffled waters of the harbor beyond the reach of sexual storms.[9]

Another physician, perhaps influenced by the moral and religious strivings pictured in *Pilgrim's Progress,* entitled his guide to woman's health, *Woman's Thirty Year Pilgrimage.*[10]

Puberty and menopause were, moreover, inseparably linked in nineteenth-century medical thought. The way in which a woman negotiated the physiological dangers of puberty was believed to determine her health not only during her childbearing years but at menopause as well. A painful, unhealthy or depressed puberty sowed the seeds for disease and trauma at menopause. Indeed so intertwined were these events that physicians used the age of puberty to predict the age when menopause would occur. Puberty and menopause were, as one nineteenth-century physician revealingly expressed it, "the two termini of a woman's sexual activity."[11] Indeed one woman physician went so far as to liken the menopausal woman to a pre-adolescent; menopause, she wrote, was "the transition of the (sexual) system from an active ovarian state to the quiet condition of a non-ovulating girl."[12]

Such medical and biological arguments helped, of course, to rationalize woman's traditional role. But they served other social purposes as well. They expressed, that is, the age-old empirical understanding that puberty and menopause were indeed periods of stress—crises both of emotional and social identification and physical health. And they served as well to provide the physician—armed with still primitive gynecological skills and an equally primitive body of physiological knowledge—a system with which to explain such biological and emotional realities. The nineteenth century was a time when pregnancies and obstetrical trauma were far more common than today. It was crucial to the physician's professional role and thus to the psychic comfort of his female patients as well that he be provided with explanations with which to counsel and to comfort.

At puberty a girl became a woman. Physicians remarked that the change was often startlingly dramatic. Many doctors indulged in romantic eulogies to the young woman's physical and anatomical attributes. They admired her newly rounded limbs, her "swelling breasts," her broadened hips, the transparent nature of her skin which reflected every blush. Her unfolding beauty was charming indeed. "How sensitive—how tremulous is now her nervous system!" one such physician remarked. "It is as if," another doctor wrote, "a new being, almost, is created."[13]

Yet this beauty, like the opening blossom to which the pubescent girl was so frequently compared, was, at the same time, weak, dependent, and fragile. Puberty, the nineteenth century never doubted, brought strength, vigor, and muscular development to boys; to women it brought increased bodily weakness, a new found and biologically rooted timidity and modesty, and the "illness" of menstruation. With puberty, English clinician Michael Ryan explained to his medical audience, "all parts of [a man's] . . . body became developed . . . the principles of life superabound in his constitution, and he vigorously performs all the noble pursuits assigned him by nature. Woman, on the contrary, delicate and tender, always preserves some of the infantile constitution."[14]

Yet the creation of this fragile and ethereal creature was frequently traumatic; female adolescence was often a stormy period. (The emotional difficulties of adolescence were hardly a discovery of the late nineteenth century; they were well known to physicians throughout the century.) Girls would suddenly became moody, depressed, petulant, capricious, even sexually promiscuous. Adolescence, explained a late nineteenth-century advice book for mothers, "is naturally a time of restlessness and of nerve irritability. Her mind is confused with vague dissatisfaction, with all about her, and vaguer desires which she vainly endeavors to define even to herself. . . . Her feelings are especially sensitive and easily hurt." It was a "period of storm and stress," of "brooding, depression and morbid introspection."[15]

Victorian physicians drew upon their "ovarian" model of female behavior both to explain such erratic behavior and to contain it within traditional social bounds. The onset of puberty, they explained, marked perhaps the greatest crisis in a woman's life—a crisis during which a new physiological and emotional equilibrium was being created, an equilibrium that would control woman's life for the next thirty years. If a girl, especially at the very outset of puberty, violated the laws of her body, a dire chain of pain and disease, of dysmenorrhoea, miscarriage, even sterility would surely follow. As one physician explained in his domestic medical text.

> It is now that every hidden germ of disease is ready to spring up; and there is scarcely a disorder to which the young and growing female is subjected, which is not at this time occasionally to be seen, and very often in a fatal form. . . . Coughs become consumptive and scrofula exerts its utmost influence in the constitution and deforms the figure of the body. . . . the dimensions of that bony outlet of the female frame is also altered and diminished on which so much of safety and comparative ease depends in childbirth. This, indeed, is the cause of almost every distressing and fatal labor that occurs and it is at this period of life. . . . that such an unspeakable misfortune may be prevented.

If a woman was to fulfill her ordained role as mother of numerous and healthy offspring, her own mother must carefully oversee her puberty—and be aware of even the slightest evidence of ill-health.[16]

Woman's body, doctors contended, contained only a limited amount of energy—energy needed for the full development of her uterus and ovaries. At the commencement of puberty, then, a girl should curtail all activity. One doctor advised the young woman to take to her bed from the first signs of a discharge until menstruation was firmly established, months or perhaps years later. Not all doctors took so extreme a position, but most did warn that a girl should not engage in any absorbing project at this time. Indeed physicians routinely used this energy theory to sanction attacks upon any behavior they considered unfeminine; education, factory work, religious or charitable activities, indeed virtually any interests outside the home during puberty were deplored, as were any kind of sexual forwardness such as flirtations, dances and party-going.[17]

There was only one right way for a young woman to behave at puberty. From the onset of menstruation until marriage, she must concentrate on the healthy development of her reproductive organs and the regulation of her menses. Physicians prescribed an elaborate regimen to maintain sexual and general health, a regimen that remained remarkably consistent throughout the nineteenth century. Young women were told to avoid the display of any strong emotions, especially anger, at puberty. They should spend much of their time in the fresh air, enjoy moderate exercise, avoid down beds, corsets, liquor and other stimulating beverages. Ample rest and a simple diet of unstimulating food were equally necessary. Indeed, the life-style most frequently advocated for the young woman consisted of a routine of domestic tasks, such as bed-making, cooking, cleaning and child-tending. These would appropriately serve, physicians argued, to provide the best regimen for the full and proper development of her maternal organs.[18]

Medical theories of puberty thus served a number of functions. Such concepts served as a way in which physicians—and society generally—could recognize the development and centrality of woman's sexual nature—while at the same time controlling and limiting that sexuality within a reproductive framework. The theories conceded the existence of sexuality and emotionality as normal aspects of adolescence, but served to warn women that they must control these emotions and limit their activities to the home; otherwise, disease, insanity, and even death would surely follow.

Even more subtly, these hypothetical physiological arguments suggest, by implication, a good deal about the social and psychic realities of female adolescence—and their latent function for the physicians who intoned them. Let me be a bit more specific. Nineteenth-century medical discussions of puberty suggested that mother-daughter relations may often have broken down at puberty, thus leaving the young girl isolated from an important emotional support system during a critical and stormy period. Physicians wrote repeatedly of girls left in culpable ignorance by their prudish mothers, terrified at what they could only construe as vaginal hemorrhaging. Many such girls, physicians reported, tried fearfully to stop the flow, immersing their bodies in icy water or wrapping wet clothes around their abdomens. Others, seized with shame and terror, ran away from home, exposed themselves to inclement weather or wandered the streets at night not wanting to return home. One woman reported that it had taken her "a life time" to forgive her mother for the fear and loneliness she had felt when she was first menstruating.[19] Indeed, so common in medical writings are versions of this traumatic first menstruation, that it becomes a kind of primal feminine scene, one encompassing in a single exemplary situation a universe of veiled emotion—emotions that nineteenth-century doctors recognized and attempted to mitigate by castigating those mothers who failed to support their daughters at so critical a period.[20]

Though warnings about rest, diet and the need for maternal supervision which mark the medical discussions of puberty may seem quaint, perhaps repressive, they tell us a good deal about the female experience of puberty; they tell us that adolescence was traumatic, that it implied an often painful restructuring of intra-familial and social identities—in short, the hypothetical pathology of the critical period and its possibly irreversible damage expressed a consciousness of the real crisis a young girl faced at this time. The emotionally charged picture of first menstruation, its isolation, fears, and dangers served, that is, to express and rationalize a rather complex insight into the several dimensions of puberty.

Insecurity and a sense of isolation and unworthiness are, of course, not peculiar to adolescent girls in Victorian America. These feelings reflect a multitude of anxieties: fear that menstrual blood might indeed be the result of injury due to masturbation, a fear probably unconscious and perhaps dating to infancy, of a growing social autonomy and sexual maturity, the reactivation of a fundamental struggle between mother and daughter for both love and independence—a struggle that psychiatrists now suggest predates any Oedipal conflict. Puberty and menstruation do, after all, force every woman to ask and attempt to answer that fundamental question: what is the nature and meaning of my femaleness?

Part of this stress surrounding female puberty was due to the ambivalent and unresolved attitudes that surrounded menstruation itself. The history of attitudes toward menstruation is age-old, varied, yet surprisingly consistent; it was a period of danger, of shame, of punishment. Judeo-Christian folk lore attributed menstruation to God's curse on the daughters of a sinning Eve. Because of Eve's transgression, women needed more forgiveness and regeneration than man, one physician argued, and thus "this special secretion was given them." "Many girls," another reported, "consider [menstruation] as a humiliating badge of their inferiority to the stronger sex." Not surprisingly, many women believed that menstrual blood was peculiarly contaminated, if retained within the body it would corrupt the blood generally and lead to disease.[21]

Physicians, or many of them, tried to counter these feelings of shame and resentment. The tactic normally chosen, of course, was to wash the menstrual blood white in the rhetorical spirituality of marriage and motherhood. "Menstruation is allied to Maternity," one doctor wrote, "leading us to regard this function with reverence." "How strange," another wrote reassuringly, "that women should regard with shame and distaste this function to which she owed health and life itself."[22] Yet, not surprisingly, such words of paternalistic reassurance were often mixed with expressions of distaste and doubt. One of America's leading gynecologists, for instance, prefaced a medical school lecture on the female reproductive system by "begging" his students, "to accompany me in this disagreeable task," while another physician commented in passing that menstrual blood had a rank smell which any man could detect. Others argued that it was not in fact blood but some strange and unclassifiable discharge.[23]

There are other indications in the medical literature that many physicians were ambivalent toward the menstruating woman. Doctors, for instance, frequently began discussions of puberty and menstruation by elaborately recounting ancient myths that granted menstrual blood distinctive and magical powers. Forcefully denying the truths of these myths, the doctors then argued that, quite the contrary, menstruation made women weak, diseased, and dependent.[24] The recurrence of this particular formulation suggests that it may well have proved psychically functional to those male physicians who so tirelessly intoned it; certain physicians may well have felt ambivalent about menstruation or female genitalia—and by implication about their own masculinity. Their elaborate and stylized exposition and then destruction of such myths might thus have served the dual psychological purpose of permitting physicians to first displace their own fears of menstruating women onto classical writers or primitive peoples—an effective distancing technique—and then consciously to ridicule and deny the validity of such displaced fears. Their coupling this denial of feminine powers with the theory that menstruating women were indeed weak and fragile supports this hypothesis.

The other patterns found in nineteenth-century medical discussions of menstruation tend to reinforce such a psychological interpretation. A significant number of physicians drew a suggestive nexus between women's sexual appetite and menstruation—seeing menstruation as either the monthly apex of women's sexual desires or as a system to aid women in controlling such impulses. George Rowe wrote in 1844: "In God's infinite wisdom . . . might not this monthly discharge be ordained for the purpose of controlling woman's violent sexual passions . . . by unloading the uterine vessels . . . so as to prevent the promiscuous intercourse which would prove destructive to the purest . . . interests of civil life . . ."[25]

The insatiate and promiscuous woman is one of man's most primitive and fearful fantasies, a fantasy which in individual men was clearly productive of anxiety such as that evident in Rowe's pious praise of menstruation. Closely parallelling the image of the sexually powerful woman is that of the maniacal and destructive woman. Menstruation, nineteenth-century physicians warned, could drive some women temporarily insane; menstruating women might go berserk, destroying furniture, attacking family and strangers alike and even killing their infants. Those "unfortunate women," subject to such excessive menstrual influence, Edward Tilt wrote, should for their own good and that of society be incarcerated for the length of their menstruating years.[26]

Like puberty, menopause was seen as a physiological crisis, its course shaped by a woman's preceding sexual experiences, its resolution determining her future health.[27] If a woman had followed a sound regimen throughout life and had no predisposition to malignant disease, menopause could bring with it a golden age of health and freedom from the periodic inconvenience, pain and depression of menstruation. The menopausal period could thus become the "Indian summer" of a woman's life—a period of increased vigor, optimism, and even of physical beauty.[28]

Far more frequently, however, menopause marked the beginning of a period of depression, of heightened disease incidence, and of early death. "There is a predisposition to many diseases, and these are often of a melancholy character," one physician noted in the 1830s. The host of diseases that might develop as a result of the cessation of menstruation included, as one doctor lamented, "almost all the ills the flesh is heir to."[29] They ranged from the classic flushes of menopause, through dyspepsia, diarrhea, severe vaginitis, vaginal inflammation, prolapsed uterus, rheumatic pains, paralysis, apoplexy, and erysipelas to uterine hemorrhaging, tumors, uterine and breast cancer, tuberculosis, scrofula, and diabetes.[30] Emotional or psychological symptoms characterized menopause as well. Irritability, depression, hysteria, melancholy, episodes of severe emotional withdrawal and insanity seemed particularly common.[31] Clearly, nineteenth-century physicians used menopause as an all-purpose explanation for the heightened disease incidence of the older female; all of her ills were directly or indirectly diseases of the uterus and ovaries.

Physicians postulated a number of mechanisms to explain this pattern of ill-health. The diseases of menopause, one theory argued, were rooted in a "plethora," which resulted after the cessation of the menses from the retention of the monthly menstrual blood. It was to such a plethora, or suffusion of the body with fluids, that physicians attributed the hot flashes, circulatory diseases, palpitations, and vaginal hemorrhaging of menopause. "The stoppage of any customary evacuations, however small, is sufficient to disorder the whole frame and often to destroy life itself," William Buchan explained in his extraordinarily influential *Domestic Medicine*.[32] By mid-century, physicians evolved additional explanations of such diseases in older women. Each month, some contended, the menstrual blood had carried off the seeds of illness and in this way repressed a host of contagious and constitutional ailments that then flourished with the repression of menstruation. Still others argued that the diseases of menopause, especially cancer of the uterus and breast, were rooted in systemic exhaustion consequent upon the unceasing cycle of menstruation, pregnancy and lactation.[33]

But the most significant cause of a woman's menopausal disease, virtually every doctor believed, lay in her violation of the physiological and social laws dictated by her ovarian system. Education, attempts at birth control or abortion, undue sexual indulgence, a too fashionable life-style, failure to devote herself fully to the needs of husband and children—even the advocacy of woman's suffrage—all might guarantee a disease-ridden menopause.[34]

One of the common causes of hemorrhaging, ovarian tumor, or insanity at menopause was not, however, a life filled with hygenic misdeeds, but rather a momentary lack of judgment in old age—that is, engaging in sexual intercourse during or after menopause. "My experience teaches me that a marked increase of sexual impulse at the change of life is a morbid impulse," Edward Tilt wrote in his widely read study of menopause. "Whenever sexual impulse is first felt at the change of life, some morbid ovario-uterine condition will be found to explain it. . . . It, therefore, is most imprudent for women to marry at this epoch without having obtained the sanction of a medical man." Female sexuality and reproduction thus formed a comforting nexus, the destruction of which clearly threatened certain Victorian physicians.[35]

Doctors warned that women must treat menopause as the beginning of old age. Women should alter their style of life and retire from the world into the bosom of their family. "We insist," wrote Walter Taylor in 1872,

> that every woman who hopes for a healthy old age ought to commence her prudent cares as early as the 40th year or sooner. . . . She should cease to endeavor to appear young when she is no longer so, and withdraw from the excitments and fatigues of the gay world even in the midst of her legitimate successes, to enter upon that more tranquil era of her existence now at hand.

"Most American mothers," he added with unintentional irony "can find at hand enough to do for their own families . . . to absorb all their energies."[36] The regimen almost universally prescribed for menopausal women closely paralleled that recommended for their pubescent daughters and granddaughters, a regimen of quiet, avoidance of mental activities, the shunning of new activities and a commitment to domesticity.[37]

Such ideas seem obviously formal and defensive. Male physicians displayed a revealing disquietude and even hostility when discussing their menopausal patients. In the medical literature, the menopausal woman often appeared as ludicrous or physically repulsive. Edward Tilt, for instance, claimed that she characteristically had a "dull stupid look", was "pale or sallow" and tended to grow a beard on her chin and upper lip. Doctors scoffed at women who, long sterile or just married at menopause, believed themselves pregnant. These women, doctors commented heartily, suffered from a little flatulence, somewhat more hysteria and, most of all, obesity. Their fantasied fetus, another doctor joked, was just their belly's double chin. More critical were their comments about women who deliberately attempted to appear young after they had reached menopause. Menopausal depression—other physicians remarked—grew out of pique at no longer being considered young and attractive.[38]

Indeed such hostility and even contempt marked male medical discussions of menopausal women that one woman physician, in a valedictory address to the 1864 class at Woman's Medical College in Philadelphia, cited such animosity as an important reason for women's becoming physicians. Referring specifically to male physicians' treatment of menopausal women she exhorted: "You will also vindicate the right, scarcely yet conceded to women, to grow *old* without reproach. . . ."[39]

But how did women view this stage of life? From what I can detect thus far from diaries, letters, and the medical literature, I would answer that women viewed menopause with utter ambivalence. Doctors routinely noted that women faced menopause with dread and depression. "Suffering at the later period of life is accepted by many women as unavoidable and proper," one doctor remarked. Another physician commented upon a woman's "fear[s] as her age warns her that she is approaching that mysterious change. Every morbid impulse of her life is discussed with her friends. . . . She anxiously dwells on every little disorder, so charged is her mind with vague fears. . . ." "Indeed," wrote a third some seventy years earlier, "so replete is this time with horrors to some that we may very justly suspect apprehension to be the cause of some of the distressing symptoms. . . ."40

There is much, however, to indicate that many women looked forward to menopause as a release from the bondage of menstruation and pregnancy. Doctors, as already mentioned, did report that despite a general pattern of disease and depression, the health of some women improved dramatically with menopause. Indeed, menopause was seen as a specific for longterm depressions, lassitude and hysteria. Other doctors remarked how fresh and lovely some menopausal women looked—with a lightness to their step and a countenance free from anxiety.

The comments of a conservative and socially prominent Philadelphia Quaker matron, Elizabeth Drinker, may throw some light on this sense of freedom. Drinker recorded in her diary a conversation she had with her daughter Sally who was about to give birth. Each of Sally's births had been protracted and painful; her youngest sister had, just the day before, almost died in childbirth, surviving only to be permanently crippled. Sally was filled with foreboding at the begining of this labor. "My poor dear Sally was taken unwell last night, . . ." Drinker wrote in October 1799.

> She is in pain at times, forerunning pains of a lingering labour, a little low spirited, poor dear Child. This day is 38 years since I was in agonies bringing her into this world of troubles; she told me with tears that this was her birth day, I endeavour'd to talk her into better Spirits, told her that the time of her birth was over by some hours, she was now in her 39th year, and that this might possibly be the last trial of this sort, if she could suckle her baby for two years to come, as she had several times done heretofore. . . .41

Elizabeth and Sally Drinker were not the only women who viewed menopause as a release from "a world of troubles." Menopause was indeed an ultimate birth-control technique and many women welcomed it for that reason. Their feelings were well captured by a woman physician when she described the obstetrical history and feelings of a representative patient at the coming of menopause. As a young woman and newly in love, the patient had believed marriage the summit of human happiness. Within a year, however, she became pregnant "and such pains as accompanied this [birth] she had never before believed that woman could endure." Many pregnancies followed this first, "until ten, twelve or even fifteen children have been born, with an accumulation of troubles to correspond. . . . Then her remarks assume a different tone. . . . She wrings her hands . . . and weeps as she begs her young friends to pause and consider before they leave home at so early an age; for marriage and maternity are not a romance. . . ." It is against a background of such experience that the nineteenth-century woman approached menopause. "She is no longer exposed to the direful risks and pain of child bearing," a male physician remarked some fifty years earlier. "She thanks God for that and takes comfort in the thought."[42]

Perhaps the most forceful mid-nineteenth-century expression of a positive view of menopause was articulated by social reformer and suffrage advocate Eliza Farnham. "My acquaintance with women of the nobler sort," Farnham wrote, "has convinced me that many a woman has experienced, at times, a secret joy in her advancing age." Indeed, Farnham continued, menopause could become woman's golden age, when she was freed from the physical and emotional demands of childbirth and child rearing, her spiritual nature could develop to its fullest. She found the post-menopausal years the period of woman's "super-exaltation" and condemned those men who had taught women to dread menopause as "an absolutely uncompensated loss of power." "That day is long since past for enlightened women," she continued, "and will be soon for their less understanding sisters. . . . For women developed enough to have opinions and take any ground, teach each other very rapidly. Their presence in the field of masculine errors is like sunlight to the mists of early dawn."[43]

Borrowing Eliza Farnham's imagery, what forms can we see shrouded in the mists of these Victorian metaphors? By examining the would-be scientific metaphors with which Victorian physicians surrounded the female crises of puberty and menopause, I believe, we can gain some insight into a number of nineteenth-century emotional realities. On the very simplest level these ideas, as I have noted, served as an absolute biological justification for woman's restricted role. They served as well to express and explain traditional empirical observations and folk wisdom concerning the real biological, emotional, and social significance—and stress—of puberty, menstruation, and menopause. They created, moreover, an ideal metaphor in which the Victorian physician could express a characteristic and revealingly inconsistent ambiguity toward woman's sexual and social nature. Within this system, woman was seen at the same time as a higher, more sensitive, more spiritual creature—and as a prisoner of tidal currents of an animal and uncontrollable nature (and in this way denied the two cardinal Victorian virtues of control and rationality). At the same time this formula also permitted Victorians to recognize the sometimes ominous force of female sexuality and to render such sexuality safe by subordinating it to the limited ends of child-bearing and nursing.

It is tempting, indeed, to elaborate a psychological interpretation of these nineteenth-century gynecological metaphors and formulations concerning puberty and menopause. They are suggestively consistent, for example, with a theory developed some years later by Karen Horney. Horney argued that male fear of woman is a basic human emotion that predates the Oedipal dread of castration. In developing this hypothesis, Horney suggested that those men fearful of woman's sexuality attempt to defend against their anxiety in two ways. First, they denigrate women, especially those aspects of woman's body most closely associated with her genitals. Secondly, they overcompensate for their fears and hostility by romanticizing women, especially those parts of a woman's body and behavior not immediately associated with genital sexuality.[44]

The conventional formulae of nineteenth-century medical writers are remarkably compatible with Horney's hypothetical male "dread of women." Woman's "disagreeable," diseased—and hidden—sexual organs contrasted unfavorably in the medical literature, that is, with her "blushing" cheeks, her parted lips, her graceful bearing, her luminous eyes. In addition to defending against primal fears, as suggested by Horney, these particular rhetorical formulae may have also served as a means through which "respectable" males could cope with sexuality in the specifically repressive moral and religious climate of mid-nineteenth-century England and the United States.[45]

But such interpretations raise serious methodological problems for the historian. I have attempted in some ways to paint a group psychological portrait of individuals at a distance of one hundred years, individuals of whom we know little more than their formal writings. These writings are suggestive, but to assert more would clearly be gratuitous. Whole segments of past societies cannot be placed upon a couch that, at best, accomodates a single individual. And contemporary psychoanalytic theory can hardly be said to have provided final statements in regard to the development of human personality. Specifically, for example, though Horney's hypothesis may indeed be plausible, it is a theory unproven and unprovable.

Thus it has not been my purpose in this article to espouse a simple psychological interpretation of such a widely supported and long-lived ideological system. I have suggested rather that the nineteenth-century medical and biological explanation of puberty and menopause may well have served a number of different functions. It served, I would argue, the broader social need of defending woman's traditional social place. It helped physicians function within their intellectual and professional role. And it may, as well, have proved functional on the level of individual psychodynamics—permitting certain Victorian males, and females, to express a deeply felt ambivalence toward sexuality.

This project was supported in part by grant 5 FO2 HG 48800-02 from the National Institutes of Health and by a grant from the Grant Foundation, New York, New York.

NOTES

[1] This article will form part of a book on woman's changing role and role conflict in nineteenth-century America to be published by Alfred A. Knopf, Inc.

[2] This is not to say that the question of adolescence and aging in women did not appear in nineteenth-century fiction; quite the contrary. Fictional discussions, however, lack the explicit physiological and sexual detail that characterized medical accounts. There were indeed so many

popular nineteenth-century medical guides for women that they may be said to constitute a specific genre; all discussed such issues with varying degrees of explicitness. This article is based on a study of popular women's medical guides and of medical literature written for a professional medical audience: gynecological textbooks, monographs, and journal articles.

3 For an expanded study of this metaphor and its implications for woman's social role see Carroll Smith-Rosenberg and Charles Rosenberg, "The Female Animal: Medical and Biological Views of Women in Nineteenth-Century America," *Journal of American History* 60 (September 1973), in press.

4 Charles West, *Lectures on the Diseases of Women*, 2 vols. (London: John Churchill, 1861), vol. 1, no. 1; A. J. C. Skene, *Education and Culture as Related to the Health and Diseases of Women* (Detroit: George S. Davis, 1889), p. 22.

5 John Wiltbank, *Introductory Lecture for the Session, 1853-54* (Philadelphia: Edward Grattan, 1854), p. 7.

6 This changing ideology reflected, of course, more than a simple improvement in medical knowledge. It reflected both a rapid growth in the prestige of science as a reference area in mid- and late-nineteenth century, as well as the growing conflict that centered around woman's role. As the traditional role of wife and mother seemed increasingly under attack, the medical and biological defenses of that role increased proportionately. For a general discussion of the role of scientific language and metaphor and the growing emotional relevance of science in dealing with such social problems see: Charles E. Rosenberg, "Science and American Social Thought," in *Science and Society in the United States*, eds., David D. Van Tassel and Michael G. Hall, (Homewood, Illinois: The Dorsey Press, 1966) pp. 135-162.

7 William Pepper, "The Change of Life in Women," *Clinical News* 1 (1880): 505; J. H. Kellog, *Ladies' Guide in Health and Disease* (Battle Creek, Michigan: Modern Medicine Publishing Co., 1895), p. 371. See as well Edward H. Dixon, *Woman and Her Diseases* (New York: author, 1846), p. 71; Charles Meigs, *Females and Their Diseases* (Philadelphia: D. G. Brinton, 1879), p. 332. A number of women physicians disagreed. Disease in women originated not in diseased ovaries, they argued, but in the unhealthy and restrained way women lived—without exercise, fresh air, or serious employment to occupy their minds. For a classic example of this "feminist" argument see Alice Stockham, *Tokology*, rev. ed. (Chicago: Sanitary Publishing Co., 1887), p. 257. With this particular exception, however, I found a remarkable uniformity in medical opinions on the specific issues discussed in this paper both in terms of chronology, that is between the late eighteenth century and the late nineteenth and between representatives of the medical establishment and so-called quack doctors.

8 Edward Tilt, *The Change of Life in Health and Disease*, 4th ed. (New York: Bermingham & Co., 1882) p. 14; P. Henry Chavasse, *Physical Life of Man and Woman* (Cincinnati: National Publishing Co., 1871), p. 155; Caleb Ticknor, *Philosophy of Living* (New York: Harper & Bros., 1836), pp. 304-305.

9 Alexander Hamilton, *A Treatise on the Management of Female Complaints* (New York: Samuel Campbell, 1792), p. 98-99; Gunning Bedford, *Lecture Introductory to a Course on Obstetrics and Diseases of Women and Children* (New York: Jennings, 1847), p. 8; Meigs, *Females and their Diseases*, p. 334; George J. Englemann, "The American Girl To-day. The Influence of Modern Education on Functional Development," *Transactions of the American Gynecological Society* 25 (1900): 9-10.

10 (W. W. Bliss), *Woman and Her Thirty Year Pilgrimage* (New York: William M. Littell, 1869).

11 This was a pattern that remained constant throughout the century. See for example: Joseph Brevitt, *The Female Medical Repository* (Baltimore: Hunter & Robinson, 1810), p. 39; John Burns, *Principles of Midwifery*, 2 vols. (Philadelphia: Edward Parker), p. 138; J. Smedley, "The Importance of Making a Physical Exploration during the Climacteric Period," *Hahnemannean Monthly* 8 (1886): p. 487; William Capp, *The Daughter* (Philadelphia: F. A. Davis, 1891), p. 65; Kellogg, *Ladies' Guide*, p. 371.

12 A. M. Longshore-Potts, *Discourses to Women on Medical Subjects* (San Diego, California: author, 1890), p. 32, 94;

13 Dixon, *Woman and Her Diseases*, p. 21; William P. Dewees, *A Treatise on the Diseases of Females* (Philadelphia: H. C. Carey & J. Lea, 1826), p. 56. Again, this pattern can be found in medical literature throughout the nineteenth century. See for example: William Buchanan, *Domestic Medicine Adapted to the Climate and Diseases of America* by Isaac Cathrall, 2nd ed. (Philadelphia: R. Folwell, 1801), pp. 356-357; Samuel Bard, *A Compendium of the Theory and Practice of Midwifery* (New York: Collins & Co., 1819), p. 39; Albert Hayes, *Physiology of Woman* (Boston: Peabody Medical Institute, 1869), pp. 86-87; Longshore-Potts, *Discourses to Women*, p. 67.

14 Michael Ryan, *Philosophy of Marriage*, 4th ed. (London: J. Bailliere, 1843), p. 143; Frederick Hollick, *The Marriage Guide, or Natural History of Generation* (New York: T. W. Strong, c. 1860), p. 111; Dewees, *Treatise*, pp. 20-21; William Alcott, *The Young Woman's Book of Health* (Boston: Tappan, Whittemore & Mason, 1850), pp. 120-121;

15 [Dr. Porter], *Book of Men, Women and Babies* (New York: DeWitt & Davenport, 1855), p. 90; Hayes, *Physiology of Women*, p. 86; Meyer Solis-Cohen, *Girl, Wife and Mother* (Philadelphia: The John C. Winston Co., c. 1911), p. 27; Capp, *The Daughter*, p. 55.

16 Edward Clarke, *Sex in Education* (Boston: James R. Osgood & Co., 1873), p. 47; J. H. Kellogg, *Plain Facts about Sexual Life* (Battle Creek, Michigan: Office of the Health Reformer, 1877), pp. 52-53; Buchan, *Domestic Medicine*, p. 357; Meigs, *Females and their Diseases*, p. 165; Hayes, *Physiology of Women*, p. 79.

17 For two classic expositions of this argument see: Clarke, *Sex in Education* and Azel Ames, Jr., *Sex in Industry* (Boston: James R. Osgood, 1875). See as well: T. A. Emmet, *The Principles and Practice of Gynecology* (Philadelphia: Henry C. Lea, 1879), p. 21; Rebecca Crumpler, *A Book of Medical Discourses, In Two Parts* (Boston: Cashman, Keating & Co., 1883), p. 121 and Smith-Rosenberg and Rosenberg, "The Female Animal."

18 Hamilton, *Treatise*, p. 100; John See, *A Guide to Mother and Nurses* (New York: author, 1833), pp. 13-14; Tulio Suzzara Verdi, *Maternity, A Popular Treatise for Young Wives and Mothers* (New York: J. B. Ford and Co., 1870), p. 347; Mrs. E. R. Shepherd, *For Girls: A Special Physiology*, 20th ed., (Chicago: Sanitary Publishing Co., 1888), pp. 132-137; Stockholm, *Tokology*, p. 254.

19 Shepherd, *For Girls*, pp. 8-9; Dixon, *Woman and Her Diseases*, p. 75; M. K. Hard, *Woman's Medical Guide* (Mt. Vernon, Ohio: W. H. Cochran, 1848), p. 6; Augustus K. Gardner, *Conjugal Sins*, (New York: G. J. Moulton, 1874), p. 22; Henry B. Hemenway, *Healthful Womanhood and Childhood* (Evanston, Illinois: V. T. Hemenway & Co., 1894), p. 16.

20 See, *Guide to Mothers*, p. 12; Lydia Maria Child, *The Family Nurse* (Boston: Charles J. Hendee, 1837, p. 43; Calvin Cutter, *The Female Guide* (West Brookfield, Mass.: Charles A. Mirick, 1844), p. 49; Potter, *How Should Girls be Educated?*, p. 5; Capp, *Daughter*, v, 2, 3.

21 Clarke, *Sex in Education*, p. 27; Elizabeth Evans, *The Abuse of Maternity* (Philadelphia: J. B. Lippincott and Co., 1875), p. 26. There was a lengthy medical debate over the nature of menstrual blood, in which these popular beliefs were discussed. See note 23.

22 Henry C. Wright, *Marriage and Parentage* (Boston, Bela Marsh, 1854), p. 32; Stockham, *Tokology*, p. 252.

23 Miegs, *Females and Their Diseases*, p. 53; Charles E. Warren, *Causes and Treatment of Sterility in Both Sexes* (Boston: International Medical Exchange, 1890), pp. 58-59. Until quite late in the nineteenth century some physicians doubted whether menstrual blood was in fact blood, or if it was not a special discharge which drew off germs and waste from the circulatory system and thus each month cleansed a woman's system. See for example: Samuel Pancoast, *The Ladies' Medical Guide*, 6th ed. (Philadelphia: John E. Potter, c. 1859) pp. 154-155; Longshore-Potts, *Discourses to Women*, p. 69; Shepherd, *For Girls*, p. 137-138 for this argument. For refutations see: A. M. Mauriceau, *The Married Woman's Medical Companion* (New York: author, 1855), pp. 30-31 and T. R. Trall, *Sexual Physiology* (New York: Miller, Wood & Co., 1866), p. 58.

24 An excellent example of this formula is found in Hayes, *Physiology of Woman*, pp. 84-85. In this passage Hayes significantly refers to menstruation as "an internal wound, the real cause of all this tragedy." For a male physician to refer to menstruation as a "tragedy" seems a bit disproportionate unless Hayes is referring unconsciously to some other primitively perceived tragedy, as for instance castration or death. For an interesting discussion of male fear of menstruation and female genitalia see Karen Horney, "Denial of the Vagina," in *Feminine Psychology*, and with an introduction by Harold Kelman (New York: Norton, 1967). The common medical argument and folk belief that menstruation spoiled the milk of a nursing mother and indeed that such milk could cause convulsions or death in the infant may also be related to a general fear of menstrual blood.

25 George Robert Rowe, *On Some of the Most Important Disorders of Women* (London: John Churchill, 1844), pp. 27-28; William Carpenter, *Principles of Human Physiology*, 4th American ed. (Philadelphia: Lea and Blanchard, 1850), p. 698; Hollick, *Marriage Guide*, p. 95.

26 Tilt, *Change of Life*, p. 13; Horatio R. Storrer and Franklin Fiske Heard, *Criminal Abortion* (Boston: Little, Brown and Company, 1868), p. 90 n.; Verdi, *Maternity*, p. 345.

27 Dixon, *Woman and Her Diseases*, p. 101; Tilt, *Change of Life*, pp. 10-12; Bard, *Compendium*, pp. 78-79.

28 Tilt, *Change of Life*, pp. 12-16; Dewees, *Treatise*, p. 94; Hayes, *Physiology of Women*, p. 95.

29 Joseph Ralph, *A Domestic Guide to Medicine* (New York: author, 1835), p. 130; L. H. Mettler, "Menopause," *Medical Register*, 2 (1887); 323.

30 Tilt, *Change of Life* contains the classic list of menopausal diseases—118 in all, pp. 106-246. See as well B. F. Baer, "The Significance of Menorrhagia recurring about or after the Menopause," *American Journal of Obstetrics* 17 (1884): 461-462; Lawson Tait, "Climacteric Diabetes in Women," *The Practitioner* 36 (June 1886): 401-408; William Pepper, "The Change of Life in Women," pp. 505-506; Dewees, *Treatise,* p. 94-103; Denman, *Introduction to Midwifery,* pp. 192-193; Sara E. Greenfield, "The Dangers of Menopause," *Woman's Medical Journal* (Toledo) 12 (1902): 183-85.

31 See, for example: C. J. Aldrich, "The Role Played by Intestinal Fermentation in the Production of the Neurosis of Menopause," *Physician and Surgeon* (Detroit) 19 (1897): 438-444; Philander Harris, "The Dangers of Certain Impressions Regarding the Menopause," *Transactions of the Medical Society of New Jersey* (1898), pp. 317-325; Dewees, *Treatise,* p. 103.

32 Buchan, *Domestic Medicine,* pp. 360. This was the most popular physiological explanation of menopausal problems. See as well: West, *Diseases of Women,* p. 44; Hayes, *Physiology of Women,* p. 96; Tilt, *Change of Life,* pp. 54, 85.

33 Denman, *Midwifery,* pp. 189-191; Dixon, *Woman and Her Diseases,* p. 103; Shepherd, *For Girls,* pp. 138-39; Mettler, "Menopause," p. 323; Longshore-Potts, *Discourses to Women,* pp. 94-95; "Change of Life in Women," pp. 505-506.

34 Dewees, Treatise, pp. 92, 95; Rowe, *On Some Common Disorders,* p. 36; George Woodruff Johnston, "Certain Facts Regarding Fertility, Utereo-Gestation, Parturition and the Puerperium in the So-Called 'Lower' or 'Laboring' Classes," *American Journal of Obstetrics and Diseases of Women and Children* 21 (May 1888): 19.

35 Tilt also reported giving menopausal women anaphrodisiacs to control their sexual impulses. *Change of Life,* pp. 93-94, 79; Kellogg, *Plain Facts,* p. 80.

36 Taylor, *A Physician's Counsels to Women,* pp. 93-94.

37 See, *Guide to Mothers and Nurses,* p. 18; Brevitt, *Woman's Medical Repository,* pp. 52-53; Longshore-Potts, *Discourses to Women,* p. 95.

38 Tilt, *Change of Life,* pp. 16, 39, 94-95; Taylor, *Physician's Counsels to Women,* p. 85, 90-92; Bard, *Compendium,* p. 80; Burns, *Principles of Midwifery,* p. 162.

39 Ann Preston, *Valedictory Address to the Graduating Class, Female Medical College of Pennsylvania at the Twelfth Annual Commencement, March 16, 1864* (Philadelphia: William S. Young, Printer, 1864), p. 9.

40 Dewees, *Treatise,* p. 92; Aldrich, "Neuroses of Menopause," pp. 153-154; Baer, "Metrorrhagia . . . Menopause," p. 451; Hal C. Wyman, "The Menopause-Gangliasthenia. A Clinical Lecture in the Michigan College of Medicine," *Michigan Medical News* 5 (1882): 313; Mauriceau, *Married Woman's Private Medical Companion,* p. 7.

41 This quote as well as many other lengthy excerpts from Elizabeth Drinker's diary are reprinted in Cecil K. Drinker, *Not So Long Ago. A Chronicle of Medicine and Doctors in Colonial Philadelphia* (New York: Oxford University Press, 1937), pp. 59-60.

42 Meigs, *Females and the Diseases,* p. 55; Longshore-Potts, *Discourses to Women,* pp. 98-102.

43 Eliza W. Farnham, *Woman and Her Era.* 2 vols. (New York: A. J. Davis & Co., 1864), pp. 56-57.

44 Horney, *Feminine Psychology.* See especially her essays on "Fear of Woman," "Denial of the Vagina" and "Female Masochism."

45 For a discussion of such issues see Charles E. Rosenberg, "Sexuality, Class and Role in Nineteenth-Century America," *American Quarterly* (May 1973): in press.

THE LADY AND HER PHYSICIAN

Regina Morantz

The Victorian period holds a particular fascination for the sympathetic historian of women. It is appealing precisely because the contention of the early feminists that women were oppressed by their domestic role is so plausible. Such a view fits nicely with what we think we know about the psychological stresses under which Victorians lived and worked. By the latter half of the nineteenth century, the harsh realities of industrialization and the competitive and un-congenial atmosphere of social Darwinism seemed to drive more and more Americans to seek refuge in the alleged tranquility of domestic life. Woman and the home were exalted accordingly. Women, it has been argued, bore the brunt of this change, as their mental and cultural burdens became more onerous even as their legal rights remained circumscribed. Woman's image was riddled with contradictions: guardian of the race, but wholly subject to male authority; preserver of civilization, religion, and culture, yet considered the intellectual inferior of men; the primary socializer of her children, but given no more real responsibility and dignity than a child herself. Inevitably, countless women were troubled by the ambiguities of their position.

Many feminists in recent years have been tempted to seek the source of present-day women's problems in the apparent injustices of nineteenth-century society. Several current investigations of the Victorian period do just that. One way or another each plays upon a single theme: woman as victim. The problem

This article was originally conceived for the *Journal of Interdisciplinary History* and has been considerably expanded for the present version.

these works present for the scholar is a vexing one: ideology too often hampers analysis; such writings cease to be history and become polemics. Few historians would deny that some women, perhaps many of them, were dissatisfied with the constraints and contradictions of their position; the more articulate may have even described themselves as victimized. However, nineteenth-century American women had other roles as well, and it is precisely the complex nature of women's position that historians ought to illuminate. Moreover, the best "women's history" is not confined to the study of women alone, but deals with the social, intellectual, and cultural context within which women lived out their lives. Therefore, the sooner we can integrate the study of women into investigations of that larger framework, the more valuable its pursuit will become.

From the beginning of the recent reemergence of interest in the history of women, one area of investigation has proved very popular: the treatment of women's diseases in nineteenth-century medicine and the response of middle-class women to a male-dominated medical profession.[1] Out of the research hitherto undertaken, a significant hypothesis is beginning to emerge. Several historians have suggested that nineteenth-century American physicians were hostile to their female patients and that their animosity was expressed in the painful and ineffective therapy they administered.[2] It will be my purpose to examine this supposition and point out its inadequacies. The aversion of doctors to women has been presumed with little effort to locate clinical procedures within the context of nineteenth-century medical therapeutics. By investigating the state of medical practice in the Victorian period, and particularly the work of the eminent neurologist, S. Weir Mitchell, who has come under especial attack, I shall attempt to put these procedures in their proper perspective. I will then examine the ideas of some of the early female physicians in order to explore how some Victorian women viewed their roles in nineteenth-century American society.

In a recent article on psychohistory, Robert Coles cautioned historians to beware of the temptation to share historical facts to coincide with psychological theory. Much recent historical writing presuming to draw on psychoanalytic principles, according to Coles, has done an injustice to the historical discipline by proving more imaginative than substantive. "Will the application of psychological 'insight' to history or the arts," Coles cogently asked, "be done in such a way as to produce caricatures of human beings—and those only to be turned into proof of some larger generalization about the 'laws' that govern the human mind?"[3]

Coles recognizes the need for psychologically sophisticated historians skilled in several disciplines who can help us view human experience more broadly. But a problem arises, he would argue, when psychologizing becomes rigid and narrow, even polemical, and when the moral judgments made are based on the biases of a narrow psychoanalytic formulation. Recent historical treatment of the male medical practitioner has suffered from just the kind of psychologizing Coles deplores. The portrait that emerges might well be termed a caricature.

Often cruel, perhaps even sadistic, the nineteenth-century physician has been accused of handling the complaints of his female patients too complacently. It has been argued that he was guilty of countless acts of torture, from leaving his patients raw and bleeding after cauterization or leeching to the even more questionable performance of drastic gynecological surgery, which included clitoridectomy, oophorectomy, and hysterectomy. Constantly engaged in complex psychological warfare with the women they treated, even the best-intentioned practitioners were partially hostile to them.[4]

"Heroic" medicine was the generic term given to the treatment used by most physicians in the early half of the nineteenth century. Usually it consisted of massive doses of extremely dangerous substances—mercury, lead, calomel, and opium. Heavy bleeding with the lancet or with leeches proved all too popular. Physicians often cauterized the cervical area by the use of hot irons or silver nitrate solution in order to treat venereal disease, as well as a host of lesser female complaints. Clitoridectomy, oöphorectomy, and hysterectomy—surgical procedures developed toward the end of the Victorian period—removed parts or all of the female genital and reproductive system to cure physical as well as emotional ailments.

It is hardly necessary to point out that in most cases the cure was worse than the disease. Yet it does not follow that the forms of treatment for women's ailments, including the drastic mutilation of women's bodies through gynecological surgery, evolved because on some unacknowledged level the doctor feared his female patient, or worried that "his sex, the constant companion of hers, was in some way menaced."[5] According to Ben Barker-Benfield, however, the Victorian male was at his best uncomfortable in his relationship with the opposite sex. His growing uneasiness is attributed by Barker-Benfield to the mounting strength of the women's rights movement and the "growing number of workless women" whose lifestyle was somehow threatening.[6] Yet Barker-Benfield views this anxiety primarily as a sexual one. The Victorian woman, he argues, represented for a man a "sperm absorber," a drain on his energies. Subordinating "desirous Woman" (apparently all women were potentially desirous) was actually a means of controlling man's own sexual irruptibility, for his forcible attraction to her made woman potentially antagonistic to the fundamental sexual and social order which men wanted to preserve.

We are told that gynecological surgery grew out of these anxieties. As the century wore on and the strains of social breakdown were felt more acutely, gynecological surgery arose as a "desperate attempt to control and shape the procreative powers as if the American body politic were literally a body." A frequent rationale for the castration of women defined as disorderly was "that they would cease to contribute to the degeneracy of the American body politic."[7]

Barker-Benfield's thesis, though fascinating, poses obvious problems for the historian, not the least of which is that it is based predominantly on impressionistic evidence. Moreover, his attempt to account for the attitudes of an entire past generation through the application of modern psychological theory—

itself under dispute—can never be more than speculative. Even assuming for the moment that his basic premises concerning the Victorian male's unconscious motivations were sound—something we can never know for sure—Barker-Benfield still cannot account for behavior. Moreover, how can the historian successfully make a connection between the culture of a given society and the unconscious feelings of certain, or even a majority of individuals living within it? Barker-Benfield has not attempted to deal with these methodological difficulties.

Barker-Benfield has argued that drastic gynecological surgery was a widespread phenomenon in the late nineteenth century; that its performance was often a result of a tacit conspiracy between insecure husbands and anxious gynecologists, both of which unconsciously viewed the operation as a way of controlling women. The historical significance of such a procedure was that it expressed a broader cultural hostility to women: "The gynecologists' underlying aims cannot be separated from the society in which they moved: these aims were retaliation against and control of women, and the assumption of as much of their reproductive power as possible, all part and parcel of the projective meaning of the subordination of 'the sex'."[8]

The evidence for such a hypothesis is at best tentative. Neither Barker-Benfield nor anyone else has yet been able to provide reliable statistical evidence of the incidence and distribution of oöphorectomy and its variations in the United States during this period. Barker-Benfield's suggestion that there were approximately 150,000 sterilized women in the country in 1906 is taken from the speculative estimate of one gynecologist—himself emphatically opposed to such procedures. Proof that such surgery was performed at all is gathered from the letters and articles of prominent physicians outspoken in their opposition to these medical practices.[9] How do we account for this vocal opposition, and in what ways do the reactions of these doctors qualify Barker-Benfield's generalizations about the anxieties of Victorian men? Though it is indisputable that drastic gynecological surgery did exist in the latter half of the nineteenth century, it is by no means possible to conclude that such therapy was routine procedure, or that it was at all representative of the medical profession's conscious or unconscious attitudes toward the female sex.

Other historians have wisely chosen not to belabor the issue of gynecological surgery. Ann Wood has turned her attention instead to various clinical treatments we know to have been more widespread. Nevertheless, she shares Barker-Benfield's assumption of male hostility and views primitive practices such as cauterization and leeching as prompted by unconscious animosity. Although she admits that by 1870 younger physicians were abandoning the most painful aspects of heroic medicine, she is equally harsh toward subsequent developments in the treatment of women's complaints. She spends a good deal of time analyzing the popular "rest cure" originated by S. Weir Mitchell, concluding that it represented an ingenious kind of psychological cruelty, a "sophisticated culmination" of earlier methods. Mitchell was still the spiritual brother of his predecessor, "the cauterizer, with his injections, leeches, and hot irons," who spitefully nurtured a "veiled but aggressively hostile male sexuality and superiority."[10]

Wood's treatment of Mitchell, one of the most prominent neurologists of the day, is based on a simplistic psychology akin to Barker-Benfield's. Mitchell, for example, is pictured as a typically anxious Victorian male who patronized his hysterical patients, nurturing a belief that they had failed to perform their feminine duties. Thus his "rest cure" was "designed both as a punishment and an agent of regeneration, for it forced her (woman) to acknowledge her womanhood, and made her totally dependent on the professional prowess of her male doctor." Much is made of the commanding personality and charismatic will of the physician. Mitchell wanted more than to be trusted by his female patients; he demanded adoration, even reverence. In fact, Wood argues, Mitchell's aim was to become "god-like" through the exercise of the will. Skating "on the edge of a theory of primitive healing through mesmeric sexual powers," Mitchell, "like his cauterizing predecessor, played the role of possessor, even impregnator in the cure process. Dominated, overfed often to the point of obesity, caressed and (quite literally) vibrating, were not his patients being returned to health—to womanhood?"[11]

It is true that Mitchell was very much the Victorian patrician—vain, stubborn, self-satisfied, and patronizing toward women. His ideal woman was well-sheltered from the degrading influences of the modern age. Yet he cannot be dismissed so easily. He conscientiously sought and relished the company of educated, intelligent, strong-minded women. He was a close friend of Agnes Repplier, who characterized their relationship as "the perfect flowering of sentiment and understanding." Nor did his disapproval of higher education for women interfere with a lifelong intimacy with Agnes Irwin, the Dean of Radcliffe College.[12] Highly critical of the weak-limbed, nervous, delicately neurasthenic ideal of Victorian womanhood, Mitchell was an early advocate of more physical activity for women. He even argued that no distinction should be made in the physical training of boys and girls until adolescence.[13] Although he clearly preferred that the majority of women should confine their interests to the home, he respected the right of individual women to opt for higher education.[14]

Mitchell was a domineering figure who believed that a self-willed and forceful personality made a better, more objective man of science. Convinced that overindulgence by well-meaning relatives exacerbated rather than cured the nervous condition of his patients, his first step was to substitute for this misplaced concern "the firm kindness of a well-trained hired nurse." His refusal to pamper his patients, and his insistence that they obey him was a deliberate part of his therapy. Nor did he feel that women would always be inferior physicians. Mitchell had apparently learned from experience that a stern, impartial demeanor was highly successful with certain kinds of patients. He doubted whether women were always capable of this "needed control," yet he was quick to assert that many male physicians also failed to achieve the proper distance. Except for these specific cases, which required the absolute obedience of the patient, women, he conceded, were "in all other ways capable doctors."

Finally, I can find no evidence that Mitchell believed that a doctor could or should become "god-like," or that he "skated on the edge of a theory of primitive healing through mesmeric sexual powers."[15]

Both authors give special status to the "sadism" of men and male doctors, though we have no reason to believe that they were inherently any more "sadistic" than women. Is it a special kind of "sadism" that leads more men than women in our own age to become surgeons? Can we label open-heart surgery, or even mastectomy "sadistic" and leave it at that? Alternatively, what *appears* as sadism may very well be a quality inherent in the physician's role, or at least in the way that the patient perceives him. It is characteristic of this questionable approach that the broadest possible conclusions concerning S. Weir Mitchell's domineering personality are based on Wood's reading of Charlotte Perkins Gilman's short story, "The Yellow Wallpaper."[16] Gilman was a patient of Mitchell's for a short time, and her experience with the "rest cure" was emphatically negative. "The Yellow Wallpaper" is the story of a young woman slowly driven insane by the treatment of her physician-husband, who forces her to submit to the "rest cure." It is a devastating piece of polemical fiction. Yet brilliant as Gilman surely was, can Wood honestly overlook the fact of Gilman's neurosis and its role in structuring her response to Mitchell, as though to deal with it were somehow to detract from her greatness? Must our heroines be utterly free from blemishes in order to retain their well-earned preeminence? Neither Gilman nor Mitchell, both impressive figures, warrant such insufficient treatment.

One further point concerning Mitchell is in order. He was, after all, a neurologist, not a "woman's doctor," as he is often labeled, and his "rest cure" was never confined to women, although the incidence of hysteria among nineteenth-century women was frequent. His first experience with rest as a treatment for acute exhaustion came during the Civil War, when he dealt with soldiers suffering from battle fatigue. In accord with the most advanced neurological thinking of his day, Mitchell saw the symptoms of exhaustion as somatic in origin, and thus it was to the physical symptoms that his cure was addressed. Too much strain and too little relaxation taxed the limited resources of energy that each individual had at his or her disposal. Absolute rest was a logical and pragmatic solution to the problem. Excessive feeding to replace the needed "red corpuscles" was proposed to counteract the loss of weight that usually accompanied nervous illness. Massage was performed by experienced women and was added as an afterthought to achieve the benefits of "exercise without exertion." Such therapy is still practiced today with long-term hospital patients. Of highly questionable value in the view of modern neurologists, Mitchell's cure was nevertheless often successful.[17] Mitchell himself saw it as a welcome departure from the excessive and indiscriminate administration of drugs and, in his case-report of the first female patient he treated in this manner, he described with utter contempt the way in which she had "passed through the hands of gynecologists, worn spinal supporters, and taken every tonic known to the books."[18]

The assumption that male physicians, like everyone else, were very much the products of their cultural milieu is unquestionably sound. But what does this mean? True enough, Victorian society exhibited a deep-seated ambivalence toward women, symbolized by its obsession with two polar images—the angel and the prostitute. There was much talk about the necessity of keeping woman confined to her "sphere." But before drawing overhasty conclusions, we need to know a great deal more about the relationship of industrialization to changes in the family structure, and how this development altered attitudes toward sex roles and practices. Increased domesticity may very well have meant that women gained power within the family. Historians have already begun to investigate the ramifications of the "feminization" of literature and morality in the nineteenth century.[19] How did this growing influence affect the relationship between the sexes? What was woman's self-image, and how and to what degree was it shaped by society's view of her? It is with questions like these that we can move beyond accusation to deeper understanding.

In her recent work, Carroll Smith-Rosenberg has covered much the same ground as Barker-Benfield and Wood, yet she has managed to avoid the major pitfalls in the first two studies by attempting to answer some of these larger questions. Two interesting studies, one on nineteenth-century hysteria and the other on Victorian attitudes toward puberty and menopause are particularly relevant.[20] Smith-Rosenberg views hysteria as a socially recognized behavior pattern for women in the nineteenth century and as such a *real* behavioral option for some American women. The question of what led these women to become hysterics is approached cautiously, and her conclusions are plausible precisely because she has carefully attempted to locate both male and female behavior patterns within the larger context of Victorian culture.

The primary area of stress for women, according to Smith-Rosenberg, was their growing power and concomitant responsibility within the family. Increasingly throughout the century, the ideal wife and mother was pictured as a self-reliant figure—a protective and efficient caretaker of children and home. Yet this portrait of American motherhood directly contradicted the equally pervasive Victorian image of woman as dependent, fragile, sensitive, and childlike. Improperly socialized for their adult role, many women might well have been overwhelmed by the burdens of housekeeping, family management, and childrearing. Hysteria, Smith-Rosenberg suggests, may have served as one kind of response for particular women otherwise unable to handle these changes in family life. She avoids the easy accusation that male domination, and the "hostility" of Victorian society "drove" such women to become hysterical. Rather she is concerned with the obvious dysfunctional aspects of female socialization in the Victorian period, and the increasing evidence of this dysfunction to be found among women who were ill.

Smith-Rosenberg is not unaware of the drastic nature of the hysterical woman's resolution of her dilemma. Though she undoubtedly achieved some alleviation of conflict and tension, "the hysteric purchased her escape from the emotional—and frequently—from the sexual demands of her life only at the cost of pain, disability, and an intensification of woman's traditional passivity and dependence. Indeed a complex interplay existed below the character traits assigned women in Victorian society and the characteristic symptoms of the nineteenth-century hysteric: dependency, fragility, emotionality, narcissism." Within this context, Smith-Rosenberg's treatment of the ambivalence of physicians to hysterical women becomes plausible. She is not afraid to label the hysteric's behavior "passive aggression," or "exploitive dependency," which often functioned to arouse a corresponding hostility in the men who cared for her or lived with her.[21] They too were burdened by Victorian society's strict and rigid definition of sex roles, and they reacted accordingly. S. Weir Mitchell and enlightened physicians like him who encountered hysteria so often among their female patients, gradually, if imperfectly, began to understand the destructive nature of female socialization in the late nineteenth century. Hence more and more of these younger physicians advocated vigorous physical and moral training for women.[22] Women physicians were also among the most outspoken critics of the frivolous upbringing of Victorian girls.

Smith-Rosenberg is less successful in treating medical attitudes toward puberty and menopause. Her description of Victorian perceptions of these critical periods in a woman's life is acute. Yet she fails to draw a sharp enough distinction between nineteenth-century rationalizations and those of previous ages. The reader is left in doubt as to what is uniquely Victorian about such reactions to woman's biological crises. Her use of Karen Horney's theory of a primordial male fear of female sexuality leads to similar difficulties. If the nineteenth-century gynecological metaphors concerning puberty and menopause which she describes do indeed reflect this primitive fear, they are not, then, necessarily reflections of Victorian culture at all. Fortunately, Smith-Rosenberg herself is aware of the pitfalls of such theorizing and concedes that Horney's hypothesis remains "unproven and unprovable."[23]

The avoidance of any account of the evolution of medical therapeutics in the studies discussed poses a problem. Treatment of disease in nineteenth-century America cannot properly be viewed apart from the broad context of scientific ignorance which was displayed throughout much of the century. Medicine was clearly in a period of transition and crisis. For decades after 1800, pioneer researchers centered in Paris had been concentrating their energies on the systematic identification and description of specific diseases in terms of a localized, structural pathology. It was slow and painstaking work: bedside symptoms uncovered through careful observation had then to be correlated with lesions discovered at autopsies. Although the future therapeutic implications of such research were momentous—medical men could not cure *any* disease until they could isolate and diagnose it—the immediate results were discouraging. One by one the traditional "heroic" methods of treatment—bleeding, and heavy dosing—were discredited. Medical practice found itself in the painful position of having advanced far enough to discard ancient methods of therapy without being able to offer anything new in their place. The patient and his or her inept but well-meaning physician were left to fend for themselves.[24]

In despair, many physicians surrendered to therapeutic nihilism. J. Marion

Sims, ultimately to become a brilliant gynecologic surgeon, described the nature of medical practice shortly after his graduation from medical school in 1835:

> The practice of that time was heroic: it was murderous. I knew nothing about medicine, but I had sense enough to see that doctors were killing their patients, that medicine was not an exact science, that it was wholly empirical, and that it would be better to trust entirely to nature than to the hazardous skill of the doctors.[25]

The problem was exacerbated in America by the social and political climate. Well-trained physicians from high-quality medical schools were ignorant enough, but only a minority of American doctors were well-trained in this period. Quality medical education had fallen victim to the leveling forces of Jacksonian democracy. Proprietary schools, operated for profit by enterprising physicians swept up in the materialism of the age, competed with each other for students. Strict requirements were relaxed as medical training was made as quick and as easy as possible. Clinical facilities were virtually non-existent, and mediocre personnel did little to advance research. Hundreds of graduates were licensed yearly without ever having treated a patient or witnessed a childbirth.[26] Nathan S. Davis, an important member of the medical profession at mid-century, described the "great mass" of his colleagues, "the ninety-nine out of every hundred," in vividly disparaging terms:

> With no practical knowledge of chemistry and botany; with but a smattering of anatomy and physiology, hastily caught during a sixteen weeks' attendance on the anatomical theatre of a medical college; with still less of real pathology; they enter the profession having mastered just enough of the details of practice to give them the requisite *self-assurance* for commanding the confidence of the public; but without either an adequate fund of knowledge or that degree of mental discipline, and habits of patient study which will enable them ever to supply their defects. Hence they plod on through life, with a fixed routine of practice, consisting of calomel, antimony, opium, and the lancet, almost as empirically applied as is cayenne pepper, lobelia, and steam, by another class of men.[27]

Poor training on the one hand and therapeutic nihilism on the other led to a widespread loss of prestige for doctors. Eventually, public opposition to the excesses of regular medicine reached alarming proportions. Controversy increased within the profession, and rival medical sects and illegitimate quacks, promising success where the regulars had failed, proliferated in the United States and abroad. Battle lines were ultimately drawn between "regulars" and "irregulars." The ranks of the rival sects, however, were seldom clearly defined. Many people opposed the medical profession, but none of them had more knowledge than ordinary physicians did of how to remedy deficiencies in treatment. Though they found many aspects of regular medicine unacceptable, it was not known how or why such procedures were undesirable. The public was left to choose only among equally unscientific alternatives available at the time.

The extremely popular health-reform movement of the mid-nineteenth century arose to fill the vacuum created by the failure of medicine to cure. Led in most cases by men and women without formal medical training, the movement sought primarily to combat public dependence on physicians by popularizing healthful dietary practices, public hygiene, physical exercise, and knowledge of physiology. Emphasis was placed on the prevention of illness, for health reformers were as helpless as physicians when disease struck. Middle-class women became avid followers of such well-known health reformers as Sylvester Graham. Soon "Ladies Physiological Reform Societies" dedicated to the study of anatomy, physiology, and sound health practices dotted the East Coast in particular. Many of the women participating in these groups were women's-rights advocates. Dress reform, the evils of tight lacing, menstrual difficulties, and the "horrors of self abuse" were favorite topics of discussion. Because of the full flowering of Victorian delicacy at mid-century, the desire to lift the veil of female ignorance by teaching women the simple functions of their bodies was decidedly radical. The writings of Catherine Beecher, Mary Gove Nichols, Paulina Wright Davis, and Harriot Hunt all exhibit a polemical flair that reflected the widespread public indignation at the failures of regular medicine. They exhibit too, however, the increasing desire of middle-class women to "modernize" and "professionalize" their roles within the family. Women, it was argued, must be "trained" to exercise their domestic responsibilities with the utmost skill.[28]

It is clear, above all, that medical men were unable to cure most diseases—not just those of women but of everyone. Indeed, they "tortured" men and women indiscriminately. Though much has been made recently of the painful procedure of cauterization for female complaints, it was actually a common therapy for the treatment of venereal disease. Male genitals were cauterized by the same complacent physicians who cauterized their female patients.[29] Yet why so many physicians persisted in the use of heroic medicine despite its obvious inefficacy is a complex question. The answer lies, not in their antipathy to women, but in ignorance, poor training, and the historical context within which they thought and worked. The historian of science, Thomas Kuhn, has argued eloquently for the necessity of viewing pre-modern science, not from the vantage point of our own day, but in relation to the internal developments within each discipline. Physicians were prisoners of their own theoretical constructs. Medical science had left them few alternatives to heroic practice in the 1850s except to admit to themselves and their patients that they were helpless. Was it not more comforting to persist in the procedures that one had taken for granted in the past? According to Kuhn, the response of scientists to such crises as medicine faced at mid-century always follows a distinctive pattern. Though scientists may lose faith in their original theories and procedures, they will not reject them until they have found and fully tested an alternative system:

> Let us then assume that crises are a necessary pre-condition for the emergence of novel theories and ask next how scientists respond to their existence. Part of the answer, as obvious as it is important, can be discovered by noting first what scientists never do when confronted by even severe and prolonged anomalies. Though they may begin to lose faith and then to consider alternatives, they do not renounce the paradigm that has led them into crisis. They do not, that is, treat anomalies as counterinstances, though in the vocabulary of philosophy of science that is what they are. In part this generalization is simply a statement of historic fact. . . . A scientific theory is

> declared invalid only if an alternative is available to take its place. . . . The decision
> to accept another, and the judgment leading to that decision involves the comparison
> of both paradigms with nature *and* with each other.[30]

Inevitably, the slowness of medical men in the nineteenth century to reject heroic medicine led to much unnecessary suffering. Yet to attribute such behavior to a veiled hostility to women, rather than to the imperfections of a pre-modern discipline, is surely misguided.

The attitudes of early female physicians have been treated with much the same distortion as the subject of medical therapeutics. Once the premise that women were being victimized by nineteenth-century physicians is accepted, it is a short step to conclude that women doctors saw themselves as the saviors of their sex—the deliverers of women everywhere from the hands of the enemy. Thus the struggle of these women for professional training is no longer a private matter. It becomes evidence that all women were oppressed, and epitomizes the Victorian woman's dilemma. Medicine, Ann Wood suggests, was used by such women "as a weapon in a social and political struggle for power between the sexes."[31] Yet again, such a portrayal, while not wholly false, is definitely one-sided.

One of the most forceful arguments put forward by feminists and female physicians alike in defense of medical training for women concerned itself with the controversial and sensitive issue of female delicacy. As Victorian prudery reached its peak at mid-century, the importance of coming to terms with feminine modesty became increasingly apparent. Middle- and upper-class women often declined to consult physicians for gynecologic problems except in extreme cases. Even when they overcame their misgivings and sought professional services, it was difficult for doctors to obtain a complete history: the embarrassment occasioned by discussing her bodily functions was simply too much for the woman of refinement to bear. Ambivalent themselves over the dictates of Victorian morality, medical men did not deal adequately with the problem. Most denounced what they termed "false modesty;" yet a minority agreed that female modesty was indeed being compromised. A few of this group advocated some sort of professional training in medicine for women as a solution.[32] Women's-rights advocates, however, had no qualms about arguing that women ought to be admitted to existing medical schools so that the modest woman would be given the opportunity to seek aid from her own sex. The argument, not without special irony, was based on a full acceptance of Victorian delicacy, which had hitherto kept woman out of the professions and confined her to the domestic sphere.

Dr. Elizabeth Blackwell faced the dilemma posed by Victorian morality squarely. Though she pledged the male medical profession her "utmost confidence and respect," she nevertheless felt it was "unnatural" for women "to have no resort but to men," in those diseases "peculiar to themselves." All women were unfortunately subject to these ailments. Yet "no woman of sensibility" could allow herself to be examined by her physician "without great reluctance." To many, "death would be preferable to the treatment to which they would be subjected." Male physicians, though they meant well, were apt to "lose all consciousness of sex in the interests of science." Unfortunately, "the patient cannot," Blackwell warned, "and bitter mortification, or a deadening of sensibility, will be the result in most cases." Dr. Ann Preston, Dean of the Woman's Medical College of Philadelphia, agreed with an English supporter that teaching women medicine was a "step not *from* but *towards* decency and decorum."[33]

It was also the hope of many female physicians that medical training for relatively few women would serve to elevate the entire sex. Indeed, they were highly critical of Victorian womanhood. What bothered them most was that girls were increasingly becoming more frivolous, weak-willed, and self-centered. They exhibited a "passion for dress and company . . . until these have become the staples rather than the stimulants of their lives."[34] Women were as responsible for this trend as were men. "Oh! I scorn men, sometimes from the bottom of my heart," raged Dr. Marie Zakrewska in a rare moment of pique. "Still, this is wrong," she reflected, "for it is the fault of the woman—of the mother—in educating her daughter to be merely a beautiful machine fit to ornament a fine establishment; not gaining this, there is nothing left but wretchedness of mind and body."[35] Harriot Hunt's contempt for such women led her to sympathize with their husbands, often plagued by the emptiness and lack of real spiritual qualities in so many Victorian marriages. Her social criticism was acute and to the point. Women were being educated as

> appendages and dead weights to husbands . . . without a knowledge of those domestic duties and responsibilities, which alone can fit them to live true to those relations, without those solid intellectual attainments and spiritual graces by which they are to educate their children and hallow the atmosphere of the home, and without those 'attractions'—enduring when youth and beauty are gone, which alone can win and keep for them the respect and love of any sensible, upright and noble man, worthy of the name of husband!

Such poor training for women was ultimately "traitorous to the virtue of both sexes;" neither suffered alone.[36]

In supporting medical training for their sex, most pioneer female physicians carefully avoided the question of woman's intellectual capabilities, preferring instead to emphasize her natural talents as nurturer. "The relative intellectual ability of the sexes," Dr. Ann Preston insisted, "is altogether an irrelevant question. You do not pretend to be something which you are not," she often reassured her students, "but you are aiming to develop your powers and to perform your duties." Mary Putnam-Jacobi, a brilliant scientist in her own right, still admitted that women required the "intellectual companionship of man," in order to attain "the highest intellectual standards." This did not mean, however, that women had no "special contributions of their own to offer." The "special capacities of women as a class," their "tact, acuteness, and sympathetic insight," enabled hundreds of women to succeed in medical practice even though "insufficiently endowed with intellectual or educational qualifications."[37]

Indeed, what is perhaps most interesting about the thinking of these women is not their putative ill-will toward men, nor even their justifiable criticisms of the medical profession, but, rather, the degree to which their own attitudes toward their sex mirrored those of their male colleagues. These professional women were not modern-day feminists, charging the barricades of male privilege, but were very much Victorian women, prisoners of their own time and culture.

Thus they advocated the training of female physicians on the grounds of propriety and morality. But even more telling was their contention that medicine was a natural extension of woman's sphere and peculiarly suited to the female character, which was self-sacrificing and empathetic. Glorifying motherhood, even those who never married viewed their own role as that of a "connecting link between the science of the medical profession and the everyday life of women."[38] Female physicians would become the professional allies of wives and mothers everywhere. In performing this task, their value to the community would be immense. The entire quality of domestic activity would improve:

> Those women who pursued this life of scientific study and practical activity, so different from woman's domestic and social life and yet so closely connected with it, could not fail to regard these avocations (housework) from a fresh standpoint, and to see in a new light the noble possibilities which the position of woman opens to her. . . .[39]

Mothers desperately needed to be educated in sanitary matters, hygiene, and physiology. This was properly the work of female physicians. Elizabeth Blackwell understood that "comparatively few" women, even when given the opportunity, would choose to "devote themselves entirely to scientific pursuits." Nevertheless, the sex was so linked together that inevitably "every woman would be benefited by the scientific development of a class."[40] As a final contribution, women, because of their superior moral qualities, would "raise the moral tone of the profession and teach reverence and purity to the grossness of the world."[41]

It is unfortunate that in their eagerness to portray nineteenth-century American women as victims, too many historians misrepresent these issues. It is clear, however, that women physicians, at least, derived great strength and support from their womanhood. They were not out to vindicate their oppressed sisters as much as to refine and purify Victorian society. Yet the contention of these women that their medical training would bring benefits to civilization as a whole was at once an extremely forceful, yet ultimately self-defeating argument. Its power lay in its embracing the concept of the separation of the spheres. Nevertheless, not until their own Victorian attitudes gave way to the more egalitarian concepts of the twentieth century would the full acceptance of women as professionals be possible. For them, however, such arguments were never a mere question of tactics. Proper Victorians themselves, thoroughly immersed in the values that their society held dear, they could see the issues in no other way.

The most intriguing aspects of woman's place in nineteenth-century American society have only begun to be explored. Surely to view the existence of Victorian women solely from the perspective of male domination has become a sterile and tedious line of inquiry. Perhaps we might profit in the future from an entirely new set of questions.

NOTES

1 Present-day feminism as well as scholarly concern lies behind this special interest in women and doctors. For within contemporary feminism, as well as in the radical youth movement which strongly influenced it, there exists a great distrust of experts and elites. In both categories doctors head the list, and they themselves have often not resisted the impulse to mystify their activities and to patronize patients, particularly women. Moreover, contemporary feminists and physicians have often been at odds over two controversial feminist demands, abortion and birth control, which are partly medical in nature.

2 Three authors have recently dealt extensively with nineteenth-century medical treatment of women's diseases: Ben Barker-Benfield, "The Spermatic Economy: A Nineteenth-Century View of Sexuality," *Feminist Studies* 1 (Summer 1972): 45-74; Ann Douglas Wood, "'The Fashionable Diseases': Women's Complaints and Their Treatment in Nineteenth-Century America," *Journal of Interdisciplinary History* 4 (Summer 1973): 25-52; Carroll Smith-Rosenberg, "The Hysterical Woman: Sex Roles and Role Conflict in Nineteenth-Century America," *Social Research* 39 (Winter 1972): 652-678, and "The Cycle of Femininity: Puberty and Menopause in Nineteenth-Century America," *Feminist Studies* 1 (Winter-Spring 1973), and reprinted in this collection. All three authors view physicians as representative Victorian males, and all three detect varying degrees of animosity in the behavior of physicians toward their female patients. Smith-Rosenberg is much more cautious than the other two, however. She is frankly tentative and views the relationship of doctor and patients in a broad cultural context   Nor is she above suggesting that Victorian women often played the dual role of the oppressor as well as the oppressed. For this reason I will deal with her work separately.

3 Robert Coles, "Shrinking History," *New York Review of Books,* February 22, 1973, p. 21.

4 Wood, "'The Fashionable Diseases," pp. 5, 7, 9; Barker-Benfield, "The Spermatic Economy," pp. 58-66. See also Ben J. Barker-Benfield, "The Horrors of the Half-Known Life," (unpublished Ph. D. thesis, University of California at Los Angeles, 1969).

5 Wood, "'The Fashionable Diseases,'" p. 13.

6 I would dispute the notion that the woman's rights movement was making much headway during this period. See Eleanor Flexner, *Century of Struggle* (New York: Atheneum, 1971), p. 164, where she describes the movement of the 1870s and 1880s as "small and divided." Thorsten Veblen's theory that workless women represented an important status symbol for their husbands appears much more plausible than Barker-Benfield's contention that they were threatening. See Thorsten Veblen, *The Theory of the Leisure Class* (New York: Macmillan, 1899).

7 Barker-Benfield is never clear on exactly who these disorderly women were.

8 Barker-Benfield, "The Spermatic Economy," pp. 54-55, 58-59, 61-62.

9 See, for example, the article and accompanying letters by Howard A. Kelly, Professor of Gynecology at Johns Hopkins, "Conservatism in Ovariotomy," *Journal of the American Medical Association* 26 (February 8, 1896): 249-251; see also Ely Van de Warker, M.D., "The Fetish of the Ovary," *American Journal of Obstetrics and the Diseases of Women and Children* 54 (July-December 1906): 366-373.

10 Wood, "'The Fashionable Diseases,'" p. 13.

11 Ibid., pp. 13, 14, 15.

12 For this and other relationships of this sort see Earnest Earnest, *S. Weir Mitchell, Novelist and Physician* (Philadelphia: University of Pennsylvania Press, 1950), pp. 128-129.

13 "To run, to climb, to swim, to ride, to play violent games, ought to be as natural to the girls as to the boy," S. Weir Mitchell, *Doctor and Patient* (Philadelphia: J.B. Lippincott & Co., 1887), p. 141. See also "Outdoor and Camp-Life for Women," ibid., pp. 155-177.

14 Ibid., p. 149. Also interesting is his good-natured confrontation with a grandniece who was a student at Bryn Mawr, in Anna Robeson Burr, ed., *Weir Mitchell: His Life and Letters* (New York: Duffield & Co., 1929), p. 374.

15 Wood, "'The Fashionable Diseases,'" p. 14; S. Weir Mitchell, *Fat and Blood* (Philadelphia: J. B. Lippincott & Co., 1902), pp. 42, 60-61, 76.

16 Wood, "The Fashionable Diseases," pp. 18-19.

17 For a time it was adapted and used by Freud. Earnest, *S. Weir Mitchell*, p. 227. Nathan Hale, Jr., *Freud and the Americans* (New York: Oxford University Press, 1971), pp. 47-68.

18 S. Weir Mitchell, "The Evolution of the Rest Treatment," *Journal of Nervous and Mental Disease* 31 (June 1904): 368-373.

19 See Mary P. Ryan, "American Society and the Cult of Domesticity," (unpublished Ph.D. thesis, University of California at Santa Barbara, 1971); Barbara Welter, "The Feminization of Religion in the Nineteenth Century," and Daniel Scott Smith, "Family Limitation, Sexual Control and Domestic Feminism in Victorian America," in this collection.

20 See note 2 above.

21 Smith-Rosenberg, "The Hysterical Woman," pp. 656, 659, 671.

22 Mitchell's perceptiveness is acute throughout his little book, *Doctor and Patient*.

23 Smith-Rosenberg, "The Cycle of Femininity."

24 Richard Shryock, *Medicine and Society in America, 1660-1860* (Ithaca: Cornell University Press, 1962), ch. 4; detailed and generally excellent is William G. Rothstein, *American Physicians in the Nineteenth Century* (Baltimore: Johns Hopkins Press, 1972), ch. 3.

25 J. Marion Sims, *The Story of My Life* (New York: Appleton and Co., 1885), p. 150. Oliver Wendell Holmes, Dean of Harvard Medical School, observed that if all the various medicines currently in use to treat disease were immediately thrown into the sea it would be so much better for mankind and so much worse for the fishes! See his *Currents and Counter Currents in Medical Science* (Boston: Ticknor & Fields, 1861), p. 39.

26 See Rothstein, *American Physicians,* ch. 5; Shyrock, *Medicine and Society,* ch. 4; idem, "Cults and Quackery in American Medical History," Middle States Association of History and Social Studies Teachers, *Proceedings* 37 (1939): 19-30; idem, "Sylvester Graham and the Popular Health Movement, 1830-1870," *Mississippi Valley Historical Review* 18 (1932): 172-183; William B. Walker, "The Health Reform Movement in the United States, 1830-1870," (unpublished Ph.D. thesis, Johns Hopkins University, 1955), p. 5; Joseph Kett, *The Formation of the American Medical Profession* (New Haven: Yale University Press, 1968).

27 N. S. D(avis), "National Medical Convention," *New York Journal of Medicine* 5 (1845): 418; quoted in Rothstein, *American Physicians,* p. 127.

28 Shryock, *Medicine and Society,* ch. 4; idem, "The Professional American Physician in 1846 and 1946, A Study in Contrasts," *Journal of the American Medical Association* 134 (1947); 417-427; idem, "Public Relations of the Medical Profession," *Annals of Medical History* 2 (1930); 319-330. See also Shryock, "Sylvester Graham;" William B. Walker, "The Health Reform Movement;" Joseph Kett, *American Medical Profession,* pp. 117-120; John B. Blake, "Mary Gove Nichols, Prophetess of Health" *Proceedings of the American Philosophical Association* 106 (June 1962): 219-234; Hebbel E. Hoff, M.D., and John F. Fulton, M.D., "The Centennial of the First American Physiological Society Founded at Boston by William A. Alcott and Sylvester Graham," *Bulletin of the Institute of the History of Medicine* 5 (1937): 687-734; Harriet Beecher Stowe, "Sermon on Your Health," *Atlantic Monthly* 18 (1865): 85; Catherine Beecher, *Letters to the People on Health and Happiness* (New York: Harper and Bros., 1855); Catherine Beecher and Harrier Beecher Stowe, *The American Woman's Home* (New York: J. B. Ford and Co., 1869).

29 For a description of this therapy see E. L. Keyes, Professor of Dermatology and Surgery at Bellevue Hospital Medical College, *The Venereal Diseases, Including the Structure of the Male Urethra* (New York: W. Wood & Co., 1880), pp. 29-33. No more pleasant was Abraham Jacobi's recommendation that a sore be raised on the penises of boys to prevent masturbation. "On Masturbation and Hysteria in Young Children," *American Journal of Obstetrics and Diseases of Women and Children* 8, 9 (1875, 1876): 603.

30 Thomas Kuhn, *The Structure of Scientific Revolutions* (Chicago: Chicago University Press, 1962), p. 77; see also Thomas Kuhn, "The Relations Between History and History of Science," *Daedalus* 100 (Spring 1971): 271-304.

31 Wood, "'The Fashionable Diseases,'" p. 28.

32 For an excellent discussion of this problem see J. P. Donegan, "Midwifery in America, 1760-1860, A Study in Medicine and Morality," (unpublished Ph.D. thesis, Syracuse University, 1972), pp. 91-111, ch. 4; Shryock, *Medicine and Society,* p. 121; Thomas Ewell, *Letters to Ladies Detailing Important Information Concerning Themselves and Infants* (Philadelphia: W. Brown, 1817); Samuel Gregory, *Letters to Ladies in Favor of Female Physicians For Their Own Sex* (New York: Fowler & Wells, 1850).

33 Elizabeth Blackwell, *Address on the Medical Education of Women* (New York: G. P. Putnam, 1856), pp. 8-9; Dr. Ann Preston, *Valedictory Address to the Graduating Class of the Female Medical College of Philadelphia* (Philadelphia: William S. Young, 1864), p. 5.

34 Blackwell, *Address,* p. 8. See also Ann Preston, *Valedictory Address* (Philadelphia: Loag, 1870). p. 6.

35 Marie Zakrewska, M.D., *A Woman's Quest* (New York: D. Appleton & Co., 1924), p. 97.

36 Harriot Hunt, *Glances and Glimpses* (Boston: John P. Jewett & Co., 1856), pp. 50-52, 408-411. See her denunciation of the leisure class woman's selfish exploitation of working women, pp. 133-134.

37 Ann Preston, *Valedictory Address* (Philadelphia: A.K. Terrlinus, 1858), p. 8; Mary Putnam-Jacobi, "Woman in Medicine," in *Woman's Work in America,* ed., Annie Nathan Meyer (New York: Holt, 1891), p. 177.

38 Elizabeth and Emily Blackwell, *Medicine as a Profession for Women* (New York: Tinson, 1860), pp. 8-9, 15-19.

39 Ibid., pp. 8-9.

40 Blackwell, *Address,* pp. 6-7. See also Preston, *Valedictory Address,* 1870, pp. 6-7, idem, *Valedictory Address,* 1864, p. 7.

41 Ann Preston, *Introductory Lecture to the Course of Instruction in the Female Medical College of Pennsylvania* (Philadelphia: Anna McDowell, 1855), p. 12; idem, *Valedictory Address,* 1864, p. 4.

VOLUNTARY MOTHERHOOD; THE BEGINNINGS OF FEMINIST BIRTH CONTROL IDEAS IN THE UNITED STATES

Linda Gordon

Voluntary motherhood was the first general name for a feminist birth control demand in the United States in the late nineteenth century.* It represented an initial response of feminists to their understanding that involuntary motherhood and child-raising were important parts of woman's oppression. In this paper, I would like to trace the content and general development of "voluntary-motherhood" ideas and to situate them in the development of the American birth-control movement.

The feminists who advocated voluntary motherhood were of three general types: suffragists; people active in such moral reform movements as temperance and social purity, in church auxiliaries, and in women's professional and service organizations (such as Sorosis); and members of small, usually anarchist, Free Love groups. The Free Lovers played a classically vanguard role in the development of birth-control ideas. Free Love groups were always small and sectarian, and they were usually male-dominated, despite their extreme ideological feminism. They never coalesced into a movement. On the contrary, they were the remnants of a dying tradition of utopian socialist and radical protestant religious dissent. The Free Lovers, whose very self-definition was built around a commitment to iconoclasm and to isolation from the masses, were precisely the group that could offer intellectual leadership in formulating the shocking arguments that birth control in the nineteenth century required.[1]

---

*The word "feminist" must be underscored. Since the early nineteenth century, there had been developing a body of population-control writings, which recommended the use of birth-control techniques to curb nationwide or worldwide populations; usually called neo-Malthusians, these writers were not concerned with the control of births as a means by which women could gain control over their own lives, except, very occasionally, as an auxiliary argument. And of course birth control practices date back to the most ancient societies on record.

The suffragists and moral reformers, concerned to win mass support, were increasingly committed to social respectability. As a result, they did not generally advance very far beyond prevalent standards of propriety in discussing sexual matters publicly. Indeed, as the century progressed the social gap between them and the Free Lovers grew, for the second and third generations of suffragists were more concerned with respectability than the first. In the 1860s and 1870s the great feminist theoreticians had been much closer to the Free Lovers, and at least one of these early giants, Victoria Woodhull, was for several years a member of both the suffrage and the Free Love camps. But even respectability did not completely stifle the mental processes of the feminists, and many of them said in private writings—in letters and diaries—what they were unwilling to utter in public.

The similar views of Free Lovers and suffragists on the question of voluntary motherhood did not bridge the considerable political distance between the groups, but did show that their analyses of the social meaning of reproduction for the women were converging. The sources of that convergence, the common grounds of their feminism, were their similar experiences in the changing conditions of nineteenth-century America. Both groups were composed of educated, middle-class Yankees responding to severe threats to the stability, if not dominance, of their class position. Both groups were disturbed by the consequences of rapid industrialization—the emergence of great capitalists in a clearly defined financial oligarchy, and the increased immigration which threatened the dignity and economic security of the middle-class Yankee. Free Lovers and suffragists, as feminists, looked forward to a decline in patriarchal power within the family, but worried, too, about the possible disintegration of the family and the loosening of sexual morality. They saw reproduction in the context of these larger social changes, and in a movement for women's emancipation; and they saw that movement as an answer to some of these large social problems. They hoped that giving political power to women would help to reinforce the family, to make the government more just and the economy less monopolistic. In all these attitudes there was something traditional as well as something progressive; the concept of voluntary motherhood reflected this duality.

Since we all bring a twentieth-century understanding to our concept of birth control, it may be best to make it clear at once that neither Free Lovers nor suffragists approved of contraceptive devices. Ezra Heywood, patriarch and martyr, thought "artificial" methods "unnatural, injurious, or offensive."[2] Tennessee Claflin wrote that the "washes, teas, tonics and various sorts of appliances known to the initiated" were a "standing reproach upon, and a permanent indictment against, American women. . . . No woman should ever hold sexual relations with any man from the possible consequences of which she might desire to escape."[3] *Woodhull and Claflin's Weekly* editorialized: "The means they (women) resort to for . . . prevention is sufficient to disgust every natural man. . . ."[4]

On a rhetorical level, the main objection to contraception* was that it was "unnatural", and the arguments reflected a romantic yearning for the "natural," rather pastorally conceived, that was typical of many nineteenth-century reform movements. More basic, however, particularly in women's arguments against contraception, was an underlying fear of the promiscuity that it could permit. The fear of promiscuity was associated less with fear for one's virtue than with fear of other women—the perhaps mythical "fallen" women—who might threaten a husband's fidelity.

To our twentieth-century minds a principle of voluntary motherhood that rejects the practice of contraception seems so theoretical as to have little real impact. What gave the concept substance was that it was accompanied by another, potentially explosive, conceptual change: the reacceptance of female sexuality. As with birth control, the most open advocates of female sexuality were the Free Lovers, not the suffragists; nevertheless both groups based their ideas on the traditional grounds of the "natural." Free Lovers argued, for example, that celibacy was unnatural and dangerous—for men and women alike. "Pen cannot record, nor lips express, the enervating, debauching effect of celibate life upon young men and women. . . ."5 Asserting the existence, legitimacy and worthiness of female sexual drive was one of the Free Lovers' most important contributions to sexual reform; it was a logical correlate of their argument from the "natural" and of their appeal for the integration of body and soul.

Women's rights advocates, too, began to demand recognition of female sexuality. Isabella Beecher Hooker wrote to her daughter: "Multitudes of women in all the ages who have scarce known what sexual desire is—being wholly absorbed in the passion of maternity, have sacrificed themselves to the beloved husbands as unto God—and yet these men, full of their human passion and defending it as righteous & God-sent lose all confidence in womanhood when a woman here and there betrays her similar nature & gives herself soul & body to the man she adores."6 Alice Stockham, a Spiritualist Free Lover and feminist physician, lauded sexual desire in men and women as "the prophecy of attainment." She urged that couples avoid reaching sexual "satiety" with each other, in order to keep their sexual desire constantly alive, for she considered desire pleasant and healthful.7 Elizabeth Cady Stanton, commenting in her diary in 1883 on the Whitman poem, "There is a Woman Waiting for Me," wrote: "he speaks as if the female must be forced to the creative act, apparently ignorant of the fact that a healthy woman has as much passion as a man, that she needs nothing stronger than the law of attraction to draw her to the male."8 Still, she loved Whitman, and largely because of that openness about sex that made him the Free Lovers' favorite poet.

According to the system of ideas then dominant, women, lacking sexual drives, submitted to sexual intercourse (and notice how Beecher Hooker

---

*Contraception will be used to refer to artificial devices used to prohibit conception during intercourse, while birth control will be used to mean anything, including abstinence, which limits pregnancy.

continued the image of a woman "giving herself", never taking) in order to please their husbands and to conceive children. The ambivalence underlying this view was expressed in the equally prevalent notion that women must be protected from exposure to sexuality lest they "fall" and become depraved, lustful monsters. This ambivalence perhaps came from a subconscious lack of certainty about the reality of the sex-less woman, a construct laid only thinly on top of the conception of woman as highly sexed, even insatiably so, that prevailed up to the eighteenth century. Victorian ambivalence on this question is nowhere more tellingly set forth than in the writings of physicians, who viewed woman's sexual organs as the source of her being, physical and psychological, and blamed most mental derangements on disorders of the reproductive organs.[9] Indeed, they saw it as part of the nature of things, as Rousseau had written, that men were male only part of the time, but women were female always.[10] In a system that deprived women of the opportunity to make extra-familial contributions to culture, it was inevitable that they should be more strongly identified with sex than men were. Indeed, females were frequently called "the sex" in the nineteenth century.

The concept of maternal instinct helped to smooth the contradictory attitudes about woman's sexuality. In many nineteenth-century writings we find the idea that the maternal instinct was the female analog of the male sex instinct; it was as if the two instincts were seated in analogous parts of the brain, or soul. Thus to suggest, as feminists did, that women might have the capacity for sexual impulses of their own automatically tended to weaken the theory of the maternal instinct. In the fearful imaginations of self-appointed protectors of the family and of womanly innocence, the possibility that women might desire sexual contact not for the sake of pregnancy—that they might even desire it at a time when they positively did not want pregnancy—was a wedge in the door to denying that women had any special maternal instinct at all.

Most of the feminists did not want to open that door either. Indeed, it was common for nineteenth-century women's-rights advocates to use the presumed "special motherly nature" and "sexual purity" of women as arguments for increasing their freedom and status. It is no wonder that many of them chose to speak their subversive thoughts about the sexual nature of women privately, or at least softly. Even among the more outspoken Free Lovers, there was a certain amount of hedging. Lois Waisbrooker and Dora Forster, writing for a Free Love journal in the 1890s, argued that while men and women both had an "amative" instinct, it was much stronger in men; and that women—only women—also had a reproductive, or "generative" instinct. "I suppose it must be universally conceded that men make the better lovers," Forster wrote. She thought that it might be possible that "the jealousy and tyranny of men have operated to suppress amativeness in women, by constantly sweeping strongly sexual women from the paths of life into infamy and sterility and death," but she thought also that the suppression, if it existed, had been permanently inculcated in woman's character.[11]

Modern birth control ideas rest on a full acceptance, at least quantitatively, of female sexuality. Modern contraception is designed to permit sexual intercourse as often as desired without the risk of pregnancy. Despite the protestations of sex counsellors that there are no norms for the frequency of intercourse, in the popular view there are such norms. Most people in the mid-twentieth century think that "normal" couples have intercourse several times a week. By twentieth-century standards, then, the Free Lovers' rejection of artificial contraception and "unnatural" sex seems to preclude the possibility of birth control at all. Nineteenth-century sexual reformers, however, had different sexual norms. They did not seek to make an infinite number of sterile sexual encounters possible. They wanted to make it possible for women to avoid pregnancy if they badly needed to do so for physical or psychological reasons, but they did not believe that it was essential for such women to engage freely in sexual intercourse.

In short, for birth control, they recommended periodic or permanent abstinence. The proponents of voluntary motherhood had in mind two distinct contexts for abstinence. One was the mutual decision of a couple. This could mean continued celibacy, or it could mean following a form of the rhythm method. Unfortunately all the nineteenth-century writers miscalculated women's fertility cycle. (It was not until the 1920s that the ovulation cycle was correctly plotted, and until the 1930s it was not widely understood among American doctors.)[12] Ezra Heywood, for example, recommended avoiding intercourse from 6 to 8 days before menstruation until 10 to 12 days after it. Careful use of the calendar could also provide control over the sex of a child, Heywood believed: conception in the first half of the menstrual cycle would produce girls, in the second half, boys.[13] These misconceptions functioned, conveniently, to make practicable Heywood's and others' ideas that celibacy and contraceptive devices should *both* be avoided.

Some of the Free Lovers also endorsed male continence, a system practiced and advocated by the Oneida community, in which the male avoids climax entirely.[14] (There were other aspects of the Oneida system that antagonized the Free Lovers, notably the authoritarian quality of John Humphrey Noyes's leadership.)[15] Dr. Stockham developed her own theory of continence called "Karezza," in which the female as well as the male was to avoid climax. Karezza and male continence were whole sexual systems, not just methods of birth control. Their advocates expected the self-control involved to build character and spiritual qualities, while honoring, refining and dignifying the sexual functions; and Karezza was reputed to be a cure for sterility as well, since its continued use was thought to build up the resources of fertility in the body.[16]

Idealizing sexual self-control was characteristic of the Free Love point of view. It was derived mainly from the thought of the utopian communitarians of the early nineteenth century,[17] but Ezra Heywood elaborated the theory. Beginning with the assumption that people's "natural" instincts, left untrammeled, would automatically create a harmonious, peaceful society—an assumption certainly derived from liberal philosophical faith in the innate goodness of man—Heywood applied it to sexuality, arguing that the natural sexual instinct was innately moderated, self-regulating. He did not imagine, as did Freud, a powerful, simple libido that could be checked only by an equally powerful moral and rational will. Heywood's theory implicitly contradicted Freud's description of inner struggle and constant tension between the drives of the id and the goals of the super-ego; Heywood denied the social necessity of sublimation.

On one level Heywood's theory may seem inadequate as a psychology, since it cannot explain such phenomena as repression and the strengthening of self-control with maturity. It may, however, have a deeper accuracy. It argues that society and its attendant repressions have distorted the animal's natural self-regulating mechanism, and have thereby created excessive and obsessive sexual drives. It offers a social explanation for the phenomena that Freud described in psychological terms, and thus holds out the hope that they can be changed.

Essentially similar to Wilhelm Reich's theory of "sex-economy," the Heywood theory of self-regulation went beyond Reich's in providing a weapon against one of the ideological bastions of male supremacy. Self-regulation as a goal was directed against the prevalent attitude that male lust was an uncontrollable urge, an attitude that functioned as a justification for rape specifically and for male sexual irresponsibility generally. We have to get away from the tradition of "man's necessities and woman's obedience to them," Stockham wrote.[18] The idea that men's desires are irrepressible is merely the other face of the idea that women's desires are non-existent. Together, the two created a circle that enclosed woman, making it her exclusive responsibility to say No, and making pregnancy her God-imposed burden if she didn't, while denying her both artificial contraception and the personal and social strength to rebel against male sexual demands.

Heywood developed his theory of natural sexual self-regulation in answer to the common anti-Free Love argument that the removal of social regulation of sexuality would lead to unhealthy promiscuity: ". . . in the distorted popular view, Free Love tends to unrestrained licentiousness, to open the flood gates of passion and remove all barriers in its desolating course; but it means just the opposite; it means the *utilization of animalism,* and the triumph of Reason, Knowledge, and Continence."[19] He applied the theory of self-regulation to the problem of birth control only as an afterthought, perhaps when women's concerns with that problem reached him. Ideally, he trusted, the amount of sexual intercourse that men and women desired would be exactly commensurate with the number of children that were wanted. Since sexual repression had had the boomerang effect of intensifying our sexual drives far beyond "natural" levels, effective birth control now would require the development of the inner self-control to contain and repress sexual urges.   But in time he expected that sexual moderation would come about naturally.

Heywood's analysis, published in the mid-1870s, was concerned primarily with excessive sex drives in men. Charlotte Perkins Gilman, one of the leading theoreticians of the suffrage movement, reinterpreted that analysis two decades later to emphasize its effects on women. The economic dependence of woman on man, in Gilman's analysis, made her sexual attractiveness necessary not only for winning a mate, but as a means of getting a livelihood too. This is the case with no other animal. In the human female it had produced "excessive modification to sex," emphasizing weak qualities characterized by humans as "feminine." She made an analogy to the milk cow, bred to produce far more milk than she would need for her calves. But Gilman agreed completely with Heywood about the effects of exaggerated sex distinction on the male; it produced excessive sex energy and excessive indulgence to an extent debilitating to the whole species. Like Heywood she also belived that the path of progressive social evolution moved toward monogamy and toward reducing the promiscuous sex instinct.[20]

A second context for abstinence, in addition to mutual self-regulation by a couple, was the right of the wife unilaterally to refuse her husband. This idea is at the heart of voluntary motherhood. It was a key substantive demand in the mid-nineteenth century when both law and practice made sexual submission to her husband a woman's duty.[21] A woman's right to refuse is clearly the fundamental condition of birth control—and of her independence and personal integrity.

In their crusade for this right of refusal the voices of Free Lovers and suffragists were in unison. Ezra Heywood demanded "Woman's Natural Right to ownership and control over her own body-self—a right inseparable from Woman's intelligent existence. . . ."[22] Paulina Wright Davis, at the National Woman Suffrage Association in 1871, attacked the law "which makes obligatory the rendering of marital rights and compulsory maternity." When, as a result of her statement she was accused of being a Free Lover, she responded by accepting the description.[23] Isabella Beecher Hooker wrote her daughter in 1869 advising her to avoid pregnancy until "you are prepared in body and soul to receive and cherish the little one. . . ."[24] In 1873 she gave similar advice to women generally, in her book *Womanhood*.[25] Elizabeth Cady Stanton had characteristically used the same phrase as Heywood: woman owning her own body. Once asked by a magazine what she meant by it, she replied: ". . . womanhood is the primal fact, wifehood and motherhood its incidents . . . must the heyday of her existence be wholly devoted to the one animal function of bearing children? Shall there be no limit to this but woman's capacity to endure the fearful strain on her life?"[26]

The insistence on women's right to refuse often took the form of attacks on men for their lusts and their violence in attempting to satisfy them. In their complaints against the unequal marriage laws, chief or at least loudest among them was the charge that they legalized rape.[27] Victoria Woodhull raged, "I will tell the world, so long as I have a tongue and the strength to move it, of all the infernal misery hidden behind this horrible thing called marriage, though the Young Men's Christian Association sentence me to prison a year for every word. I have seen horrors beside which stone walls and iron bars are heaven. . . ."[28] Angela Heywood attacked men incessantly and bitterly; if one were to ignore the accuracy of her charges, she could well seem ill-tempered. "Man so lost to himself and woman as to invoke legal *violence* in these sacred nearings, *should have solemn meeting with, and look serious at his own penis until he is able to be lord and master of it, rather than it should longer rule, lord and master, of him and of the victims he deflowers."*[29] Suffragists spoke more delicately, but not less bitterly. Feminists organized social purity organizations and campaigns, their attacks on prostitution based on a critique of the double standard, for which their proposed remedy was that men conform to the standards required of women.[30]

A variant of this concern was a campaign against "sexual abuses"—a Victorian euphemism for deviant sexual practices, or simply excessive sexual demands, not necessarily violence or prostitution. The Free Lovers, particularly, turned to this cause, because it gave them an opportunity to attack marriage. The "sexual abuses" question was one of the most frequent subjects of correspondence in Free Love periodicals. For example, a letter from Mrs. Theresa Hughes of Pittsburgh described:

> ... a girl of sixteen, full of life and health when she became a wife .... She was a slave in every sense of the word, mentally and sexually, never was she free from his brutal outrages, morning, noon and night, up almost to the very hour her baby was born, and before she was again strong enough to move about ... Often did her experience last an hour or two, and one night she will never forget, the outrage lasted exactly four hours.[31]

Or from Lucinda Chandler, well-known moral reformer:

> This useless sense gratification has demoralized generation after generation, till monstrosities of disorder are common. Moral education, and healthful training will be requisite for some generations, even after we have equitable economics, and free access to Nature's gifts. The young man of whom I knew who threatened his bride of a week with a sharp knife in his hand, to compel her to perform the office of 'sucker,' would no doubt have had the same disposition though no soul on the planet had a want unsatisfied or lacked a natural right.[32]

From an anonymous woman in Los Angeles:

> I am nearly wrecked and ruined by ... nightly intercourse, which is often repeated in the morning. This and nothing else was the cause of my miscarriage ... he went to work like a man a-mowing, and instead of a pleasure as it might have been, it was most intense torture. . . .[33]

Clearly these remarks reflect a level of hostility toward sex. The observation that many feminists hated sex has been made by several historians,[34] but they have usually failed to perceive that feminists' hostility and fear of it came from the fact that they were women, not that they were feminists. Women in the nineteenth century were, of course, trained to repress their own sexual feelings, to view sex as a duty. But they also resented what they experienced, which was not an abstraction, but a particular, historical kind of sexual encounter—intercourse dominated by and defined by the male in conformity with his desires and in disregard of what might bring pleasure to a woman. (That this might have resulted more from male ignorance than malevolence could not change women's experiences.) Furthermore, sexual intercourse brought physical danger. Pregnancy, child-birth and abortions were risky, painful and isolating experiences in the nineteenth century; venereal diseases were frequently communicated to women by their husbands. Elmina Slenker, a Free Lover and novelist, wrote, "I'm getting a host of stories (truths) about women so starved sexually as to use their dogs for relief, and finally I have come to the belief that a CLEAN dog is better than a drinking, tobacco-smelling, venerally diseased man!"[35]

"Sex-hating" women were not just misinformed, or priggish, or neurotic. They were often responding rationally to their material reality. Denied the possibility of recognizing and expressing their own sexual needs, denied even the knowledge of sexual possibilities other than those dictated by the rhythms of male orgasm, they had only two choices: passive and usually pleasureless submission, with high risk of undesirable consequences, or rebellious refusal. In that context abstinence to ensure voluntary motherhood was a most significant feminist demand.

What is remarkable is that some women recognized that it was not sex per se, but only their husbands' style of making love, that repelled them. One of the women noted above who complained about her treatment went on to say: "I am undeveloped sexually, never having desires in that direction; still, with a husband who had any love or kind feelings for me and one less selfish it *might* have been different, but he cared nothing for the torture to *me* as long as *he* was gratified."[36]

Elmina Slenker herself, the toughest and crustiest of all these "sex-haters," dared to explore and take seriously her own longings, thereby revealing herself to be a sex-lover in disguise. As the editor of the *Water-Cure Journal,* and a regular contributor to *Free Love Journal,*[37] she expounded a theory of "Dianaism, or Non-procreative Love," sometimes called "Diana-love and Alpha-abstinence." It meant free sexual contact of all sorts except intercourse.

> We want the sexes to love more than they do; we want them to love openly, frankly, earnestly; to enjoy the caress, the embrace, the glance, the voice, the presence & the very step of the beloved. We oppose no form or act of love between any man & woman. Fill the world as full of genuine sex love as you can . . . but forbear to rush in where generations yet unborn may suffer for your unthinking, uncaring, unheeding actions.[38]

Comparing this to the more usual physical means of avoiding conception—*coitus interruptus* and male continence—reveals how radical it was. In modern history, awareness of the possibilities of nongenital sex, and of forms of genital sex beyond standard "missionary-position" intercourse has been a recent, post-Freudian, even post-Masters and Johnson phenomenon. The definition of sex as heterosexual intercourse has been one of the oldest and most universal cultural norms. Slenker's alienation from existing sexual possibilities led her to explore alternatives with a bravery and a freedom from religious and psychological taboos extraordinary for a nineteenth-century Quaker reformer.

In the nineteenth century, neither Free Lovers nor suffragists ever relinquished their hostility to contraception. But among the Free Lovers, free speech was always an overriding concern, and for that reason Ezra Heywood agreed to publish some advertisements for a vaginal syringe, an instrument the use of which for contraception he personally deplored, or so he continued to assure his readers. Those advertisements led to Heywood's prosecution for obscenity, and he defended himself with characteristic flair by making his position more radical than ever before. Contraception was moral, he argued, when it was used by women as the only means of defending their rights, including the right to voluntary motherhood. Although "artificial means of preventing conception are not generally patronized by Free Lovers," he wrote, reserving for his own followers the highest moral ground, still he recognized that not all women were lucky enough to have Free Lovers for their sex partners.[39]

> Since Comstockism makes male will, passion and power absolute to *impose* conception, I stand with women to resent it. The man who would legislate to choke a woman's vagina with semen, who would force a woman to retain his seed, bear children when her own reason and conscience oppose it, would waylay her, seize her by the throat and rape her person.[40]

Angela Heywood enthusiastically pushed this new political line.

> Is it "proper", "polite", for men, real *he* men, to go to Washington to say, by penal law, fines and imprisonment, whether woman may continue her natural right to wash, rinse, or wipe out her own vaginal body opening—as well legislate when she may blow her nose, dry her eyes, or nurse her babe. . . .Whatever she may have been pleased to receive, from man's own, is his gift and her property. Women do not like rape, and have a right to resist its results.[41]

Her outspokenness, vulgarity in the ears of most of her contemporaries, came from a substantive, not merely a stylistic, sexual radicalism. Not even the heavy taboos and revulsion against abortion stopped her: "To cut a child up in woman, procure abortion, is a most fearful, tragic deed; but *even that* does not call for man's arbitrary jurisdiction over woman's womb."[42]

It is unclear whether Heywood, in this passage, was actually arguing for legalized abortion; if she was, she was alone among all nineteenth-century sexual reformers in saying it. Other feminists and Free Lovers condemned abortion, and argued that the necessity of stopping its widespread practice was a key reason for instituting voluntary motherhood by other means. The difference on the abortion question between sexual radicals and sexual conservatives was in their analysis of its causes and remedies. While doctors and preachers were sermonizing on the sinfulness of women who had abortions,[43] the radicals pronounced abortion itself an undeserved punishment, and a woman who had one a helpless victim. Woodhull and Claflin wrote about Madame Restell's notorious abortion "factory" in New York City without moralism, arguing that only voluntary conception would put it out of business.[44] Elizabeth Cady Stanton also sympathized with women who had abortions, and used the abortion problem as an example of women's victimization by laws made without their consent.[45]

Despite stylistic differences, which stemmed from differences in goals, nineteenth-century American Free Love and women's rights advocates shared the same basic attitudes toward birth control: they opposed contraception and abortion, but endorsed voluntary motherhood achieved through periodic abstinence; they believed that women should always have the right to decide when to bear a child: and they believed that women and men both had natural sex drives and that it was not wrong to indulge those drives without the intention of conceiving children. The two groups also shared the same appraisal of the social and political significance of birth control. Most of them were favorably inclined toward neo-Malthusian reasoning (at least until the 1890s, when the prevailing concern shifted to the problem of under-population rather than over-population).[46] They were also interested, increasingly, in controlling conception for eugenic purposes.[47] They were hostile to the hypocrisy of the sexual double standard and, beyond that, shared a general sense that men had become over-sexed and that sex had been transformed into something disagreeably violent.

But above all their commitment to voluntary motherhood expressed their larger commitment to women's rights. Elizabeth Cady Stanton thought voluntary motherhood so central that on her lecture tours in 1871 she held separate afternoon meetings for *women only* (a completely unfamiliar practice at the time) and talked about "the gospel of fewer children & a healthy, happy maternity."[48] "What radical thoughts I then and there put into their heads & as they feel untrammelled, these thoughts are permanently lodged there! That is all I ask."[49] Only Ezra Heywood had gone so far as to defend a particular contraceptive device—the syringe. But the principle of woman's right to choose the number of children she would bear and when was accepted in the most conservative sections of the women's rights movement. At the First Congress of the Association for the Advancement of Women in 1873, a whole session was devoted to the theme "Enlightened Motherhood," which had voluntary motherhood as part of its meaning.[50]

The general conviction of the feminist community that women had a right to choose when to conceive a child was so strong by the end of the nineteenth century that it seems odd that they were unable to overcome their scruples against artificial contraception. The basis for the reluctance lies in their awareness that a consequence of effective contraception would be the separation of sexuality from reproduction. A state of things that permitted sexual intercourse to take place normally, even frequently, without the risk of pregnancy, inevitably seemed to nineteenth-century middle-class women as an attack on the family, as they understood the family. In the mid-Victorian sexual system, men normally conducted their sexual philandering with prostitutes; accordingly prostitution, far from being a threat to the family system, was a part of it and an important support of it. This was the common view of the time, paralleled by the belief that prostitutes knew of effective birth-control techniques. This seemed only fitting, for contraception in the 1870s was associated with sexual immorality. It did not seem, even to the most sexually liberal, that contraception could be legitimized to any extent, even for the purposes of family planning for married couples, without licensing extra-marital sex. The fact that contraception was not morally acceptable to respectable women was, from a woman's point of view, a guarantee that those women would not be a threat to her own marriage.

The fact that sexual intercourse often leads to conception was also a guarantee that men would marry in the first place. In the nineteenth century women needed marriage far more than men. Lacking economic independence, women needed husbands to support them, or at least to free them from a usually more humiliating economic dependence on fathers. Especially in the cities, where women were often isolated from communities, deprived of the economic and psychological support of networks of relatives, friends and neighbors, the prospect of dissolving the cement of nuclear families was frightening. In many cases children, and the prospect of children, provided that cement. Man's responsibilities for children were an important pressure for marital stability. Women, especially middle-class women, were also dependent on their children to provide them with meaningful work. The belief that motherhood was a woman's fulfillment had a material basis: parenthood was often the only creative and challenging activity in a woman's life, a key part of her self-esteem.

Legal, efficient birth control would have increased men's freedom to indulge in extra-marital sex without greatly increasing women's freedom to do so. The pressures enforcing chastity and marital fidelity on middle-class women were not only fear of illegitimate conception but a powerful combination of economic, social and psychological factors, including economic dependence, fear of rejection by husband and social support networks, internalized taboos and, hardly the least important, a socially conditioned lack of interest in sex that may have approached functional frigidity. The double standard of the Victorian sexual and family system, which had made men's sexual freedom irresponsible and oppressive to women, left most feminists convinced that increasing, rather than releasing, the taboos against extra-marital sex was in their interest, and they threw their support behind social-purity campaigns.

In short, we must forget the twentieth-century association of birth control with a trend toward sexual freedom. The voluntary motherhood propaganda of the 1870s was associated with a push toward a more restrictive, or at least a more rigidly enforced, sexual morality. Achieving voluntary motherhood by a method that would have encouraged sexual license was absolutely contrary to the felt interests of the very group that formed the main social basis for the cause— middle-class women. Separating these women from the early-twentieth-century feminists, with their interest in sexual freedom, were nearly four decades of significant social and economic changes and a general weakening of the ideology of the Lady. The ideal of the Free Lovers—responsible, open sexual encounters between equal partners—was impossible in the 1870s because men and women were not equal. A man was a man whether faithful to his wife or not. But women's sexual activities divided them into two categories—wife or prostitute. These categories were not mere ideas, but were enforced in reality by severe social and economic sanctions. The fact that so many, indeed most, Free Lovers in practice led faithful, monogamous, legally-married lives is not insignificant in this regard. It suggests that they instinctively understood that Free Love was an ideal not be realized in that time.

As voluntary motherhood was an ideology intended to encourage sexual purity, so it was also a pro-motherhood ideology. Far from debunking motherhood, the voluntary motherhood advocates consistently continued the traditional Victorian mystification and sentimentalization of the mother. It is true that at the end of the nineteenth century an increasing number of feminists and elite women—that is, still a relatively small group—were choosing not to marry or become mothers. That was primarily because of their increasing interest in professional work, and the difficulty of doing such work as a wife and mother, given the normal uncooperativeness of husbands and the lack of social provisions for child care. Voluntary motherhood advocates shared the general belief that mothers of young children ought not to work outside their homes but should make mothering their full-time occupation. Suffragists argued both to make professions open to women and to ennoble the task of mothering; they argued for increased rights and opportunities for women *because* they were mothers.

The Free Lovers were equally pro-motherhood; they only wanted to separate motherhood from legal marriage.[51] They devised pro-motherhood arguments to bolster their case against marriage. Mismated couples, held together by marriage laws, made bad parents and produced inferior offspring, Free Lovers said.[52] In 1870 *Woodhull and Claflin's Weekly* editorialized, "Our marital system is the greatest obstacle to the regeneration of the race."[53]

This concern with eugenics was characteristic of nearly all feminists of the late nineteenth century. At the time eugenics was mainly seen as an implication of evolutionary theory and was picked up by many social reformers to buttress their arguments that improvement of the human condition was possible. Eugenics had not yet become a movement in itself. Feminists used eugenics arguments as if they instinctively felt that arguments based solely on women's rights had not enough power to conquer conservative and religious scruples about reproduction. So they combined eugenics and feminism to produce evocative, romantic visions of perfect motherhood. "Where boundless love prevails. . .," *Woodhull and Claflin's Weekly* wrote, "the mother who produces an inferior child will be dishonored and unhappy . . . and she who produces superior children will feel proportionately pleased. When woman attains this position, she will consider superior offspring a necessity and be apt to procreate only with superior men."[54] Free Lovers and suffragists alike used the cult of motherhood to argue for making motherhood voluntary. Involuntary motherhood, wrote Harriet Stanton Blatch, daughter of Elizabeth Cady Stanton and a prominent suffragist, is a prostitution of the maternal instinct.[55] Free Lover Rachel Campbell cried out that motherhood was being "ground to dust under the misrule of masculine ignorance and superstition."[56]

Not only was motherhood considered an exalted, sacred profession, and a profession exclusively woman's reponsibility, but for a woman to avoid it was to choose a distinctly less noble path. In arguing for the enlargement of woman's sphere, feminists envisaged combining motherhood with other activities, not rejecting motherhood. Victoria Woodhull and Tennessee Claflin wrote:

Tis true that the special and distinctive feature of woman is that of bearing children, and that upon the exercise of her function in this regard the perpetuity of race depends. It is also true that those who pass through life failing in this special feature of their mission cannot be said to have lived to the best purposes of woman's life. But while maternity should always be considered the most holy of all the functions woman is capable of, it should not be lost sight of in devotion to this, that there are as various spheres of usefulness outside of this for woman as there are for man outside of the marriage relation.[57]

Birth control was not intended to open the possibility of childlessness, but merely to give women leverage to win more recognition and dignity. Dora Forster, a Free Lover, saw in the fears of underpopulation a weapon of blackmail for women:

> I hope the scarcity of children will go on until maternity is honored at least as much as the trials and hardships of soldiers campaigning in wartime. It will then be worth while to supply the nation with a sufficiency of children . . . every civilized nation, having lost the power to enslave woman as mother, will be compelled to recognize her voluntary exercise of that function as by far the most important service of any class of citizens.[58]

"Oh, women of the world, arise in your strength and demand that all which stands in the path of true motherhood shall be removed from your path," wrote Lois Waisbrooker, a Free Love novelist and moral reformer.[59] Helen Gardener based a plea for women's education entirely on the argument that society needed educated mothers to produce able sons (not children, sons).

> Harvard and Yale, not to mention Columbia, may continue to put a protective tariff on the brains of young men: but so long as they must get those brains from the proscribed sex, just so long will male brains remain an 'infant industry' and continue to need this protection. Stupid mothers never did and stupid mothers never will, furnish this world with brilliant sons.[60]

Clinging to the cult of motherhood was part of a broader conservatism shared by Free Lovers and suffragists—acceptance of traditional sex roles. Even the Free Lovers rejected only one factor—legal marriage—of the many that defined woman's place in the family. They did not challenge conventional conceptions of woman's passivity and limited sphere of concern.[61] In their struggles for equality the women's-rights advocates never suggested that men should share responsibility for child-raising, housekeeping, nursing, cooking. When Victoria Woodhull in the 1870s and Charlotte Perkins Gilman in the early 1900s suggested socialized child care, they assumed that only women would do the work.[62] Most feminists wanted economic independence for women, but most, too, were reluctant to recommend achieving this by turning women loose and helpless into the economic world to compete with men.[63] This attitude was conditioned by an attitude hostile to the egoistic spirit of capitalism; but the attitude was not transformed into a political position and usually appeared as a description of women's weakness, rather than an attack on the system. Failing to distinguish, or even to indicate awareness of a possible distinction between women's conditioned passivity and their equally conditioned distaste for competition and open aggression, these feminists also followed the standard Victorian rationalization of sex roles, the idea that women were morally superior. Thus the timidity and self-effacement that were the marks of women's powerlessness were made into innate virtues. Angela Heywood, for example, praised women's greater ability for self-control, and, in an attribution no doubt intended to jar and titillate the reader, branded men inferior on account of their lack of sexual temperance.[64] Men's refusal to accept women as human beings she identified, similarly, as a mark of men's incapacity: ". . . man has not yet achieved himself to realize and meet a PERSON in woman. . . ."[65] In idealistic, abstract terms, no doubt such male behavior is an incapacity. Yet that conceit failed to remark on the power and privilege over women that the supposed "incapacity" gave men.

This omission is characteristic of the cult of motherhood. Indeed, what made it a cult was its one-sided failure to recognize the privileges men received from women's exclusive responsibility for parenthood. The "motherhood" of the feminists' writings was not merely the biological process of gestation and birth, but a package of social, economic and cultural functions. Although many of the nineteenth-century feminists had done substantial analysis of the historical and anthropological origins of woman's social role, they nevertheless agreed with the biological-determinist point of view that women's parental capacities had become implanted at the level of instinct, the famous "maternal instinct." That concept rested on the assumption that the qualities that parenthood requires—capacities for tenderness, self-control and patience, tolerance for tedium and detail, emotional supportiveness, dependability and warmth—were not only instinctive but sex-linked. The concept of the maternal instinct thus also involved a definition of the normal instinctual structure of the male that excluded these capacities, or included them only to an inferior degree; it also carried the implication that women who did not exercise these capacities, presumably through motherhood, remained unfulfilled, untrue to their destinies.

Belief in the maternal instinct reinforced the belief in the necessary spiritual connection for women between sex and reproduction, and limited the development of birth-control ideas. But the limits were set by the entire social context of women's lives, not by the intellectual timidity of their ideas. For women's "control over their own bodies" to lead to a rejection of motherhood as the *primary* vocation and measure of social worth required the existence of alternative vocations and sources of worthiness. The women's rights advocates of the 1870s and 1880s were fighting for those other opportunities, but a significant change had come only to a few privileged women, and most women faced essentially the same options that existed fifty years earlier. Thus voluntary motherhood in this period remained almost exclusively a tool for women to strengthen their positions within conventional marriages and families, not to reject them.

[1] There is no space here to compensate for the unfortunate general lack of information about the Free Lovers. The book-in-progress from which this paper is taken includes a fuller discussion of who they were, the content of their ideology and practice. The interested reader may refer to the following major works of the Free Love cause:

R. D. Chapman, *Freelove a Law of Nature* (New York: author 1881).

Tennessee Claflin, *The Ethics of Sexual Equality* (New York: Woodhull & Claflin, 1873).

———, *Virtue, What Is It and What It Isn't; Seduction, What It Is and What It Is Not* (New York: Woodhull & Claflin, 1872).

Ezra Heywood, *Cupid's Yokes: or, The Binding Forces of Conjugal Life* (Princeton, Mass.: Co-operative Publishing Co., n.d., probably 1876).

———, *Uncivil Liberty: An Essay to Show the Injustice and Impolicy of Ruling Woman Without Her Consent* (Princeton, Mass.: Co-operative Publishing Co., 1872).

C. L. James, *The Future Relation of the Sexes* (St. Louis: author, 1872).

Juliet Severance, *Marriage* (Chicago: M. Harman, 1901).

Victoria Claflin Woodhull, *The Scare-Crows of Sexual Slavery* (New York: Woodhull & Claflin, 1874).

———, *A Speech on the Principles of Social Freedom* (New York: Woodhull & Claflin, 1872).

———, *Tried as by Fire; or, the True and the False Socially* (New York: Woodhull & Claflin, 1874).

[2] Heywood, *Cupid's Yokes, p. 20.*

[3] Claflin, *The Ethics of Sexual Equality,* pp. 9-10.

[4] *Woodhull & Claflin's Weekly* 1, no. 6 (1870): 5.

[5] Heywood, *Cupid's Yokes,* pp. 17-18.

[6] Letter to her daughter Alice, 1874, in the Isabella Beecher Hooker Collection. Beecher Stowe Mass. This reference was brought to my attention by Ellen Dubois of SUNY-Buffalo.

[7] Alice B. Stockham, M.D., *Karezza, Ethics of Marriage* (Chicago: Alice B. Stockham & Co., 1898), pp. 84, 91-92.

[8] Theodore Stanton and Harriot Stanton Blatch, eds., *Elizabeth Cady Stanton as Revealed in Her Letters, Diary and Reminiscences* (New York: Harper & Bros., 1922), 2:210 (Diary, 9-6-1883).

[9] Ben Barker-Benfield, "The Spermatic Economy: A Nineteenth Century View of Sexuality," *Feminist Studies* 1, no. 1 (Summer 1972): 53.

[10] J.J. Rousseau, *Emile* (New York: Columbia University Teachers College, 1967), p. 132. Rousseau was, after all, a chief author of the Victorian revision of the image of woman.

[11] Dora Forster, *Sex Radicalism as Seen by an Emancipated Woman of the New Time* (Chicago: M. Harman, 1905), p. 40.

[12] Norman E. Himes, *Medical History of Contraception* (New York: Gamut Press, 1963).

[13] Heywood, *Cupid's Yokes,* pp. 19-20, 16.

[14] Ibid., pp. 19-20; *Woodhull & Claflin's Weekly* 1, no, 18 (September 10, 1870): 5.

[15] Heywood, *Cupid's Yoke,* pp. 14-15.

[16] Stockham, *Karezza,* pp. 82-83, 53.

[17] See for example, *Free Enquirer,* ed. Robert Owen and Frances Wright, (May 22, 1830), pp. 235-236.

[18] Stockham, *Karezza,* p. 86.

[19] Heywood, *Cupid's Yoke,* p. 19.

[20] Charlotte Perkins Gilman, *Women and Economics* (New York: Harper Torchbooks, 1966), pp. 38-39, 43-44, 42, 47-48, 209.

[21] In England, for example, it was not until 1891 that the courts first held against a man who forcibly kidnapped and imprisoned his wife when she left him.

[22] Ezra Heywood, *Free Speech: Report of Ezra H. Heywood's Defense before the United States Court, in Boston, April 10, 11, and 12, 1883* (Princeton, Mass.: Co-operative Publishing Co., n.d.), p. 16.

[23] Quoted in Nelson Manfred Blake, *The Road to Reno, A History of Divorce in the United States* (New York: Macmillan, 1962), p. 108, from the *New York Tribune,* May 12, 1871 and July 20, 1871.

[24] Letter of August 29, 1869, in Hooker Collection, Beecher-Stowe Mss. This reference was brought to my attention by Ellen Dubois of SUNY-Buffalo.

[25] Isabella Beecker Hooker, *Womanhood: its Sanctities and Fidelities* (Boston: Lee and Shepard, 1873), p. 26.

26 Elizabeth Cady Stanton Mss. No. 11, Library of Congress, undated. This reference was brought to my attention by Ellen Dubois of SUNY-Buffalo.

27 See for example, *Lucifer, The Light-Bearer*, ed. Moses Harman (Valley Falls, Kansas: 1894-1907) 18, no. 6 (October 1889): 3.

28 Victoria Woodhull, *The Scare-Crows*, p. 21. Her mention of the YMCA is a reference to the fact that Anthony Comstock, author and chief enforcer for the U.S. Post Office of the anti-obscenity laws, had begun his career in the YMCA.

29 *The Word* (Princeton, Mass.) 20, no. 9 (March 1893): 2-3. Emphasis in original.

30 See for example, the National Purity Congress of 1895, sponsored by the American Purity Alliance.

31 *Lucifer* (April 26, 1890), pp. 1-2.

32 N. a. *The Next Revolution: or Woman's Emancipation from Sex Slavery* (Valley Falls, Kansas: Lucifer Publishing Co., 1890), p. 49.

33 Ibid., pp. 8-9.

34 Linda Gordon et al., "Sexism in American Historical Writing," *Women's Studies* 1, no. 1 (Fall 1972).

35 *Lucifer* 15, no. 2 (September 1886): 3.

36 *The Word* 20 (1892-1893).

37 (Slenker) *Lucifer*, May 23, 1907; *Cyclopedia of American Boigraphy* 8: 488.

38 See for example *Lucifer* 18, no. 8 (December 1889): 3; 18, no. 6 (October 1889): 3; 18, no. 8 (December 1889): 3.

39 Heywood, *Free Speech*, pp. 17, 16.

40 Ibid., pp. 3-6. "Comstockism" also is a reference to Anthony Comstock. Noting the irony that the syringe was called by Comstock's name, Heywood continued: "To name a really good thing 'Comstock' has a sly, sinister, wily look, indicating vicious purpose; in deference to its N.Y. venders, who gave that name, the Publishers of *The Word* inserted an advertisement . . . which will hereafter appear as 'the Vaginal Syringe'; for its intelligent, humane and worthy mission should no longer be libelled by forced association with the pious scamp who thinks Congress gives him legal right of way to and control over every American Woman's Womb." At this trial, Heywood's second, he was acquitted. At his first trial, in 1877, he had been convicted, sentenced to two years, and served six months; at his third, in 1890, he was sentenced to and served two years at hard labor, an ordeal which probably caused his death a year later.

41 *The Word* 10, no. 9 (March 1893): 2-3.

42 Ibid.

43 See for example Horatio Robinson Storer, M.D., *Why Not? A Book for Every Woman* (Boston: Lee and Shepard, 1868). Note that this was the prize essay in a contest run by the A.M.A. in 1865 for the best anti-abortion tract.

44 Claflin, *Ethics;* Emanie Sachs, *The Terrible Siren, Victoria Woodhull, 1838-1927* (New York: Harper & Bros., 1928), p. 139.

45 Elizabeth Cady Stanton, Susan Anthony, Matilda Gage, eds., *History of Woman Suffrage*, 1:597-598.

46 Heywood, *Cupid's Yokes*, p. 20; see also *American Journal of Eugenics*, ed. M. Harman 1, no. 2 (September 1907); *Lucifer* (February 15, 1906; June 7, 1906; March 28, 1907; and May 11, 1905).

47 I will deal with early feminists' ideas concerning eugenics in my book.

48 Elizabeth Cady Stanton to Martha Wright, June 19, 1871, Stanton Mss. This reference was brought to my attention by Ellen Dubois of SUNY-Buffalo; see also Stanton, *Eight Years After, Reminiscences 1815-1897* (New York: Schoeken, 1971), pp. 262,297.

49 Stanton and Blatch, *Stanton as Revealed in Her Letters*, pp. 132-133.

50 *Papers and Letters*, Association for the Advancement of Women, 1873. The AAW was a conservative group formed in opposition to the Stanton-Anthony tendency. Nevertheless Chandler, a frequent contributor to Free Love journals, spoke here against undesired maternity and the identification of woman with her maternal fuction.

51 *Woodhull & Claflin's Weekly* 1, no. 20 (October 1, 1870): 10.

52 Woodhull, *Tried as by Fire*, p. 37; Lillian Harman, *The Regeneration of Society*. Speech before Manhattan Liberal Club, March 31, 1898 (Chicago: Light Bearer Library, 1900).

53 *Woodhull & Claflin's Weekly* 1, no. 20 (October 1, 1870): 10.

54 Ibid.

55 Harriot Stanton Blatch, "Voluntary Motherhood," *Transactions*, National Council of Women of 1891, ed. Rachel Foster Avery (Philadelphia: J. B. Lippincott, 1891), p. 280.

56 Rachel Campbell, *The Prodigal Daughter, or, the Price of Virtue* (Grass Valley, California, 1885), p. 3. An essay read to the New England Free Love League, 1881.

57 *Woodhull & Claflin's Weekly* 1, no. 14 (August 13, 1870): 4.

58 In addition to the biography by Sachs mentioned above, see also Johanna Johnston, *Mrs. Satan* (New York: G. P. Putnam's Sons, 1967), and M. M. Marberry, *Vicky, A Biography of Victoria C. Woodhull* (New York: Funk & Wagnalls, 1967).

59 From an advertisement for her novel, *Perfect Motherhood; Or, Mabel Raymond's Resolve* (New York: Murray Hill, 1890), in *The Next Revolution*.

60 Helen Hamilton Gardener, *Pulpit, Pew and Cradle* (New York: Truth Seeker Library, 1891), p. 22.

61 Even the most outspoken of the Free Lovers had conventional, role-differentiated images of sexual relations. Here is Angela Heywood, for example: "Men must not emasculate themselves for the sake of 'virtue,' they must, they will, recognize manliness and the life element of manliness as the fountain source of good manners. Women and girls demand strong, well-bred generative, vitalizing sex ability. Potency, virility, is the grand basic principle of man, and it holds him clean, sweet and elegant, to the delicacy of his counterpart." From *The Word* 14, no. 2 (June 1885): 3.

62 Woodhull, *The Scare-Crows;* Charlotte Perkins Gilman, *Concerning Children*.

63 See for example Blatch, "Voluntary Motherhood," pp. 283-284.

64 *The Word* 20, no. 8 (February 1893): 3.

65 Ibid.

SALON, FOYER, BUREAU:
WOMEN AND THE PROFESSIONS IN FRANCE

Catherine Bodard Silver

During the great revolution of 1789—rhetorically dedicated to abstract equality—the women of France rioted, demonstrated, and struggled in the cause. However, apart from references to *citoyennes*—the female version of the new, universal social rank, *citoyen*—women received no substantive benefits from the redistribution of rights after the destruction of the monarchy and aristocracy.[2] Such a pattern has long characterized the situation of women in France—not least those women who seek to enter the most skilled and prestigious occupational positions, the professions. France has long been characterized by abstract commitments to equality—but also by strong familistic traditions stressing women's subordinate and domestic role. Since 1900, higher education has been available to women in proportions that compare favorably with other European societies; yet today they are minimally represented at the highest professional levels. At the same time, French women have wider access to professional careers than do their counterparts in many other Western societies.

Thus, French women are very far indeed from that "equality" proclaimed in the Republic's motto, but simplistic images of "repression" or "discrimination" are insufficient for an adequate sociological understanding of the professional aspirations, frustrations, and achievements of women in France. The situation of professional women in France reveals some of the complex interactions among economy, polity, and culture defining "women's place," illuminating by comparison and contrast the more familiar situation in English-speaking societies.

The Class and Occupational Setting

Some distinctive characteristics of French social and occupational structure must be understood as a prologue to analysis. Professional occupations in

This article first appeared in *The American Journal of Sociology* 78, no. 4 (January 1973): 836-851, and is reprinted with the permission of the publisher.

France cannot be taken as the direct equivalents of American ones. They include, of course, the classic "liberal professions"—law, medicine, the professoriat; but in France, *professeurs* are found not only in universities but at the educational level just below, the *lycées*. High government administrators—*cadres supérieurs*—are more highly professionalized in France, both in occupational style and educational requirements (roughly equivalent to American graduate studies short of the doctoral dissertation). For this reason, as well as the traditional dignity and prestige of the higher public administration in France, government administration is appropriately regarded as a profession.

Other occupations, too, are more readily accorded professional status in France. This is true of some in which women are numerous, such as teachers below the *lycée* level (*instituteurs*), and middle-level administrators; such strata comprise the *cadres moyens*. Both *cadres supérieurs* and *cadres moyens* are classifications used by the French census, but they are also terms of daily speech used to describe social distinctions in French society.

These distinctions suggest how inapplicable to France is the American notion of a broad middle class which—however heterogeneous in occupational, educational, and ethnic terms—nonetheless shares core social values which widely serve as models for other strata. The term *bourgeoisie,* often translated misleadingly as "middle class," refers to about 26 percent of the French population (in 1962), a group sharply distinguished both from manual workers (*ouvriers*) and white-collar personnel (*employés*). Within the *bourgeoisie* must be distinguished the 4 percent or 5 percent of the population forming the *grande bourgeoisie*—*cadre supérieurs,* the liberal professions, and the most wealthy property owners, employers, investors, and businessmen. The *grande bourgeoisie* differs significantly not only in wealth and status but also in values and style of life from the *petite bourgeoisie* (10 percent of the population) and the *bourgeoisie moyenne* (12 percent) (who include the *cadres moyens,* i.e., *instituteurs,* nurses, administrators, and smaller businessmen and property owners). As we shall see, distinctions between the values of the *grande bourgeoisie* and other strata are important in understanding the position and opportunities of professional women.[3]

Professional Women in the Occupational Structure

Compared with other Western nations, the proportion of women employed in nonagricultural occupations in France ranks among the highest—36 percent.[4] However, the extent of women's participation in the labor force is an ambiguous indicator of equality between the sexes; a high rate may denote women's large-scale relegation to low-paying, unskilled, and dead-end positions, whose major social function is to supplement low family incomes or to support families without male heads of households. The nature of women's participation in professional occupations partakes of analogous ambiguities. In the nonagricultural labor force, the proportion of each sex who are professionals (the liberal professions, *cadres supérieurs, cadres moyens*) is essentially identical—17 percent for women, 17.8 percent for men. But distinguishing within professional occupations, only 18 percent of professional women are in the higher-status positions (liberal professions, *cadres supérieurs*) compared with 42 percent of the men. The absolute number of French professional women is about half that of men—in 1968 there were 1,002,940 such women, compared with 2,003,960 men.

Although French women enjoy considerable access to the professions, they tend to cluster in the middle ranks. Yet this state of affairs is in some ways not so unsatisfactory as the comparable one in the United States. The relatively high status of middle-level professionals in France, and some distinctive characteristics of professional occupations like teaching and public administration—in which women are heavily concentrated—work to modify somewhat what would otherwise be a position of very marked inferiority in professional life.

The most important case in point is that of *lycée professeurs,* of whom 55 percent were women in the school year 1968-69. In all, 46,307 were *lycée professeurs,* constituting one-quarter of all women in the *cadre supérieur* and liberal professions. *Lycées,* although the stage before university studies, are hardly the same as American high schools. Academically, their last two years are comparable with the the first two in superior American colleges. The selection of teachers is rigorous, and requirements are intellectually strenuous. Candidates receive specialized educations in the Ecoles Normales Supérieures, at academic levels higher than that provided in university faculties attended by students of the same age. Both *lycée* and university *professeurs* usually pass a difficult competitive examination, the *agregation,* requiring several years of preparation and testing general culture as well as specialized knowledge. Teaching staffs in *lycées* are organized in a hierarchy of ranks, and high rank is achieved both by seniority and by indications of professional achievement. These schools are understood to be vehicles of high culture, and successful completion of such a school provides an automatic entitlement to university admission. Thus, *lycée* teaching is clearly assimilated to university education rather than lower education; it represents an arduous and prestigious achievement. *Lycée professeurs* are widely regarded as representatives of science and culture in a society where official values accord high status to these domains. That half of these *professeurs* are women meets an abstract criterion of equality without devaluating the profession by "overfeminizing" it, in a society in which women are not admitted on equal terms to the highest occupational ranks. In both qualitative and quantitative senses, then, *lycée* teaching represents a most significant professional area available to women, one essentially lacking in American society.[5]

Similar considerations apply to *instituteurs.* In 1962, 72 percent of these were women (Ministère de l'Education National 1968-69)—certainly a high proportion but lower than the comparable figure for primary school teachers in the United States, which is more than 90 percent. As representatives of culture in a society which officially holds its culture to be a national treasure, their prestige benefits; also, their professional preparation is clearly superior to that of their American counterparts.[6] Thus, at all levels of state-supported teaching below the university, but particularly in *lycées,* teaching careers open to women are significantly more professionalized than their American counterparts.

There remain the universities. As is well known, the distinction between academic ranks is far sharper than in the United States, with the professoriat constituting by far a smaller fraction of the total teaching staff, and exercising distinctive kinds of authority.[7] In these ranks, women are indeed few—less than 2 percent in the faculties of law and medicine, 4.5 percent in the *facultés des lettres* (teaching literature, philosophy, and social science), and 6 percent in the science faculties. However, below the professorial rank—at instructional levels which in rights and relative compensation rank below associate and assistant professors in the American system—the proportion of women jumps to 25 percent (reaching 35 percent in the *facultés des lettres*). In the United States in 1961, 9 percent of university full professors were women, and 16 percent of the associate professors.[8] Once again, a characteristic pattern emerges—a tiny participation of women at the very highest professional levels but a very considerable presence at the middle levels, one comparing favorably indeed with other Western societies.

Given the significance of academic intellectuals in defining and interpreting the nature of social problems, it is curious that this discrepancy between women's participation at high and low levels of instructional authority within the university has not produced in France an ideological focus upon the special problems of academic women, as it has in the United States. Data are lacking to show how long this sort of discrepancy has characterized French university faculties, but, in any case, the general problems of French universities—overcrowding, concentration of authority in the professorial "mandarinate," restricted opportunities for nonprofessorial staff, and others—have overshadowed concern with the problems of women. None of the major competing interpretations of the universities' difficulties—financial, administrative, Marxist, *gauchiste,* or other—stresses discrimination against women, as compared with such issues as class inequality, generational conflict, disputes about intellectual authority, or insufficient resources.

Apart from teaching, public administration is the other large-scale set of professional opportunities sponsored by the state. Its significance is very great, given the long tradition in France of centralized state administration, the high qualifications required for it, and the prestige surrounding it. Women were first admitted into the civil service at the end of the last century, but it was the First World War which significantly widened their opportunities in the state sector and led to a formal equality of treatment and conditions in most respects. Only after the Second World War, however, were the highest administrative positions made accessible to women, who were admitted to the Ecole Nationale d'Administration, the intellectually rigorous and key point of entry into these posts. As of 1962, 11.2 percent of the highest administrative positions—finance inspectors, members of the Conseil d'Etat, and others—were women. In the United States as of 1961, the proportion of women in the highest grades of the civil service was 4.4 percent. Nonetheless, whole ministries—Justice, Foreign Affairs, Finance—have very few women in higher positions, and admission to some administrative careers remains formally closed.[9] Women are still formally barred from the office of *préfet*—the extremely important representatives of central government in the *départements* into which France is administratively divided. Indeed, the very law which established equal rights for women in the public service provided also for exceptions due to the "physical unfitness" of women and "psychological difficulties which the presence of women might provoke."[10] Nonetheless, public administration clearly represents an important professional opportunity for women. Among women in positions of high administrative responsibility, three-quarters are in the public service. Furthermore, the rate at which the number of women administrators among the *cadres supérieurs* is increasing is the highest of any profession; and this rate is double that of the increase among males.[11] As of 1962, 21,000 women were at administrative ranks corresponding to the *cadres supérieurs* compared with 172,740 men. The major significance of public administration as a profession for women lies in the *cadres moyens,* where in 1962 there were 79,600 women (and 168,700 men).

We have already observed that the high qualifications and prestige of public administration in France lend it both the aura and the substance of a professional career.[12] But this rather high participation of women professionals in public administration occurs in the context of their low participation in the liberal professions. Law and medicine remain heavily masculine (15 percent of French physicians are women); and engineeering even more so (3 percent of the latter are women).[13] The achievement of professional women in France is thus very much weighted on the side of public employment, especially in teaching and government administration, at the expense of accomplishment in entrepreneurial and private professions.

Given the "statist" tradition of France—in which, historically, public administration and education have played central roles as stabilizing and conservatizing forces—this means that professional women are largely engaged in the least dynamic and change-oriented aspects of French life. As we shall see below, when analyzing aspects of French culture, this is but one way in which French professional women are particularly affected by the most conservative tendencies in French society. At this point, it is sufficient to point out that in the context of France, professional achievements by women do not necessarily contribute to accelerated social change.

Access to Higher Education in Professional Career Lines

Higher education being an indispensable prerequisite for entry to professional occupations, it is necessary to consider women's access to universities. In these terms, France emerges as among the most egalitarian of European nations: in 1963, 43 percent of university students were women, compared with 32 percent in Britain, 35 percent in Denmark, 24 percent in Germany, and 22 percent in Norway. And the significant proportion of women among French university students has not been a recent development: from 2.5 percent in 1900, it grew to 12.5 percent in 1920, 26 percent in 1930, and fully 34 percent at the start of the Second World War. The postwar period saw a slowing of the growth of female representation as the total university population began to expand considerably; from 38 percent in 1959 it moved to 43 percent in 1963, where it has roughly remained.[14]

France has thus made higher education available to women on a larger scale, and over a longer period, than has been the case in many other, if not all, Western European countries. However, access of women to higher education in France is largely a function of class inequality. The *grande bourgeoisie* in 1962 represented 4 percent of the population but 29 percent of the university students; the *cadres moyens* amounted to 7.8 percent of the population but 18 percent of the students. Among women university students, the proportion of *bourgeois* origin is higher than among men. Thus, higher education in France consolidates the class position of the *bourgeoisie* more often among women than among men.[15] The daughters of the *bourgeoisie* are more likely to go to universities than the sons of nonmanual occupational strata, let alone of *ouvriers*. Women in France are by no means denied access to professions because they are blocked off from university education. There is a marked discrepancy between their educational opportunities and the extent of their professional achievement. This situation, now developing on a large scale in the United States and some other nations for the first time, has existed in France for decades. Yet women in France have displayed less overt discontent on this account or indeed on any other account that involves woman's place. Tellingly, Simone de Beauvoir's subtle and powerful *Le deuxième sexe,* published in 1949, was the first notable occasion on which the problem of women's role was comprehensively raised; by no means restricted to France, it analyzes those aspects of French society which women of Beauvoir's stamp find particularly irksome. In France today, this book can still be regarded as ahead of its time—its impact having been limited to some intellectual and ideological circles—while, in translation, it has been widely read in the English-speaking societies, where the problem was raised decades earlier in both intellectual and agitational terms. To understand why feminist formulations and movements have been so slow to develop in France, we may begin with a discussion of some cultural factors particularly distinctive to French society.

Cultural Definitions of Women

If it is true that everywhere images of women's nature play a large role in defining and reinforcing "appropriate" roles for them, in no Western society is this more palpably obvious than in France. Surely no other Western culture has developed more elaborated and intricate ideas about women and more closely interwoven them with the "high culture" and the style of life of whole social classes. The two centuries that produced the classical culture of France, the seventeenth and eighteenth, also produced a series of women eminent as both sponsors and creators of high culture. Beside such names as la duchesse de Rambouillet, la marquise de Sevigné, Madame de Lafayette, Madame de Maintenon, Mademoiselle de Lespinasse, and Madame de Staël, corresponding figures in Anglo-American culture (Jane Austin and Emily Dickinson, for example) are comparatively pale and late. Women helped shape the core values and the very language that are crucial to the substance of French culture. Such women, of course, were few and highly privileged, flourishing in the setting of an aristocratic social order. The rise of commercial society in the nineteenth century demoted women from the highest reaches of cultural creativity and participation as key sponsors of culture. Balzac and Flaubert, among others, described the emergence of a new type of woman—a highly elaborated aesthetic object, the property of men, and seeking expression as wife or mistress. "The destiny of woman and her sole glory," writes Balzac in his *Physiologie du mariage,* "is to excite the hearts of men. Woman is a property acquired by contract; she is disposable property, . . . in short, woman properly speaking is only an annex of man."[16] Older themes portraying woman as an idealized erotic object, finding fulfillment and power over men in love, certainly persisted; but more significant by far was the new dominance of the domestic ideal, associated above all with the most prosperous *bourgeoisie.* The focus of emotional life became the *foyer*—an idea for which "home" is a weaker equivalent; as an arena for women, the *foyer* was far more restricted and passive than the aristocratic milieu.[17]

It would be anachronistic to regard this development solely as a decrease of *bourgeois* women's power. On the contrary, their enhanced role within the family—the expectation of being loved, some responsibility for the rearing and education of children—represented a significant improvement. Until about the middle of the eighteenth century, *bourgeois* and aristocratic women had little or nothing to do in these terms. On the whole, they neither reared children nor administered households; these tasks were discharged by servants, nurses, and tutors under the ultimate direction of husbands. Ironically, in view of later developments, among the first conquests and achievements of higher-status women in France was the role of *maîtresse de maison.*[18] (The very phrase, the counterpart of *maître de maison,* differs from the English "housewife" (*ménagère*); it implies an important and distinct role in the administration of the home as a social and moral entity.) We shall see that the impact of this "achievement" is still meaningful among *bourgeois* women in contemporary France. To appreciate this we must understand the historical and cultural aspects of prevalent ideology about the family and women's place in it as they evolved in France.

After the Bourbon Restoration of 1815, conservative ideologists elaborated a social philosophy which defined the domestic, nuclear family as a major element of social stability. This represented a shift in the alleged basis of social stability from earlier emphases upon the extended aristocratic lineage, public ties of dependence and obligation based upon locality, the "corporations" of artisans and merchants, the parish, and other groupings—all of them larger than the domestic family and, of course, excluding women from significant power. The influential conservative Bonald, for example, worked out such a theory, comparing domestic authority with fundamental social and political authority, and assigning to women a subordinate but vital place in the newly significant domestic scheme.[19]

Such values, however, were very far from the exclusive property of the Catholic reaction. Rousseau, seminal both for Romanticism and the Enlightenment, called for domesticated, loving motherhood, even to the point of having mothers nurse their own children—a suggestion ridiculed in the aristocratic *salons* as an expression of "les vanités de la mamelle."[20] The apostle of rational progress, Comte, saw women as inferior by reason of their "biological childishness" (*infantalisme biologique*). He rather vaguely sentimentalized them as morally superior to men, but saw men as stronger "not only in body, but also in intellect (*espirit*) and character. . . . We must above all act and think, struggling against the difficulties of our real destiny; thus, men must command, despite their lesser morality." Comte, like Rousseau and Bonald, saw woman's chief role and contribution as lying in the *foyer,* in the education of children and the refinement of emotional impulses. Like Rousseau's, his definition of women's role was not seen as reactionary and retrograde but was linked to a vision of progress. "In order to assure [women's] emotional destiny," Comte wrote, man must make woman's life "more and more domestic," and "above all detach her from all outside work. . . . *The man must feed the woman:* this is the natural law of our species." To grasp how such a vision could possibly be understood as expressing a kind of liberating progress, the briefest excursion into Comtean thinking is necessary. For him, the domestication of women was a phase of progress in emotional life—part of the grand Comtean vision—in which society would pass from family arrangements, like those of aristocracy, linking it to the past; move on to the new type of voluntary, conjugal, and domestic arrangement linking it to the present and the living; and finally arrive at "paternal" impulses expressing a "universal sociability" linking humanity to the future.[21] Such perspectives may seem obscure, muddled, or quaint; but only by grasping them do we understand how the domesticizing of higher-status women in France was understood as a form of progress rather than a regressive and reactionary development.

Perhaps the most indigenously French founder of the European Left, Proudhon, was a fervent mysogynist. Woman was fit only to choose between being "mistress or housewife" (*courtisane ou ménagère*).[22] Her inferiority was intrinsic, not conditioned; in the family—as much the cell of social stability, in Proudhon's thought, as in the reactionary Bonald's—her task was to educate children in moral duty, but "under paternal sanction," since she was only a "living reflection, her mission [being] to embody, simplify and transmit to young minds the father's thought."

Even Emile Durkheim, later in the century, explained some sex differences in suicide rates as a function of women's less complex and sensitive emotional character, requiring lessened dependence upon social control.[23]

Neither a radical thinker like Fourier nor, more important, writers in the mainstream of French Marxism or socialism subscribed to these perspectives. Attacking the *bourgeois* family, they included women's subjection among the evils of capitalist society. But French Marxism has always interpreted the subjection of women in a context of class conflict. The powerful emphasis on class themes in French social protest has operated to discourage specifically "feminist" diagnoses of women's situation such as those characteristic of England and America. As we have seen, such advantages as higher-status women do enjoy in France—in state employment and access to higher education—are indeed strongly linked to the political and social status quo. The problems of lower-status women have characteristically been assimilated to a class- rather than a women-centered definition of the situation.

We see that important representatives of widely diverse and opposed French thought—Catholic conservatives, Romantic individualists, scientific progressivists, antibourgeois polemicists—have all agreed, in different tones and in different perspectives, on the value or necessity of women's domestic and subordinate mission. There was no French counterpart to the role played by a John Stuart Mill in the struggle for women's rights in the nineteenth century. The dominant conservative impulses found wide echo, and still do. "She is to charm, console, understand. Her role is that of a helpful, available assistant, but without initiative. She exists essentially in relation to others; her place in the scheme of things is not in the outside world of action, but in the privacy of the home, where she arranges and prepares the times of relaxation."[24] Thus does a sociologist, summing up contemporary research findings, describe the modal image of women in France.

To assess this image only as passive and self-effacing is to underestimate its strength and appeal. It also provides a positive role for woman, interpreting her familial functions as crucial rather than ornamental, dignified rather than subordinate. Thus, the woman becomes the agent of high culture within the domestic circle—not only in substantive terms that provide a function for women's education—but also as teacher and exemplar of *la politesse* to children—a concept of far greater social scope and cultural resonance than its American analogues, "politeness" or "good manners." This value complex is strongest in the *bourgeoisie.* Thus, we will see below, familistic definitions of woman's role are strongest precisely in that stratum which, in Anglo-American societies, is among the least familistic.

Such values were, until very recently, strongly reflected in French laws. The Napoleonic Code, drawing often on Roman models, found both precedent and conceptual imagery for reaffirming the domestic hegemony of the *pater,* and conceiving of women only in a domestic context. Until 1938, women could not work, attend universities, or participate in decisions about children's education, without their husbands' permission; husbands were administrators of their wives' property and wealth; women were defined, with the criminal, the insane, and children, as legally "unfit." The Napoleonic Code defined the obedience of wives to husbands as a legal obligation. After 1938, only a successful request for a special form of marriage contract could prevent husbands from being invested with total ownership of family property, including that owned by women before marriage; in recent years, about three-quarters of French women have been married without making such requests. Husbands are still legally defined as the *chef de la communauté* and *chef de famille*—both much more extensive notions than "head of the family." In France, it has been secular law, not religious ritual, that proclaimed the wife's duty to "obey the man." As *chef de la communauté* he was entitled to make major financial, educational, and other decisions without consulting the wife. Until 1965, when some reforms were introduced, wives needed the formal consent of husbands to work outside the home or to buy on credit; even those reforms left many of the husbands' privileges untouched.[25]

Thus, married women in France have long suffered from legal disabilities. Yet French values assign far higher social esteem to the married than the unmarried woman; the single state is regarded as deeply anomalous for women, and nowhere except in deviant subcultures is it identified with notions of freedom and self-determination. These values are not peculiar to France, of course, but are especially deep there. A forceful indicator of their strength is found in a recently enacted law providing that all women over the age of 25 are entitled to be addressed as *Madame,* even if unmarried; and that an unmarried woman above that age who is persistently addressed as *Mademoiselle* may bring legal action for slander.[26] Thus, single women in France have traditionally been subject to social deprivations, and married women, to legal ones. Expressive of these attitudes were debates that occurred in the French Assembly after World War I, on the subjct of enfranchising women: it was argued, in opposition, that the vote should be given to unmarried but not to married women, on the grounds that married women could not be "political individuals" with wills other than those of their husbands. This reverses the view, conventional in England and America, that the married are in general more "mature" or "responsible" than the unmarried.[27]

To call these perspectives "traditional" would suggest an unbroken continuity that, as we have seen, distorts history. In fact, they are linked above all to a class which only developed in the nineteenth century, the *bourgeoisie;* and this historical association is strongly manifested in contemporary data on the distribution of family values and behavior in French society. Repeatedly, the *bourgeoisie* emerges as *more* "traditional" in these areas than the *classe moyenne* or the working class. Thus, *the very class whose cultural, economic, and social advantages are such as to render many of its women qualified candidates for professional careers is that least disposed to approve and provide for women's work outside the home.*

The data are striking indeed—perhaps especially to American readers who are likely to think of higher social status and education as implying greater approval for the equality of women. In France, the percentage of women who play significant roles in decisions about the family budget is 15 percent among the *bourgeoisie,* 53 percent for the *classe moyenne,* and 78 percent in the working class. The lower the social class, the more likely men are to help in domestic tasks. The higher the class, the more women's working outside the home is perceived as incompatible with the obligations of family life.[28]

In professional strata, the strength of the *femme au foyer* image remains very strong. Among professional women with at least one child, two-thirds think it wise to remain at home while children are small. It is not unduly speculative to imagine the psychic cost to those professional women who, accepting this ideology, continue careers through this stage of the life cycle. The great majority of these women regard their family roles as requiring a full-time commitment. Not only familistic but "women-of-cultivated-leisure" imagery is very strong: 59 percent of professional women express the desire to cease work in order to pursue cultural interests after children have left the home.[29] Thus, professional commitments among French women are accompanied both by familistic commitments and the attractions of a consummatory attitude to culture as a substitute for a professional career.

That this "traditionalism" is apparently especially strong among the *bourgeoisie* means that there is a greater tendency for women professionals to come from the *classe moyenne,* who are more disposed to utilize higher education as a means of social mobility and comparatively less inhibited by such values. Thus, the greatest opportunities for professional advances have been made available to those women whose class and family styles are least likely to encourage serious professional commitments. Indeed, among the few women who have achieved the highest positions in the professional civil service, the proportion of unmarried ones is extremely high—50 percent.[30] In France, the claims of family and profession are incompatible for women to a degree extraordinary in a modern society. Each is treated as sovereign, making the kind of claims upon life and being that do not easily tolerate the coexistence of the other.

Conclusions

Characterized by strong commitments to abstract equality and universalism, France has long evolved a richly wrought set of conservatively defined roles and values governing the social existence of women. These values have continuing and compelling influence.[31] Their fulfillment is conceived as rewarding, not merely as restrictive and constraining, by many French women. The role of the women in the *foyer,* especially in the more advantaged classes likely to furnish higher proportions of professionals, is charged with satisfying content, psychologically and culturally. Even among those who choose professional life, the competing tug of the *femme au foyer* remains strong.

But French women have also achieved considerable professional success and have long enjoyed access—within the limits of overarching class inequalities—to free higher education. As we have seen, many of their successes are within the context of state-sponsored activity. Indeed, there is a sense in which the state has created the professional women in France. Thus, the extent and nature of women's professional activities reflects the characteristic French cleavage between the society's modal social values, on the one hand, and those of the French state, on the other—a difference that has led some to describe France as an "administered" rather than a "governed" society. In these respects, the professional successes of French women run against the grain of the culture, in much the same way as the universalism of the French government has often ignored or overridden the localism, Catholicism, and individualism of the French people.

This sort of state-sponsored success for women's professional aspirations involves considerable costs. It fails, of course, to eliminate the tensions and limits imposed by the continuing cultural conservatism of French society with respect to women's place and role. Indeed, given the great gap in France between those values suffusing government and public administration and those of the society, the professional aspirations of many women can be seen as diverted into insulated and conservative sectors of French life.

We saw earlier that French women made a large advance into the professional labor market after the First World War, but that there were signs of a decline or stagnation in the situation after the Second World War. Rapid defeat and occupation meant that France did not experience prolonged mobilization of the domestic economy, unlike other Western nations during 1939-45. The French economy since 1945 has grown at a rate that has not compelled a major "talent hunt" among women for scarce aptitudes required in newly emerging specialties. Men have only slowly, if at all, "abandoned" the less dynamic professional careers to women, as might happen to a greater extent in a more rapidly growing economy (we have seen a few signs of this in the sex patterns of professional employment in government and the private sector).

Despite the holding of an "Estates-General" of Women at Versailles in the fall of 1970—an event which surprised many by the vigor and clarity of the complaints and demands that the delegates and leaders manifested—there is little sign of the emergence of a modern women's movement in search of expanded opportunities. Forces of the Left—above all, the Communist party—are slow to deal with the question of women's rights, least of all those of women professionals. Themes of protest center on the rigidities of administration in government and institutions; the insufficiency of resources for education, housing, and transport; inflation and the slow rate of economic growth; and the maldistribution of wealth and income in a society that has not become significantly less socially hierarchical in the postwar period. The few groups—among them, weak and scattered *gauchistes*—who raise the issue of women's role as such, often in accents borrowed from contemporary American polemic, are barely heard and widely ignored.

In such a setting, the prospects for an expansion of professional opportunities for women are not encouraging. Whether one defines the situation as depressing or moderately promising is a matter of personal style and social ideology. But, in any event, it seems unlikely that the weight of French tradition in the matter of women will be rapidly lightened in the decades to come. The limited and deeply ambiguous "success" of French professional women is likely to endure for some time.

[1] I wish to acknowledge the help of Elinor Barber and Allan Silver in the preparation of this paper.

[2] See Paul-Marie Duhet, *Les femmes et la Révolution* (Paris: Julliard, 1971). The Constitution of 1791 treated women as *passif* rather than *actif* citizens; the legislative committee of the Convention in 1793 excluded women—together with minors, the mad, and the criminal—from political rights; shortly after, they were prohibited from attending any political assembly (Duhet, pp. 165-66). The Revolution's unprecedented provision for divorce, however, formally conferred equal rights on both spouses.

[3] The status and life styles of professions and the *bourgeoisie* in France are also affected by the continuing presence of very large proportions of rural and manual workers. Of the labor force, 15 percent (a proportion applying to both sexes) are in the agricultural sector—three times that of Britain, and almost twice that of the United States. Fully 39 percent of the total labor force are manual workers, *ouvriers;* of working women, 22 percent are *ouvrières*. (All descriptive statistics not otherwise attributed have been drawn from 5 percent samples of census data; these figures are drawn from the 1968 census.)

[4] Organisation Internationale du Travail, *Annuaire statistique du travail* (Paris, 1967). Other "leaders" in this respect are Finland (42 percent in 1960), Denmark (38 percent in 1967), and the United States (36 percent in 1967).

[5] Conditions of employment and compensation have been equal for men and women in *lycée* teaching since 1927. It is important to add, however, that positions of higher administrative authority within *lycées* are dominated by men. *Lycées* are sexually segregated, both as to students and teaching staff—a circumstance that has offered women "built-in" *entrée* to this important profession.

[6] Institut National de la Statistique et des Etudes Economiques (INSEE), *Annuaire statistique de la France* (Paris, 1970). Equality of working conditions among *instituteurs* of both sexes was achieved in 1882. We may note that women staffing the *écoles maternelles*—caring for children between the ages of three and six years—must have achieved essentially the same educational qualifications as *instituteurs* and have often begun advanced studies. See Ida Berger, *Les maternelles* (Paris: Centre d'Etudes Sociologiques, 1952).

[7] The rank of university professor usually requires the completion of the *thèse d'Etat*—a degree more strenuous than the American Ph.D. that normally requires ten years for completion.

[8] Francine Dumas, "La femme dans la vie sociale," in *Femmes du XXᵉ siècle* (Paris: Presses Universitaires de France, 1965); Michael Fogarty et al., *Sex, Career and Family* (Beverly Hills, Calif.: Sage, 1971).

[9] Ibid. Women are excluded from the Ecole des Mines, Ecole du Génie Rural, and the Ecole des Eaux et Forêts. On the other hand, although data are lacking, their presence at responsible levels in the Ministries of Education, of Labor, and of Health appears to be significant.

[10] "L'inaptitude physique," "les difficultés psychologiques que|pourraient|soulever une présence féminine," Andrée Michel and Geneviève Texier, *La condition de la française aujourd'hui* (Paris: Gauthier, 1964), p. 39.

[11] Anon., "Les carrieres feminines," *Avenir* (April-May 1965): 10; Organisation de la Coopération et du Développment Economique, *L'Emploi des femmes* (Paris: Seminaire Syndicale Régional, 1970). The rate is even higher in the private sector, where the absolute number of women is smaller.

[12] The substantive benefits are described by Claude Vimont, "Un enquête sur les femmes fonctionnaires," *Population* (January-February 1965): pp. 23-55.

[13] One percent of architects are women.

[14] Organisation de la Coopération, *L'emploi des femmes;* UNESCO, World Survey of Education (Paris: UNESCO, 1968).

[15] Organisation de la Cooperation et du Development Economique, *Origines sociales des professeurs et instituteurs* (Paris: Direction des Affaires Scientifiques, 1965); Pierre Bourdieu and J. C. Passeron, *Les héritiers* (Paris: Editions de Minuit, 1964).

[16] Simone de Beauvoir, *Le deuxième sexe* (Paris: Gallimard, 1949).

[17] A succinct contrast of *bourgeois* and aristocratic notions of women and family life is found in Elinor Barber, *The French Bourgeoisie in the Eighteenth Century* (Princeton, N.J.: Princeton University Press, 1955), pp. 78-81. For more extended statements, see the essays by Xavier Lannes and Jean Maitron on the eighteenth and first half of the nineteenth centuries, respectively, in Robert Prigent, ed., *Renouveau des idées sur la famille* (Paris: Presses Universitaries de France, 1954). A large historical view is offered by Phillipe Ariès, *Centuries of Childhood* (London: Cape, 1962), esp. pt. 3.

18 See Evelyne Sullerot, *Histoire et sociologie du travail féminin* (Paris: Presses Universitaires de France, 1968).

19 "L'homme est à la femme ce que la femme est à l'enfant; ou le pouvoir (sovereign authority) est au ministre, ce que le ministre est au sujet." Cited by Beauvoir, *deuxième sexe*, p. 186. As we have observed it was a *gain* for women to be regarded as "ministers" in Bonald's sense. (This did not prevent Bonald from describing the adultery of men as a cause only of personal unhappiness to wives, while that of wives represented the destruction of the family—a widespread French perspective.) On the distinctive contribution of the domestic family to social order in Bonald's thought, see his "Du divorce considéré au xixᵉ siècle relativement à l'état domestique et à l'état public de la société," in Louis de Bonald, *Oeuvres complètes* (Paris: Migne, 1864), II, esp. chaps. 2, 3, 4. At more popular levels, comparable images of the family and women's role were promulgated during the Restoration with unprecedented scope and intensity. See Raymond Deniel, *Une image de la famille et de la société sous la Restauration (1815-1830)* (Paris: Éditions Ouvrières, 1965).

20 Awkwardly translated, at best, as "the conceit of breasts." Sullerot, *Travail feminin,* p. 80. Rousseau's family doctrine is found chiefly in his didactic novels, *Emile* and *La nouvelle Héloise,* and included, it must be noted, a parallel domestication of men.

21 Auguste Comte, *Discours sur l'ensemble du positivisme* (Paris: Mathias, 1848), pp. 204; 242-43; 91.

22 Proudhon did not regard the woman question lightly. In his *De la justice dans la Révolution et dans l'Eglise,* written in 1858, he devoted three hundred pages to "Amour et mariage"; just before his death, he wrote another 270 pages replying to female critics, under the title *La pornocratie; ou les femmes dans les temps modernes.* See Jean Maitron, "Les penseurs sociaux et la famille dans la première moitié du XXᵉ siècle," in *Renouveau des idées sur la famille,* ed. Robert Prigent (Paris: Presses Universitaires de France, 1954).

23 "Her sensibility is rudimentary rather than highly developed. As she lives outside of community existence more than man, she is less penetrated by it; society is less necessary to her because she is less impregnated by sociability. With a few devotional practises and some animals to care for, the old unmarried women's life is full. . . . Man, on the contrary, is hard beset in this respect. . . . Because he is a more complex social being, he can maintain his equilibrium only by finding more points of support outside himself." Emile Durkheim, *Suicide,* trans. John Spaulding and George Simpson (Glencoe, Ill.: Free Press, 1951, orig. pub., 1897), pp. 215-216.

24 Paul-Henry Chombart de Lauwe, *La femme dans la société: Son image dans différents milieu:* (Paris: Centre Nationale de la Recherche Scientifique, 1963), p. 120.

25 A good summary of these aspects of French law is given in Michael and Texier, *Condition de la française,* pp. 71-106. They led, in the words of these authorities, to a situation in which "a sane wife is never the [legal] equal of a mad husband." Michael and Texier, p. 73. The concept of the *foyer* and of women's place in it is clearly expressed in an aspect of French marriage law which provided that adultery by husbands was punishable only by light sanctions, unless the offense was actually committed in his home, in which case it was cause for divorce. Adultery by wives anywhere was cause for divorce and sometimes imprisonment. The backwardness of French law on women is hardly restricted to family life. Women did not receive the right to vote until 1945, when their participation in the Resistance was frequently cited as justification for enfranchising them. They thus received, after the Second World War, what American and British women received after the First World War without having had to become heroines or martyrs to do so.

26 These provisions contrast sharply with the emergence of "Ms." as a form of address that ignores marital status, in the United States, or the general use of "Miss" as a way to gain the attention of receptionists, sales personnel, and waitresses.

27 In Britain the vote was, in fact, extended during the 1920s to women in two stages, beginning with those above the age of 28, with no attention paid to marital status. Thus, in Britain it was considered anomalous for *younger* women, and in France, for *married* women, to vote.

28 Chombart de Lauwe, *La femme dans la société,* p. 158.

29 Cécile Andrieux, "Idéologies traditionelles et modernes dans les attitudes sociales féminines," (Thèse de troisieme cycle, Université de Paris, 1962), pp. 351ff.

30 Chombart de Lauwe, *La femme dans la société,* pp. 197-205; Vimont, "femmes fonctionnaires," 23-52.

31 The continuing social conservatism of French women can be shown by their disproportionate electoral support for the parties of order and hierarchy in postwar France, regardless of age or social class. The number of women in elective office at all levels has, in fact, declined considerably since a high point after the Liberation. See Alain Duhamel, "Les femmes et la politique," *Monde,* March 10, 1971, p. 1.

THE SEXUAL POLITICS OF VICTORIAN
SOCIAL ANTHROPOLOGY

Elizabeth Fee

Some modern anthropologists have characterized the work of their nineteenth-century forebears as politics masquerading as science. The systems of evolutionary anthropology, riddled as they were with blatant racism, are now written off as the pseudo-scientific apologetics of early imperialism; *modern* anthropology is assumed to be value-free. But historical anthropology—indeed history itself—is inevitably, dialectically intertwined with politics. The analysis of the past is shaped by the present; our choice of questions, our selection of evidence, our analyses, all are influenced by contemporary concerns. The reconstruction of the past in turn serves present needs, as it clarifies or justifies the contours of present reality.

In the past fifty years, social anthropology has not escaped from politics; it has merely succeeded in gaining the appearance of political neutrality at the cost of a retreat into cautious microanalysis. But earlier anthropologists, attempting to come to grips with a changing political world, boldly sought for answers in grand syntheses of the past. They aimed at nothing less than an understanding of the entire history of the human race; and if in the end they succeeded in telling us more about themselves than about human pre-history or the cultures they ostensibly studied, we may still admire their daring, their forthrightness, and their intellectual ambition.

The reassessment of the past becomes particularly important when social conventions are threatened or the future appears uncertain. When, in the late nineteenth century, feminists challenged complacent assumptions about the timeless quality of women's role, the theoretical underpinnings of the status quo were reexamined. They were found partially unsatisfactory and had to be revised and recast in a modern form. Until about 1860, marriage, the family, and sexual roles were assumed to belong to the natural condition of man, institutions beyond and above any mere geographical or historical accident. Between 1860 and 1890, however, social anthropology demonstrated that the idealized family of the Victorian middle class was dictated by no law of nature, that monogamous marriage was only one of various human sexual possibilities and that women were not necessarily born only to domestic and decorative functions. Yet the scholarly work of the anthropologists also supported the conventional vision of perfection in family life; it was not, perhaps a natural institution, but it was the result of a long and painful evolutionary struggle away from nature. Current social arrangements should be seen as the final culmination, the glorious end-product of man's whole social, sexual, and moral evolution from savagery to civilization. Other forms of marriage and the family were still surviving remnants of worn-out cultural patterns that had long been superseded. By thus presenting "civilized" marriage as the end-point of social evolution, these men provided a solid, historical, evolutionary justification for the role of women in their own culture. To illustrate this process of theoretical reformulation, I will examine the work of six men whose theories were critically important: Henry Maine, Johann J. Bachofen, John McLennan, John Lubbock, Lewis Henry Morgan, and Herbert Spencer.

One of the main traditional theoretical justifications for English political authority had been a body of thought known as patriarchalism. In the seventeenth century, men like James I and Sir Robert Filmer had advanced the concept that royal authority could be legitimated by arguing, analogically, its paternal character. The vast bulk of the populace, it was suggested, were like the women and children of a patriarchal family. In that institution, the father possessed natural authority over his wife, children and slaves. So, too, the argument went, the king held a natural authority over the subjects of his realm. This political model, of course, accepted, indeed drew strength from, the widespread assumption that the patriarchal family was a natural, i.e. God-given, and a just institution.

By the nineteenth century, patriarchal theory had been profoundly challenged by emergent liberal concepts of democracy and individualism. While some conservatives clung to an attenuated patriarchalism as a means of defending the status quo, the doctrine had been seriously eroded as a prop to political authority by Whig contractualists and Benthamite liberals. But the old tradition maintained force in other arenas. Imperialists delighted in legitimating, indeed applauding their sway over non-whites by comparing themselves to benevolent parents seeking the well-being of infantile natives. And patriarchalism still seemed of use in justifying the subordination of women.

But there were problems with patriarchalism. For one thing, in the 1860s the feminist challenge raised severe questions about the nature of the "natural family" itself—most specifically about the subordinate position of women within it. The elemental source of authority in the tradition was thus questioned: if the power of father-husbands were proved not to be a natural, God-given, timeless fact of life, then might not the basis of sexual, imperial, and, to some extent, even political authority be undermined?

Another difficulty arose from the archaic, sweeping quality of the claims of patriarchal theory. Most of the anthropological community (and all of my sample with the exception of Maine) were liberals; they repudiated the claims of arbitrary, naturally inherent authority in political leaders; to rest the case for the subordinate position of women on such a harsh doctrine—to imply that women and children were virtual slaves or extensions of the head of the household—seemed reactionary and crude. The scientists were great believers in contract as the basis for human and political interrelationships, and so patriarchalism made them uneasy; it did not square with their economic, political, or social outlook and self-image as progressives. Yet it seemed somehow improper for slogans such as "Individualism" and "The Rights of Man" (so useful in combating governmental interference with free trade or capitalist enterprise) to be taken up by women or by non-whites. Certainly there could be no merit to the feminist charge that existing social arrangements were both unjust and unnecessary, the product of arbitrary, essentially political decisions, that could in turn be reversed. Somehow the essence of patriarchal theory still seemed particularly relevant to the woman question; if only it could be shorn of its archaic harshness. A generation of social anthropologists turned to a consideration of these fascinating intellectual and political problems. Perhaps they might discern the proper role of women by an examination of the past. Social anthropology, then, turned to a study of the role of women in the history of mankind *(sic)*.

In 1861, Sir Henry Maine, a successful lawyer and Corpus Professor of Jurisprudence at Oxford University, had summed up the state of conventional wisdom concerning the patriarchal family. His *Ancient Law* attempted to demonstrate that the power of the father had always been the basis of law and of society; as Filmer had before him, he denounced liberal assumptions about the State of Nature as ahistorical nonsense: patriarchs had *always* ruled. The patriarchal father had always held absolute authority over his wife, children, servants and slaves: only in modern times had the family begun to disintegrate, with yet unrealized consequences for social order. The French Revolution had been only the first result of the new-fangled disregard for history and tradition; long political experience could not be so easily tossed aside.

In order to prove the timeless and inherent nature of patriarchal authority, Maine, a legal historian, turned to written records, using as his sources the Old Testament, the Hindu Laws of Manu, and the Twelve Tables of Rome. These were, he claimed, the earliest reliable records of man's history; the sources usually used by ethnologists he discounted as "the slippery testimony concerning savages which is gathered from travelers tales."[1] From a brilliant reconstruction of fragmented ancient histories and legal codes, Maine built a case for the foundation of all known societies from the same, patriarchal basis: "The effect of the evidence of comparative jurisprudence is to establish the view of the primeval condition of the human race which is known as the Patriarchal Theory."[2]

This accurate summation of the basis of patriarchal theory worried the anthropological community. From their perspective, Maine's work demonstrated severe methodological inadequacies. Maine had made no use of the available ethnological data: he had ignored field work. His formulation of patriarchal theory reflected the narrow range of his source material. For one thing, he had reconstructed only a fair case for a very small geographical area, and a very restricted historical period, and then blithely extrapolated to the rest of human history. Then, too, the anthropologists preferred the direct or indirect observation of tribal society to Maine's reliance on written sources. As Spencer explained: "I see no reason to ascribe to the second-hand statements of modern explorers."[3] It seemed that Maine had unintentionally demonstrated the weakness of the patriarchal theory's evidential base; the very inadequacies of his work, at least from an anthropological perspective, led others to an awareness of its problematic character. As Donald McLennan later explained: "The patriarchal theory . . . was most simple, and agreeable to current prejudices. It used to be accepted as palpably true, like the fact of the sun moving daily round the earth. No one thought of proving it, and but few of seriously doubting it."[4]

The second problem with Maine's theory was that it was a static, non-evolutionary view in an era of Darwinism, an age when evolutionary thinking permeated all of the social sciences. In considering the history of "civilized" man, Maine had assumed that his conclusions could be extrapolated to man's entire history. Yet those attuned to work in primitive societies were aware that a great dichotomy existed between "savage" and "civilized" man. It seemed to go almost without saying that unless the two types had developed in a parallel manner, one was in reality the remnant of an "earlier stage"; and Victorians had no doubt about the direction in which history was flowing. Every contact of British imperialists with "primitive" cultures proved how far Victorian England had risen above the savage state; much of anthropology in this period was given over to documenting and glorifying the triumph of man over nature. Rousseau's savage was no longer noble, rather a living testament to civilized man's rude origins; Victorians gloried in the fact that economic, technological and cultural progress in the West had all but vanquished the remnants of natural man. But civilized man had to go beyond self-congratulatory affirmations of his superiority. It was the business of the anthropologists particularly to develop a theory that would tell him how that superiority had been achieved.

The consideration of remaining "primitive" social orders, then, was of utmost importance, and when anthropologists turned to consider the primitive family, they found material that both raised problems for Maine's simplistic, static model, and provided the means to transcend it. The experience of "primitive" societies made it clear that patriarchalism was *not* an immutable fact of nature. It became apparent that sexual control, marital fidelity, the centering of the emotional life around the home and children, the exaggerated respect shown to wives and mothers—these were *not* natural to man. Did this mean that patriarchal theory rested on false foundations? Not at all. One need only suggest that the contrast between savage and civilized family and sexual life could be accounted for by postulating that the former had evolved into the latter. That, in other words, if the male and female roles of the nineteenth-century middle class were not natural, they were something better: they were the final culmination of a millennia-long development—the very point to which all recorded history had been heading. They were, in short, not natural, they were *civilized*.

The theorist who opened up this promising line of analysis was J. J. Bachofen. In his most notorious work, *Das Mutterrecht* (published in 1861), Bachofen provided patriarchal theory with a novel, indeed a romantic account of social evolution. Bachofen saw the continuing struggle between male and female as the central theme in social evolution; each stage of human society could be described in terms of the balance of power between the sexes. He believed human history to have consisted of three main stages: the hetaerist-aphroditic, the matriarchal, and the patriarchal. During the hetaerist-aphroditic stage, marriage was unknown. Sexual relationships were unregulated: women were at the mercy of male lust; promiscuity and sexual exploitation triumphed. Eventually, however, the women had rebelled and had staged a worldwide Amazonian revolt. Following their military success, they established the second stage of human history, the matriarchal stage. Women, as mothers, dominated social and cultural institutions; female sexuality triumphed; now they could force marriage and monogamy onto the reluctant males. In the final stage, men rebelled in their turn, triumphed, and replaced matriarchy with the patriarchal system. Women were dethroned and male supremacy everywhere recognized. Each stage had its religious or ideological basis. In the matriarchal period, the female fertility principle had been glorified, while the transition to patriarchalism represented the emancipation of man from material nature, "the sublimation of earthly existence to the purity of the divine father principle."[5] Echoing much of mythological thought, woman to Bachofen represented materialism, and man, spirituality.

Indeed, Bachofen was a student of mythology, and argued that it was a valuable source of historical reconstruction: "Multiform and shifting in its outward manifestation, myth nevertheless follows fixed laws, and can provide as definite and secure results as any other source of historical knowledge."[6] Bachofen also made extensive use of other forms of symbolism from painting and sculpture to architecture, all freely interpreted. His approach was intuitive; he discounted the laborious approach of English scientists with their piling up of minute pieces of data in favor of a creative use of the imagination: "Aroused by direct contact with the ancient remains, the imagination grasps the truth at one stroke, without intermediary links."[7]

Neither Bachofen's methods nor his sources held any appeal for most English anthropologists. Like Maine, Bachofen had ignored the necessary hard work in the field; instead he constructed what seemed to be fairy tales. Worse, his mechanism of the transition to matriarchy seemed founded on obvious absurdities, given what every Victorian knew about the eternal nature of woman. His armed Amazonian rebellion seemed preposterous—women (as everyone knew) would never take up arms in open warfare with their men; and if they did, they could—it was patently clear—never have been successful. Nor was it plausible that within the structure of monogamous marriage women would have absolute authority over their children. Natural authority was represented by the father; only under extraordinary conditions could the mother attempt to take over his role. Women—it was well known—were the gentle sex, physically weak, and constitutionally timid; men *must* always have held social and political power.

Bachofen's theory, then, was badly flawed by unorthodox sources, an alien methodology, and absurd notions of ancient feminine superiority; still, there were many facets of this thought that held great appeal. Bachofen had, after all, argued that the modern Victorian family had to be understood as the end result of a long historical struggle against the crude desires of nature. This dovetailed with the contemporary identification of sexuality with animality; brute passions struggled with man's rationality—the sexual instinct was the "animal" part of man which had to be kept under control by the higher dictates of conscience and the active striving of the will. The struggle that took place in the individual had once taken place in society; as Freud in *Totem and Taboo* postulated an actual Oedipal struggle in the history of man, so many anthropologists were to see the struggle against sexual instincts as the earliest triumph of man against nature. The evolution of moral feeling had led from sexual anarchy to the rigid mores of the Victorian middle class.

Anthropologists, then, could find congenial Bachofen's story which began with a period of promiscuity, when man's sexual desires were unhampered by social restraints. Women were the possessions of men, human property was communally shared. But then, just as a child learned sexual control, so did primitive man. According to Bachofen, the restraints were instituted by the women themselves, through the power of woman as mother. Matriarchy was a necessary stage in maturation, later to be supplanted by patriarchy as the more abstract "masculine" values and activities supplanted the concrete "feminine" ones.

Bachofen's thesis, then, clearly resolved some of the problems of Maine's work. Yet surely the evolutionary model could be freed from the assumption that the wheel of progress had been largely turned by women. It was, after all, well known that woman was a passive being whose role was to complement the aggressive creativity and achievements of the male through her altruism and selfless devotion to the cares of the home. In the end, those aspects of Bachofen's theory that accorded with Victorian sexual and racial mythology were accepted. In the next twenty-five years, John McLennan, Lewis Henry Morgan, John Lubbock, and Herbert Spencer reconstructed his model to reflect more closely their social and intellectual needs and those of their middle-class audience.

Unlike Maine or Bachofen, these men used the accounts of primitive societies brought back by travelers, colonial administrators, and missionaries as their main sources of evidence. Of the four, only Morgan had direct contact with the peoples about whom he was writing; his theories and data were correspondingly more sophisticated than those of men who worked primarily in their studies and in libraries. Yet all saw themselves as empirical scientists, carefully weighing the evidence at hand, comparing and evaluating contradictory reports and applying sound judgment to the results; they were often painstakingly careful in their scholarship as in their "science." They were also aware that many of their informants viewed other cultures in a highly prejudiced manner; they worked as best they could with the data available. And they all worked toward a similar end: the construction of a refurbished, scientific patriarchalism, based now on the evolutionary perspective suggested by Bachofen.

John McLennan, like Maine, a lawyer, devoted his three major works *Primitive Marriage* (1865), *Studies in Ancient History* (1876), and *The Patriarchal Theory* (1885) to demolishing the static version of patriarchalism. He constructed in its place a dynamic three-stage evolution that developed from primitive promiscuity through group marriage with descent in the female line, to monogamous marriage with male descent; at the same time he avoided Bachofen's absurdities.

McLennan had three types of evidence that suggested three distinct forms of social organization. There was, first of all, the evidence of the nature of contemporary primitive cultures. Ethnological studies revealed one very vivid fact about primitive societies: they were steeped in sex and sin. A recurrent theme of the missionaries, explorers and administrators was the lax or non-existent moral standards of the savages. Their lack of clothing, their apparent sexual freedom offended; specific customs such as wife-lending and the public defloration of virgins seemed clear evidence of a degraded moral sensitivity. The evident lack of female modesty shocked; as McLennan stated: "Women are usually depraved and inured to scenes of depravity from their earliest infancy."[8]

Secondly, kinship studies certainly demonstrated that the reckoning of descent through the female, or matrilineality, was a common enough custom to be accepted as evidence of a distinct type of social organization. (McLennan distinguished this from matriarchy, however; it was surely explicable without the improbable assumption that it stemmed from the actual social power or authority of women themselves, as Bachofen had assumed.) Thirdly, there was the monogamous, patrilineal, patriarchal, civilized family of McLennan's own culture.

Since the aims of historical anthropology were first, to isolate stages of development, and then, to arrange them in a plausible evolutionary sequence, McLennan postulated promiscuity as the earliest stage, and placed the monogamous family at the apex of evolutionary development.

He had, however, to account for the existence of matrilineal succession without the aid of Amazonian warriors. Bachofen's theory in that regard seemed even more improbable than matriarchy itself: "That the children of a man and a woman living together as husband and wife should be subject to the mother's authority and not the father's, be named after her and not after the father, be her heirs and not the father's is simply incredible; and it is surely not rendered credible by the statement that these singularities were the direct consequences of women having been victorious in a war with men."[9]

Kinship through women could have occurred only if kinship through men was impossible, that is, if paternity were uncertain. McLennan tied matrilineal succession directly to the prevalence of promiscuity. Savages, he reminded his reader, were "unrestrained by any sense of delicacy from a copartner in sexual enjoyments."[10] If tribal groups of men had held their wives in common, the children produced would belong to the horde rather than to the individual. In the absence of individual paternity, they would have been forced to reckon descent through the mother. Thus McLennan cleansed Bachofen's theory of the unseemly notion of matriarchal power.

But McLennan had still many identifiable social forms and customs which had to be fitted into his evolutionary sequence somewhere between the promiscuous horde and the patriarchal family. He had to explain exogamy (the custom of marrying outside one's own tribe or totem), polyandry and polygamy as transitional stages in the development of human marriage, and to show how the transitions from one stage to the other might have occurred.

Where Bachofen had made women responsible for a sudden shift to monogamy, McLennan postulated a gradual transition, created and engineered by male activity. His mechanism is worth following in some detail. First, he "demonstrated" that women were less useful to society than were men. This was easy, for as all bourgeois Victorians knew, women could not support themselves, nor could they contribute by their labor to "the common good." In McLennan's theoretical system, women seem completely passive social units of property who may be either individually or collectively owned by men, but who initiate no action of their own.[11] Since women were of relatively little use to society, McLennan concluded that in times of scarcity, female infanticide would be common. Unfortunately, this in turn would result in a scarcity of wives, leaving the men only two alternatives: either several men could peaceably agree to share one woman (polyandry) or they would have to steal wives from other tribes (exogamy).[12] Through the single assumption of female infanticide, which he assumed to have been a generally universal practice, McLennan had explained both polyandry and exogamy, thus satisfying the scientific desire for simplicity of explanation. As long as polyandry was the most common form of marriage, descent would of course continue in the female line. To make the transition to male descent, either the polygamous or monogamous form of the family must have come into existence

McLennan explained this transition through the mechanism of the capture of wives. He had compiled an enormous quantity of evidence of the practice of marriage-by-capture; marriage ceremonies which symbolized the forcible abduction of a woman by her husband were assumed to be survivals of a once universal system of the actual capture of women. This practice, thought McLennan, must have been responsible for the fragmentation of the horde into individual families. A man who had captured his wife would treat her as an individual possession. Neither the woman nor her children could now belong to her matrilineal group; they must now become the individual property of their captor. Once the practice of capturing wives became well established, polyandry would vanish, since each man would want to venture into the jungle to find a wife of his own. When women were individually owned, paternity would no longer be uncertain and patriarchal succession would follow as a matter of course. As McLennan says, ". . . the superiority of the male sex must everywhere have tended to establish that system."[13]

At this stage, McLennan introduced a new factor into his social history: an economic motive. The transition from matrilineal to patrilineal succession must have been aided, he thought, by the growth of private property. Fathers would for the first time have a real motive for desiring to identify their sons, since they would, of course, want them to inherit the family property, lest it be returned to the matrilineal line. Even if wife capture later became impractical, men would be sufficiently eager for male descent that they would be prepared to acquire their wives by purchase from the matrilineal group. The purchase price would cover the wife and her unborn children; today this is symbolized by "giving away" the bride in the marriage ceremony.

As had Bachofen, McLennan had incorporated Maine's patriarchal family as the last of a succession of historical forms; yet Bachofen's theory had now been rewritten to exclude the Amazons and matriarchs who had been such unwelcome intruders in the history of man.

Sir John Lubbock, one of the most widely known pre-historians of his day, specialist in both anthropology and archeology, a prominent member of many scientific societies and the author of numerous articles and books, added further refinements to McLennan's theory. In his work—particularly *The Origin of Civilization and the Primitive Condition of Man* (1870)—Lubbock emphasized the emerging theme: the patriarchal family was not *natural,* but the proud product of millennia of development. The system whereby males ruled their families was *better* than natural (i.e., primitive, i.e., savage, i.e., disgusting); it was *civilized.*

In *Primitive Times* (1865) Lubbock had graphically described the immorality of savages and the horrors of their lives, dwelling particularly on their treatment of women. This degradation of women was best demonstrated by the fact that some tribes had no word for "love." Love, apparently, was a by-product of civilization, and respect for women a modern invention. Since savages knew nothing of "love," they could not know the pleasures of monogamous marriage; instead, they practiced various objectionable customs which Lubbock delicately summarized in the term "communal marriage." He did not care for the careful distinctions between polygamy, polyandry, serial pairing, and the like; all these came under the general rubric of "lax morality." He strongly objected to the central importance that McLennan had given to polyandry. This he saw as an odd and exceptional marriage form. "I cannot," he stated, "regard polyandry as having been a general and necessary stage in human development," though he nowhere gave reasons for this feeling.[14] The prevalence of matrilineal succession simply showed, he said, how little faith was placed in the virtue of women in those barbarian days. Besides, the men had so many wives and children that they could have cared little about any of them. Matriarchal power he thought particularly implausible since—it was well known—women do not assert themselves, and savage women would be particularly unlikely "to uphold their dignity."[15] Matrilineal succession was only the consequence of the indifference of savage men to their progeny, certainly no evidence of female supremacy. In "communal marriage," savage men shared their wives; individual marriage could have arisen only when individual men took wives by force: "Capture and capture alone, could give a man the right to monopolise a woman, to the exclusion of his fellow clansmen."[16] The sheer physical effort involved in wife-capture must have made the men proud of their new possessions. This pride and consequent possessiveness led to the strengthening of the bond between man and wife and to the beginning of marital "love." At the same time, paternal "love" also became possible, because men would now be able to identify their own children. Marriage was born in "brutal violence and unwilling submission," yet the very control of man over woman opened the possibility of love between the sexes.[17] The male loved the female not in spite of her weakness and vulnerability, but because of it; possessiveness was not an outgrowth of love, but love a consequence of possession. For Lubbock and doubtless many of his contemporaries, the essence and beauty of the male-female relationship resided in inequality.

Finally, Lubbock elaborated on the connection that McLennan had perceived between the monogamous family and private property. The first socially important consequence of the blossoming paternal affections was the father's desire to transmit his property to his sons. Apparently, these paternal feelings were not extended to daughters. In view of the fact that the association of monogamous marriage and male descent with the transmission of property is usually attributed to Engels, it is interesting to see how widely this idea was held by the most conservative anthropologists. None of them considered the possibility that property might have been held by women, although instances of female ownership are often cited (with surprise) in the ethnological monographs.

Lewis Henry Morgan is now best known as the immediate authority for Engels's *Origin of the Family, Private Property, and the State* (1884). Perhaps because he was an American, Morgan enjoyed little esteem among English anthropologists, though his work now seems more sophisticated than that of either Lubbock or McLennan. Morgan had been trained as a lawyer and had made a modest fortune in the practice of law, but his avocation was the study of Indian culture and system of kinship. Of his three major works, only two concern us here: *Systems of Consanguinity and Affinity* (1871) and his more developed thesis, *Ancient Society* (1877). Morgan's evolutionary scheme (consisting of fifteen or sixteen distinct stages) was considerably more complicated than those already sketched. His first stage is now the familiar one, "primitive promiscuity"; the final one is monogamy. The story he relates is one of the gradual emplacement of restrictions on the natural passions of man; the evolution is a moral one, each stage an "unconscious reformatory movement" testifying to the "growth of the moral idea." Morgan did not hide his consciousness of the superiority of monogamy which he saw as one of the higher cultural achievements of mankind: ". . . upon the family, as now constituted, modern civilized society is organized and reposes. The whole previous experience and progress of mankind culminated and crystallised in this one great institution."[18] Morgan was not immune to the widespread moral distaste for "primitive" man, yet he clearly admitted that the evidence for primitive promiscuity was, at best, indirect. In no existing society was there completely unregulated sexual conduct; the assumption of a promiscuous stage was however a logical deduction from knowledge of the consaguine family, in which intermarriage between brothers and sisters was permitted. "Promiscuity may be deduced theoretically as a necessary condition antecedent to the consanguine family; but it lies concealed in the misty antiquity of mankind beyond the reach of positive knowledge."[19]

According to Morgan, the very first organization of society was made on the basis of sex; the division between male and female was the first class division. Through a long succession of subdivisions, too complex to detail here, tribal organizations and various primitive forms of the family evolved. Morgan's comments on the systems of polygamy and polyandry are, however, amusing and instructive. Despite his admiration for monogamy, Morgan still had some sympathy for an institution in which each man might have several wives. Polygamy he considered "essentially modern," a "reformatory" and not a "retrograde" movement. Polygamy, after all, implied a settled condition and a plentiful means of subsistence since a single male was able to support many individuals. With the polygamous family came the emergence of a single powerful family authority and therefore the rudiments of a system of government.

If polygamy constituted an advanced stage on the road to civilization, polyandry was worthy only of deep scorn. "An excrescence of polygamy, and its repulsive converse," it was "scarcely entitled to the rank of a domestic institution."[20] Polyandry could only be the result of economic scarcity; men were unable to feed and maintain the standard of one wife and one set of children and so were forced to share. Morgan, like others, assumed that women had no productive function; large numbers of women and children existed as the result of surplus production. When the man was unable to support a wife and children he was dishonored; the state of polyandry was both economically and sexually "repulsive."

Morgan was no foe to the emancipation of women; he left a large sum of money to the University of Rochester for the furthering of female education and he optimistically predicted that equality of the sexes would be the result of the next great change in the history of the family. Since Morgan welcomed sexual equality in the future, he did not react with the usual derision to Bachofen's postulate of matriarchy in the past. Gyneocracy, the social power of women, would be a predictable consequence of matrilineal succession and the social arrangments of the matrilineal household: ". . . gyneocracy seems to require for its creation descent in the female line. Women thus entrenched in large households, supplied with common stores, in which their own gens so largely predominated in numbers, would produce the phenomena of mother-right and gyneocracy, which Bachofen has detected and traced with the aid of fragments of history and tradition."[21] As far as Morgan was concerned, the transition to patrilineality had had a very unfavorable influence on the position of women— thus, Engels could derive from Morgan the world historical defeat of the female sex.

Morgan was not impressed with Lubbock's attempt to document the first appearance of paternal love in human history, but he was deeply convinced of the vast importance of private property to civilized man. He emphasized its role as a crucial one in the transition from mother-right to father-right; through this concern with the inheritance of property, men came to the realization of the advantages of monogamy: ". . . property, as it increased in variety and amount, exercised a steady and constantly augmenting influence in the direction of monogamy."[22] The family, said Morgan, was a creation of the social and economic system; as society advanced, the family would continue to change and evolve to new forms.

Unlike other anthropologists, then, who tended to see their own form of the family as the final culmination of evolution, the most perfect possible form, Morgan left his evolutionary scheme open-ended, but moving toward more perfect monogamy and greater sexual equality.

Herbert Spencer held no such hopes or expectations; he was quite happy with things the way they were. Spencer, perhaps England's most revered nineteenth-century philosopher, polymath, and staunch supporter of the harsher bourgeois values, clearly believed that since evolution had placed women in the home, there they should stay. Spencer gathered the full weight of anthropological theory behind this opinion. A dilettante in social anthropology, he brilliantly summarized the findings of others, and integrated them within his own system of synthetic philosophy, thus carrying anthropological theories to a wider intellectual audience.

Spencer did more. In his *Principles of Sociology* (1876) he provided the now dynamic version of patriarchal theory with new support. Not only was the patriarchal Victorian family supported by and supportive of private property, decency, order, civilization, and love; it was now scientifically shown to be the inevitable product of natural selection.

Forms of marriage and the family, Spencer argued, like biological species, had to prove their superiority in the struggle for survival. A form that might have been adapted to the environment in the past could have become maladaptive when environmental conditions changed; in the long run, the fittest survived. Certainly, the patriarchal family based on monogamous marriage had survived the test and been proved most worthy. The development of rigidly defined sex roles (with males dominant) and the tight controls clamped on sexuality (particularly female sexuality) were not historical accidents but adaptations to social survival.

Civilization, Spencer would argue, rested on the control of sensuality. And there were few more fit than he to be the chronicler of the culture of repression, for he was, by all reports, its epitome. He was a man whose emotions and "passions" appeared to have been completely subjugated to his intellect. As

Francis Gribble said, in reviewing his autobiography for the *Fortnightly Review,* "What is almost uncanny about Herbert Spencer is his triumphant superiority to natural instincts."[23] Spencer, we are told, never unbent; he never loved or hated, he merely judged; his only expressed emotion was intellectual pride.

Spencer's survey of the evolution of the family in the *Principles of Sociology* began in the now standard fashion, positing promiscuity as the initial condition of humanity. Through "logic" alone, Spencer decided that "union of the sexes must have preceded all social laws." This was a most unsatisfactory state of affairs. For one thing, the lower forms of domestic life were characterized by "the abject condition of women" and an "entire absence of the higher sentiments that accompany the relations of the sexes."[24] Another difficulty with the "unregulated relations of the sexes" had been the fact that it led to no settled political control; the establishment of subordination was hindered. In addition, Spencer thought that children must suffer from the lack of individual fathers because mothers would be unable to give them adequate support and protection. Women must also suffer since, after maturity, they would decline and die without male protection. Promiscuity was evidently a highly inefficient form of social organization; clearly things had to change.

Spencer saw three possibilities open to social evolution: polyandry, polygamy, or monogamy. Humanity experimented with these various familial forms; the evolutionary tree branched out in a variety of ways; yet finally only monogamy proved successful in the competitive struggle.

Polyandry, he felt sure, would have fared poorly in the race for survival. With several fathers in one family, the resulting authority conflicts must have created serious evils. The first result would be poor family cohesion; poor family cohesion would have inhibited the development of social cohesion; poor social cohesion meant a disordered society and such societies would have lost out in warfare or economic competition with more disciplined cultures. Spencer also disputed McLennan's suggestion that the practice of wife-capture developed from an acute shortage of women (a demographic state conducive to polyandry). No, said Spencer, wife-capture arose because women *had* to be captured to overcome their feminine modesty and coyness: "Coyness, either real or affected for reputation's sake, causes resistance of the woman herself."[25] Natural man may have been at the mercy of his passions, but natural woman zealously guarded her reputation. She too, perhaps, was repulsed by polyandry, for certainly the idea of one woman having several husbands was—from the English perspective—a highly unnatural one.

Polygamy, says Spencer, does not create as much "surprise and repugnance"; we are more used to the idea of one man with many women. And it seemed a more logical outcome of the earlier stage: the men who were strongest simply appropriated as many women as they desired. An additional motive for polygamy (surprising in that it clearly admitted the important economic function of women) was suggested by several polygamous chieftains whom Spencer quoted. They explained that many wives were desirable because the more women, the more food; their wives did all the agricultural labor. The emergence of polygamy, then, seemed dictated by the unrestrained sexual instincts of savage men, and by economic advantages.

Once established, polygamy had many advantages in the race for survival. Under polygamy, there was but one head of the household; order was more easily maintained. The single head of the household, this polygamous patriarch, would establish family cohesion and eventually patriarchal inheritance. With patriarchal inheritance would come economic stability and social control. The reverence due to the lord of the family would, after his death, generate ancestor worship, and with the development of religion, law and order would become firmly grounded. The logical progression here is fairly convincing if the following assumptions are granted: that the only authorities are male authorities, that men care only for their own children, that economic power has always been, and can only be, in the hands of males, and that only males could have been the subjects of ancestor worship and sacred authority. Polygamy, argued Spencer, was admirable for biological as well as social and political reasons: it maximized human fertility. Sons lost in battle could be easily replaced. Indeed, polygamy would be ideally suited to a military social organization; if many men were engaged in warfare, the surplus women could still be easily absorbed. Polygamy, however, could never have raised society to the stage of civilization, since for civilization to be attained, (as his colleagues had already agreed), marital love and respect for women were necessary.

Monogamy emerged from polygamy when the husband of many wives began to make one the favorite. He subsequently demoted the others to the status of slaves or concubines; a survival of this custom may be seen, Spencer said, where married men support a mistress or patronize a prostitute. Alternatively, since the state of having two wives must always be preceded by the state of having one, monogamy may sometimes have resulted from the unavailability of second wives. True monogamy, however, required not only that a man should have one wife, but that he should desire only one. Probably, men had come to place a higher value on their wives when they were forced to purchase them; the concept of wife as valuable property would also lead to a constraint on divorce.

When monogamy did appear, its superiority would become evident; a variety of indices showed the superiority of monogamous relationships. For one thing, when stable couples did form, the children would be well looked after and would be much healthier than the sickly offspring of unmarried mothers. Through the survival of the fittest, the healthy children would then in turn transmit, through the inheritance of acquired characteristics, the tendency toward forming stable couples to their own children. Moreover, the children with protective fathers would grow up healthier and better soldiers, so that societies with monogamous marriage must triumph over societies of "lower domestic arrangements." Then again, all of the benefits accruing to polygamy would follow even more strongly from monogamy: stronger ancestor worship, increased social cohesion and greater political control.

The greatest boon of the monogamous family, however, was that it alone created the conditions for the strict definition of sex roles. This was, to be sure, of value to the children: with a diminished family size and a thoroughly domesticated mother, the father could devote his attention to breadwinning, and the mother to child rearing. But still more was it of value to the adults: it allowed for the replacement of sexual instinct by "the sentiments which characterise the relations of the sexes in civilised peoples."

In the monogamous family, women could finally be placed on the pedestal on which they belonged. They were emancipated from physical labor and from the burden of male "passions;" with settled family life, women lived longer because their husbands continued to support them even after their sexual attractiveness and general usefulness were long dead; in monogamous marriage, women came to be protected, respected, and insulated from the necessity of production and the evils of the marketplace. In primitive societies, Spencer reminded his readers, women had received brutal and cruel treatment; eye-witnesses testified to women's fishing, carrying and pitching tents, digging up roots, planting, plowing and reaping, building houses, climbing trees for small animals, and even hunting and going to war. We should, Spencer argued, congratulate ourselves on "the improvement of women's status implied by limitation of their labors to the lighter kinds."[26] The less a woman worked, the higher her status, and the less all women worked, the better for society, since the health of the future generation would then be improved.

At least in the wealthier middle-class circles of Victorian society, the pinnacle of female evolution had been reached. Women had ascended the pedestal to become "the angels of the home"; no longer sexually or economically exploited, the women were safe in their drawing rooms, far removed from the frightful realities of "natural" life. Men, of course, were firmly in control. Though the demands of marital fidelity might sometimes conflict with their own "natural passions," they, too, felt far removed from the savage state. And the rewards of civilized life compensated for any lingering sympathy for the primitive freedoms.

Spencer proceeded to draw the moral and political conclusions that social anthropology dictated. In the light of these evolutionary achievements, feminism appeared distinctly reactionary. The course of domestic evolution in the future, he cautioned, must be determined by the best interests of children. Besides, if "in some directions the emancipation of women has to be carried further, we may suspect that in other directions their claims have already been pushed too far."[27] Absolute equality with men could not be achieved; the law must continue to give supremacy to the husband, since he is more "judicially-minded" than his wife. Besides, thought Spencer, if women would only perceive the glory of the domestic sphere, they would wish for none other. Probably all the fuss was being raised by spinsters who had no opportunity to enjoy the feminine role; normal women should be pleased to have no worries other than their domestic duties.

With Spencer the anthropological invigoration of a moribund patriarchalism reached a peak; here we should take note of the nature of the final achievement. The anthropologists had jettisoned a key provision of the old theory that had appeared increasingly untenable in the light of investigations of alien cultures:

no longer did they posit that patriarchal monogamy was the natural, eternal human family order. Quite the reverse: in the beginning there was natural, and despicable licentiousness, and, if not female power, certainly female independence from male control. But they argued that the course of history and evolution flowed inexorably *away* from such an unnatural nature in the direction of patriarchal monogamy. Indeed patriarchalism was now inextricably linked with the progress of civilization; Victorian culture and its attendant social relations represented the capstone of all evolution. Male superiority, then, was sanctified not by nature, but by civilization.

More than that: the anthropologists had managed to harness a whole series of sacred concepts to help pull the patriarchal vehicle. Male dominance was now bound up with decency, the refinement and control of the passions, private property, and natural selection. But perhaps the strongest underpinning of male domination was to be found in the quintessential characteristic of the civilization it had produced—the thorough domestication of women (that is to say, male dominance). Admittedly not all women were angels; some were still slaves to economic production and others allowed themselves to be sexually used. The real vicissitudes of the lives of working women caused no great perturbation however; the lives of these women were pronounced anthropological survivals of an earlier stage. Like the savages, the lower classes had simply not advanced very far in evolutionary terms. But if Victorian society had not attained perfection, at least its civilized members could reassure themselves that they were aware of the evils yet lurking in the recesses of the culture, whereas savages had not sufficient moral sensitivity to know that their activities could be the cause of righteous indignation: as Lubbock observed, "that which is with us the exception, is with them the rule; that which with us is condemned by the general verdict of society, and is confined to the uneducated and the vicious, is among savages passed over almost without condemnation, and treated as a matter of course."[28]

This Victorian morality drama was, of course, a massive exercise in circular reasoning—despite the technical nature of many of the discussions and the impressive scholarly apparatus used. Their own culture provided the model by which all others had to be compared; the more divergent another culture from the "civilized" ideal, then the more "primitive" it must be. And "primitive" was often synonomous with "evil"; for if the Victorians had produced the most perfect of all social systems, they had also evolved the most sensitive perception for unveiling moral laxity in others. "Primitive promiscuity" was more projection than fact, as Morgan himself almost admitted. In fact projections abounded throughout the scholarly studies. In their speculations about primitive man, Victorians projected fantasies of his enormous physical and sexual power; the untamed brute often seemed fashioned out of their own repressed psyches. Primitive woman emerged as an odd mixture of blushing bride and lascivious whore; since she was both "primitive" (sensual) and "woman" (pure and innocent). The stage was now set; it remained only to turn the psychic dichotomy between primitive and civilized into a evolutionary tale by filling in the intermediate links. In doing so, cultural anthropologists utilized the prevailing worship of progress and brilliantly confirmed their own social order by constructing an appropriate past.

NOTES

[1] Sir Henry Summer Maine, *Village Communities in the East and West* (orig. 1841, London: John Murray, 1887), p. 17.

[2] Maine, *Ancient Law: Its Connection with the Early History of Society, and its Relations to Modern Ideas*, 4th ed. (London: J. Murray, 1870), p. 123.

[3] Herbert Spencer, *The Principles of Sociology, Works* (Osnabrück: Otto Zeller, 1966, reprint ed.), p. 683n.

[4] Donald McLennan, ed., *The Patriarchal Theory; based on the papers of the late John Ferguson McLennan* (London: Macmillan and Co., 1885), p. 3.

[5] J. J. Bachofen, *Myth, Religion and Mother Right*, trans. R. Manheim (Princeton: Princeton University Press, 1967), p. 119.

[6] Ibid., p. 76.

[7] Ibid., p. 12.

[8] John McLennan, *Primitive Marriage: An Inquiry into the Origin of the Form of Capture in Marriage Ceremonies* (Edinburgh: A & C Black, 1865).

[9] John Ferguson McLennan, *Studies in Ancient History* (London: Macmillan, 1886), p. 324.

[10] McLennan, *Primitive Marriage*, p. 167.

[11] Much attention was paid to the psychology of natural man, but natural woman is a strangely shadowy figure in evolutionary anthropology, remarkable only for her ubiquitous "maternal instinct."

[12] Note the conventional descriptive form: in polyandry several men agree to share one woman; polygamy results when one man possesses a number of women. The reverse description would have been inconceivable: in polyandry one woman possesses a number of men; polygamy results when a number of women agree to share one man.

[13] McLennan, *Primitive Marriage*, p. 228.

[14] Sir John Lubbock (Lord Avebury), "Review of McLennan's *Studies in Ancient History*," *Nature* 15 (1876): 133.

[15] Sir John Lubbock, *The Origin of Civilization and the Primitive Condition of Man* (London: Longmans Green and Co., 1870), p. 68.

[16] Ibid., p. 72.

[17] Ibid., p. 73.

[18] Lewis Henry Morgan, *Systems of Consanguinity and Affinity of the Human Family*, Smithsonian Contributions to Knowledge, Vol. 17 (Washington: Smithsonian Institution, 1871), p. 493.

[19] Morgan, *Ancient Society*, ed. Leslie A. White (1877-1878; reprint ed., Cambridge, Mass.: Harvard University Press, 1964), p. 424.

[20] Morgan, *Systems*, p. 477.

[21] Morgan, *Ancient Society*, pp. 297-298.

[22] Ibid., p. 426.

[23] Francis Gribble, "Herbert Spencer, His Autobiography and His Philosophy," *Fortnightly Review*, N.S. 75 (1904), p. 987.

[24] Spencer, *Works*, Vol. 6, p. 629.

[25] Ibid., p. 623.

[26] Ibid., p. 724.

[27] Ibid., p. 755.

[28] Lubbock, *Prehistoric Times* (London: Williams and Norgate), p. 561.

THE POWER OF WOMEN THROUGH THE FAMILY
IN MEDIEVAL EUROPE: 500-1100

Jo Ann McNamara and Suzanne Wemple

The concept of public power was more highly developed under the Roman Empire than in any other society before modern times. The role of women in the civic life of the Empire was uncompromisingly clear: "Women are to be excluded from all civil and public offices; and therefore they cannot be judges or act as magistrates, nor can they undertake pleas nor intervene on behalf of others, nor act as procurators."[1] But the same state actively promoted the augmentation of the private rights of Roman women. Under the Republic, the family had held extensive power on every level and women lived in complete subjection to the *patria potestas* (paternal power), being classed as *alieni juris* (minors). Should their fathers die, they were placed under the control of a guardian. Should they marry, they were transferred at the end of a year to the control of their husbands.[2] But, as the bureaucracy of the Empire extended its authority systematically over virtually every aspect of life, the power of the family and of the father was correspondingly weakened and the private rights of wives and children came to be protected by the laws of the state.[3] A woman's right to property was protected. The dowry she brought with her into marriage had to be returned intact if her husband repudiated her. The growing custom of marriage *sine manu* enabled a woman to remain under the power of her own family rather than being transferred to her husband's on the simple condition that she live for three days of every year in her father's house. She then had the right to own jointly with her father property over which her husband had no control.[4] After her father's death, the obligatory guardian or tutor was still given power over her but his authority steadily weakened, and he became a figurehead.[5] By the beginning of the third century, Ulpian said that a woman had to have a tutor to act for her at law, to make contracts, to emancipate slaves or to undertake civil business. But he added that a woman who had borne three children was no longer subject to this regulation.[6] Thus, the Roman woman, entirely powerless within the public structure, could exercise very considerable power in private life as a result of the wealth and property that she might accumulate by herself or through her family.

In the same period, the Germanic woman appears to have occupied an exceptionally important place in the rudimentary public life of the barbarian tribes. Tacitus, to whom we also owe the saga of the warrior queen, Boudicca, informed the Romans that girls of noble families would provide the best surety from the Germans if held as hostages. He continued: "they believe that there resides in women an element of holiness and prophecy, and so they do not scorn to ask their advice or lightly disregard their replies."[7] At a somewhat later period, Ammianus Marcellinus wrote of the barbarians: "A whole band of foreigners will be unable to cope with one of them in a fight if he calls in his wife, stronger than he by far and with flashing eyes; least of all when she swells her neck and gnashes her teeth and, poising her huge white arms, proceeds to rain punches mingled with kicks."[8]

Yet this awe-inspiring creature enjoyed very few private rights outside the authority of her family. She was barred from the inheritance of any property and she came to her husband as the object of sale or capture. Whether these practices illustrate the great value that the Germans placed upon their women — Tacitus, for example, praised them for paying for their wives rather than taking a dowry from them[9] — or demonstrates the contempt in which they were held as individuals, it is clear that their economic position was weak indeed, since the bride price went to the woman's family, not to her.

By the fifth and sixth centuries, when the Germanic tribes were setting up kingdoms in the western parts of the decaying Roman empire, the economic position of the women had improved somewhat. Germanic kings, assisted by the growing strength of the *comitatus* (personal followers of the ruler), were gradually weakening the power of the kindred. As the smaller family group began to replace the tribe as the basic social unit, the incapacity of women to inherit property began to disappear along with the old customs of marriage by sale and capture. This process was probably hastened by the influence of the opposing precepts of Roman law and Christianity.

With her position within the family thus enhanced, a woman of that age could expect to share actively in the social role of her family. The Germans drew no distinction between private and public power, or between public and private rights. As a result, women whose families were economically powerful, or who held extensive property in their own names, occupied the public sphere as well as the private. In this investigation of the economic and political power of women, we shall rely heavily on the Germanic codes to chart the changes that occurred in the early Middle Ages. Since most of the aristocratic families who exercised power at that time were Germanic, Roman law will figure only insofar as its influence penetrated those codes.

The Germanic tribes did not impose their own laws uniformly upon the areas they occupied. Instead of territoriality of law, they followed the principle of personality of law, which meant in practical terms that each individual was allowed to live under the law of his ancestors.[10] In areas close to the Mediterranean, where there was a population of Roman descent, Roman law continued to be observed in a simplified codification mixed with Germanic customs. In the Frankish kingdom the population was heterogeneous. But as more and more areas that had never been Romanized were added to the kingdom, Germanic customs came to predominate. In turn, to be sure, these codes were somewhat influenced by Roman precepts as they became the foundation of the feudal customs that were to prevail in the medieval West from the late ninth century on.

Studies of early medieval property and family law, a field that owes much to German scholarship, provide us with valuable information on the extensive area of bride price, marriage settlements, widows rights and inheritance. The importance of women's legal position was recognized by the Jean Bodin Society which devoted two conferences in 1956 and 1957 to women throughout the world from ancient times to the present.[11] Sometimes, however, the laws create problems for scholars. The carefully devised conditions for marriage and its economic arrangements that we find in the codes date from a period when the Germanic tribes were already partially Romanized and Christianized. In actual deeds of settlement and wills and in the accounts of events recorded in chronicles, a more chaotic reality is apparent. Customs barely noticed in the codes died out only gradually. Practices actively condemned by the church continued unabated for some centuries.

Although no trace of the old marriage by capture appears even in the earliest codes, the blood-stained pages of Gregory of Tours, a historian of the late sixth century, are all too full of marriages made on the battlefield.[12] Again and again, the conquering king espouses the widow or daughter of his defeated rival, apparently as part of the loot. But Gregory's care in distinguishing between wives and concubines leaves us in no doubt that these were marriages indeed.

While the codes entirely ignore the possibility of marriage by capture, they do show remnants of the practice of purchasing a bride from her kindred. The German historians of the Nazi period argued in vain that their ancestors never undertook such barbarous arrangements:[13] the careful work of Noel Senn has isolated the traces of the old purchase price *(pretium uxoris, puellae or nuptialis)* in the codes and traced the slow process by which the sale of the bride was converted to sale of the family's rights over her, to a token payment balanced by a growing custom of giving money to the bride herself.[14]

The woman continued to be an object of value for which her suitor was expected to pay a price, but the price itself moved through a series of steps into the hands of the woman rather than those of her family. In the early Germanic kingdoms, a suitor no longer haggled over the price the family would get for the girl herself but the price to be paid for her *mundium,* the power the father or guardian held over her, which passed to the husband at the time of the marriage.[15] This sum gradually became a symbolic payment and the bride received as her own an increasingly large portion of the bride gift *(wittemon, meta or dos)* contributed by the bridegroom. For example, Salic law required that the groom pay the bride's father or guardian only the token sum of a gold solidus and one denarius.[16] But if the groom had not already turned a bride gift over to the bride, with written guarantees, she was to receive, on her husband's death, twenty five or sixty two and a half solidi, depending on her status, under Salic law and fifty solidi under Ripuarian law.[17] The Burgundian code, issued in the early sixth century, shows a transitional stage with the bride receiving only a third of the bride gift and the rest going to her father or nearest relative.[18] A woman was allowed to keep the entire bride gift only if she married for a third time.[19] The Visigothic,[20] Bavarian,[21] and Alemannic[22] codes awarded the whole bride gift to the bride. In the earliest version of the Lombard code, issued by Rothari (636-652), the father retained the bride gift but in the later version, revised by Liutprand (712-744), the bride gift was turned over to the bride and the relatives were given only a token indemnity.[23] The Saxons, who remained farthest outside the Roman sphere of influence, with their customs being codified only under Charlemagne (768-814), continued to award a substantial sum, three hundred solidi to the bride's father.[24] It was, however, conceded that the wife could keep the bride gift she was given in movable goods.[25] In England, the practice of giving the parents or the guardian a payment was abolished by Cnut (1016-1035) who ruled that: "No woman or maiden shall ever be forced to marry a man whom she dislikes, nor shall she ever be given for money unless the suitor wishes to give something of his own free will."[26]

Although the codes usually expressed the amount of the bride gift in money, the formulas and deeds show that, most frequently, real property was turned over to the wife as her bride gift.[27] For example, according to a marriage settlement drawn up in the reign of Cnut, a certain Godwin, when he wooed Brihtric's daughter, "gave her a pound of gold to induce her to accept his suit and he granted her the estate at Street and whatever belongs to it, and 150 acres at Burmash and also 30 oxen and 20 cows and 10 horses and 10 slaves."[28] Deeds frequently gave her unrestricted ownership of this property although some codes and donations stipulated that she had only the usufruct of her bride gift, which, upon death, would be passed to her children or revert back to her husband's heirs, if she should have no children.[29]

In addition to her bride gift, a woman received a *morgengabe,* or morning gift, after the consummation of her marriage. That settlement usually consisted of real property, and customs varied as to whether she held the usufruct or had outright possession of the gift.[30] Through the bride gift and the morning gift, women were able to acquire impressive personal domains and concommitant economic and political power. Probably for that reason, in periods of fairly effective royal power—at the beginning and again at the end of the period we are discussing—efforts were made to restrict their extent. The Lombard code tried to limit the amount of the property that passed into the hands of women by stipulating that the morning gift would not exceed a quarter of the husband's patrimony. Nobles were forbidden to give more than 300 solidi of gold though an exception was made for judges who could give up to 400 solidi.[31]

When the Merovingian prince, Chilperic I (561-584), married Galswintha in 556-557, he gave her the cities of Limoges, Bordeaux, Cahors, Bearn, and

Bigorre as a morning gift. After the murder of Galswintha, that property did not revert to her husband but went to her sister, Brunhilda, wife of Sigibert, Chilperic's brother.[32]

Although, according to Germanic customs, a father was not obliged to give a dowry to his daughter, we know that many doting parents did provide their daughters with generous dowries, perhaps imitating the Roman practice. Riguntha, the daughter of Chilperic and Fredegunda, his third wife, was sent off to her Visigothic fiance with so astounding a quantity of goods that the Frankish nobles objected, fearing that the royal fisc had been stripped to outfit her. This was in fact the case, but the girl's mother claimed that she had provided for the girl out of the property she had amassed as a result of her husband's generosity.[33] Such resources should have meant that a Merovingian queen could well afford to support her own retainers and that a man in her service could not be harmed with impunity since she had the power to take reprisals. However, it required a strong hand and constant vigilance to retain wealth in those times. Riguntha's fortune never reached Spain. The girl was robbed repeatedly along the road by members of her diminishing entourage, the last of whom finally abandoned her in Toulouse with nothing left. All the formidable rage of her mother was ineffectual in recouping the losses.

This tale acquires additional interest in light of the fact that Fredegunda had nothing of her own when she married Chilperic. All her wealth and power came to her through her marriage. Nor was she unusual among the wives of the Merovingian kings. Among the several wives of Chilperic's brother, Charibert, were two sisters whom he discovered in the service of yet another wife. One of these, "who wore the robe of a nun," attempted to discourage his advances by taking him to see her father, a weaver, at his work. This did nothing to kill his appetite, and the amorous king, who had already married a shepherd girl, added the sisters to his harem. The shepherd's daughter, incidentally, was in possession of vast treasures at his death, though many of them were stolen from her and she came to a sorrowful end in a convent.[34]

Misalliances on such a scale are astonishing today and the motivations of those early kings in choosing their marriage partners are obscure. King Sigibert is said to have married the Visigothic princess, Brunhilda, because he "saw that his brothers were taking wives unworthy of them, and to their disgrace, were actually marrying slave women."[35] But when a bishop taunted Chilperic with this fact, claiming that the king's sons "could not inherit the kingdom because their mother had been taken to the king's bed from among the slaves of Magnachar," Gregory states that the bishop spoke, "not knowing that the families of the wives are now disregarded and they are called the sons of a king who have been begotten by a king."[36] The lack of a noble origin does not, in this period, appear to have been a substantial barrier to the unlimited exercise of power by women. The history of the Frankish monarchy in the late sixth century is dominated by the ferocious rivalry between Fredegunda, the former slave, and Brunhilda, the Visigothic princess. Their titanic struggle stemmed originally from Brunhilda's sense of family—she was determined to avenge the murder of her sister Galswintha—but the progress of the contest suggests that the power of women in this period was derived from their own personal force rather than from legal protection or from the position of their family.

Only in the tenth century, when the family had entered its age of glory, does the blooodline become a significant factor in determining the position of women. When Hugh Capet advanced his claim to the throne of France against the Carolingian claimant, Charles of Lorraine, his supporters argued that Charles should be disqualified because he had married beneath his station, the daughter of a mere knight. "How could the powerful duke suffer that a woman, coming from the family of one of his vassals, should become queen and rule over him? How could he walk behind one whose equals and, even whose superiors, bend the knee before him?" On the other side, Hugh's wife was the daughter of the Empress Adelaide by her first marriage, and the powerful hand of her mother was guiding her husband's party.[37]

A woman's opportunities to achieve a position of power through marriage were increasingly enhanced as time went on, if she controlled inherited property of her own. In the early period, when royal power was still relatively strong in the Germanic kingdoms, women were generally discriminated against in favor of their brothers. In contrast to Roman law, which provided equal rights of succession to the family's property by daughters and sons, the general principle upheld by the Burgundian, Alemannic, Bavarian and Ripuarian codes was that daughters could inherit only if there were no sons.[38] Lombard law made similar provision, although it enabled fathers to give a third of their property to their daughters.[39] Only the most Romanized of the Germanic codes, the Visigothic law,[40] allowed equal rights of succession to daughters. As Ganshof has demonstrated, the most restrictive laws were those that prevailed in the least Romanized areas of the Germanic lands.[41] The Thuringian code excluded women altogether from the inheritance of immovable property,[42] and the Saxon code conceded that daughters could succeed only if there were no uncles or brothers on the father's side.[43]

As can be seen from the evolution of the Salic Law, the tendency in the sixth and seventh centuries was to relax the inheritance laws designed to keep property intact for the benefit of sons. The most ancient version of the code, issued in the late fifth century, excluded women completely from the inheritance of Salic land.[44] In the late sixth and seventh centuries, the Salic law was somewhat mitigated to allow women to inherit land which had not come to their parents as part of the patrimony. Chilperic admitted women even to the inheritance of Salic land, provided that they had no brothers. Lands acquired by means other than inheritance were equally divided between sons and daughters.[45] In any case, as we have seen, a forceful woman occupying a favorable position was not generally vulnerable to these legal restrictions. Merovingian women, like their men, took what power they could and held it as long as they were not forcibly dispossessed.

Deeds show that the restrictions on inherited Salic land were frequently disregarded, and indeed even resented, by the fathers. In one deed of the late eighth century, a father complained against the "impious custom" which discriminated between his children and which ran contrary to their equality before God and the love he felt for them.[46] Lombard law, while holding to the principle that daughters could succeed only where there were no sons, allowed fathers to leave one-third of their property to their daughters.[47] In England, Alfred the Great (870-899) recognized the intentions of his grandfather in excluding women from the inheritance of his family's land. In his own testament, however, he defended the equal rights of his own daughters. He respected the earlier custom only in his stipulation that if the male heirs wished to keep the land intact they could purchase the portion of land inherited by the females.[48]

By the mid eighth century, when the Carolingians succeeded to the Frankish throne and began to dominate the West, the restrictive Germanic customs of marriage by purchase and female incapacity to inherit immovables were thus nearly obliterated. The private rights of women to the control of property had been established, giving them, as daughters, sisters, mothers and wives, a position of economic equality within the family. As we shall see, this condition held inherent difficulties for the family itself, difficulties Charlemagne himself may have perceived—he apparently solved the potential problems of divided inheritances by preventing the marriage of any of his daughters, turning a blind eye to their more informal sexual alliances. Few families, however, followed his example. Most women continued to marry, bringing property of their own with them to strengthen their claims to power within the household they were entering. For the aristocracy, in an age when private power was almost synonymous with public power, this meant that there would be few restrictions on the power of women in any sphere of activity.

In theory, the married woman in Carolingian times did no more than adopt the role that has always been regarded as proper to women. Carolingian queens were housewives. But the houses they kept were the imperial domain itself. In the *Capitulare de villis*, Charlemagne delegated extensive authority to the queen for the regulation of the domestic concerns of the empire and the direction of the royal servants. The breadth of this power is apparent in the fact that persons bearing the humble domestic titles of chamberlain, butler and steward, for example, were in reality the ministers of the Carolingian state. The emperor was therefore giving his wife very great power indeed when he ordered: "We wish that anything ordered by us or by the queen to one of our judges, or anything ordered by the ministers, seneschals or cupbearer . . . be carried out to the last word. . . . And if someone, through negligence fails to do this, he must abstain from drink . . . until such time that he gains admission to our presence or that of the queen and asks to be absolved."[49]

Two generations after Charlemagne, describing the administration of the palace, Hincmar of Rheims gave the queen, with the assistance of the chamberlain, charge of the royal treasury, arguing that the king, who had to concern himself with the ordering of the entire kingdom, should not be burdened with such domestic trifles.[50] When, under Charlemagne's successors, domestic revolt and armed rivalry once more disturbed Europe, the housewifely role became even more extensive. Like any wife on the American frontier, a woman was expected to defend her home if her husband was absent. It is therefore only worthy of a passing mention by the chroniclers that the wives, mothers and sisters of the Carolingian kings and their vassals were frequently engaged in holding cities under siege or directing military operations against troublesome subordinates when their lords were engaged elsewhere.

The importance of the queen's role was recognized by the Carolingians and their successors through their practice of having their queens anointed and crowned, to make them sharers in the rather mystical aspects of the king's power. Along with Pepin, the first Carolingian monarch, whose own claims needed all the reinforcemnt that could be devised, his wife, Queen Bertha, was formally crowned and continued to exercise considerable political power after his death.[51] Praise of the queen was also incorporated into the *Laudes* (hymns of praise), which comprised part of the royal liturgy.[52] The importance of the queen's position in the early medieval empire was recognized by contemporaries not only in the use of such lofty titles as *consors regis* (royal consort), but by the complaints of some writers against queens who were not regarded as capable of the satisfactory performance of their duties. Agobard of Lyons, for example, in his writings against Judith of Bavaria, the wife of Louis the Pious (814-840), complained that in her the emperor did not have a wife "who can be to him a help in administering the palace and the realm."[53]

As a matter of course, these women were also expected to raise their children and protect their heritage when necessary. Here a complication of the greatest magnitude arose. The protecting mother was all too often found to be simultaneously acting the wicked stepmother. In this age, when primogeniture had yet to be introduced, royal patrimonies, and others, were already suf- ficiently disturbed by the practice of making provision for all sons. But to this, Carolingian conditions commonly added the problem of providing for children of a second marriage. The sons of the first wife of Louis the Pious were sufficiently quarrelsome to do untold damage to the fabric of the empire. But even the hope of a peaceful succession secured by the division of the empire was destroyed by the determination of his second wife, Judith of Bavaria, to secure a favorable place for her own son, the future Charles the Bald.[54] In England, an even more decisive role in the future of the kingdom was played by Elfreda, the mother of Ethelred the Unready (978-1016), who secured the crown for her son by the murder of his half-brother, Edward the Martyr.[55] Similarly, the great German empire of Otto the Great (936-973) came close to foundering on the rock of his second wife's ambition. Here, too, the elder son was driven to rebellion, though, fortunately for all, he met an early death, making place for Adelaide's child, Otto II.[56]

But the quarrels and ambitions of queens, however interesting, are not the most important aspect of the growing power of women in the ninth and tenth centuries. As the great empire of Charlemagne began to lose its cohesion, power slipped from the hands of the monarchs and was seized by the great nobles of the realm. In the development of this "first feudal age," the family entered its age of glory. The key to power in this period was control of landed property, whether through private ownership or through control of royal property received as a fief. Initially, the fief was designed to equip a man for knightly service and was regarded as indivisible. But in 870, Charles the Bald was obligated to issue the

Capitulary of Quierzy, acknowledging the heritability of fiefs and therefore subjecting them to the inheritance laws that governed private property.[57] The subsequent development of *franc-parage* provided for the possibility of dividing the income from a fief among the heirs, although rights over the fief as such remained with the eldest son. When a family held several fiefs, it was customary to divide them among younger sons and daughters. As the power of the Frankish monarchy continued to disintegrate, families developed the custom of willing fiefs to daughters when there were no sons to inherit them.[58]

In addition to this growing freedom in disposing of royal fiefs, the aristocratic families of the ninth and tenth centuries were expanding their control of allodial—free hold—land by force and purchase and through land clearance. There were no serious restrictions on the family's power to distribute such land as it saw fit. Few families were inclined to exclude their daughters from the capacity to inherit allodial land. When such land came into the hands of a woman, it remained her property and did not pass to her husband or her husband's family unless she willed it to do so. It was common for a wife to leave the management of her property to her husband, although he could not alienate it, as is attested by joint signatures on deeds of this type. Forceful women, however, like Matilda of Tuscany in the eleventh century, insisted on excluding their husbands from the management of their property and taking it into their own control.

The most dramatic instance of the movement of a woman's inheritance is the case of Eleanor of Aquitaine. Though Eleanor lived in the twelfth century, her situation conforms with the practices of the tenth and eleventh centuries. When she married the King of France, her great duchy nearly doubled the extent of that monarchy. But when she divorced him and married the King of England, the duchy went with her. When she quarreled with her second husband, she had no hesitation in returning to Aquitaine as an independent ruler and designating her second, and favorite, son as her heir rather than her elder son, for whom the crown of England had been destined. The career of Eleanor affected the highest seats of power in the Middle Ages. That similar powers were exercised by women of less magnificence is becoming increasingly clear as modern social histories, particularly in England, France and Belgium, broaden the trails blazed by the great Marc Bloch. Out of this growing volume of work, based on the patient examination of local records, the living outlines of medieval society in such areas as the Maconnaise, Bavaria and Catalonia emerge. Though much remains to be learned, a recent attempt at a synthesis has been made by Georges Duby,[59] and Doris Stenton has begun to apply the findings to the history of women.[60] From collections of English records we have many examples of women able to dispose freely of their property, and in at least one case, in the late tenth century, to disinherit a son in favor of a more distant female relative.[61]

Through their control of the land, lords of various degrees came to control most of the regalian rights formerly held by the kings. They administered justice, made laws, coined money, raised armies and carried on all the normal responsibilities of government. Like Charlemagne's queen, their female partners shared in such responsibilities. However, when a woman inherited her own estate, she inherited the political power that went with it, and frequently exercised it in her own right. To this, she might add independent exercise of her husband's power when she became a widow. Such activities of women were not accepted without complaint. An assembly of bishops at Nantes in 895 demonstrated that they were one at heart with their Roman ancestors when they proclaimed:

> It is astounding that certain women, against both divine and human law, with bare-faced impudence, act in general pleas and with abandon exhibit a burning passion for public meetings, and they disrupt, rather than assist, the business of the kingdom and the good of the commonweal. It is indecent and reprehensible, even among barbarians, for women to discuss the cases of men. Those who should be discussing their woolen work and weaving with the residents of the women's quarters, should not usurp the authority of senators in public meetings just as if they were residents of the court.[62]

But the indignation of the bishops was quite without effect, for the public power at the behest of the Roman Empire was gone. Within a century, the successors of the censorious bishops had to bear the humiliation of women's inheriting the advocacies even of churches.[63] For a period in the tenth century the power of the papacy itself was under the control of the noble Roman ladies Theodora and her daughter Marozia, who bore the proud title "senatrix."[64]

If the capacity to inherit property gave extensive power to women, the freedom to leave the same property wherever they liked put the seal on that power. When a woman married and had children she had to be counted as a member of at least two families and it was by no means inevitable that she would identify primarily with that of her husband. As a wife or as a widow, she could administer her power to further projects that were conceived mutually with her husband. But she might as easily pursue her own ends, or those of her original family.

Ethelfleda, the Lady of the Mercians, was the widow of the king of Mercia and the daughter of Alfred the Great of Wessex (871-899) and sister of Edward the Elder. Even during the lifetime of her ailing husband, she took over the active role of governing Mercia and continued in that capacity for years after his death. After a life of campaigning against invading Danes, Irish and Norwegians to defend her frontiers, Ethelfleda deliberately excluded from succession to the kingdom of Mercia her daughter (whom she had prevented from marrying with that purpose in mind) and brought it into union with her brother's kingdom ot Wessex.[65] As regent for her son, the future Henry IV (1056-1106), Agnes of Poitou earned the epithet "the tears of Germany" because she used her power to further policies objectionable to the German nobility.[66] Perhaps it was his awareness of such possibilities that determined Otto II (973-983) to entrust the regency of Germany, during his absences, neither to his Italian mother nor to his Greek wife, both of whom proved to be capable regents after his death, but to his German sister, Matilda Abbess of Quedlinburg.[67]

Archibald Lewis has provided many examples of the power of women as heads of families in southern France in the ninth to the eleventh century. Indeed Lewis believes that this conglomeration of power in the hands of women was the major cause of the breakdown of the family system in the tenth century

Languedoc.[68] Wherever we look during this period, we find no really effective barriers to the capacity of women to exercise power. They appear as military leaders, judges, castellans, controllers of property.[69] Though barred from the priesthood, they even exercised vast power over the church as a result of their family positions.

Before the church required celibacy of its ministers, the wives of priests took ecclesiastical property into their own hands, as is shown by the complaints registered by Atto, Bishop of Vercelli, in the second quarter of the tenth century.[70] In addition, the power of secular women to donate or withhold property and their power to appoint candidates to church offices through exercise of their magisterial powers was an integral part of their general position. In this way, the Roman lady Marozia came to exercise control over the papacy itself for a period in the early tenth century. The proprietary rights of the family of Theophylactus and their great political influence passed first into the hands of Theodora, his wife. Their daughter, Marozia, became mistress of one pope and mother of another, leader of the famous pornocracy which Liutprand of Cremona attacked so violently. The same lady, at one point, nearly succeeded in uniting all of northern Italy under her power only to be thwarted by the anger of one of her sons, who feared the loss of his entire inheritance.[71]

On the other side, the reformed church of the eleventh century owed an incalculable debt to the powerful Countess of Tuscany, Beatrice, and her daughter, Matilda. It was in Matilda's castle of Canossa that the great drama of Pope Gregory's subjection of the Emperor Henry IV was played out. During that pope's lifetime and for decades after his death, it was the armies of Matilda that defended the liberated church in Italy. And when she died, she willed her great Tuscan inheritance to the church to form the bulwark of the papal state.[72]

These extensive powers exercised by women were, as we have seen, largely derived from the rather irregular powers held by the great families of the age. In the eleventh century, throughout Europe, the process of reconstituting some of the institutions of public power was begun, a process that accelerated throughout the twelfth century. Vogelsang,[73] studying the German Empire, called the tenth century the "golden age" of the *consortium regni*. He demonstrated that by the eleventh century the Empire had largely ceased to be governed on a personal basis and, as a result, the empress's power was severely diminished. The same process became apparent in France and England in the next century. In the church, the imposition of celibacy and the prohibition of lay investiture restricted the power of the family, and therefore of women, in the late eleventh century. The resumption of some control of the fief system by contemporary princes weakened their position in the feudal system. In 1037, Konrad II issued the *Constitutio de feudis,* excluding women from the inheritance of fiefs. Although there was a perceptible decrease in the influence and power of women in Germany after this date, Herlihy argued that the Constitution was applied with indifferent success.[74] Other historians point out that only after 1156, when Barbarossa invested Henry of Babenberg and his wife with the Duchy of Austria and granted that in Austria sons and daughters could succeed equally after that date, were women occasionally admitted to the inheritance of fiefs in other areas of Germany.[75] In France, where the consolidation of royal power was far more gradual and the restoration of royal control of fiefs far more difficult, women were never categorically excluded from their inheritance. If they were lucky enough not to have brothers, they could continue to inherit great wealth and play a correspondingly important role.[76] In England, William the Conqueror, following Norman custom, was content to control the succession of fiefs by controlling the marriage of their heirs, both male and female.[77]

Meanwhile, the families themselves had become alarmed at the effects of their inheritance practices. Duby has described their widespread efforts to halt the erosion of estates through split inheritances and thereby protect the position of the family in this period of renewed royal power.[78] As the idea of primogeniture and the indivisibility of the patrimony was again entrenched, the daughters of the nobility suffered a severe diminution of their rights. A daughter's claim on the inheritance gradually gave way to the dowry provided by her family at the time of her marriage, the *maritagium*. Throughout western Europe, by the twelfth century, we find that the dowry was becoming considered a sufficient settlement for a married woman. In some areas, even that right was restricted or simply not recognized. In Normandy, where women's rights were quite restricted, a woman could receive only up to a third of the total patrimony as dowry and her parents had the right to exclude her altogether if they wished to do so.[79]

During the late tenth and eleventh centuries, the bride gift, given by the husband, came to be transformed into the dower. The bride gift, as we saw it in its earlier form, whether given as usufruct, which had to be passed on to the children after the wife's death, or as property, which the wife owned outright and could alienate or leave to whomever she wished, was turned over to her on her wedding day and usually represented a specific piece of land.[80] But in the tenth and eleventh centuries, fewer deeds gave the wife outright ownership and even the usufruct was generally restricted to the use of the husband and wife jointly, not to the wife exclusively. Instead of specifying a given piece of property, some deeds spoke only of a fraction of the income derived from the husband's patrimony. That type of agreement was replaced in the twelfth century by the dower arrangement, which gave a widow the usufruct of a portion, usually one-third, of her husband's patrimony. She was thus provided for in case of her husband's decease but her economic independence during his lifetime, and, to some extent, after his death, had vanished.[81]

With the power of their women thus severely reduced, the aristocratic family was in better condition to face the ensuing period of struggle with the resurgent monarchies—a struggle that continued well into modern times. But by the twelfth century, public power was gradually being recaptured from the great aristocratic families by kings and princes. Institutions outside the household were being created to administer public affairs. The success of the aristocracy as a class in adjusting itself to this broad political change was accomplished largely at the expense of the aristocratic women. As the families were resisting princely encroachment upon their rights by insisting upon the indivisibility of the patrimony, the economic rights of women were restricted. Concurrently, as rulers slowly developed an impersonal machinery for government, queens and empresses, as well as ladies on a somewhat more modest level, were excluded from public life. This meant that the heads of the great families—both men and women—were losing the power they had derived from the private power of the family. But, while it was possible for aristocratic men to retain the same power by acting as the administrators of the new institutions, such positions were not open to noble women. Their activities were confined to the role of housekeeper, a role whose boundaries were shrinking. With the return of public power and the corresponding loss of family power, women were moving back to the conditions that had existed under the Roman Empire.

NOTES

1 Digest, 50, 17, 2. *Corpus Iuris Civilis,* ed. Georgius Gebaver (Göttingen: Ioan Christian Dieterich, 1776), p. 1137.

2 Robert Villiers, "Le statut de la femme à Rome jusqu'à la fin de la Republique," Société Jean Bodin, *Recueils* 11 (1959): 179.

3 Jean Gaudemet, "Le statut de la femme dans l'empire romaine," ibid., p. 191.

4 Villiers, "Le statut," p. 187.

5 Gaudemet, "Le statut."

6 Ulpian, Regula IX, *Corpus Iuris Civilis,* ed. Galisset (Paris: Cotelle, 1853), p. 6.

7 Tacitus, *Germania,* 8, trans. H. Mattingly (Harmondsworth: Penguin 1960), p. 107.

8 Ammianus Marcellinus, *History* 15: 12, ed. J. C. Rolfe (Cambridge, Mass.: Harvard University Press), vol. 1, p. 195.

9 Tacitus, *Germania,* pp. 18, 115.

10 L. Stouff, "Etude sur le principe de la personnalité des lois depuis les invasions barbares jusqu'au XIIe siecle," *Rev. bourguignonne de l'Enseignement supérieur* 4, 2 (1894); F.L. Ganshof, "L'étranger dans la monarchie franque," Société Jean Bodin, *Recueils* 10 (1958): 19-20.

11 "La femme," Société Jean Bodin, *Recueils* 11-12 (1959-1962).

12 Gregory of Tours, *History of the Franks,* ed. E. Brehaut (New York: Norton, 1969).

13 Although the feminist movement of the Weimar Republic was eradicated under the National Socialists, supporters of that regime retained an interest in this aspect of women's studies. One extremist went so far as to say that belief in such a practice was "rassfeindlich," inimical to the race: Gerda Merschberger, *Die Rechtsstellung der germanischen Frau* (Leipzig: Rabitzsch, 1937), p. 47.

14 Noel Senn, *Le contrat de vente de la femme en droit matrimonial germanique* (Portentruy: Jura, 1946).

15 Louis-Maurice-André Cornuey, *Le régimè de la 'dos' aux époques merovingienne et carolingienne* (Thèse Univ. d'Alger, La Typolitho, 1929).

16 *Formulae Salicae Merkelianae,* ed. K. Zeumer, no 15. *Monumenta Germanicae Historica, Legum sectio V: Formulae* (henceforth cited as *MGH FORM.),* p. 247. "idcirco ego in Dei nomine ille, filius illius, puellam ingenuam nomine illa, filiam illius, per solidum et denarium secundum legem Salicam . . ." see also, *Formulae Salicae Bignonianae,* no. 6, p. 230 and *Formulae Salicae Lindenbrogianae,* no. 7, p. 271.

17 *Capitula Legi Salicae addita, Pactus Legis Salicae,* 100, 1-2; *MGH Legum sectio I, Legum nationum germanicarum* IV, I, pp. 256-257 (henceforth cited as *MGH, Leg. nat. germ.). Lex Ribuaria,* 41 (37), 2; *MGH Leg. nat. germ.* III, II, p. 95.

18 *Leges Burgundiorum,* 86, 2; *MGH Leg. nat. germ.* II, I, p. 108. See also no. 66, 1-3, pp. 94-95.

19 *Leg. Burg.* 69, 2 *MGH Leg. nat. germ.* II, I, p. 96. As to a woman's right when she married a second time, see 69, 1, p. 95, and Ganshof, "La femme dans la monarchie franque," Jean Bodin Société, *Recueils* 12 (1962): 21, n. 47.

20 *Lex Visigothorum* III, 1, 6; ed. Zeumer, *MGH Leg. nat. germ.* I, p. 130.

21 *Lex Baiuvariorum,* 8, 14. *MGH Leg. nat. germ.* V, II, p. 359.

22 *Leges Alemanorum,* 54, 1, *MGH Leg. nat. germ.* V,I, p. 112.

23 Rothari, 215; Liutprand, 103; ed. Franz Beyerle, *Die Gesetze der Langobarde* (Weimar: Böhlaus, 1947) pp. 84 and 268.

24 *Leges Saxonum,* 40, ed. von Richthofen, *MGH Leg. nat. germ.* V, pp. 60-70; ed. Claudius von Schwerin, *Leges Saxonum und Lex Thuringorum, MGH, Fontes iuris germanici antiqui in usum scholarum* (Hanover: Hansche Buchhandlung, 1918) pp. 27-28; ed. Karl A. Eckhardt, *Germanenrechte* II: *Die Gesetze des Karolinger-Reiches* III (Weimar: Verlag H. Böhlaus, 1934), 40.

25 *Leges Saxonum* 47, ed. von Richthofen, pp. 73-74; ed. von Schwerin, pp. 29-30; ed. Eckhardt, p. 26.

26 II Cnut 76, A. J. Robertson, *The Laws of the Kings of England from Edmund to Henry I* (Cambridge: University Press, 1925), p. 216.

27 According to Cornuey, *Régime de la dos,* p. 46, dowry in the fifth century was usually in the form of moveable goods but, in the sixth, it was more commonly given as real property.

28 *Anglo-Saxon Charters,* ed. A. J. Robertson (Cambridge: University Press, 1939), pp. 150-151.

29 Cornuey, *Régime de la dos,* p. 53 ff.

30 Ibid., pp. 127-131.

31 *Liuprandi Leges,* p. 89, ed. Beyerle, p. 254.

32 Gregory of Tours, *History of the Franks,* pp. 9, 20.

33 Ibid., pp. 6, 45.

34 Ibid., pp. 4, 26.

35 Ibid., pp. 4, 27.

36 Ibid., pp. 5, 20.

37 Richer, *Histoire de France,* 4, ed. R. Latouche (Paris: Champion, 1936), pp. 9-11.

38 See Biondo Biondi, *Il diritto romano christiano* III (Milan: Giuffre, 1954), pp. 339-341; *Leges Burg.,* 14, 1-2, *MGH, Leg. nat. germ.* II, I, p. 52; *Leges alam.,* 55 *MGH Leg. nat. germ.,* V, I, pp. 114-115; *Lex Bai.,* 15, 9-10, *MGH Leg. nat. germ.* V, II, pp. 428-429; *Lex Rib.,* 57-(56), 4, *MGH Leg. nat. germ.* III, 11, p. 105.

39 *Liutprandi Leges,* 1 and 65, ed. Beyerle, *Gesetze der Langobarden* 170, 230.

40 *Lex Vis.* IV, 3, De successionibus, 1, Antiqua. *MGH Leg. nat. germ.* I, p. 174.

41 Francois Ganshof, "La femme dans la monarchie franque," Société Jean Bodin, *Recueils,* 12, (1962): 33-40.

42 *Lex Thur.,* 26-27, ed, von Schwerin, p. 60; ed. Eckhardt, p. 38.

43 *Lex Saxonum,* 41, 44, 46, ed. von Richthofen, pp. 71-72; ed. von Schwerin, 28-29.

44 *Pactus Legis Salicae,* De alodis 6, ed. Eckhardt, II, 1: *65 Titel-Text* (Göttingen: Musterschmidt, 1955) also in *MGH Leg. nat. germ.* IV, I, p. 222. Text A is most ancient, dating to 507-511, Chlodovech's reign; on this Eckhart, *Pactus Legis Salicae,* vol. I: Einführung (Göttingen, 1954), p. 207.

45 *Capitulare IV ad Legem Salicam,* 108; *MGH Leg. nat. germ.* IV, I, p. 262.

46 *Marculfi formularum II,* 12, ed. Zeumer, *MGH Form.,* p. 83: see also *Cartae senonicae* (dated 768-775), 45, ed. Zeumer, Ibid., p. 205, and the testament of Burgundofara, dated 632, ed. B. Mayer, "Das Testament der Burgondofara," *Mitteilungen des Instituts für Oesterreichische Geschichtsforschung, Ergänzungsband* 14 (1939), 11-12.

47 *Liutprandi Leges* 1 and 65, ed. Beyerle, pp. 170, 230.

48 F. E. Harmer, ed., *Select English Historical Documents* (Cambridge: University Press, 1914), no. 9.

49 *Capitulare de villis* 16; *MGH Capitularia regum francorum,* I, p. 84.

50 Hincmar of Rheims, *De ordine palatii,* 22; *MGH Capt. reg. franc.,* II, p. 525.

51 P. Krull, *Die Salbung und Krönung der deutschen Königinnen und Kaiserinnen im Mittelalter* (Diss. Halle: Wulfert, Shönebeck a.e., 1911).

52 Ernst Kantorowicz, *Laudes Regiae* (Berkeley: University of California Press, 1947).

53 Agobard of Lyons, ed. Migne *Patrologia latina* (cited as *PL),* 104, p. 310.

54 On Judith of Bavaria, see translations of contemporary chronicles by Allen Cabaniss, *Charlemagne's Cousins* (Syracuse: University Press, 1967) and *Son of Charlemagne* (Syracuse: University Press, 1965); and by Bernard Scholz, *Carolingian Chronicles* (Ann Arbor: University Press, 1972).

55 Frank M. Stenton, *Anglo-Saxon England*, 3rd ed. (Oxford: Clarendon Press, 1971), p. 373, casts doubt upon the evidence for Elfreda's guilt but concedes that she was popularly believed to be guilty. The event gave rise to another tradition recorded in the fourteenth century life of St. Edith of Wilton: C. Horstmann, ed., *St. Editha* (Heilbronn: Henniger, 1883). There the shocked nobles are said to have tried to avoid bestowing the crown on Ethelred by offering it to the sister of the murdered king who was living with her mother in the convent at Wilton.

56 The life of Adelaide was written by Odilo of Cluny, *Epitaphium Adelheidae Imperatricis, PL*, 142, pp. 974-75. The marriage of Adelaide and Otto also offers us another problem regarding the inheritance of land by women. After the death of Adelaide's first husband, she was regarded as the sole heiress of his lands and titles in Italy, which she carried to her second husband, the German Emperor. Perhaps it was in recognition of this authority that Otto took the unusual step of stamping her image on the reverse of his coins.

57 Capitulary of Quierzy. *MGH Leges* II, pp. 343-344.

58 As Ganshof, "La femme dans la monarchie franque," p. 29, points out, a married woman's incapacity under the Germanic laws presents a problem whose solution the laws themselves do not demonstrate. Only the *Lex Burg.* 100, *MGH Leg. nat. germ.* II, V, p.113 is explicit on the subject. Deeds are few and do not necessarily show that a married woman's incapacity was a general principle in all the codes.

59 Georges Duby, *Rural Economy and Country Life in the Medieval West* (London: Edward Arnold, 1968).

60 Doris Stenton, *The English Woman in History* (London: Allen & Unwin, and New York: Macmillan, 1957).

61 Robertson, *Anglo-Saxon Charters,* pp. 150 ff. Domesday Book lists a woman named Asa in Yorkshire who held her land separate and free from the domination and control of her husband, Beornwulf, even when they were together, so that he could neither give nor sell nor forfeit it. They had separated and she had withdrawn all her land and possessed it as its lady. Quoted from Dorothy Whitelock, *The Beginnings of English Society,* 2nd. ed. (Penguin, 1971), 95.

62 Council of Nantes, 895, canon 19, *Acta Conciliorum,* ed. Harduin (Paris, 1714), VI[1], p. 461.

63 Duby, *Rural Economy,* 493, reprinted a particularly interesting document in which Cunegonde, advocate of Plauen, left her extensive holdings to a sisterhood of which she was a member.

64 Flodoard, *De Christi triumphis apud Ital.* XII, 7, in *Liber pontificalis,* ed. L. Duchesne, 2 (Paris, 1892).

65 *The Anglo-Saxon Chronicle,* ed. G. N. Garmonsway (London: J. M. Dent, 1953), pp. 94-97; 100-101; 103. Her contribution to the unification of England is examined in detail by F. T. Wainwright, "Aethelflaed, Lady of the Mercians," in *The Anglo-Saxons* ed. P. Clemoes (London: Bowes and Bowes, 1959).

66 Marie Luise Bulst-Thiele, *Kaiserin Agnes,* (Leipzig and Berlin: Teubner, 1933).

67 An account of her regency, which shows the abbess performing all the secular duties of ruling the empire is to be found in *Annales Quedlinburgenses; MGH SS* 3, pp. 75-76.

68 Archibald Lewis, *The Development of Southern French and Catalan Society* (Austin: University of Texas Press, 1956), pp. 170 and 210.

69 Aimee Ermolaef, *Die Sonderstellung der Frau im französischen Lehnrecht,* (Bern: Dürig, 1930), pp. 56 ff. gives numerous examples for the tenth and eleventh centuries of women leading military expeditons, going on crusade, dispensing justice, etc.

70 Atto of Vercelli, *Epistolae, PL,* 134, pp. 115-119.

71 Liutprand of Cremona, *Tit-for-tat,* III *et passim,* ed. F. Wright (London: Routledge, 1930).

72 Matilda's role in the great reform of the eleventh century was noticed by all the annalists of the age. Her life was recorded in a lengthy poem by Donizo of Canossa, *Vita Matildis,* ed. L. Simeoni, *Rerum italicarum scriptores,* rev. ed., V, 2 (Bologna: Lanichelli, 1930), and also in *MGH SS* 12. Alfred Overmann, *Gräfin Mathilde von Tuscien* (Innsbruck, 1895. Reprinted Frankfurt a.M., Minerva, 1965), has brought together all the texts relating to her history.

73 Thilo Vogelsang, *Die Frau als Herrscherin im hohem Mittelalter; Studien zur "consors regni" Formel* (Göttingen: Musterschmidt, 1954).

74 David Herlihy, "Land, Family and Women in Continental Europe, 701-1200." *Traditio,* 18 (1962), 89-113.

75 Hans Thieme, "Die Rechtstellung der Frau in Deutschland," Société Jean Bodin, *Recueils,* 12 (1962): 351-376. He noted that following Barbarossa's precedent, *Weiberlehen* became more common, women holding Brabant in 1204 and Lünenburg in 1235.

76 Ermolaef, *Die Sonderstellung der Frau.*

[77] The condition of women of the aristocracy in 11th century Normandy is presently being examined by Anne Prah-Pérochon under the direction of Georges Duby, Collège de France (written communication).

[78] Duby, *Rural Economy,* p. 183.

[79] In Roman Law, the father of the bride, not her husband, provided the dowry and in areas influenced by Roman Law this arrangement was never abandoned. As early as the first codification of Lombard Law, it stipulated that if a father or brother married off a girl and gave her a dowry she should remain satisfied and should ask for no more. F. Niccolai, *La formazione del diritto successario* (Milan: Giuffre, 1940), shows the substitution of a *maritagium* for the daughter's share. This was the prevailing practice in Italy and Rothari's edict was incorporated into the statutes of the Italian cities. *Exclusio propter dotem* meant that preference was given to male descendants. See also, G. Rossi, "Statut juridique" in Société Jean Bodin, *Recueils,* 12, (1962), 115-133.

[80] Roger Bataille, *Le droit des filles dans la succession de leurs parents en Normandie* (Paris: Jouve, 1927).

[81] Even crown lands were alienated in this manner when kings turned them over to their brides with the right of unrestricted ownership. For example, Charles the Simple in 907, gave his bride extensive property from the royal fisc as her irrevocable property. The change is traced in great detail by Cornuey, *Le régime de la dos.*

FAMILY LIMITATION, SEXUAL CONTROL, AND DOMESTIC FEMINISM IN VICTORIAN AMERICA

Daniel Scott Smith

The history of women is inextricably connected with the social evolution of the family. The revitalization of the American feminist movement and the surge of interest in social history among professional historians during the past decade have combined to make the study of women in the family a crucial concern. The central insight of the new feminism—the critical relationship of family structure and roles to the possibilities for full participation by women in the larger society—provides an immediate impetus to the historical study of that relationship. To isolate a central historical question conceptually, however, is far easier than to examine it empirically. Women in the family do not generate written documents describing their ordinary life experiences. It is easier, for example, to describe historical attitudes toward women's proper role than to determine what the roles actually were at any given time. Only painstaking research into local history, a systematic study of personal documents describing ordinary behavior, and tracing life histories of women through manuscript lists can bridge this major gap in the historiography of American women.[1] At this point, then, a different approach seems necessary and useful.

An examination of three rather well-established quantitative indicators showing the relationship of the entire population of American women to the family suggests the hypothesis that over the course of the nineteenth century the average woman experienced a great increase in power and autonomy *within* the family. The important contribution women made to the radical decline in nineteenth-century marital fertility provides the central evidence for this hypothesis. Empirical data on the details of family limitation and the control of sexuality in the nineteenth century unfortunately are limited. However, an analysis of nineteenth century sexual ideology supports the theory that women

I wish to thank Carl Degler, A. William Hoglund, Peter Stearns, and especially Ellen Dubois for their comments and suggestions on an earlier version of this analysis; none of the above should be held responsible for its flaws and errors.

acquired an increasing power over sex and reproduction within marriage. The hypothesis that women's power increased within the nineteenth-century family also accords well with such important themes as the narrow social base of the women's movement in America before the late nineteenth century, the flourishing of women's groups opposed to female suffrage, and the centrality of the attack on aspects of male culture in such movements as temperance. A long-term perspective is essential for understanding the history of women in the family. I shall suggest how the situation of women varied in three periods: the pre-industrial (seventeenth and eighteenth century); industrial (nineteenth century); and the post-industrial (recent) phases of American society.

From the colonial period to the present, *an overwhelming majority*—from 89 to 96 percent—*of American women surviving past the age of forty-five have married* (Table 1). The proportion who never married was highest for those born in the last four decades of the nineteenth century. Small percentage changes represent, of course, thousands of women. While marriage was overwhelmingly the typical experience for American women, before the present century roughly a third of all females did not survive long enough to be eligible for marriage.[2] In addition, the numerically tiny minority who remained single had a far larger historical importance than their percentage would suggest. For example, 30.1 percent of 45-49-year-old native-white female college graduates in 1940 were unmarried.[3] Before the marked increase in life-expectancy in the late nineteenth and early twentieth century, the average American woman married in her early-to-mid-twenties, survived with her husband for some three decades, and, if widowed, spent an additional decade or so in widowhood.[4]

The implications of these figures for historians of women are obvious but must still be emphasized. Labor historians now realize that most workers historically did not belong to unions, black historians have been conscious that most Negroes were not in civil-rights organizations, and urban historians have discovered that groups other than politicians and elites dwell in cities. The search for the history of "anonymous Americans" has generally focused on population elements that in one sense or another have been defined as "social problems." For these groups there exists at least some information imbedded in contemporary myths and prejudices. It will be more difficult to write the history of the average or modal American woman, a person substantively akin to William Graham Sumner's Forgotten Man. She was, in 1880, for example, a 38-year-old white wife of a farmer living eight miles west-by-south of Cincinnati and the mother eventually of five or six children.[5] Intensive study of local records may reveal a surprising degree of social participation in church and voluntary associations and perhaps performance in other roles as well. Yet the primary statuses of the modal woman were those of wife and mother.

While nearly all American women have married, *married American women did not work outside the home until the twentieth century,* with the major increase coming in the last three decades (Table 2). Only one white married woman in forty was classified in the labor force in 1890 and only one in seven in 1940; today two-fifths of all married women are working according to official

TABLE 1
Percentage of American Women Who Never Married

Census or survey, and birth cohort		Age at enumeration	Percentage never-married
1910	1835-38	70-74	7.3
	1840-44	65-69	7.1
	1845-49	60-64	8.0
	1850-54	55-59	7.7
	1855-59	50-54	8.9
	1860-64	45-49	10.0
1940	1865-69	70-74	11.1
	1870-74	65-69	10.9
	1875-79	60-64	10.4
	1880-84	55-59	8.7
	1885-89	50-54	8.8
	1890-94	45-49	8.6
1950	1895-99	50-54	7.7
	1900-04	45-49	8.0
1960	1905-09	50-54	7.6
	1910-14	45-49	6.5
1965	1915-19	45-49	4.8
1969	1921-25	45-49	4.5
	1926-30	40-44	5.0

SOURCE: Calculated from Irene B. Taeuber, "Growth of the population of the United States in the Twentieth Century," Table 11, p. 40 in *Demographic and Social Aspects of Population Growth*, eds., Charles F. Westoff and Robert Parke, Jr., vol. 1, U.S. Commission on Population Growth and the American Future (Washington: Government Printing Office, 1972).

definition.[6] The increase in labor-force participation for single women in the twentieth century has been less dramatic. More generally, many indicators (an increase in single-person households for the young and widowed, the disappearance of boarders and lodgers from family units, the decline in the age at marriage, an increase in premarital intercourse, and the legalization of abortion and no-fault divorce) point to an emerging post-industrial family pattern in the post-World-War-II period. This major shift in the family has important implications for the periodization of women's history.

The final statistical trend presents an interesting historical problem. During the nineteenth century, some ninety percent of women got married, over ninety-five

TABLE 2
Female Participation in the Labor Force (in percentage)

Year	Total	White only		Native-white, age 35-44	
		Single	Married	Single	Married
1830[a]	(7)	---	---	---	---
1890[a]	12.1	35.2	2.5	39.3	2.3
1940[a]	26.9	47.9	14.6	73.6	17.9
1960[a]	34.1	45.5	29.6	76.5	29.9

	All Women			Age 35-44		
	Single	Married, husband present	Widowed, divorced, separated	Single	Married, husband present	Widowed, divorced, separated
1950[b]	50.5	23.8	37.8	83.6	28.5	65.4
1960[b]	44.1	30.5	40.0	79.7	36.2	67.4
1972[b]	54.9	41.5	40.1	71.5	48.6	71.7

[a] Stanley Lebergott, *Manpower in Economic Growth* (New York: McGraw Hill, 1964), Table A-10, p. 519.

[b] Bureau of Labor Statistics, summarized in *The New York Times,* January 31, 1973, pp. 20.

percent of the married were not employed outside the home, yet *women progressively bore fewer and fewer children*. The average number born to a white woman surviving to menopause fell from 7.04 in 1800 to 6.14 in 1840, to 4.24 in 1880, and finally to 3.56 in 1900 (Table 3). The same decline is also apparent in U.S. census data on completed fertility.[7] Between 1800 and 1900 the total fertility rate decreased by half. By the late nineteenth century, France was the only European country whose fertility rate was lower than America's.[8] Despite the demographic effects of a later marriage age and of more women remaining permanently single, from one-half to three-fourths of the nineteenth-century decline in fertility may be attributed to the reduction of fertility within marriage.[9]

The decline in marital fertility is of critical importance in structuring the possibilities open to the average woman. A fifteen-to-twenty-year cycle of conception-birth-nursing-weaning-conception (broken not infrequently by

TABLE 3

Total Fertility Rates (TFR) for Whites, 1800-1968

Year	TFR	Year	TFR	Year	TFR
1800	7.04	1860	5.21	1920	3.17
1810	6.92	1870	4.55	1930	2.45
1820	6.73	1880	4.24	1940	2.19
1830	6.55	1890	3.87	1950	3.00
1840	6.14	1900	3.56	1960	3.52
1850	5.42	1910	3.42	1968	2.36

SOURCES: For 1800-1960, Ansley J. Coale and Melvin Zelnik, *New Estimates of Fertility and Population in the United States* (Princeton: Princeton University Press, 1963), Table 2, p. 36; 1968 calculated from Irene B. Taueber, "Growth of the Population of the United States in the Twentieth Century," in *Demographic and Social Aspects of Population Growth,* eds. Charles F. Westoff and Robert Parke, Jr., U.S. Commission on Population Growth and the American Future, vol. 1 (Washington, D.C.: Government Printing Office, 1972), Table 7, p. 33.

spontaneous abortions) at the height of active adulthood obviously limits chances for social and economic participation as well as for individual development. Child-rearing must be added to this onerous cycle. The great transition in fertility is a central event in the history of woman. A dominant theme in the history is that women have not shaped their own lives. Things are done to women, not by them. Thus it is important to examine the extent to which nineteenth-century women did gain control over their reproductive lives.

Many forces, to be mentioned later, were clearly at work in curbing fertility, but the power of the wife to persuade or coerce her husband into practicing birth control deserves examination. While women did employ contraceptive methods in the nineteenth century (principally douching and the sponge), the major practices involved the control of male sexuality—*coitus interruptus* (withdrawal) and abstinence.[10] Following Kraditor's excellent definition of the essence of feminism as the demand for autonomy, sexual control of the husband by the wife can easily be subsumed under the label of "domestic feminism."[11]

Before marshalling empirical data showing the strengthening of the position of women within the nineteenth-century American family, it is first necessary to consider certain misconceptions about women's place in the industrial and pre-industrial periods. Many of the recent interpretations of the history of American women have been devoted to an autopsy of the "failure" of women's suffrage. According to Kraditor, late nineteenth-and early-twentieth-century American women became conservative and were co-opted into the general progressive movement.[12] In Degler's view, women lacked an ideology that could properly guide them to full status as human beings.[13] For O'Neill, the "failure" lay in the refusal of the movement to assult the ideology and reality of the conjugal family structure that sustained women's inferior position.[14] This "what-went-wrong" approach implicitly assumes the constancy of woman's role within the family, and, more damagingly, interprets the behavior and responses of women as deviations from a preconceived standard rather than as responses to their actual situations. The turn toward conservatism in the leadership of active American women, for example, is seen as a tactical mistake rather than as the result of interaction between the leaders and their female constituency.

The extremely low percentage of married women in the nineteenth-century labor force suggests that the domestic-sphere versus social-participation dichotomy is not appropriate for the interpretation of women's history during the industrial period. If the average woman in the last century failed to perceive her situation through the modern feminist insight, this did not mean she was not increasing her autonomy, exercising more power, or even achieving happiness within the domestic sphere. Rather than examining Victorian culture and especially the Victorian family at its heart through a twentieth-century perspective, it is more useful and revealing to contrast nineteenth-century values and institutions with their pre-industrial antecedents.

Misconceptions about women in the pre-industrial family fit integrally into the pessimistic view of the Victorian era derived from the modern feminist perspective. Having portrayed the nineteenth century as something of a nadir for women, by implication, all other eras must be favorable by comparison. In order to show that women are not inevitably entrapped by the family, it has seemed important to emphasize that somewhere or sometime the status and role of women were quite different. While cross-cultural evidence supports this argument adequately, more compelling are conclusions drawn from as little as two centuries ago in American or Western culture. Historians, however, have been properly cautious about more than hinting at a Golden Age for the pre-industrial American woman. There is, to be sure, a sharp difference between the pre-industrial and industrial family and the corresponding position of women in each. A conjugal family system, in the sense of the centrality of the married pair, in contrast to the dominance of the family line, did emerge in the United States during the early nineteenth century.[15]

The effects of this shift for women are complex. The conventional belief in the more favorable position of the average woman in pre-industrial society rests on three arguments: the intimacy and complementary nature of sex roles in an undifferentiated economy; Aries' thesis that the boundary between the pre-industrial family and society was very permeable; and finally, in the American case, the favorable implications for women of the relative female and labor scarcity on the frontier. The first argument may be compared to George Fitz-hugh's defense of slavery, but extreme subordination and superordination do not require a highly differentiated economy and society. The very absence of complexity in the pre-industrial family doubtless contributed to the subordination of women. While the identity of the place of work and residence in an agricultural economy inevitably meant some sharing of productive tasks by husband and wife, the husband's presence, given the prevailing ideological and cultural values, deterred the wife from gaining a sense of autonomy. Just as the gender stereotypes of masculine and feminine were not as rigidly defined as in the Victorian period, the prestige attached to the status of wife and mother was less than in the nineteenth century. Social prestige depended on the position of the woman's family in the hierarchical structure of pre-industrial society. Daughters and wives shared in the deference paid to important families. When this system collapsed in the nineteenth century, women of high-status families experienced considerable deprivation compared to their high-ranking colonial counterparts. Women born to more modest circumstances, however, derived enhanced status from the shift away from deference and ascription.

Although Aries has little to say about women, his thesis that the line between the Western pre-industrial family and community was not sharply delineated is of considerable importance here.[16] There does exist scattered evidence of women's nonfamilial activity, e.g., voting, operating businesses, etc., in the pre-industrial period. The incidence of women's nonfamilial activity over time, its relationship to family and conventional sex roles, and finally, its importance in the social structure as a whole have not been explored. The existing social history of colonial women has successfully demonstrated that wider participation was not unknown.[17] The details of such nonfamilial participation have been much more fully researched for the colonial period than for the nineteenth century. Spinsters almost certainly were more marginal and deviant in pre-industrial American society than during the nineteenth century. Only widows who controlled property may have been in a more favorable position. While changes in colonial America law permitted a married woman to exercise certain rights, these innovations related mainly to acting as a stand-in for a husband.[18] By negating the impact of male absence because of travel and death, these modifications in colonial law made the family a more efficient economic unit; historians should not confuse a response to high mortality and slow transportation with normative support for women's being outside the family. In fact, nonfamilial participation by pre-industrial women must generally be viewed as a substitution for the activities of absent husbands. In effect, a woman's activity outside the pre-industrial family was a *familial* responsibility.

Systematic evidence comparing the position of women in the pre-industrial and industrial phases of American society is scarce; what exists points to the comparatively unfavorable place of women in the earlier stage. In most populations, for example, women live considerably longer than men. Yet this was not the case in four (Andover, Hingham, Plymouth and Salem) of the five seventeenth-century New England communities studied to date. Only in seventeenth-century Ipswich did the typical pattern of longer survival for adult females exist.[19] In Hingham, furthermore, an inverse relationship between family wealth and mortality is apparent only for eighteenth-century married women, not for their husbands or children.[20] Literacy is a good index of the potential to perform complex tasks. The scattered published data on the frequency of signatures on documents suggest that there may have been some narrowing of the historic differential between male and female literacy during the eighteenth century. The gap, however, was not fully closed until the nineteenth century.[21] The sex differential in literacy is, of course, also a class differential. Compared to those of pre-industrial men, the burdens of life were harsh for women, particularly those of low status. Finally, the resemblance in that era of the sexual act itself to the Hobbesian state of nature is revealing. Marital sex, succinctly summarized by Shorter as "simple up-and-down, man on top, woman on bottom, little foreplay, rapid ejaculation, masculine unconcern with femine orgasm,"[22] perhaps mirrored the broader social relationship men and women.

It may be argued that America was not Europe and that the relative strength of the woman's movement in nineteenth-century America can be attributed to a decline from a more favorable situation during the colonial period. The existence of protest, however, is not an index of oppression, but rather a measure of the ambiguities and weaknesses of the system of control. It is ironic that the Turnerian frontier theory, implicitly biased by its emphasis on male experience, survives most strongly in the field of women's history.[23] As Domar has shown, however, labor scarcity and free land are intimately related to the institutions of slavery and serfdom.[24] The economic factor associated with the exceptional freedom of white American males was a precondition of the equally exceptional degree of suppression of blacks. For a group to gain from favorable economic conditions, it must be able to benefit from the operation of the market. While this was true for single women in the nineteenth century (but not in the pre-industrial period), it decidedly was not true for married women. Wives were not free to strike a better bargain with a new mate. What appears to be crucial in determining the turn toward freedom or suppresion of the vulnerable group are the ideology and values of the dominant group.[25] Neither the position of the labor force nor of women can be mechanistically reduced to simple economic factors.[26]

The empirical basis for the importance of the frontier in the history of women is not impressive. On the nineteenth-century frontier at least, the high male-to-female sex ratio was a transitory phenomenon.[27] For the entire American population, the high rate of natural increase during the colonial period quickly narrowed the differential in the sex ratio created by immigration.[28] The truth left in the frontier argument is also ironic. Women's suffrage undeniably came earlier in the West. That development, as Grimes has argued, reflected the potential usefulness of women as voters along the conservative wife-mother line rather than a recognition of Western women as citizens per se.[29] Farber's interesting analysis of the East-Midwest variation in marriage prohibition statutes points to a relative emphasis on the conjugal family in the newer areas of the country. Midwestern states tend to prohibit marriages of cousins while certain affinal marriages are illegal in the East and South.[30] In summary, then, the frontier and the general newness of social institutions in America benefitted women chiefly as part of the elevation of conjugality in family structure.

The majority of women in nineteenth-century families had good reason to perceive themselves as better off than their pre-industrial forebearers. This shift involved not merely the level of material comfort but, more importantly, the quality of social and familial relationships. Since being a wife and mother was now evaluated more positively, women recognized an improvement within their "sphere" and thus channeled their efforts within and not beyond the family unit. It is not surprising that contemporary and later critics of the Victorian family referred to it as patriarchal, since that was the older form being superseded. If a descriptive label with a Latin root is wanted, however, "maritarchal" would be more suitable for the nineteenth-century family. Men had inordinate power within the Victorian family, but it was as husbands—not as fathers. The conservative conception of woman's role focused, after all, on the submissive wife rather than the submissive daughter.[31] Nineteenth-century women, once married, did not retain crucial ties to their family of birth; marriage joined individuals and not their families.[32]

While the interpretation being advanced here stresses the significance of the new autonomy of women within the family as an explanation of the decline of fertility during the nineteenth century, this is not to deny the importance of economic, instrumental, or "male" considerations. The shift from agriculture, the separation of production from the family, the urbanization of the population, and the loss of child labor through compulsory education doubtless also contributed. Indeed, the wife's demand for a smaller family may have been so successful precisely because it was not contrary to the rational calculations of her husband. Since the fertility decline was nationwide and affected urban and rural areas simultaneously, attitudes and values as well as structural factors are obviously of relevance.[33] The romantic cult of childhood, for example, may have induced a change from quantitative to qualitative fertility goals on the part of parents.

The social correlates of lower fertility found in modern populations are relevant to this discussion of the history of American fertility. A common finding of cross-national studies, for example, is a strong negative relationship between fertility and female participation in the labor force.[34] The American historical record, however, does not provide much support for this theory. During the 1830-1890 period, there was probably only a slight increase in the labor-force participation of married women and yet marital fertility continuously declined.[35] During both the post-World-War-II baby boom and the fertility decline since 1957, labor-force activity of married women increased.[36] For lower fertility, what is important is the meaning women assign to themselves and their work, either in or out of the home.[37] Since work is compatible with a traditional orientation for women,[38] the converse may also be true. Finally, the strong relationship between lower fertility and the educational attainment of a woman may involve more than a response to the higher financial return of nonfamilial activity for the better educated.[39] Education may be a proxy variable for the degree to which a woman defines her life in terms of self rather than others.

Some quantitative support for the hypothesis that the wife significantly controlled family planning in the nineteenth century derives from a comparison of sex ratios of last children in small and large families, and an analysis of the sex composition of very small families in Hingham, Massachusetts. Most studies indicate that men and women equally prefer boys to girls.[40] Given a residue of patriarchal bias in nineteenth-century values, it is not an unlikely assumption that women would be more satisfied than men with girl children. A suggestive psychological study supports this notion. In a sample of Swedish women expecting their first child, those preferring a boy were found to have less of a sense of personal autonomy. Of the eleven of the eighty-one women in the sample who considered themselves dominant in their marriages, only two wanted sons. The "no-preference" women were better adjusted psychologically and scored higher on intelligence tests.[41] In short, the less autonomous and adjusted the woman, the more likely she is to want her first child to be a boy.

In Hingham marriages formed between 1821 and 1860, the last child was more likely to be a girl in small families and a boy in the larger families (see Table 4). The difference between the sex ratios of the final child in families with one to four children as compared to those with five and more is statistically significant only at the 0.1 level. Given the complexity of the argument here, this is not impressive. Small families, however, tended to contain only girls. Sixty percent of only children were girls (21 of 35); 27 percent and 17 percent of two-child families were both girls (14) and boys (9) respectively; and 14 percent and 6 percent of three-child families were all girls (9) and all boys (4) respectively. The independent probability of these differences is less than one in ten, one in four, and one in twenty respectively. With a slight biological tendency toward males in births to young women, these figures suggest that differing sex-preferences of husbands and wives may explain the pattern. On the other hand, twentieth-century sex-ratio samples show either no difference or a bias toward males in the sex ratio of the last-born child.[42] In the absence of very marked differences in the preference of husband and wives and with less than perfect contraceptive methods available to nineteenth-century couples, no extreme relationship should appear. This quantitative pattern does suggest that the Victorian family had a domestic-feminist rather than a patriarchal orientation.

TABLE 4

Sex ratio of last versus other children of stated parity and the probability of having another child according to sex of the last child: Hingham women in complete families marrying before age twenty-five between 1821 and 1860.

| Parity | Sex ratio | | Parity progression ratios | | |
	Last	Not last	Male last	Female last	Difference
1	57(22)	124(242)	.944	.885	+.059
2	113(32)	82(211)	.848	.855	—.037
3	69(49)	83(165)	.789	.756	+.033
4	83(42)	114(124)	.776	.716	+.060
5	107(31)	114(94)	.758	.746	+.012
6	237(22)	74(66)	.596	.826	—.230
7	150(20)	77(46)	.625	.764	—.139
8& +	124(47)	105(86)	.628	.667	—.039

NOTE: Sample sizes in parentheses. Chi-Square (1-4) vs. (5 and more) 2.882, significant at 0.1 level.
SOURCE: Daniel Scott Smith,"Population, Family and Society in Hingham, Massachusetts, 1635-1880," (unpublished Ph.D. dissertation, University of California, Berkeley, 1973), p. 360.

Recognition of the desirability and even the existence of female control of marital sexual intercourse may be found in nineteenth-century marital advice literature. In these manuals, "marital excess," i.e., too-frequent coitus, was a pervasive theme. Although conservative writers, such as William Alcott, proclaimed that "the submissive wife should do everything for your husband which your strength and a due regard to your health would admit,"[43] women rejected submission. In fact, Dio Lewis claimed that marital excess was the topic best received by his female audience during his lecture tours of the 1850s. The Moral Education Society, according to Lewis, asserted the right "of a wife to be her own person, and her sacred right to deny her husband if need be; and to decide how often and when she should become a mother."[44] The theme of the wife's right to control her body and her fertility was not uncommon. "It is a woman's right, not her privilege, to control the surrender of her person; she should have pleasure or not allow access unless she wanted a child.[45]

It should be emphasized that both the husband and the wife had good (albeit different) reasons for limiting the size of their family. In most marriages, perhaps, these decisions were made jointly by the couple. Nor is it necessarily true that the wife imposed abstinence on her husband. While *coitus interruptus* is the male contraceptive par excellence, the wife could assist "with voluntary [though unspecified] effort."[46] Withdrawal was, according to one physician, "so universal it may be called a national vice, so common that it is unblushingly acknowledged by its perpetrators, *for the commission of which the husband is even eulogized by his wife and applauded by her friends* [italics added]."[47] In the marriage manuals, withdrawal was the most denounced means of marital contraception and, it may be inferred, the most common method in actual practice.

There are serious questions about the applicability of this literary evidence to actual behavior. Even among the urban middle classes (presumably the consumers of these manuals and tracts) reality and ideology probably diverged considerably. Historical variation in sexual ideology doubtless is much greater than change in actual sexual behavior.[48] The anti-sexual themes of the nineteenth century should not, however, be ignored. One may view this ideology as the product of underlying social circumstances—the conscious tip, so to speak, of the submerged iceberg of sexual conflict. While the influence of this literature is difficult to assess, its functions can be examined. It can be argued that anti-sexual themes had little to do with family limitation. Nor was contraception universally condemned by respectable opinion. The *Nation* in June 1869 called family limitation "not the noblest motive of action, of course; but there is something finely human about it."[49] Male sexual self-control was necessary, it has been suggested, to produce ordered, disciplined personalities who could focus relentlessly on success in the marketplace.[50] The conventional interpretation of these anti-sexual themes, of course, is that Victorian morality was but another means for suppressing women. The trouble with these arguments is that men more than women should be expected to favor, support, and extend the operation of this morality.

To understand the function of this ideology we must examine the market system involving the exchange of services between women and men. In historical, pre-industrial, hierarchical society, male control and suppression of female sexuality focused especially on the paternal control of daughters. This system of control existed for the establishment of marriage alliances and for the protection of one's females from the intrusions of social inferiors. Sexual restrictiveness need not, however, imply direct male domination. In a system of equality between males in which females are denied access to other resources, a sexually restrictive ideology is predictable. Nineteenth-century mate-choice was more or less an autonomous process uncontrolled by elders. American women, as Tocqueville and others noted, had considerable freedom before marriage. Lacking economic resources, however, they could bargain with their only available good—sex. The price of sex, as of other commodities, varies inversely with the supply. Since husbands were limited by the autonomy of single women in finding sexual gratification elsewhere, sexual restrictiveness also served the interests of married women. Furthermore, in a democratic society, men could not easily violate the prerogatives of their male equals by seducing their wives. Thus Victorian morality functioned in the interest of both single and married women.[51] By having an effective monopoly on the supply of sexual gratification, married women could increase the "price" since their husbands still generally expressed a traditional uncontrolled demand for sex. Instead of being "possessed," women could now bargain. Respectable sexual ideology argued, it is true, that men should substitute work for sex. This would reduce the price that wives could exact. At the same time, according to the prevailing sexual ideology, marital sex was the least dangerous kind. In contrast to masturbation or prostitution, marital intercourse was evaluated positively. But, contrary to these ideological trends, prostitution appears to have increased during the nineteenth century. Whether or not prostitution was a substitute for marital sex or merely a reflection of the relative increase in the proportion of unattached males created by late marriage and high geographical mobility is uncertain. This brief economic analysis of the supply and demand of sex at least suggests the possibility that Victorian morality had distinctly feminist overtones.

In principle, Victorian sexual ideology did advance the interest of individual women. Whether or not this represented a genuine feminist ideology depends to some extent on the behavior of women as a group. The evidence seems to be fairly clear on this point. If women as individuals had wished to maximize their advantage, they could have furthered the devaluation of non-marital sex for men by drawing more firmly the line between "good" and "bad" women, between the lady and the whore. While mothers may have done this on an individual basis, for example, by threatening their daughters with the dishonor of being a fallen woman, collectively they tended to sympathize with the prostitute or fallen woman and condemn the male exploiter or seducer.[52] The activity of the New York Female Moral Reform Society is an instructive case in point.[53]

Historians have had some difficulty in interpreting the anti-sexual theme in nineteenth-century women's history. Although Rosenberg recognizes the implicit radicalness of the assault on the double standard and the demand for a reformation in male sexual behavior, she tends to apologize for the failure of sexual reformers to link up with the "real" feminism represented by Sarah Grimke's feminist manifesto.[54] More serious is the distortion of the central question of the periodization of women's history. Cott's labeling of the first half of the nineteenth century as a question of "the cult of domesticity vs. social change," Kraditor's similar choice of "the family vs. autonomy," and Lerner's dichotomy of "the lady and the mill girl" all perpetuate the half-truth that the family served only as a source of social stability and change for women occurred only outside of the family.[55] I am arguing here, however, that the domestic roles of women and the perceptions that developed out of these roles were not an alternative to social change but presented a significant and positive development for nineteenth-century women.

Linking the decline of marital fertility to women's increasing autonomy within the family—the concept of "domestic feminism"—conflicts with several other theories held by scholars. To stress the failure of the woman's movement to support family limitation, as the Bankses do in their analyses for England, ignores the possibility of a parallel domestic feminist movement. It may be more to the point that anti-feminists blamed the revolt against maternity and marital sexual intercourse on the public feminists.[56] The Bankses suggest that individual feminists may have fought a battle to gain control over their own reproduction.[57] The nineteenth-century neo-Malthusians and the woman's movement had different purposes; the former attempted to control the fertility of "others," i.e., the working classes, while the latter sought reforms in its own interest. Since mechanical means of contraception were associated with non-marital sex of a kind exploitative of women, the opposition of women to these devices was an expression of the deeper hostility to the double standard.

A more serious objection to identifying the increasing power and autonomy of women within the family as feminism is, of course, the existence of the parallel tradition of "real" or "public" feminism. This tradition—linking Wollstonecraft, Seneca Falls, Stanton, Anthony, and Gilman—at least partially recognized the centrality of the role and position of women in the family to the general subjugation of women in society. In contrast, the goals of domestic feminism, at least in its initial stage, were situated entirely within marriage. Clearly some explanation is needed of why both strands of feminism existed. A possible answer relates to the evolution of the family in the process of modernization. With the democratization of American society, prestige ascribed by birth declined. Women born into families of high social status could not obtain deference if they remained single; even if a woman married a man of equally high status, his position would not assure her prestige; his status depended on his achievement. The satisfactory and valued performance in the roles of wife and mother could not compensate for the loss of status associated with the family line in pre-industrial society. Thus public feminism would be most attractive to women of high social origin.[58] This conception of the woman as an atomistic person and citizen naturally drew on the Enlightenment attack on traditional social ties. The modeling of the Seneca Falls manifesto on the Declaration of Independence is suggestive in this regard.[59]

The liberal origins of public feminism were both its strength and its weakness. Because it emphasized a clear standard of justice and stressed the importance of human individuality, it was consistent with the most fundamental values in American political history. But it was also limiting as a political ideology in that it cast its rhetoric against nearly obsolete social forms that had little relevance in the experience of the average American woman, i.e., patriarchalism and arbitrary male authority. Paradoxically, public feminism was simultaneously behind and ahead of the times. Resting on eighteenth-century notions, it clashed with the romantic and sentimental mood of the nineteenth century. The social basis of the appeal of public feminism—the opportunity for married women to assume both family and social roles—would not be created for the average woman until the post-industrial period.

Domestic feminism, on the other hand, was a nineteenth-century creation, born out of the emerging conjugal family and the social stresses accompanying modern economic growth. Instead of postulating woman as an atom in competitive society, domestic feminism viewed woman as a person in the context of relationships with others. By defining the family as a community, this ideology allowed women to engage in something of a critique of male, materialistic, market society and simultaneously proceed to seize power within the family. Women asserted themselves within the family much as their husbands were attempting to assert themselves outside the home. Critics such as de Tocqueville concluded that the Victorian conjugal family was really a manifestation of selfishness and a retreat from the older conception of community as place. As one utopian-communitarian put it, the basic social question of the day was "whether the existence of the marital family is compatible with that of the universal family which the term 'Community' signifies."[60]

Community—"that mythical state of social wholeness in which each member has his place and in which life is regulated by cooperation rather than by competition and conflict,"[61]—is not fixed historically in one social institution. Rather, as Kirk Jeffrey has argued, the nineteenth-century home was conceived of as a utopian community—at once a retreat, refuge and critique of the city.[62] Jeffrey, however, does not fully realize the implications of his insight. He admits that the literature of the utopian home demanded that husbands consult their wives, avoid sexual assault on them, and even consciously structure their own behavior on the model of their spouses. Yet he still concludes that "there seems little doubt that they (women) suffered a notable decline in autonomy and morale during the three-quarters of a century following the founding of the American republic."[63] He suggests that women who engaged in writing, social activities, political reform, drug use, and sickliness were "dropping out" of domesticity. On the contrary, these responses reflect both the time and autonomy newly available to women. The romantic ideal of woman as wife and mother in contrast to the Enlightenment model of woman as person and citizen did not have entirely negative consequences—particularly for the vast majority of American women who did not benefit from the position of their family in society.

The perspective suggested above helps to explain why the history of the suffrage movement involved a shift from the woman-as-atomistic-person notion toward the ideology of woman as wife-and-mother. Drawing on the perceptions gained from their rise within the family, women finally entered politics in large numbers at the turn of the twentieth century. Given the importance of family limitation and sexual control in domestic feminism, it is not surprising that women were involved in and strongly supported the temperance and social purity movements—reform attempts implicitly attacking male culture. Since these anti-male responses and attitudes were based on the familial and social experience of women, it seems beside the point to infer psychological abnormality from this emphasis.[64]

In an important sense, the traditions of domestic and public feminism merged in the fight for suffrage in the early twentieth century. In a study of "elite" women surveyed in 1913, Jensen found that mothers of completed fertility actually exhibited more support for suffrage than childless married women.[65] Women in careers involving more social interaction, for example, medicine, law, administration, tended to favor suffrage more strongly than women in more privatistic occupations, for example, teaching, writing, art.[66] In short, the dichotomy between women trapped or suppressed within marriage and women seeking to gain freedom through social participation does not accurately represent the history of American women in the nineteenth century.

It has been argued that historians must take seriously the changing roles and behavior of women within the Victorian conjugal family. That women eventually attained a larger arena of activity was not so much an alternative to the woman-as-wife-and-mother as an extension of the progress made within the family itself. Future research doubtless will qualify, if not completely obviate, the arguments presented in this essay. Although power relationships within contemporary marriages are poorly understood by social scientists, this critical area very much needs a historical dimension.[67] The history of women must take into account major changes in the structure of society and the family. During the pre-industrial period, women (mainly widows) exercised power as replacements for men. In the industrializing phase of the last century, married women gained power and a sense of autonomy within the family. In the post-industrial era, the potentiality for full social participation of women clearly exists. The construction of these historical stages inevitably involves over-simplification. Drawing these sharp contrasts, however, permits the historian to escape from the present-day definition of the situation. Once it is clear just what the long-run course of change actually was, more subtlety and attention to the mechanism of change will be possible in the analysis of women's history.

[1] The attempt to examine systematically the lives of ordinary women is well under way; for example, see Theodore Hershberg, "A Method for the Computerized Study of Family and Household Structure Using the Manuscript Schedules of the U.S. Census of Population," *Family in Historical Perspective Newsletter* 3 (Spring 1973): 6-20.

[2] For a suggestive illustration of the impact of changing mortality on the average female, see Peter R. Uhlenberg, "A Study of Cohort Life Cycles: Cohorts of Native-Born Massachusetts Women, 1830-1920," *Population Studies* 23 (November 1969): 407-420.

[3] Wilson H. Grabill, Clyde V. Kiser, and Pascal K. Whelpton, *The Fertility of American Women* (New York: John Wiley & Sons, Inc., 1958), Table 67, p. 145.

[4] Robert V. Wells, "Demographic Change and the Life Cycle of American Families," *Journal of Interdisciplinary History* 2 (Autumn 1971): Table 2, p. 282.

[5] This modal woman was constructed from the median age of household heads (less four years) from U.S. Bureau of the Census, *Historical Statistics of the United States, Colonial Times to 1957* (Washington, D.C.: Government Printing Office, 1960), Series A-263, p. 16; from the center of population gravity, from *U.S. Statistical Abstract* (87th ed., 1966), Table 11; from the mean number (5.6) of children born to rural-farm women in the north-central region born between 1835 and 1844 and married only once, U.S. Bureau of the Census, Sixteenth Census., *Population; Differential Fertility 1940 and 1910, Women by Number of Children ever Born* (Washington: Government Printing Office, 1945), Table 81, p. 237; and from the fact that 51.3 percent of the workforce in 1880 was employed in agriculture, Stanley Lebergott, *Manpower in Economic Growth* (New York: McGraw Hill, 1964), Table A-1, p. 510.

[6] Some working women may have been counted as housewives by the census takers. Lebergott, *Manpower*, pp. 70-73, however, makes a cogent case for accepting the census figures.

[7] Grabill *et al.*, *Fertility*, Table 9, p. 22.

[8] Ansley J. Coale and Melvin Zelnik, *New Estimates of Fertility and Population in the United States* (Princeton: Princeton University Press, 1963), p. 41.

[9] Yasukichi Yasuba, *Birth Rates of the White Population in the United States, 1800-1860* (Baltimore: Johns Hopkins Press, 1961), Table IV-9, p. 119, attributes 64.3 percent of the Connecticut fertility decline between 1774 and 1890 and 74.3 percent of the New Hampshire decline between 1774 and 1890 to change in marital fertility. Longer birth intervals and an earlier age at the termination of childbearing contributed nearly equally to the decrease in marital fertility. See Daniel Scott Smith, "Change in American Family Structure before the Demographic Transition: The Case of Hingham, Massachusetts," (unpublished paper presented to the American Society for Ethnohistory, October 1972), p. 3.

[10] For a summary of the importance of withdrawal in the history of European contraception, see D. V. Glass, *Population: Policies and Movements in Europe* (New York: Augustus M. Kelley, Booksellers, 1967), p. 46-50.

[11] For this definition, see Aileen S. Kraditor, *Up from the Pedestal* (Chicago: Quadrangle Books, 1968), p. 5.

[12] Aileen S. Kraditor, *The Ideas of the Woman Suffrage Movement* (New York: Anchor Books, 1971).

[13] Carl N. Degler, "Revolution without Ideology: The Changing Place of Women in America," *Daedalus* 93 (Spring 1964): 653-670.

[14] William L. O'Neill, *Everyone was Brave* (Chicago: Quadrangle Books, 1969).

[15] My use of the term conjugal is intended to be much broader than the strict application to household composition. On the relatively unchanging conjugal (or nuclear) structure of the household see Peter Laslett, ed., *Household and Family in Past Time* (Cambridge: Cambridge University Press, 1972). For an empirical demonstration of the types of changes involved see my article, "Parental Power and Mariage Patterns: An Analysis of Historical Trends in Hingham, Massachusetts," in the special historical issue of *Journal of Marriage and the Family* 35 (August 1973).

[16] Phillipe Aries, *Centuries of Childhood: A Social History of Family Life*, trans. Robert Baldick (New York: Vintage Books, 1962).

[17] Julia Cherry Spruill, *Women's Life and Work in the Southern Colonies* (Chapel Hill: University of North Carolina Press, 1938) and Elisabeth Anthony Dexter, *Colonial Women of Affairs* (Boston: Houghton Mifflin Company, 1924).

[18] Richard B. Morris, *Studies in the History of American Law*, 2nd ed. (Philadelphia: Joseph M. Mitchell Co., 1959), pp. 126-200.

19 Maris Vinovskis, "Mortality Rates and Trends in Massachusetts before 1860," *Journal of Economic History* 32 (March 1972): 198-199. In the eighteenth century women began to live longer than men with the exception again of Ipswich.

20 Daniel Scott Smith, "Population, Family and Society in Hingham, Massachusetts, 1635-1880," (unpublished Ph.D. dissertation, University of California, Berkeley, 1973), pp. 225-227.

21 Scattered American data are available in Lawrence A. Cremin, *American Education: The Colonial Experience, 1607-1783* (New York: Harper Torchbooks, 1970), pp. 526, 533, 540. Also see Carlo M. Cipolla, *Literacy and Development in the West* (Baltimore: Penguin Books, 1969), Table 1, p. 14. Professor Kenneth Lockridge of the University of Michigan, who is undertaking a major study of literacy in early America has written me, however, that women using a mark may have been able to read.

22 Edward Shorter, "Capitalism, Culture and Sexuality: Some Competing Models," *Social Science Quarterly* 53 (September 1972): 339.

23 David M. Potter, "American Women and the American Character," in *History and American Society: Essays of David M. Potter*, ed. Don E. Fehrenbacher (New York: Oxford University Press, 1973), pp. 227-303.

24 Evsey D. Domar, "The Causes of Slavery or Serfdom: A Hypothesis," *Journal of Economic History* 30 (March 1970): 18-32.

25 See Edmund S. Morgan, "Slavery and Freedom: An American Paradox," *Journal of American History* 59 (June 1972): 3-29.

26 Stanley Engerman, "Some Considerations Relating to Property Rights in Man," *Journal of Economic History* 33 (March 1973): 56-65.

27 Jack E. Eblen, "An Analysis of Nineteenth Century Frontier Populations," *Demography* 2 (1965): 399-413.

28 See Herbert Moller, "Sex Composition and Correlated Culture Patterns of Colonial America," *William and Mary Quarterly* 2 (April 1945): 113-153 for data on sex ratios.

29 Alan P. Grimes, *The Puritan Ethic and Woman Suffrage* (New York: Oxford University Press, 1967).

30 Bernard Farber, *Comparative Kinship Systems* (New York: John Wiley & Sons, Inc., 1968), pp. 23-46.

31 Walter E. Houghton, *The Victorian Frame of Mind* (New Haven: Yale University Press, 1957), pp. 348-353.

32 See Smith, "Parental Power and Marriage Patterns . . ." *Journal of Marriage and the Family* (August 1973).

33 Grabill *et al., Fertility*, pp. 16-19. For insights based on differentials in census child-woman ratios see Yasuba, *Birth Rates*, as well as Colin Forster and G. S. L. Tucker, *Economic Opportunity and White American Fertility Ratios, 1800-1860* (New Haven: Yale University Press, 1972). For a brief statement of the structural argument see Richard Easterlin, "Does Fertility Adjust to the Environment?" *American Economic Review* 61 (1971): 394-407.

34 John D. Kasarda, "Economic Structure and Fertility: A Comparative Analysis," *Demography* 8 (August 1971): 307-317.

35 Lebergott, *Manpower*, p. 63.

36 Kingsley Davis, "The American Family in Relation to Demographic Change," in *Demographic and Social Aspects of Population Growth*, eds. Charles F. Westoff and Robert Parke, Jr. (Washington, D.C.: Government Printing Office, 1972), p. 245.

37 One study involving seven Latin American cities has suggestively concluded that the "wife's motivation for employment, her education, and her preferred role seem to exert greater influence on her fertility than her actual role of employee or homemaker." Paula H. Hass, "Maternal Role Incompatability and Fertility in Urban Latin America," *Journal of Social Issues* 28 (1972): 111-127.

38 Virginia Yans McLaughlin, "Patterns of Work and Family Organization: Buffalo's Italians," *Journal of Interdisciplinary History* 2 (Autumn 1971): 299-314.

39 For the relationship between fertility and individual characteristics see the special issue of the *Journal of Political Economy* 81, pt. 2 (March/April 1973) on "new economic approaches to fertility."

40 See the summary by Gerald E. Markle and Charles B. Nam, "Sex Determination: Its Impact on Fertility," *Social Biology* 18 (March 1971): 73-82.

41 N. Üddenberg, P. E. Almgren and A. Nilsson, "Preference for Sex of Child among Pregnant Women," *Journal of Biosocial Science* 3 (July 1971): 267-280.

42 In a study of early twentieth century *Who's Who*, cited by Markle and Nam, the sex ratio of the last child was 117.4 in 5,466 families, No differences appear in Harriet L. Fancher, "The

Relationship between the Occupational Status of Individuals and the Sex Ratio of their Offspring," *Human Biology* 28 (September 1966): 316-322.

[43] William A. Alcott, *The Young Man's Wife, or Duties of Women in the Marriage Role* (Boston: George W. Light, 1837), p. 176.

[44] Dio Lewis, *Chastity, or our Secret Sins* (New York: Canfield Publishing Company, 1888), p. 18.

[45] Henry C. Wright, *Marriage and Parentage* (Boston: Bela Marsh, 1853), pp. 242-255.

[46] Anon, *Satan in Society* (Cincinnati: C. V. Vent, 1875), p. 153.

[47] Ibid., p. 152.

[48] For a discussion of the gradualness of change in sexual behavior see Daniel Scott Smith, "The Dating of the American Sexual Revolution: Evidence and Interpretation," in *The American Family in Social-Historical Perspective,* ed., Michael Gordon (New York: St. Martin's Press, 1973), pp. 321-335.

[49] Quoted by George Humphrey Napheys, *The Physical Life of Women* (Philadelphia: H. C. Watts Co., 1882), p. 119.

[50] Peter C. Cominos, "Late Victorian Sexual Respectability and the Social System," *International Review of Social History* 8 (1963): 18-48, 216-250.

[51] Although the basic argument here was formulated independently, Randall Collins, "A Conflict Theory of Sexual Stratification," *Social Problems* 19 (Summer 1971): 3-21; and David G. Berger and Morton C. Wenger, "The Ideology of Virginity," (paper read at the 1972 meeting of the National Council on Family Relations) were very helpful in developing this theme.

[52] On attitudes toward prostitution, see Margaret Wyman, "The Rise of the Fallen Woman," *American Quarterly* 3 (Summer 1951): 167-177; and Robert E. Riegel, "Changing American Attitudes Toward Prostitution," *Journal of the History of Ideas* 29 (July-September 1968): 437-452.

[53] Carroll Smith-Rosenberg, "Beauty, the Beast and the Militant Woman: a Case Study in Sex Roles in Jacksonian America," *American Quarterly* 23 (October 1971): 562-584.

[54] Ibid.

[55] Nancy F. Cott, *Root of Bitterness* (New York: E. P. Dutton & Co., Inc., 1972): 11-14; Kraditor, *Up from the Pedestal,* p. 21; Gerda Lerner, "The Lady and the Mill Girl: Changes in the Status of Women in the Age of Jackson," *Midcontinent American Studies Journal* 10 (Spring 1969): 5-14.

[56] J. A. and Olive Banks, *Feminism and Family Planning in Victorian England* (Liverpool: Liverpool University Press, 1964); esp. pp. 53-57.

[57] Ibid., p. 125.

[58] In his book, *Daughters of the Promised Land* (Boston: Little, Brown, 1970), Page Smith argues that many prominent feminists had strong fathers. It might be that the true relationship, if any in fact exists, is between public feminism and high status fathers.

[59] Robert A. Nisbet, *The Sociological Tradition* (New York: Basic Books, 1966), ch. 3, esp. pp. 47-51.

[60] Quoted by John L. Thomas, "Romantic Reform in America, 1815-1865," *American Quarterly* 17 (Winter 1965): p. 677.

[61] Charles Abrams, *The Language of Cities* (New York: Viking Press, 1971), p. 60.

[62] Kirk Jeffrey effectively develops this theme in "The Family as Utopian Retreat from the City: The Nineteenth Century Contribution" in *The Family, Communes and Utopian Societies,* ed. Sallie Teselle (New York: Harper Torchbooks, 1972), pp. 21-41.

[63] Ibid., p. 30.

[64] For a psychological emphasis see James R. McGovern, "Anna Howard Shaw: New Approaches to Feminism," *Journal of Social History* 3 (Winter 1969-70): 135-153.

[65] Richard Jensen, "Family, Career, and Reform: Women Leaders of the Progressive Era," in *The American Family in Social-Historical Perspective,* Table 7, p. 277.

[66] Ibid., Table 2, p. 273.

[67] An analysis of recent literature of this important topic is presented by Constantina Safilios-Rothschild, "The Study of Family Power Structure: A Review 1960-1969," *Journal of Marriage and the Family* 32 (November 1970): 539-552.

THE FEMINIZATION OF AMERICAN
RELIGION: 1800-1860

Barbara Welter

The relationships among nineteenth-century reform movements in the United States, their overlapping of personnel, and their disparity and similarity in motivations and results are popular themes in social history.[1] In the women's movement, which concentrated on obtaining suffrage but had more specific and more diffuse goals as well, almost all of the leaders and most of the followers were active in other reforms. Indeed, the abolitionist, temperance, and peace societies depended on their women members to lick envelopes, raise money through fairs, and influence their husbands and fathers to join in the good work. Although sometimes frustrated and even betrayed by these other reform movements, the woman's movement on the whole benefitted from the organizational experience, political knowledge, and momentum generated by other reformers. At the same time American religion, particularly American Protestantism, was changing rapidly and fundamentally. Although not overtly tied to the woman's movement, these religious changes may have had more effect on the basic problems posed by women than anything which happened within the women's organizations or in related reform groups. Because of the nature of the changes and the importance of their results to women's role, American religion might be said to have been "feminized." The term is used here, like the term "radicalization," to connote a series of consciousness-raising and existential, as well as experiential, factors which resulted in a new awareness of changed conditions and new roles to fit these new conditions.

For the historian to attempt an analysis of the relationships between in-

This article is reprinted from *Problems and Issues in American Social History,* ed. William O'Neill (Minneapolis: Burgess Publishing Co., 1974), with the permission of the publisher.

stitutions and movements at a given point in time is a fascinating exercise in social history. It may well be an exercise in futility, however, because she lacks sufficient knowledge of the society she studies, or because the theories of change and social dynamics are applicable only to the present, or at least not to the particular segment of the past which she explores. The hazards of the sociological vocabulary, the limited number of sources (or the overwhelming magnitude of sources in some areas), and the difference between sociological and historical logistics and time are significant barriers.[2] Within these limitations this article proposes to discuss the process of "feminization," to apply this definition to religion in America in the first half of the nineteenth century, and to explore the results of a "feminized" religion.

In some ways the allocation of institutions or activities to one sex or another is a continuation of the division of labor by sex which has gone on since the cave dwellers. At certain times survival required that the strongest members of society specialize in a given activity. Once the basic needs of survival were met, other activities, not of current critical importance, could be engaged in. These more expendable institutions became the property of the weaker members of society which, in western civilization, generally meant women.[3] In the period following the American Revolution, political and economic activities were critically important and therefore more "masculine," that is, more competitive, more aggressive, more responsive to shows of force and strength. Religion, along with the family and popular taste, was not very important, and so became the property of the ladies. Thus it entered a process of change whereby it became more domesticated, more emotional, more soft and accommodating—in a word, more "feminine."

In this way the traditional religious values could be maintained in a society whose primary concerns made humility, submission, and meekness incompatible with success because they were identified with weakness. At the same time American Protestantism changed in ways which made it more useful to American society, particularly to the women who increasingly made up the congregations of American churches. Feminization, then, can be defined and studied through its results—a more genteel, less rigid institution—and through its members—the increased prominence of women in religious organizations and the way in which new or revised religions catered to this membership.

American churches had regarded it as their solemn duty to lead in building a godly culture, and the "city on the hill" which symbolized American aspirations had clusters of church steeples as its tallest structures.[4] In the nineteenth century the skyscraper would replace the steeple as a symbol of the American dream, and the ministers of God fought against this displacement. Politics captured the zeal and the time once reserved to religion, and the pulpits thundered against those men who mistakenly served power itself and not the Source of Power. The women's magazines and books of advice also warned against politics as a destroyer of the home. Cautionary tales equated the man who squandered his energy in political arguments with the man who drank or gambled; both were done at the expense of the home and religion.[5] Women and ministers were allies against this usurper, from which they were both excluded. Women were forbidden to go into politics because it would sully them; the church was excluded for similar reasons. Increasingly, in a political world, women and the church stood out as anti-political forces, as they did in an increasingly materialistic society, dominated by a new species, Economic Man. For women and the church were excluded from the pursuit of wealth just as much as they were kept out of the statehouse, and for the same rhetorical reasons. Both women and the church were to be above the counting house, she on her pedestal, the church in its sanctuary. Wealth was to be given them as consumers and as reflections of its makers.[6]

Democracy, the novel by Henry Adams, gives a fascinating insight into what happens when a woman ventures near the source of power, politics, and Washington. In venturing so near the sun she burns her wings and, limping badly, heads for home.[7] Human nature as defined by the church and human nature as defined by the state seemed totally different in the eighteenth century when the idea of original sin conflicted with the Jeffersonian hopes for perfectability through democracy. During the nineteenth century the churches moved toward the eighteenth-century premise of progress and salvation. Democracy, on the other hand, seems to have reverted to a more cynical or perhaps realistic view of human nature, closer to the Calvinist tradition. Women, however, precisely because they were above and beyond politics and even beyond producing wealth, much less pursuing it, could maintain the values of an earlier age. If women had not existed, the age would have had to invent them, in order to maintain the rhetoric of eighteenth-century democracy. As the religious view of man became less harsh, it meshed nicely with the hopes of Jefferson and Jackson.

The hierarchy, ministers, and theologians of most religions remained male. There were almost no ordained female ministers—Antoinette Brown Blackwell was an exception and not too happy a one—and few evangelical or volunteer female ministers.[8] When Orestes Brownson growled about a "female religion" he was referring largely to the prominent role which women played in congregations and revivals. However, he was also sniping at the tame minister, whom he caricatured with such scorn as a domesticated pet of spinsters and widows, fit only to balance teacups and mouth platitudes. Brownson's solution, to join the Church of Rome, undoubtedly was motivated by a number of personal and ideological reasons. Not the least of these, however, in the light of his contempt for feminine and weak Protestantism, was the patriarchal structure of the Catholic church.[9]

Besides their prominence during services, women increasingly handled the voluntary societies which carried out the social office of the churches, by teaching Sunday school, distributing tracts, and working for missions. This was only the external sign of the internal change by which the church grew softer and the religious life less rigorous. Children could be baptized much earlier. The idea of infant damnation, which Theodore Parker rightly said would never have been accepted had women been in charge of theology, quietly died around the middle of the century.[10] These changes were of great benefit to women's peace of mind.

Now, if a diary recorded the loss of a child, at least the loss was only a temporary one. Women who believed in heaven had found the prospect of parting forever from a beloved child because there had been no baptism or sign of salvation almost unbearable. The guilt with which these women so often reproached themselves at least need not concern eternal suffering, and the difference mattered to a believer.

The increasing softness and flexibility in the American churches was reflected in their role in social stratification as well as in their theology. The highly touted classless society of the Revolution was becoming increasingly stratified and self-conscious. The churches represented all different stages in the transition from wilderness to social nicety. The revivals had to fight not only hardness of heart but the lack of social prestige they entailed. Anglo-Catholicism had stood for a softer life both materially and spiritually since at least the time of the Glorious Revolution. It was also at least partially identified with higher social and economic status. The Episcopal church and the Presbyterian church were increasingly the churches of the well-to-do, and they offered their members a higher social status to correspond with their wealth. Women used their membership in a more prominent church as an important means of establishing a pecking order within the community.[11]

The male principle was rarely challenged by Trinitarians or Unitarians—whether three or one, God was male (and probably white). However, during the first half of the nineteenth century two ideas gained popularity which showed an appreciation for the values of femaleness—the first was the idea of the father-mother God and the second was the concept of the female Saviour. The assignation to God of typically female virtues was nothing new. Presumably a God who was defined as perfect would have all known virtures, whether or not he had a beard. The Shakers went farther, however, and insisted that God had a dual nature, part male and part female.[12] Theodore Parker used the same theme, in pointing out the need for female virtues, particularly the lack of materialism, and finding these virtues in a godhead which embodied all the symbols of mother's mercy along with father's justice.[13] Joseph Smith consoled his daughter with the thought that in heaven she would meet not only her own mother, who had just died, but she would also "become acquainted with your eternal Mother, the wife of your Father in Heaven." Mormon teaching posited a dual parenthood within the godhead, a father and a mother, equally divine.[14]

This duality of God the father with a mother God almost necessitated the idea of a female counterpart of Christ. Hawthorne in *The Scarlet Letter* has Hester muse on the coming of a female saviour. She reflects that because of her sin she is no longer worthy to be chosen.[15] The female saviour is an interesting amalgam of nineteenth-century adventism, the need for a Protestant counterpart to the cult of the Virgin, and the elevation of pure womanhood to an almost supernatural level. If the world had failed its first test and was plunging into an era of godlessness and vice, as many were convinced, then a second coming seemed necessary. Since the failure of the world also represented a failure of male laws and male values, a second chance, in order to effect change, should produce a different and higher set of laws and values.[16] The role was typecast for the "true woman," as the Shakers and the mystical feminists (and later the Christian Scientists) were quick to point out.

The changes in interpretation of Christ which made him the greatest of humans and stressed his divinity in the sense that all men are divine were also interpreted as feminine. The new Christ was the exemplar of meekness and humility, the sacrificial victim.[17] Woman too was the archetypal victim, in literary and religious symbolism. If Christ was interpreted as a human dominated by love, sacrificing himself for others, asking nothing but giving everything and forgiving his enemies into the bargain, he was playing the same role as the true woman in a number of typical nineteenth-century melodramatic scenarios. As every reader of popular fiction knew in the early nineteenth century, woman was never more truly feminine than when, on her deathbed, the innocent victim of male lust or greed, she forgave her cruel father, profligate husband, or avaricious landlord. A special identification with suffering and innocence was shared by both women and the crucified Christ. "She was a great sufferer," intoned one minister at a lady's funeral, "and she loved her crosses."[18]

The minister who interpreted this feminized Christ to his congregation spoke in language which they understood. By 1820 sermons were being preached on the "godless society" which spent its time and money on politics and the pursuit of wealth, "and were seen in church only at weddings and funerals."[19] Observers of the American scene noted frequently that American congregations were composed primarily of women and that ministers spoke to their special needs. Mrs. Trollope cast her cold eye over the flounce-filled pews and remarked that "it is only from the clergy that the women of America receive that sort of attention which is so dearly valued by every female heart through the world . . . I never saw, or read, of any country where religion had so strong a hold upon the women, or a slighter hold upon the men."[20] One reason for this prominence was, she felt, that only the clergy listened to women, all other ranks of man's society and interests were closed to them.

The hymns of this period also reflect the increasing stress on Christ's love and God's mercy. The singer is called upon to consider Christ his friend and helper. (To some degree, if the period before the Civil War is seen as one of feminization for Protestantism, the period following it might be termed a period of juvenilization, for increasingly the child as the hope and redeemer of his parents and society is stressed.) Woman's active role in the writing of hymns used in the Methodist, Presbyterian, Episcopal and Congregational hymnals at this time is very small. They contributed almost no music but did quite a few translations, particularly from the German. They were represented best in the lyrics to children's hymns.[21] It is perhaps significant that a hymn which became extremely popular at weddings had words written by a woman. "O Perfect Love" exhorts the young couple to emulate the perfect love of Christ in their own marriage:

O perfect life, be thou their full assurance
Of tender charity and steadfast faith,

Of patient hope, and quiet, brave endurance,
With childlike trust that fears not pain nor death.[22]

This was a pattern for domestic bliss much favored by women and the church, since it required the practice of those virtues they both cherished so highly—and which were found increasingly in only one partner of marriage. The implication is one which was made more explicit in the women's magazines: the burden of a marriage falls on the wife; no matter how hard her bed, it is her duty to lie on it. Marriage, and life itself, were at best endurance contests and should be entered in a spirit of passive acceptance and trust.

Another great favorite, "Nearer My God, to Thee," written by Sarah Adams in 1841, carried the same message: "E'en though it be a cross, that raiseth me; Still all my song would be, Nearer, my God, to thee, Nearer to thee." The hymns of the Cary sisters, Phoebe and Alice, repeated this theme with variations: "No Trouble Too Great But I Bring It to Jesus," and "To Suffer for Jesus Is My Greatest Joy," for example.[23] Another favorite stressed the total dependence of the singer on Jesus: "I Need Thee Every Hour."[24] The lyrics to this lend themselves all too well to the *double entendre* as those of us forced to sing it in Sunday schools remember to our shame, but in fairness to our interpretations it is true that the imagery in many of these hymns seems very physical. In the desire to stress the warmth and humanity of Christ, he becomes a very cozy person; the singer is urged to press against him, to nestle into him, to hold his hand, and so forth. A love letter to Christ was the only kind of love letter a nice woman was allowed to publish, and sublimation was as yet an unused word. If Julia Ward Howe had called her book of love lyrics a book of hymns even Hawthorne (who thought her husband should have whipped her for the book) would have approved.

The ultimate in such expressions of total absorption in Christ and a yielding up of an unworthy body and soul to his embrace is the widely-sung "Just As I Am, Without One Plea."

Just as I am, without one plea,
But that thy blood was shed for me,
And that thou bidd'st me come to thee,
O Lamb of God. I come. I come.

Just as I am, though tossed about
Without many a conflict, many a doubt;
Fightings and fears within, without,
O Lamb of God, I come, I come.

Just as I am, poor, wretched, blind;
Sight, riches, healing of the mind,
Yea, all I need, in thee to find,
O Lamb of God, I come, I come . . .

Just as I am: thy love unknown
Has broken every barrier down;
Now to be thine, yea, thine alone,
O Lamb of God, I come, I come.[25]

Since so many of women's problems were presumably physical and thus, like the weather, beyond help, it behooved them to endure what they could not cure. The "natural" disasters of childbirth, illness, death, loss of security through recurrent financial crises—all made "thy will be done" the very special female prayer, especially since submission was considered the highest of female virtues. In their hymns women expressed this theme of their lives, as a kind of reinforcement through repetition. However, the woman who wanted a more active role in religion than enduring, or even than teaching Sunday school, had several possibilities open to her at this time. She could become a missionary, she could practice an old religion in a new setting, or she could join a new religion which gave women a more active role.

The Christianizing of the West, indeed the domesticating of the West, was probably the most important religious, cultural, and political event of the first half of the nineteenth century.[26] So long as the West was unhampered by the appurtenances of civilization, including women with their need for lace curtains, for coffee cups and Bibles and neighbors within chatting distance—it was an unknown and possibly dangerous phenomenon. All the Protestant religions and Catholicism as well considered it their special duty to bring God and women westward as soon as possible. Law, order, and consumers were enhanced by the presence of churches and women. Missionary work appealed to women as a way to have an adventure in a good cause, although the Mission Boards which passed on applications were firm in ruling out "adventuring" as a satisfactory motive. Missions to far off China or Burma were usually denied to the single woman, but the determined girl could quickly find a husband in other zealous souls determined on the same career. The majority of American missionaries in the period before the Civil War stayed within the continent, taking the Christianizing of the Indians as their special challenge and duty.[27]

Mary Augusta Gray reflected on the interior dialogue with which she came to her missionary vocation:

> Ever since the day when I gave myself up to Jesus, it had been my daily prayer, "Lord, what wilt thou have me do?" and when the question, "Will you go to Oregon as one of a little band of self-denying missionaries and teach these poor Indians of the Saviour?" was suddenly proposed to me, I felt that it was the call of the Lord and I could not do otherwise.[28]

The missionaries to China usually went with a sense of doom and impending martyrdom, and the heroic exploits of such women as Ann Hasseltine Judson were fodder for this belief. Mrs. Judson had died, as she knew she would, far from home but near to Jesus, and thus her story became one much favored in children's biographical literature.[29] However, even the home missions carried the same possibility for martyrdom, as the fate of Narcissa and Marcus Whitman proved.[30] There is no question but that the aspiring missionary was aware of this possibility and that he welcomed it. Part of the reason for this is perhaps the theology of the period which taught that the death of a martyr assured heaven. The desire for death in the service of the Lord seems in the cases of some missionary women to be their strongest motive.

Eliza Spaulding, a Connecticut girl who had been converted at an early age, found that distributing tracts and doing visiting among the poor was not enough for her. She asked divine guidance about her future and received the impulse to go to Oregon. When her husband tried to dissuade her she replied: "I like the command just as it stands, 'Go ye into all the world' with no exception for poor health. The dangers in the way and the weakness of my body are his; duty is mine." Mrs. Spaulding survived the trip, leaving the following diary entry:

> Oh, that I had a crust of bread from my mother's swill pail. I cannot sit on that horse in the burning sun any longer. I cannot live much longer. Go on, and save yourself and carry the Book of the Indians. I shall never see them. My work is done. But bless God that He has brought me thus far. Tell my mother that I am sorry I came.

Her husband wrote to the Mission Board: "Never send another white woman over these mountains, if you have any regard for human life," but of course they did, for the women clamored to come to the Indians and to death, if need be.[31]

Although the West has been seen as a fertile ground for democratic innovations, this was not necessarily true for women's role. Simply because of the lack of numbers, most western churches gave women the freedom to participate in church services, and the West was the natural breeding place for such women evangelists as Carry A. Nation and Aimee Semple MacPherson. However, there was still pressure to conform to the traditional female role within religion, as Narcissa Whitman wrote shortly before her death:

> In all the prayer meetings of this mission the brethen only pray. I believe all the sisters would be willing to pray if their husbands would let them. We are so few in number, it seems as if they would wish it, but many prefer the more dignified way. My husband has no objection to my praying, but if my sisters do not, he thinks it quite as well for me not to.[32]

In the West, but especially in the East, the spirit of revival was strong during this period. The language, like that of the hymns, was sexual in its imagery and urged the penitent to "stop struggling and allow yourself to be swept up in His love." Obviously this kind of imagery had a familiar ring to women, for it was in similar language that they were encouraged to submit to their husbands. Whether in the divine or human order, woman was constantly urged to be swept away by a torrent of energy, not to rely on her own strength which was useless, to sink into the arms of Jesus, to become absorbed and assimilated by the Divine Will—in other words, to relax and enjoy it. The fantasies of rape were nourished by this language and by the kind of physical sensations which a woman expected to receive and did receive in the course of conversion. "A trembling of the limbs," " a thrill from my toes to my head," "wave after wave of feeling," are examples of female reaction to the experience of "divine penetration."[33]

Mrs. Maggie N. Van Cott, who called herself the first lady licensed to preach in the Methodist Episcopal church in the United States, told in her autobiography of receiving the "great blessing of fullness" as a result of which she was "perfectly emptied of self and filled with the Spirit of God." In showing her the way, God had announced "I am a jealous God; thou shalt have no other Gods before me," which she interpreted to mean that her Master wanted her complete devotion.[34]

Ellen G. White had a similar vision in which she was shown a steep frail staircase, at the top of which was Jesus. As she fell prostrate, her guide gave her a green cord "coiled up closely," which she could uncoil to reach Him. From that time "my entire being was offered to the service of my Master."[35]

Particularly interesting are those first-person accounts which discuss these experiences and then go on to say how little her husband understands her and how he tries to interfere with this wholehearted commitment to Christ. "Oh, the bliss of that moment, when my soul was enabled to cast all her care upon Jesus and feel that *her* will was lost in the will of God," rhapsodized Myra Smith at 4:14 a.m. one Sunday. Soon after she wrote: ". . . I find sweet comfort in doing the will of God instead of my own . . . I feel that God calls me to labor in a more special manner than he usually does female . . . I am not understood by my husband and children but I don't murmur, or blame them for it. I know they can't tell why I seem at times lost to everything around me."[36] Richard Hofstadter points out that revivalism was one of the manifestations of a pervasive anti-intellectualism in mid-nineteenth-century America.[37] However, it can be further annotated by means of the popular custom of dividing qualities into male and female categories. By this nomenclature all the intuitive and emotional qualities are most natural to women, all the cerebral and intellectual policies of linear thought the prerogative of men. When in terms of religion a more intuitive, heartfelt approach was urged it was tantamount to asking for a more feminine religious style.[38]

Although at the intellectual and, therefore, presumably "masculine" end of the scale, Transcendentalism might also be considered representative of certain feminine standards. One hanger-on to Transcendental circles and ardent feminist, Caroline Dall, saw Anne Hutchinson as the first Transcendentalist and, by extension, the first feminist in the American colonies.[39] Her argument was that antinomianism was an open door to the exercise of individual rights, by either sex or by any group. If God, not the ordained clergy, picks his spokesmen, then women are as likely as any to be among the chosen, for as any popular novel or sermon would have it, women are more religious, more noble, more spiritual than men—so all the more likely to be a vehicle for God's message. Besides, if one adheres to the principle of autonomous conversion, then there is no way to second-guess the Almighty; any soul may receive him, no sex barred. In the Quaker religion the Inner Light was expected to be equally indiscriminate in the choice of vessels to illuminate, and the Society of Friends practiced theoretical religious equality from its beginnings.

The Transcendentalists accepted a similar definition of equality before God. All souls were equally divine, without regard to sex or race. As Nathaniel Frothingham points out, Transcendentalism was a part of the woman's rights movement in the most profound sense in that it posited her as an innate equal, whose potential had been hampered by society. Ralph Waldo Emerson went through a number of phases in the formulation of his own position on women. His theoretical approach, contained in a number of essays, was sometimes at variance with the way in which he actually coped with his Aunt Mary, his two wives, and the irritatingly untheoretical presence of Margaret Fuller. In an essay, "Woman," Emerson tried to analyze the religious style of females. He concluded that ". . . the omnipotence of Eve is in humility." This, he continued, was the direct opposite of male style, which was to stress the necessity and potency of the male to the object loved. Religion perforce requires humility, since God does not depend on human strength. Women also, according to Emerson, possess to a high degree that "power of divination" or sympathy which the German romantics prized so highly. They have "a religious height which men do not attain" because of their "sequestration from affairs and from the injury to the moral sense which affairs often inflict . . ." It was therefore not surprising that "in every remarkable religious development in the world, women have taken a leading part."[40]

The idea of a regenerated reconstituted society was important to most members of the Hedge Club, and they looked optimistically toward an America in which man would leave behind his chains and emerge closer to nature and nature's God. The concept of ideal manhood and of ideal womanhood was often discussed at these meetings, and, of course, in Margaret Fuller's Conversations.[41] Womanhood was believed to be, in principle, a higher, nobler state than manhood, since it was less directly related to the body and was more involved with the spirit; women had less to transcend in their progress. "I trust more and more every opportunity will be offered to women to train and use their gifts, until the world finds out what womanhood is," wrote William Henry Channing. "My hope for society turns upon this; the regeneration of the future will come from the exalting influence of woman."[42] Most of these Transcendentalists were unconvinced about woman's role in politics, but they were totally convinced that she represented the highest and best parts of man.

Margaret Fuller contributed another important idea to the feminization of religion in her stress on the importance of the will. As historians such as John William Ward have pointed out, this belief in the power of the American will was typical of Jacksonian America. Like other aspects of the so-called American character, however, it did not necessarily hold true for all groups within the society. (David Riesman, for example, has reconsidered some of his statements about American character because of the remoteness of the female half of the population from his producer economy.)[43] For Margaret Fuller the will was the instrument to power for women even more than for men, and she set out to convince her world of this fact. Woman traditionally was urged to negate her will, or at least to yield it up to her father, her husband, and her God, Margaret Fuller told her to actively pursue her goals, to "elect" her destiny. Miss Fuller possessed Emerson's "spark of divinity" by which she was able to convince the young girls and wives who flocked to her that they too were divine and could go out and accomplish great (but unnamed) things. This preaching to women of their worth before God and man was sound Transcendental doctrine, but the stress on female worth, on transcendent womanhood, was a personal interpretation of Margaret Fuller. She gloried in her role of Sibyl, and relished all references to her as Delphic and/or oracular.[44] The cult of the will, as Donald Myers writes, found its triumph in Christian Science, also the religion of a woman, in which even death bows to positive thought.[45] Margaret Fuller's intent and fervid preoccupation with the making-over of the self presented a considerable threat to the men in her circle. For if sex itself, as well as health, family, education, income, all counted for nothing—what standards remained? It was perhaps the vicious circle of antinomianism after all; a religion open to the vagaries of God's choice or the boundaries of the human will is a religion without class lines and certainly without sex discrimination.

The Transcendentalists sought concrete expression of their philosophy in the community of Brook Farm, and the setting up of ideal communal societies was one way in which nineteenth-century religion expressed its dissatisfaction with past religious styles and its hope for the future. The equal rights of Transcendentalism were much in evidence at Brook Farm. One participant in that noble experiment recalled hearing a lecture on women's rights during his time in residence. The young lady speaker:

> . . . was much put out, after orating awhile, to note that her glowing periods were falling on dull ears. Our womenfolk had all the rights of our men-folk. They had an equal voice in our public affairs, voted for our offices, filed responsible positions, and stood in exactly the same footing as their brethen. If women were not so well off in the outer world, they had only to join our community or to form others like it.[46]

In the constitution of Brook Farm, as in many other communal societies, there are promises to the women members that they would be liberated from the tyranny of men and of the stove, and given greater freedom to develop their own identities. Charles Nordhoff, writing on the influence of women in utopian communities in 1875, found that women's participation in discussions gave them "contentment of mind, as well as enlarged views and pleasure in self-denial." Women in communal life found stability, which they needed and wanted, and many small comforts provided by the men for which "the migrating farmer's wife sighs in vain." The simplicity of dress typical of many groups was "a saving of time and trouble and vexation of spirit." Their greatest contribution to communal society was their "conservative spirit," which operated in the aggregate as it had in family life. Nordhoff concluded that women expressed the basic excuse for being of the communist society, for her "influence is always toward a higher life."[47]

When the commune moved from the planning stages to the land itself, somehow or other, women ended up in the kitchen or the laundry. Men might serve on these committees, but the overriding principle of the division of labor mandated their presence outdoors. In the communal societies whose records I studied, there is no record of any complaint on the part of the women, nor was there any recorded instance of women challenging their husbands on a given vote. There seems also to be no pattern of a woman's bloc.[48] But the actual role of women is less important than the way in which the changed pattern of social life was supposed to bring true equality to both sexes and liberate man from his own tyranny at the same time woman was freed from the conventional bonds of family life.

The Fourierist philosophy, which, so far as recorded sources tell, was never completely followed in the United States, provided for a good deal of sexual freedom within a definition of human nature which relied on "natural affinities." Parts of the human race were exempted from monogamy because they had "natural affinities" toward several members of the opposite sex. The fact that women, as well as men, might be expected to have these preferences was regarded as "peculiarly French," and not relevant to the American phalanx.[49]

Within the Americanized version of Fourierism there was much "wholesome intercourse" between the sexes. The opportunity to work and study and talk together was rare enough for middle-class American youth, and the phalanxes gave them much more freedom than most families allowed. The great charm of the communal life, one remembered fondly long after the community itself was a thing of the past, "was in the free and natural intercourse for which it gave opportunity, and in the working of the elective affinities."[50] The young women who participated in these experiments were emboldened to pursue lives as teachers or reformers after they left the phalanx. The Transcendental idea of the infinite worth of the individual and his ability to work out his destiny was greatly appealing to these young women. Even if women continued to do woman's work and find their greatest individual destiny in monogamous marriage, there was a statement of equality and of alternatives on the record.

The experiment at Oneida, conducted by John Humphrey Noyes as an example of his Perfectionist religion, was a particularly interesting application of new religion to women. One of the avowed purposes of the Oneida community was to give women "extended rights" within "an extended family." The way in which Noyes defined these rights was sharply criticized by his contemporaries and has not received very sympathetic treatment from historians. In many ways he really was, as he claimed to be, "woman's best friend." Noyes believed that the search for complete perfection began with control over one's own body. For women this was a complicated phenomenon, involving not only the marital rights but the right to choose whether she wished to have children. Noyes spoke very cogently about the trauma of the nineteenth-century woman, who bore her children with such pain and hope, and saw them die as infants.[51] In a society which defined woman as valuable largely in relation to her ability to bear children, it was logical that women thought of their own worth in those terms. When a child died it was an affirmation of personal guilt and possibly sin. What have I done, the bereaved mother asked her God, that I should be punished? Pages of women's diaries are filled with personal recriminations. For months she flagellated herself with the remedies she might have used, the errors of judgment she could have avoided, the ways in which she might have offended a jealous God. Noyes proposed to define her worth in different terms: she was a loving companion and "yoke-fellow" on the road to perfection. Childbearing was only part of her duty, to be engaged in sparingly and under controlled conditions, and to be separated from sex.[52] In terms of woman's self-image this proposal was one of the most radical of the century.

The form of birth control used by Noyes, which he called "male continence," consisted in "self-control" which prolonged intercourse but stopped the act short of ejaculation. Interestingly enough, this insistence on control was only for the man; there was no limit to the amount of pleasure a woman was allowed to get from the act. Moreover, sexual intercourse was accepted as a good in itself, completely outside the propagation of the species, and as an important means of self-expression for both sexes. Noyes went so far in identifying the sex act with Perfectionism as to assert that sexual intercourse was practiced in heaven. This insistence on the joys of sex was rare enough, but, couched in terms of a conjugal relation which promised equal rights of choice and no penalty of child-bearing on the woman, it was extraordinary. Perfectionism stressed the "giving, not the claiming," the act of loving, rather than the social and economic benefits of marriage.[53] In these ways, it acceded to the feminine spirit and role. The nineteenth-century belief that "love is a game, nothing more to a man/But love to a woman is life or death," that "love is woman's whole existence," was applied by Noyes to both sexes. "We should pray, give us this day our daily love, for what is love but the bread of the heart. We need love as much as we need food and clothing, and God knows it. . . ."[54] In the popular jargon of phrenology, Noyes separated "amativeness" from both "union for life" and "procreativeness." In the phrenological manuals, amativeness was considered to be particularly well developed in men; the other two qualities, along with "philoprogenitiveness" to be peculiarly suited to female skulls.[55] Noyes stressed love for both sexes and freedom of choice for both, which gave to women the continuation of her preoccupation with love plus the right to a repetitive use of her loving. Marriage at Oneida was a working out of the feminine rhetoric of love on a sequential basis.

Although Mormonism was treated as a great foe of women's rights, and even its female proponents agreed that it placed the male in a dominant role, it had certain components which made it part of the overall movement toward "feminization." Like Perfectionism it claimed to be acting in the name of a better life for women. "No prophet or reformer of ancient or modern times has surpassed, nay, has equalled, the Prophet Joseph Smith in the breadth and scope of the opportunities which he accorded womanhood," wrote a dutiful and satisfied daughter of both the Prophet and Zion.[56] Mormonism required its followers to accept the words of their spiritual father, without murmur, and to obey the precepts of authority. The important concept of the Mormon priesthood is one which excludes women (as well as blacks by some interpretations). However, Joseph Smith, when the women of this group asked him for a written constitution for their relief society, told them he would give them "something better for them than a written constitution . . . I will organize the sisters under the priesthood after a pattern of the priesthood . . . The Church was never perfectly organized until the women were thus organized."[57]

Thus the women of the Church of Jesus Christ of the Latter Day Saints claimed that they were admitted as "co-workers and partners" in its important work of attaining salvation. They were in the priesthood only when taken by their husbands, and only with their husband could they enter into a special heaven. Their consent was required for plural marriage, which became their passport—again, only with their husbands—to the highest stages of celestial bliss. And yet, patriarchal as it was, women were not ignored by this new religion. Indeed, they were given explicit and critical directions for salvation. No man could get to heaven alone, by any combination of faith or good works; he had to come bringing his family with him. Women could legitimately claim that Mormonism recognized their importance more than any other religion because it tied them to their husbands for all time and eternity. Motherhood was stressed in Utah even more than in the rest of American society, but it was the importance of producing souls not bodies that counted. Since every woman, in theory, could be united to the man of her choice, she could go to heaven with her love, not her forced compromise. Recognizing the fact that society gave women status only as a married woman and as a mother, the Mormons gave each woman the opportunity to have that coveted status in this life and in the next. What is surprising is not the formulation of celestial marriage, but the fervor with which Mormon women defended it as important to their ideas of themselves as valuable and valid persons.[58]

Like the Church of the Latter Day Saints, Roman Catholicism during this pre-Civil War period had both masculine and feminine manifestations. The patriarchal system of authority, which so pleased Orestes Brownson, has already been mentioned. The diatribes against Rome which were prevalent in the 1830s and 1840s stressed this authoritarian and anti-democratic aspect of the church. In other words, Catholics were not allowed to exercise their masculine prerogatives of intellectual autonomy and independent judgment. When a modest number of conversions to Roman Catholicism occurred during the last days of Brook Farm, some observers found the cause to be the discouragement and disappointment which the failure of that experiment created in its members. Most of the converts were female, and disparaging statements were made about the need to abandon the heritage of the New England Protestant (masculine) church to find solace in a more soothing, structured (feminine) religion.[59]

The letters of the converted Fourierists do nothing to deny that they found the Church of Rome more suitable to their needs, but their emphasis is not on feminine dependence but on womanly warmth. Sophia Ripley wrote to a sympathetic friend that she found "the coldness of heart in Protestantism and my own coldness of heart in particular" to be repugnant. After her conversion she saw herself clearly for the first time: "I saw that all through life my ties with others were those of the intellect and imagination, and not human heart ties; that I do not love anyone. I never did, with the heart, and of course never could have been worthy in any relation." Catholicism united her for the first time with humanity, and that chill intellectual pride which New Englanders wore like Lady Eleanor's mantle at last melted away. "I saw above all that my faith in the Church was only a reunion of my intellect with God," and not a union of hearts. To her mentor Bishop Hughes she poured out her fears that "this terrible deathlike coldness" had produced a "heart of stone" which even the love of

Christ could not melt. He reassured her that if she had been born in the Church perhaps her nature would have been softened, but she must offer to God not the heart she coveted but the heart she had: "Oh God, take this poor cold heart of mine, and make of it what thou wilt . . . This heart of yours is a cross which you must bear to the end if needs be."[60] Catholicism, then, at least to some of its members, incorporated the love and warmth so characteristic of women and so necessary to them.

Like Mormonism, Roman Catholicism was also regarded as a religion for the many, not the few. This sense of religion as a means of keeping down intellectual arrogance and spiritual pride is one which accords with a subtle but important aspect of female definition during this period. In Hawthorne's stories and novels the woman is the symbol of the earth, the tie with domestic detail and bodily warmth which prevents man from soaring too high or sinking too low.[61] Louis Auchincloss has called women "guardians and caretakers" because of their role in preserving literary and cultural traditions.[62] Inasmuch as religion is concerned they might as well be termed "Translators and Vulgarizers." In the Transcendental novel, *Margaret*, Sylvester Judd says of woman: "She translates nature to man and man to himself."[63] Women, in religion, as in popular taste, take the bold and bitter and make it bland. One critic of American conformity blames the low standards of American culture on the fact that women are the audience and arbiters. "Averse to facing the darker brutal sides of existence, its uncertainty and irrationality, they prefer the comforting assurance that life is just bitter enough to bring out the flavor of its sugared harmonies."[64] Women in the first half of the nineteenth century took Christianity and molded it to their image and likeness.

"The curse of our age is its femininity," complained Orestes Brownson. "Its lack, not of barbarism, but of virility."[65] These changes, which annoyed Brownson as much in literature as in religion, made women as well as men conscious of their virtues. Womanhood and virtue became almost synonymous. Although the values of the nineteenth century have predominated during the twentieth century, it becomes increasingly more clear that they are not the only values and that the so-called feminine virtues may assume more than rhetorical significance. The giving over of religion to women, in its content and in its membership, provided a repository for these female values during the period when the business of building a nation did not immediately require them. In order to do this, it was necessary first to assign certain virtues to women and, then, to institutionalize these virtues. The family, popular culture, and religion were the vehicles by which feminine virtues were translated into values.

Religion carried with it the need for self-awareness, if only for the examination of conscience. Organizational experience could be obtained in many reform groups, but only religion brought with it the heightened sense of who you were and where you were going. Women in religion were encouraged to be introspective. What they found out would be useful in their drive towards independence. The constant identification of woman with virtue and with religion reinforced her own belief in her power to overcome obstacles, since she had her own superior nature and God's own Church, whichever it might be, behind her. Religion in its emphasis on the brotherhood of man developed in women a conscious sense of sisterhood, a quality absolutely essential for any kind of meaningful woman's movement. The equality of man before God expressed so effectively in the Declaration of Independence had little impact on women's lives. However the equality of religious experience was something they could personally experience, and no man could deny it to them.

NOTES

[1] Martin Duberman has done this very effectively in his introduction to *The Anti-Slavery Vanguard: New Essays on the Abolitionists* (Princeton: Princeton University Press, 1965) and his biography of James Russell Lowell (Boston: Houghton Mifflin Co., 1966). Alice Felt Tyler, *Freedom's Ferment: Phases of American Social History to 1860* (Minneapolis: University of Minnesota Press, 1944) and Arthur M. Schlesinger, Sr., *The American as Reformer* (Cambridge: William H. Wise and Co., 1951) attempt a synthesis of the reform movements of the nineteenth century. A contemporary account of the nature of the reformer by Ralph Waldo Emerson, "Man the Reformer," in Ralph Waldo Emerson, *Nature, Addresses, and Lectures,* ed. Edward Waldo Emerson (Boston: William H. Wise and Co., 1903) is the first and perhaps the best attempt at this kind of social history.

[2] For example, Max Weber, *The Theory of Social and Economic Organization,* trans. A. M. Henderson (Glencoe, Ill.: The Free Press, 1957); Robert Merton, *Social Theory and Social Structure,* rev. ed. (Glencoe, Ill.: The Free Press, 1960); Talcott Parsons, *Structure and Process in Modern Society* (Glencoe, Ill.: The Free Press, 1960); Richard H. Tawney, *Religion and the Rise of Capitalism* (New York: Harcourt, Brace and Co., 1922); W. Seward Salisbury, *Religion in American Culture* (Homewood, Ill.: The Dorsey Press, 1964); Hadley Cantril, *The Psychology of Social Movements* (New York: Wiley, 1941); Cyclone Covey, *The American Pilgrimage* (Stillwater, Oklahoma: Oklahoma State University Press, 1960), and David O. Moberg, *The Church As a Social Institution: The Sociology of American Religion* (Englewood Cliffs, N.J.: Prentice-Hall, 1962).

[3] See especially Robert Briffault, *The Mothers: The Matriarchal Theory of Social Origins* (New York: The Macmillan Co., 1931) and Johann Jakob Bachofen, *Myth, Religion and Mother Right,* trans. Ralph Manheim (Princeton, New Jersey: Princeton University Press, 1967).

[4] For basic histories of American religion see Winthrop Hudson, *American Protestantism* (Chicago: University of Chicago Press, 1961); W.W. Sweet, *The Story of Religions in America* (New York: Harper and Brothers, 1930); W.L. Sperry, *Religion in America* (New York: The University Press, 1946); T.C. Hall, *The Religious Background of American Culture* (Boston: Little, Brown, and Co., 1930); J.W. Smith and A.L. Jamison, eds., *Religion in American Life* (Princeton: Princeton University Press, 1961), and E.S. Bates, *American Faith: Political and Economic Foundations* (New York: W.W. Norton and Co., 1940).

[5] For example, Eliza W. Farnham, *Woman and Her Era,* 2 vols. (New York: A.J. Davis and Co., 1964), and Charlotte Perkins Stetson Gilman, *His Religion and Hers: A Study of the Faith of Our Fathers and the Work of Our Mothers* (New York and London: The Century Co., 1923).

[6] A classic account is in Thorstein Veblen, *The Theory of the Leisure Class* (New York: The Macmillan Co., 1919). In nineteenth-century tariff policy, women are urged to consume only goods manufactured at home. In his report on manufactures in 1790, Alexander Hamilton urged the adoption of manufacturing as a means of providing employment for women, an argument approved of by the nineteenth-century economist Matthew Carey. However, the use of women as cheap labor

paid scarcely any lip service to these rhetorical rationalizations, and Veblen's theory of women as consumers and symbols of prosperity increasingly applied only to the middle classes.

[7] Henry Adams, *Democracy: An American Novel* (New York: H. Holt and Co., 1882).

[8] The best brief sketch of Antoinette Brown Blackwell is by Barbara M. Solomon in *Notable American Women: 1607-1950*, 3 vols., 1: 158-160 (Cambridge, Mass.: The Belknap Press for Harvard University Press, 1970), hereafter referred to as NAW. Other biographies are Laura Kerr, *Lady in the Pulpit* (New York: Woman's Press, 1951) and Elinor Rice Hays, *Those Extraordinary Blackwells* (New York: Harcourt, Brace and World, 1967). Blackwell became increasingly dissatisfied with pastoral work and the Congregational Church and by 1854, after one year's service, resigned her pulpit to do volunteer work among the poor and mentally disturbed. In later life, after her family was raised, she returned to the ministry, where she campaigned for woman suffrage. Blackwell was a philosopher rather than a theologian and, like her sister-in-law Elizabeth, was more concerned with the application of her profession to women's life than in achieving distinction in her own field.

[9] *The Works of Orestes A. Brownson, Collected and Arranged by Henry F. Brownson*, 20 vols. (New York: AMS Press, 1966) give a complete picture of Brownson's views on women. Briefly, he was opposed to the "woman worship" of his age, and horrified at the woman's movement because it preached interference with marriage and procreation. "Of course we hold that the woman was made for the man, not the man for the woman, and that the husband is the head of the wife, even as Christ is the head of the Church. . . ." (18:386). He saw the weakening of American family life as the greatest crisis of the age, and the women's movement, in its stress on individual rights, hastened the dissolution of the family as a social unit and contributed to the disastrous trend of isolation (18: 388). Moreover, the woman's movement was yet another indication of the increasing "spirit of insubordination" in society and like other such movements required "no self-sacrifice or submission of one's will (18:416). He was convinced that its leaders were not only opposed to the Christian family, "but to Christianity" itself" (18:414).

[10] Quoted in Henry Steele Commager, *Theodore Parker* (Boston: Little, Brown and Co., 1936), p. 150 and in Theodore Parker, *A Discourse of Matters Pertaining to Religion* (Boston: C.C. Little and J. Brown, 1842), p. 201. The issue of infant damnation led several Congregational ministers into the more permissive theology of Unitarianism, including Sheba Smith and Antoinette Brown Blackwell. Barbara M. Cross, *Horace Bushnell: Minister to a Changing America* (Chicago: University of Chicago Press, 1958) deals with one minister's solution to the tensions of change. Unitarian theology is covered fully in E.M. Wilbur, *History of Unitarianism*, 2 vols., (Cambridge, Mass.: Harvard University Press, 1945-1952).

[11] E. Digby Baltzell, *The Protestant Establishment: Aristocracy and Caste in America* (New York: Random House, 1964); Henry F. May, *Protestant Churches and Industrial America* (New York: Harper and Brothers, 1949); Louis Wright, *Culture on the Moving Frontier* (Bloomington, Indiana: University of Indiana Press, 1955), and Moberg, *Church As a Social Institution*.

[12] *Testimony of the Life, Character, Revelations and Doctrines of Our Ever Blessed Mother, Ann Lee and the Elders With Her; Through whom the word of eternal life was opened on this day of Christ's Second Appearing; Collected from living witnesses, by order of the ministry, in union with the Church* (Hancock, Massachusetts: The Society Press, 1816). A basic history of the Shakers is Marguerite Melcher, *The Shaker Adventure* (Princeton: Princeton University Press, 1941).

[13] Theodore Parker, "A Sermon of the Public Function of Woman," preached at the Music Hall, March 27, 1863 (Boston: Little, Brown, and Co.; 1853), and in many other sermons.

[14] Susa Young Gates, *History of the Young Ladies' Mutual Improvement Association of the Church of Jesus Christ of Latter Day Saints* (Salt Lake City: The Desert News, 1911), pp. 16ff. Eliza R. Snow Smith, wife of both Joseph Smith and Brigham Young, wrote a hymn on this theme, "O My Father," in *Poems, Religious, Historical and Political* (Salt Lake City: Latter Day Saints Printing and Publishing Establishment, 1877), p. 173.

[15] Nathaniel Hawthorne, *The Scarlet Letter* (Boston: Ticknor, Reed, and Fields, 1850), "Earlier in life, Hester had vainly imagined that she herself might be the destined prophetess, but had long since recognized the impossibility that any mission of divine and mysterious truth should be confided to a woman stained with sin, bowed down with shame, or even burdened with a life-long sorrow. The angel and apostle of the coming revelation must be a woman indeed, but lofty, pure, and beautiful; and wise, moreover, not through dusky grief, but the ethereal medium of joy; and showing how sacred love should make us happy, by the truest test of a life successful to such an end" (240). This new saviour will reveal "a new Truth" to re-order the relations between men and women.

[16] This idea is set out most clearly in Eliza W. Farnham, *Woman and Her Era*, 2 vols. (New York: A.J. Davis and Co., 1964).

[17] A history of the major theological and social changes in Christianity could be written in which the primary sources were biographies of Christ. A perceptive treatment of this subject is Edith Hamilton, *Witness to the Truth: Christ and His Interpreters* (New York: W.W. Norton, 1948). Another sort of survey is *Christ In Poetry*, an anthology compiled and edited by Thomas Curtis Clark and Hazel Davis Clark (New York: Association Press, 1952). Two popular nineteenth-century biographies were Lyman Abbott, *Jesus of Nazareth: His Life and Teachings* (New York: Harper and Brothers, 1869) and Frederic William Farrar, *The Life of Christ* (New York: World Publishing Co., 1874). A sample of the "Sunday School" biography is Caroline Wells Dall, *Nazareth* (Washington, D.C.: Privately Printed, 1903). Dall saw the mission of the Saviour as the revelation of "the universal Fatherhood of God, the common brotherhood of man" and the repudiation of the "old dogma of a corrupt nature by showing how Godlike human life could be" (p. 24).

[18] C.A. Bartol, "The Image Passing Before Us: A Sermon After the Decease of Elizabeth Howard Bartol," (Boston: Cupple, Upham and Co., 1883).

[19] Theodore Parker had several sermons on this subject, including "A Sermon of Merchants" (November 22, 1846); "A Sermon on the Moral Condition of Boston" (February 11, 1849); "A Sermon on the Spiritual Condition of Boston" (February 18, 1849); and "A Sermon on the Moral Dangers Incident to Prosperity," (November 5, 1854).

[20] Frances Trollope, *Domestic Manners of the Americans* (1832; New York: The Viking Press, 1949), p. 75. This American phenomenon (which has parallels in most Western countries) of women forming the majorities of church congregations, has been explained in various ways. The way most favored by the nineteenth century involved the natural predelection of women for good and therefore for religion. One twentieth-century writer believes that church-going is accounted for largely by a "Psychology of Bereavement." The Puritans were bereft of England, the nineteenth-century woman was bereft of her children (or her personhood), and so forth. Therefore insofar as the individual American was pleased with himself, self-confident, and victorious over nature or property he had, presumably, increasingly less need for church (Covey, *American Pilgrimage*, pp. 44-69). Another sociological explanation believes that women are "conditioned to react in terms of altruism and cooperation rather than egocentrism and competition," and therefore are prime candidates for submission to external authority in both worlds. W. Salisbury, *Religion in American Culture*, p. 88. Other explanations stress the supposed attraction of children to authority figures of the opposite sex. God is the father, ergo Oedipus aeternus. Woman's supposed innate masochism might, it could be argued, produce more guilt feelings than are produced in males, and religion is supposed to remove feelings of guilt. In any case, whether psychological or cultural, the historic fact of female-dominated churches and male-dominated clergy remains.

[21] Hymn books consulted were: Baron Stow and S.F. Smith, *The Psalmist: a new collection of hymns for the use of the Baptist Church* (Boston: The Baptist Church, 1843); *Psalms and Hymns Adapted to Social, Private and Public Worship in the Presbyterian Church in the United States of America: Approved and authorized by the General Assembly* (Philadelphia: The Assembly Press, 1843); *Hymns of the Protestant Episcopal Church in the United States of America: Set Forth in the General Convention of Said Church in the Year of Our Lord, 1789, 1808, 1826* (Philadelphia: The General Convention, 1827); *Collection of Hymns for Public and Private Worship: Approved by the General Synod of the Evangelical Lutheran Church* (Columbus, Ohio, 2nd edition: Evangelical Lutheran Publishers, 1855); Abiel A. Livermore, ed., *Christian Hymns for Public and Private Worship* (Boston: Ticknor and Fields, 1846); Samuel Longfellow and Samuel Johnson, *A Book of Hymns for Public and Private Devotion* (Cambridge: Ticknor and Fields, 1846) (Unitarian); *Plymouth Collection of Hymns and Tunes; for the use of Christian Congregations* (New York: The Plymouth Press, 1855); *Hymnal of the Presbyterian Church: Ordered by the General Assembly* (Philadelphia: The Assembly Press, 1866); *The Hymnal: Published by the Authority of the General Assembly of the Presbyterian Church in the United States of America* (Philadelphia: The Assembly Press, 1895); *Hymns of the Faith with Psalms* (Boston: Ticknor and Fields, 1887) (Congregational); *The Baptist Hymn and Tune Book* (Philadelphia: The Baptist Press, 1871); *Hymns: Approved by the General Synod of the Lutheran Church in the United States* (Philadelphia: Lutheran Publishers, 1871, revised from the edition of 1852); *Hymns for Church and Home* (New York: World Press, 1860) (Episcopal); and *Hymnal: According to the Use of the Protestant Episcopal Church in the United States of America printed under the authority of the General Convention* (Oxford: The University Press, 1892; original edition 1872).

[22] "O Perfect Love" was written by Charlotte Elliott, a pious English invalid, who also wrote the popular revival hymn "Just As I Am" [Harvey B. Marks, *The Rise and Growth of English Hymnody* (New York, London and Edinburg: Fleming H. Revell Co., 1937), p. 127].

[23] Sarah Adams, perhaps the most famous of the nineteenth century hymn writers, had the

dubious distinction of seeing her most popular hymn, "Nearer, My God to Thee" identified with imperialism and patriotism. It was reputedly quoted by McKinley on his deathbed, was Theodore Roosevelt's favorite hymn, and was sung by the gallant men on the sinking *Titanic* [Louis F. Benson, *The English Hymn: Its Development and Use in Worship* (1915; Richmond, Virginia: John Knox Press, 1962), p. 272]. Mary Clemmer, ed., *The Poetical Works of Alice and Phoebe Cary: With a Memorial of Their Lives* (New York: Hurd and Houghton, 1876), p. 172; Alice Cary, *Ballads, Lyrics and Poems* (New York: Hurd and Houghton, 1866), p. 276.

24 "I Need Thee Every Hour" was written by Annie S. Hawks, and was considered a particularly appropriate hymn for Women's Circles and Mothers' Meetings [Edward S. Ninde, *The Story of the American Hymn* (Cincinnati: The Abingdon Press, 1921), p. 150].

25 Charlotte Elliott in Marks, *Rise and Growth of English Hymnody,* p. 128.

26 The Christianizing of the West is seen as a central theme in virtually all standard accounts of the American religious experience. T. Scott Miyakawa, *Protestants and Pioneers: Individualism and Conformity on the American Frontier* (Chicago and London: University of Chicago Press, 1944) applies Frederick Jackson Turner's frontier thesis to the religious life of the West, and agrees with Turner that in this, as in other areas, the frontier "either drastically altered or rejected the older cultural traditions" (p. 226). Nineteenth-century witnesses to the propagation of the faith included the travel accounts of Robert Baird, *Religion in America: or, an Account of the Origins, Progress, Relation to the State and Present Condition of the Evangelical Churches in the United States* (New York: Harper and Brothers, 1844); Caroline Kirkland, *The Evening Book: Or, Fireside Talk on Morals and Manners, with Sketches of Western Life* (New York: C. Scribner, 1852); Harriet Martineau, *Retrospect of Western Travel,* 3 vols. (London: Saunders and Otley, 1838) and *Society in America,* 3 vols. (London: Saunders and Otley, 1837), as well as the critical Mrs. Trollope.

27 Robert F. Berkhofer, Jr., *Salvation and the Savage: An Analysis of Protestant Missions and American Indian Response,* 1787-1862 (Lexington, Kentucky: University of Kentucky Press, 1965) and R. Pierce Beaver, *Church, State, and the American Indians: Two and a Half Centuries of Partnership in Missions Between Protestant Churches and Government* (St. Louis: Concordia Publishing House, 1966).

28 Mrs. Owens, ed., "Diaries of Pioneer Women in Clatsop County," *Oregon Pioneers Association,* 24 (1896): pp. 89-94.

29 Adoniram Judson, a baptist missionary, brought three wives to join him in his labors in Burma: Ann Hasseltine (1789-1826), followed by Sarah Hall Boardman (1803-1845) and Emily Chubbuck (1817-1854) who returned to the United States after her husband's death in 1850. The combined trials of these three women culminating in their early deaths were considered excellent propaganda for the Mission Boards [James D. Knowles, *Memoir of Mrs. Ann H. Judson, Late Missionary to Burma* (New York: Lincoln and Edmands, 1829); Arabella W. Stuart, *The Lives of Mrs. Ann H. Judson and Mrs. Sarah B. Judson, with a Biographical Sketch of Mrs. Emily C. Judson* (New York: Miller, Orton, 1851); Gordon L. Hall, *Golden Boats from Burma* (New York: Macrae Smith Co., 1961); Emily Forester (Judson), *Memoirs of Sarah B. Judson* (New York: L. Colby and Co., 1848); Walter N. Wyeth, *Sarah B. Judson* (Boston: Published by the Author, 1889); Asahel Clark Kendrick, *The Life and Letters of Mrs. Emily C. Judson* (New York: Sheldon and Co., 1860). Another popular missionary heroine was Harriet Atwood Newell (1793-1812), who was the first American to die on a foreign mission (Mary Sumner Benson, "Harriet Atwood Newell," NAW 2:619-620; Harriet Newell, *The Life and Writings of Mrs. Harriet Newell* (Boston: American Sunday School Union, 1831)].

30 The Whitmans were married in 1836 and almost immediately embarked for Oregon. Narcissa survived the hazards of frontier life, the loss of her daughter by drowning, increasing blindness and constant harassment by Indians and rival religious groups only to die with her husband in a massacre at Waiilatpu in 1847 [Clifford M. Drury, *The First White Women over the Rockies,* 3 vols. (New York: The Caxton Printers, 1963-66); Jeanette Eaton, *Narcissa Whitman* (New York: Harcourt, Brace and Co., 1941); Opal Sweazea Allen, *Narcissa Whitman* (New York: Binfords and Mort, 1959), and the *Proceedings* of the Oregon Pioneers Association, *passim*)].

31 Eliza Spalding, whose health continued to decline with each year in the West, died of tuberculosis in 1851 at the age of forty-three [Clifford M. Drury, *The First White Women over the Rockies* 1: 173-233; "Diary of Mrs. E.H. Spaulding," *Oregon Pioneers Association,* 24 (1896):106-110)].

32 T.E. Elliott, ed., *Narcissa Prentiss Whitman: The Coming of the White Woman,* 1836, as told in the *Letters and Journals of Narcissa Prentiss Whitman* (Portland: Oregon Historical Society, 1937), p. 108.

33 Histories of revivalism in the United States are numerous. One of the best is Timothy L. Smith, *Revivalism and Social Reform in Mid-Nineteenth Century America* (New York and Nashville: The

Abingdon Press, 1957). An interesting psychological study is Sidney George Dimond, *The Psychology of the Methodist Revival: An Empirical and Descriptive Study* (London: Oxford University Press, 1926). Other sources are Paulus Scharpff, *History of Evangelism: Three Hundred Years of Evangelism in Germany, Great Britain, and the United States of America,* trans. Helga Bender Henry (Grand Rapids, Michigan: Eerdmas, 1966); F.G. Beardsley, *A History of American Revivals* (The Tract Society, no publisher, 1912); Bernard A. Weisberger, *They Gathered At the River: The Story of the Great Revivals and Their Impact Upon Religion in America* (Boston and Toronto: Little, Brown, and Co., 1958); C.A. Johnson, *The Frontier Camp Meeting* (Dallas, Texas: Southern Methodist University Press, 1955) and Whitney R. Cross, *The Burned-over District: The Social and Intellectual History of Enthusiastic Religion in Western New York, 1800-1850* (Ithaca, New York: Cornell University Press, 1950). The most famous nineteenth-century account of revivals was by the man who made them, Charles G. Finney, *Lectures on Revival* (Cambridge, Mass.: W.G. Loughlin, 1836).

34 Mrs. Maggie N. Van Cott, *The Harvest and the Reaper: Reminiscences of Revival Work* (New York: G.A. Sparks, 1883), pp. 49, 67-69.

35 Ellen G. White, *Life Sketches* (1860; Mountain View, California: Pacific Press Publishing Association, 1915) , pp. 32-34.

36 MS Diary of Myra S. Smith, June 19, 1859, Elizabeth and Arthur Schlesinger Library, Radcliffe College, Cambridge, Massachusetts.

37 Richard Hofstadter, *Anti-Intellectualism in America* (New York: Alfred A. Knopf, 1963).

38 Barbara Welter, "Anti-Intellectualism and the American Woman: 1800-1860," *Mid-America,* 48 (October 1966): 258-270.

39 Caroline Dall, "Transcendentalism in New England: A Lecture Given before the Society for Philosophical Enquiry, Washington, D.C., May 7, 1895, in *The Journal of Speculative Philosophy,* 23, no. 1 (1897): 1-38. C. Gregg Singer, *A Theological Interpretation of American History* (Nutley New Jersey: Craig Press, 1964) saw Transcendentalism as a direct repudiation of Puritanism, because it glorified man instead of God.

40 Octavius Brooks Frothingham, *Recollections and Impressions,* 1822-1890 (New York and London: G.P. Putnam's Sons, 1891), p. 136. Ralph Waldo Emerson, *The Complete Writings of Ralph Waldo Emerson,* (1875; New York, 1929), "Woman," pp. 1178-1184.

41 An informal collection of these conversations was compiled by Caroline Dall but was not published.

42 Octavius Brooks Frothingham, *Memoir of William Henry Channing* (Boston and New York: Houghton, Mifflin and Co., 1886), p. 296.

43 David Riesman, Introduction to Jessie Bernard, *Academic Women* (New York: World Publishing Co., 1966). The late David Potter also reconsidered his assessment of the American character in his essay, "American Women and the American Character" in John A. Hague, ed., *American Character and Culture* (De Land, Florida: Edward Everett Press, 1964), pp. 65-84.

44 See in particular Margaret Fuller (Ossoli), *Woman in the Nineteenth Century* (New York: Greeley and Co., 1845), A.B. Fuller, ed., *Life Without and Life Within* (Boston: J.P. Jewett and Co., 1859), and Caroline W. Healey (Dall), *Margaret and Her Friends: Or, the Conversations with Margaret Fuller Upon the Mythology of the Greeks and Its Expression in Art* (Boston: Roberts Brothers, 1896).

45 Donald Meyer, *The Positive Thinkers* (Garden City, New York: Doubleday and Co., 1965).

46 John Van Der Zee Sears, *My Friends at Brook Farm* (New York: D. FitzGerald, Inc., 1918), p. 89.

47 Charles Nordhoff, *The Communist Societies of the United States* (1875; New York: Harper and Brothers, 1912), p. 412.

48 New Harmony (Indiana), Yellow Springs Community (Ohio), Brook Farm (Massachusetts), North American Phalanx (New Jersey), Ceresco (Wisconsin), Northampton Association (Massachusetts), Fruitlands (Massachusetts), Oneida (New York), and Modern Times (New York).

49 John Thomas Codman, *Brook Farm: Historic and Personal Memoirs* (Boston: Arena Publishing Co., 1894), p. 111, and articles in *The Dial* and *The Harbinger,* throughout their publication, translating and commenting on Fourier. Fourier's ideas on the role of women in the new society can be found in Francois Marie Charles Fourier, *Theory of Social Organization* (New York: C.P. Somerby, 1876).

50 Amelia Russell, "Home Life of the Brook Farm Association," *The Atlantic Monthly,* 42 (October 1878): 457-466, and (November 1878): 556-563, 561.

51 Robert Allerton Parker, *A Yankee Saint; John Humphrey Noyes and the Oneida Community* (New York: G.P. Putnam's Sons, 1935), is an excellent biography with many quotations from Noyes'

writings.

[52] Ibid., p. 67.

[53] Ibid., p. 182-183.

[54] Ibid., p. 183.

[55] Phrenology was a nineteenth-century mixture of science, religion, and cultural reinforcement; both conservatives and liberals used its terminology, sometimes seriously, sometimes with tongue in cheek. Among the most popular phrenological manuals were Jessie A. Fowler, *A Manual of Mental Science* (London and New York: Fowler and Wells, 1897); G. Spurzheim, *Outlines of Phrenology* (Boston: Marsh, Caper and Lyon, 1832), and Lorenzo N. Fowler, *Marriage* (New York: Fowler and Wells, 1847).

[56] Gates, *History,* p. 2.

[57] *History of the Relief Society of the Church of Jesus Christ of Latter Day Saints* (Salt Lake City: The Desert News, 1966), p. 18.

[58] For example, see the testimony of Joseph Smith's wives in Don Cecil Corbett, *Mary Fielding Smith: Daughter of Britain; Portrait of Courage* (Salt Lake City: The Desert Press, 1966), and the women in Edward W. Tullidge, *The Women of Mormonism* (New York: Published by the author, 1877). Tullidge quotes Eliza Snow Smith as saying that the Mormon Church "is the oracle of the grandest emancipation of womanhood and motherhood" (p. 194). Mrs. Hannah T. King, in 1870, proposed a resolution opposing the federal bill outlawing polygamy which ended with an acknowledgment of the Church of the Latter Day Saints "as the only reliable safeguard of female virtue and innocence; and the only sure protection against the fearful sin of prostitution . . ." (p. 385). There is also a considerable literature of anti-Mormonism, in which the Mormons are portrayed as despoilers of female virtue and degenerates of the worst sort, very much in the Maria Monk tradition.

[59] Octavius Brooks Frothingham, *George Ripley* (Boston: Houghton, Mifflin and Co., 1882), pp. 236-237.

[60] MSS Letters of Sophia Dana Ripley and Charlotte Dana, Dana Papers, Massachusetts Historical Society, Boston, Massachusetts; March 1848.

[61] For example, Ellen in *Fanshawe,* Phoebe in *The House of the Seven Gables,* and Annie in "The Artist of the Beautiful" all represent the principle of the common humanity of the ordinary man rather than the singular arrogance of the individual.

[62] Louis Auchincloss, *Pioneers and Caretakers: A Study of Nine American Women Novelists* (Minneapolis: University of Minnesota Press, 1965).

[63] Sylvester Judd, *Margaret: A Tale of the Real and Ideal* (1851; Boston: Phillips, Sampson and Co., 1882), pp. 378-379.

[64] Morris Raphael Cohen, *American Thought: A Critical Sketch* (1954; New York: The Macmillan Co., 1962), p. 41.

[65] Orestes Brownson, *Works,* "Literature, Love and Marriage," 14: 421.

THE TENDER TECHNICIANS:
THE FEMINIZATION OF
PUBLIC LIBRARIANSHIP, 1876-1905

Dee Garrison

"The law of nature destines and qualifies the female sex for the bearing and nurture of the children of our race and for the custody of the homes of the world," stated the Wisconsin Supreme Court in 1875 when ruling that women could not be admitted to their bar. The judges conceded that the "cruel chances of life" might leave some women free of the sacred female duties. "These may need employment, and should be welcome to any not derogatory to their sex and its proprieties."[1] Most Americans of the time would have agreed with the Court that only financial need justified a woman's going to work and that only limited jobs should be opened to her. But in the decades immediately before and after 1900 Americans became the unobservant participants in a social revolution, as profound changes took place in the attitudes toward women and their work. The American public libraries played an important role in the revolution, for the feminization of librarianship proceeded rapidly. In 1852 the first woman clerk was hired at the Boston Public Library;[2] by 1878 fully two-thirds of the library workers there were female.[3] In 1910 78½ percent of library workers in the United States were women; only teaching surpassed librarianship as the most feminized "profession."[4]

Educated women, while meeting resistance in more established professions, flooded into library work during the last quarter of the nineteenth century for a variety of reasons. Librarianship was a new and fast-growing field in need of low-

This article is a slightly revised version of "The Tender Technicians: The Feminization of Public Librarianship, 1876-1905, *Journal of Social History* (Winter 1972-1973); 131-159, and is reprinted with the permission of the publisher.

paid but educated recruits. With a plentiful number of library jobs available, male librarians offered no opposition to the proliferation of women library workers, partly because women agreed that library work matched presumed femine limitations. Librarianship was quickly adjusted to fit the narrowly circumscribed sphere of women's activities, for it appeared similar to the work of the home, functioned as cultural activity, required no great skill or physical strength, and brought little contact with the rougher portions of society. For all these reasons, Melvil Dewey could predict, when writing at the turn of the century of the ideal librarian, that "most of the men who achieve this greatness will be women."[5] The feminization of librarianship, however, had unexpected long-range results. The prevalence of women would profoundly affect the process of professionalization and the type of service the library would provide. The nature of library work itself, one of the few sources of economic opportunity open to educated women in the late nineteenth century, would serve to perpetuate the low status of women in American society. Above all, female dominance of librarianship did much to shape the inferior and precarious status of the public library as an important cultural resource and to cause it to evolve into a marginal kind of public amusement service.[6]

The rapid growth of libraries in size, number and complexity between 1876 and 1905 was an important cause of the feminization of librarianship. The monumental 1876 "Report on Public Libraries" listed 3,682 libraries containing a little over twelve million volumes.[7] Total yearly additions of library books in the nation passed the one million mark in 1876.[8] A conservative estimate raised the total to forty million volumes held in 8,000 libraries in 1900.[9] Because a heavy demand for trained librarians coincided with other national developments, particularly the advance of women's education and the increase of women workers, many women found employment in library service. Very probably, women would have flocked into any new field into which their entry was not opposed. Because male librarians heartily welcomed women into library service, the eventual feminization of the library staff was assured.

The low cost of hiring women was perhaps the most important reason why male library leaders welcomed women assistants. The public library, supported by taxes and voluntary donations, was by necessity obliged to practice thrifty housekeeping. Trustees and taxpayers expected that the major portion of the yearly income would be invested in books. Because women were notoriously low-paid, the annual cost of library administration could be appreciably lowered by the introduction of women workers. Frederick Perkins, in an 1876 article entitled "How to Make Town Libraries Successful," recommended that "women should be employed as librarians and assistants as far as possible." Perkins was no crusader for women's equality; he only pointed out that the hiring of women, along with the use of "mechanical appliances . . . better arrangements of book rooms and other sufficient contrivances of that American ingenuity," would lessen the excessive cost of library administration.[10] Justin Winsor, speaking at the 1877 conference of British and American librarians in London, emphasized the importance of women workers in American libraries.

In American libraries we set a high value on women's work. They soften our atmosphere, they lighten our labor, they are equal to our work, and for the money they cost—if we must gauge such labor by such rules—they are infinitely better than equivalent salaries will produce of the other sex. . . .We can command our pick of the educated young women whom our Colleges for Women are launching forth upon our country—women with a fair knowledge of Latin and Greek, a good knowledge of French and German, a deducible knowledge of Spanish and Italian, and who do not stagger at the acquisition of even Russian, if the requirements of the catalogue service make that demand. It is to these Colleges for Women, like Vassar and Wellesley, that the American library-system looks confidently for the future.[11]

The limited opportunities open to educated women for paid employment served to bring larger numbers of competent women than competent men into low-paid library jobs during this period. Of the eight leading women librarians of the time, four had some college and the rest at least a high school education.[12] In view of the constant references made in library literature to the necessity of finding workers with an educated knowledge of books, a high intelligence and preferably a familiarity with a few languages, it is safe to assume that most women entering library service at this time were either self- or formally-educated to at least the extent expected of an urban schoolteacher.[13] The same economic factors were at work in librarianship and teaching, for educated women, with few other job opportunities, flocked into both fields, with a depressing effect on wages. Library work required similar qualifications to teaching and was little worse in pay. In librarianship women could exercise their presumed special feminine talents and could, besides, remain isolated, in a way teachers could not, from the rough workaday world.[14]

The woman's movement into such new occupations as nursing and teaching or clerical and industrial employment began in the middle of the nineteenth century when both the right to individuality and the myth of women's sphere held extremely important places in American popular thought. Two such conflicting ideas could not exist together unless individualism was reserved for man alone. Thus man took the world and all its activities as his "sphere," while confining women to domesticity and the guardianship of culture. Women were just as guilty of inconsistency. The gradual expansion of women's claim to the right of individual choice was on the whole unaccompanied by any feminine calls for radical social change. Instead, as each new job became filled by women, charming theories were developed by both sexes to explain why the feminine mind and nature were innately suited to the new occupation. Thus it was decided that teaching was much like mothering; women, it was said, were uniquely able to guide children into piety, purity and knowledge. Women were cleared to work as writers, musicians and artists because of their inherent sensitivity, elevated moralism and love of beauty. Women doctors and nurses were intuitively kind, sympathetic and delicate of touch. The woman social worker expressed inborn feminine qualities of love, charity and idealism. Factory, business and clerical work fit the feminine nature, for women were naturally industrious, sober and nimble-fingered, as well as better able than men to endure the boredom of detailed or repetitive tasks. These various expansions of the work of women served to modify the concept of woman's proper sphere, but the process was gradual and involved no radical threat to traditional social ideals.[15] Yet each expansion led to others, with a snowballing effect, so that within a hundred years the limits of woman's claim to individual freedom of choice had undergone considerable and drastic change.

This redefinition of woman's sphere, always in accord with the characteristics presumed to be innately feminine, also came to encompass librarianship as one of the proper fields open to women. The course to library work had already been cleared for women because libraries held books and books denoted Culture with a capital "C." By the late nineteenth century, woman's sphere decidedly included the guardianship and enjoyment of culture. It was believed that through their refining and spiritualizing influence women could exalt all human society. It would be almost impossible to overemphasize the Victorian conviction that men were physically tamed and morally elevated by the sway of the gentle female. Moreover, by the 1870s American popular literature was consciously designed to please feminine readers. Therefore the advent of women to library work required little stretching of the popular ideal regarding the female, for "books . . . should be treated by reverent hands . . . should be given out as a priest dispenses the sacrament, and the next step to this ideal ministry is to have them issued by women."[16]

> The librarian . . . is becoming . . . the guardian of the thought-life of the people. . . . The library, in its influence, is whatever the librarian makes it; it seems destined to become an all-pervading force . . . moulding [sic] public opinion, educating to all of the higher possibilities of human thought and action; to become a means for enriching, beautifying, and making fruitful the barren places in human life. . . . Librarians have an important part to play in the history of civilization and in the conservation of the race.[17]

Women in librarianship were merely making more visible the female position as the guardian of cultural ideals.

Just as the concept of "culture" had been generally accorded to the care of women, so the functions of providing education and of overseeing charity to the poor had been deemed suitable fields for female concern. The provision of education and moral uplift to the masses was a prominent mission of the early library; thus, women library workers, with their presumed inborn talents and temperaments, seemed uniquely suited to the new field of librarianship. The popular library brought the librarian "in hourly contact with her constituency of readers, advising, helping and elevating their lives and exerting a far-reaching influence for good not to be exceeded in any profession open to women. . . ."[18] The great mass of men in all fields worked to secure prestige or a higher income but the librarian worked "with as distinct a consecration as a minister or missionary. . . . The selfish considerations of reputation or personal comfort, or emolument are all secondary."[19] For Melvil Dewey, library work offered more opportunity to the altruistic than did the work of the clergyman or teacher. The library would reach those who never entered a church or who did not go to school.

> It is not true that the ideal librarian fills a pulpit where there is service every day during all the waking hours, with a large proportion of the community frequently in the congregation. . . . [The library is] a school in which the classes graduate only at death.[20]

Dewey encouraged educated women who might ordinarily have become teachers to consider a library career. Physically the library was less exacting than the school. The librarian avoided the "nervous strain and the wear and tear of the classroom" and escaped the bad air of crowded rooms. Dewey could think of no other profession "that is so free from annoying surroundings or that has so much in the character of the work and of the people which is grateful to a refined and educated woman."[21] The genteel nature of library work would compensate, he believed, for the regretable fact that women librarians normally received half the pay of men librarians and often received even less than urban teachers did.

As women became dominant in library work, library literature began to reflect the concept that the ideal library would offer the warmth and hospitality of the home to its patrons. To nineteenth-century man, of course, woman's sphere was, above all, the home, for which she was originally intended and which she was so exactly fitted to adorn and bless. Not surprisingly, it was anticipated that the feminine influence of the librarian would soften the library atmosphere. Like a visitor to a home, the reader must be welcomed; he must be given kind and individual attention; he must be treated with tact and gentle manners. Not the cold impersonality of the business world should pervade but rather the warmth of the well-ordered home, presided over by a gracious and helpful librarian. Counsel like the following is pervasive in the library literature of the 1870s and 1880s:

> Something may be said of the desirableness of making the library wear a pleasant and inviting look. The reading-room offers perhaps the best opportunity for this. A reading-room lately seen has a bright carpet on the floor, low tables, and a few rocking-chairs scattered about, a cheerful, open fire on dull days, attractive pictures on the walls, and one can imagine a lady librarian filling the windows with plants. Such a room is a welcome in itself, and bids one come again.[22]

It was this ideal of the librarian as the accommodating and heartily receptive hostess which Theresa West had in mind when she said that "the personal equation of the librarian may easily become the exponent of the power of the library."[23] On the surface the likening of the library to the home was but one of several devices which library leaders used to entice the reluctant patron and to make the library into a more "popular" institution. Operating more subtly, underground, were the effects of the prevalence of women in library work. Just as the school had been likened to the home, in order to make more acceptable the dominance of women teachers, so did the library readjust to reflect the widening of woman's sphere. The position of librarian required a certain "gracious hospitality" and here "women as a class far surpass men." Women would not feel humiliated by serving, by playing in the library the part they played in the home: "Here it is said her 'broad sympathies, her quick wits, her intuitions and her delight in self-sacrifice' give her an undoubted advantage."[24]

Women workers were also preferred, it was generally conceded, for the tedious job of cataloging. Again, it was the unique nature of woman which qualified her for this work because of her "greater conscientiousness, patience and accuracy in details."[25] Because women had greater ability than men to bear pain with fortitude, women had stored great reserves of patience and thus could perform the most monotonous tasks without boredom. All the routine, repetitive work of the library was quite generally agreed to fall within the scope of women's special talents.[26]

It is evident that the role of domesticity imposed upon women also worked to create the emphasis which was early given to library service for children.[27] By 1900 the children's library had "passed its first stage—all enthusiasm and effervescence—"[28] and had moved into its current position as a major department of the public library. From the beginning, the supervision of children's reading was given over to the woman librarian.

> The work for children in our libraries, like many other of our best things, is woman's work. To them it owes its inception, its progress and present measure of success, and its future is in their hands.[29]

Here in the children's sections was woman's undisputed domain. And here the librarians waxed eloquent over the attributes and accomplishments of the reigning queen. Work with children is "the most important, and in its results, the most satisfactory of all library work," reported Minerva Sanders. "As our personal influence is exerted, in just such a proportion will our communities be uplifted."[30] Another librarian commented that woman, alone, has "that kind of sympathetic second-sight that shall enable her to read what is often obscure in the mind of the child."[31] Edwin M. Fairchild summed up the prevailing attitude toward woman's natural role in library work—not as a bluestocking, but as a traditionally defined female with intrinsic traits.

> The chief source of enthusiasm for the children's library is the librarian. . . . [She] needs to be . . . . a woman grown, herself the realization of the educational ideal, which by the way is not the smart, but the intelligent, great souled woman. . . .[32]

Originally conceived and theoretically maintained as an educational institution, the children's department was, in fact, even by the turn of the century, becoming mainly a provider of recreational reading for pre-adolescents.[33] Misgivings over the nature of library service to children were rarely expressed, however. Most often, sentimentality over-ruled any attempt at a realistic assessment of the work being accomplished in the children's department. The romantic air of enthusiastic tenderness so prominent in any discussion of children in the library is in sharp contrast to the more normal tendency of librarians to indulge in searching self-criticism in every other phase of library work. This incongruity becomes more understandable when it is remembered that the children's section of the library was created and shaped by women librarians. Here, as in no other area, library women were free to express, unchallenged, their self-image. Because their activities did not exceed the Victorian stereotype of the female, their endeavors remained substantially unquestioned and unexamined by male library leaders.

Despite the respect paid them, however, women soon learned that they were seldom paid the same as men who were doing the same work; and that even though women easily dominated the library field in numbers, male librarians headed the largest and most prestigious libraries. In the library literature of this period there is hardly a hint that the hundreds of women librarians across the country were seriously disturbed at the inequality which was freely admitted to be their lot.[34] Rather, one finds feminine pride repeatedly expressed over the prevalence of women in the library, at the increased participation of women in the national association and of America's flattering contrast with England where women were meeting resistance in library work. A situation which really amounted to the exploitation of women in the American library was publicly touted as a liberal concession to women in America and was contrasted with women's supposedly less favorable position in the Old World to indicate the superiority of American freedoms and the liberal attitudes of the male leaders of the American library movement.[35]

The twelve women present at the 1876 American Library Association meeting set the submissive tone which few women librarians were to challenge. They were "the best of listeners, and occasionally would modestly take advantage of gallant voices, like Mr. Smith's, to ask a question or offer a suggestion."[36] The next year Caroline Hewins had the distinction of being the first woman to speak up at the national convention; she asked if the dog tax were used to support a library outside Massachusetts. Perhaps this small temerity earned her the reputation of fearless spokesman for it was Hewins who presented in 1891 the first general discussion of the "woman question" in the Library Journal.

Library work was difficult for women, Hewins said. For a salary varying from three to nine hundred dollars annually, a library assistant must write steadily six or seven hours a day, know half a dozen languages, be absolutely accurate in copying, "understand the relation of all arts and sciences to each other and must have . . . a minute acquaintance with geography, history, art and literature." A successful woman librarian would work eight to ten hours a day and "those who are paid the highest salaries give up all their evenings." Hewins added that "librarians and library attendants sometimes break down from overwork." With unconscious humor, the intrepid Hewins had a remedy for impending exhaustion—"plenty of sleep and nourishing food, with a walk of two or three miles every day."[37] Presumably this stroll was to be taken in the hours of early dawn or late evening.

The year after Hewin's article appeared there was an abortive attempt to establish a Woman's Section in the national organization. The sole meeting of women in 1892 was a tame affair, with only the barest expression of stifled rage at women's low wages and subordinate position. An official statement secured from twenty-five of the nation's most prominent libraries revealed that "women rarely receive the same pay for the same work as men."[38] But no matter. "The palm of honor and of opportunity waits for her who shall join a genius for organization . . . to the power of a broad, rich, catholic and sympathetic womanhood." In "the long run" the woman librarian "will win appreciation."[39]

The Woman's Section of the American Library Association did not meet again, although the 1892 session appointed a committee to report at the next conference in Chicago. There was no formal explanation of the failure of this committee to report, but it may be that a protest movement, sparked by Telsie Kelso of the Los Angeles Public Library, would explain the demise of the Woman's Section. Kelso study disapproved of any deference paid to women as a group.[40]

> In the . . . 14th American Library Association Conference I note that there is a movement toward establishing a woman's section. . . . For years woman has worked, talked, and accepted all sorts of compromises to prove her fitness to hold the position of librarian, and to demonstrate that sex should have no weight where ability is equal. In all these years the accomplishment is seen in the table of wages paid women librarians in comparison with those paid men. . . . For women to now come forward with the argument that a woman librarian has a point of view and such limitation that they must be discussed apart from the open court of library affairs is a serious mistake. . . . The use of the name of the association should not be permitted in such direction. . . .[41]

Such a truculent defense of women's equality, however, was not in accord with the expressed attitude of most women librarians. They accepted with little protest the traditional view of women as inherently limited in the working world. Certain women library leaders had no utopian plans for woman's sexual and social emancipation. Of course they wanted to do things not customary for women in the past, such as managing a library with pay equal to men's, but this they considered as no more than a slight modification of the traditional ideal, and certainly not as a basic change in the male-structured view of women. As late as 1896 the influential Mary Ahern, editor of *Public Libraries,* warbled that "no woman can hope to reach any standing . . . in the library profession . . . who does not bring to it that love which suffereth long and is kind, is not puffed up, does not behave itself unseemly, vaunteth not itself, thinketh no evil. . . ." Every woman owes it to herself to live up to the ideals expected of womanhood; "no woman striving ever so hard to play the part of a man has ever succeeded in doing more than to give just cause for a blush to the rest of her kind." Every woman in library work should seek not "to detract from the reputation so hardly earned of being faithful conscientious workers."[42]

In 1904 one hundred representative libraries were asked by the American Library Association to comment on the limitations of women library workers.[43] Economic reasons were most often cited to explain women's low pay scale; women who did not demand as much salary as men were in abundant supply. Women were generally acknowledged to be hampered by their "delicate physique" and "inability to endure continued mental strain." Mary Cutler (now Mary Fairchild), an important woman library leader, commented that she could not see how women's physical disability could ever be eliminated. Whether women would ever hold high positions in the library "may remain perhaps an open question." While having decided advantage wherever "the human element predominates," Fairchild went on, women too frequently lacked the will to discharge executive power and most trustees "assume that a woman would not have business capacity." Reviewing all the facts, she concluded that "on account of natural sex limitations, and also actual weakness in the work of many women as well as because of conservatism and prejudice, many gates are at present closed to women."[44]

Recognition of women's limited potential was probably justified when applied to women library workers in general. The average woman accepted the current ideal which taught that her success in life would be judged by her marriage and not by her work. With this concept central in her mind, she was being wholly practical if she spent much of her time in conforming to the popular ideal of "femininity" rather than in thinking about business achievement. Women librarians who had given up hope for marriage were also less apt to strain for advancement since they realized that society would discourage them from a display of "male" aggressiveness. Of course, some talented and energetic women librarians did realize their ambitions to a considerable degree, primarily because these ambitions were exceedingly modest and did not threaten the prevailing notion of woman's place.

Perhaps the most striking point to be made about women's adaptation to library work is the extent to which they supported the traditional feminine concern for altruism and high-mindedness. They invoked the Victorian definition of proper female endeavors at the same time as they were widening it. Librarianship, when defined as self-denying and spiritual, offered women the opportunity not to change their status but to affirm it, not to fulfill their self but their self-image. When women's advance became justified in terms of the good they could do, rather than of their human right to equality, it became conditional in nature.

Even if some librarians did not subscribe to the concept of woman's sphere, with all its connotations, they had to appear to do so in order not to offend the many who did. Not to surrender to the Victorian mystique was to run the terrible risk of being judged deviants in their society, of being judged abnormal because of a challenge to well-established norms. Perhaps, too, both men and women librarians wished to avoid any real discussion of the injustice which library women suffered because of the eagerness of all library leaders to establish librarianship as a profession. To publicize the prevalence of women in the library or to increase their influence could only harm the drive toward professionalization. A woman-dominated profession was obviously a contradiction in terms.

Librarians have been absorbed to a marked degree, from 1876 to the present, with the question of professionalization. Melvil Dewey and other early library leaders made repeated claims to professional status.[45] Not until the Williamson report of 1923 was there open and general admission among librarians that significant elements common to professional work were lacking in librarianship.[46] In the effort to win professional standing, librarians have concentrated upon improvements in their system of library schools. The education of librarians, it has been commonly lamented, includes too much detail and attention to method, only producing good craftsmen and technicians. True professional education, on the other hand, should present a systematic body of theory and a scientifically-based abstract knowledge upon which the profession rests.

Throughout the debate among librarians as to how best to receive recognition as professionals, the dominant influence of women on librarianship has been strangely shunted, buried under a multitude of words concerning recruitment, accreditation, curriculums and other factors thought to be inhibiting professionalization. There has been no systematic consideration given to the way in which feminization has shaped, in a most significant way, the development of library education and the entire range of activities associated with the field of library work. Carl White, who has written the best study of library education as it developed before 1923, gives thoughtful and scholarly attention to the social and educational setting in which library education began and relates it brilliantly to the traditions which remain today from that early inheritance.[47] Yet White curiously refrains from considering the effect of the prevalence of women workers upon the shaping of those traditions. Only sociologist Peter Rossi, in a symposium of 1961, has tackled the existence of feminization head-on and applied it to library development. Rossi commented upon the puzzling absence of any real consideration being given to the influence of women upon library history.

> I kept expecting . . . some comment on *the major reason* (italics added) why librarians find it difficult to achieve a substantial spot in the array of professions. Any occupation in which there is a high proportion of women suffers a special disability. . . . Women depress the status of an occupation because theirs is a depressed status in the society as a whole, and those occupations in which women are found in large numbers are not seen as seriously competing with other professions for personnel and resources. It is for this reason that professions such as education, social work, and librarianship develop within themselves a division of labor and accompanying status along sex lines.[48]

Rossi added that the status of librarianship could be raised by a radical division of labor such as that accomplished in medicine where nursing was done by females and doctoring by males. This sharp differentiation between male and female librarians, however, runs counter to the central development of library history. Once formed, the solutions—both planned and accidental—found workable by nineteenth-century librarians closed the possibility of starting over with a clean slate. For this reason it is important that librarians assess the basic meaning of feminization and give precise attention to their early history, for the dominance of women is surely the prevailing factor in library education, the image of librarianship and the professionalization of the field. Women's role in the library was established in the last quarter of the nineteenth century. An examination of the principal factors in this period of library history should include an emphasis upon the underrated effect of women students in library schools and its relationship to the constant search of librarians for professional standing.

The process of professionalization has received increasing attention by sociologists and historians in recent years.[49] Although it is generally agreed that professions have certain characteristics differentiating them from other occupations, there is no agreement on the precise nature of these characteristics. The conceptual model developed here will be discussed under three headings: service orientation, knowledge base and degree of autonomy. These components will be examined, first as they apply to nineteenth-century librarianship in general and then as they relate to the feminization of the field.

The service orientation of librarianship exhibits most of the qualities expected in the ethical code of a profession. The professional, in contrast to the non-professional, is primarily concerned with his client's needs or with the needs of society, rather than with his own material interests. A profession also has direct relevance to basic social values on which there is widespread consensus. In law and medicine, for example, the services provided by the professional are justice and health. In librarianship the basic social value served is education. Early library leaders were firm in their commitment of the library to educational purposes; they definitely relegated the recreational function of the library to a secondary place. William Poole's comment typifies this view.

> Our public libraries and our public schools are supported by the same constituencies, by the same methods of taxation, and for the same purpose; and that purpose is the education of the people. . . . If public libraries shall, in my day, cease to be educational institutions, and serve only to amuse the people and help them to while away an idle hour, I shall favor their abolition.[50]

The librarian also showed a professional acceptance of the ideal of sacrificial service to the community. Librarianship was deemed to be second only to the ministry in its aims and standards.[51] Additionally, librarians had the sense of community which is common to professionals. They felt an affinity with other librarians in a way which the plumber, for example, does not feel for all other plumbers. Librarians, like the ministers with whom they liked to compare themselves, sensed an identity as a group, sharing a common destiny, values and norms.

The service and collectivity orientation of librarianship, then, conform to certain important characteristics of a profession. The characteristics used in the definition of the term "profession" are variables, forming a continuum along which an occupation's rise to professionalism can be measured. Although librarianship certainly showed a number of professional traits, significant elements of a truly professional code of service were missing. Specifically lacking in the librarian's professional service code are a sense of commitment, a drive to lead rather than to serve, and a clear-cut conception of professional rights and responsibilities. The feminization of library work is a major cause of these deficiencies.

The concentration of women served to lower a professional work-commitment within librarianship. The culture defined woman's responsibility to the home as her primary one and this definition was all-pervasive before 1900. It was perfectly understandable, for example, that Theresa West would in 1896 leave her job as the leading woman librarian heading an important library when she married. Indeed, it would have been shocking if she had chosen otherwise. Nineteenth-century complaints of high employee turnover and of low commitment to excellence among library workers are directly related to the place which women accepted in society. For the library assistant of the nineteenth century to become highly work-committed would require from her an atypical value orientation.[52] The majority of librarians were no doubt eager to marry and to leave library work. Of the eight women leaders selected for this study, five were unmarried and one was a widow. Of the two who married, late in life, both continued to work in the library field, although not as head librarians. All eight of these women were highly educated by the standards of their time. In each case, professional success, high status, extensive training and spinsterhood served to increase their vocational commitment. Despite the positive work commitments demonstrated by these women leaders, it remains generally true that within the field of librarianship, from 1876 to the present, the dominance of women significantly lessened a trend toward professional, life-long commitment to the field of library service.[53]

In established professions the practitioner assumes the responsibility for deciding what is best for his client. Whether or not the client agrees with him is theoretically not a factor in the professional's decision. Thus in the medical field, the doctor does not give the patient whatever treatment he requests, but instead prescribes the treatment which, for professional reasons, the doctor thinks is correct. In contrast to this professional attitude, librarians tended to "serve" the reader, rather than to help him. They felt a strong obligation to meet the needs of the public and were self-consciously sensitive to requests and complaints of the client.[54] This is partly a result of the tax-supported nature of the library and of its early efforts to attract a large public following. But this passive, inoffensive and non-assertive "service" provided by the librarian is also a natural acting-out of the docile behavioral role which females assumed in the culture.[55]

Theoretically the nineteenth-century library could have developed a less demand-oriented code of service. John Dana, Melvil Dewey, William Fletcher and William Poole often urged the librarian to lead her community, to educate the reader and the public. These men felt strongly that the librarian's role was to teach the standards that the public *should* want, not merely to provide access to what the public *did* want. Dewey argued that it was unwise "to give sharp tools or powerful weapons to the masses without some assurance of how they are to be used."[56] The public library, said William Fletcher,

> . . . has too often been regarded somewhat as a public club, a purely democratic association of the people for mutual mental improvement or recreation. . . . The public library is an educational and moral power to be wielded with a full sense of its mighty possibilities and the corresponding danger of their perversion.[57]

The assumption of a definitive intellectual leadership, however, did not come to characterize the public librarian. Modern librarians have laid the blame for their general passivity and inferior status upon various factors: the lack of a scientifically-based abstract body of knowledge; the public's lack of differentiation between the "professional" librarian and the library clerk, and the inherently weak position of the librarian as implementor rather than creator of intellectual and cultural advance. Rarely given its due as a determinant is the overwhelming presence of women in librarianship. The negative traits for which librarians indict themselves—excessive cautiousness, avoidance of controversy, timidity, a weak orientation toward autonomy, little business sense, tractability, over-compliance, service to the point of self-sacrifice and willingness to submit to subordination by trustees and public—are predominantly "feminine" traits.[58] Dana and others who sought to give librarianship a position of community leadership and intellectual authority were vastly outnumbered by the thousands of women who were shaping library development across the country. There is no evidence to indicate that these women opposed society's views of woman's nature and function. The traditional ideals of feminine behavior held by women librarians and the reading public had a profound impact upon the development of the public librarian's non-assertive, non-professional code of service.

The second component of library professionalization—the body of knowledge—does not contain as many professional attributes as does the service ideal of librarians. Professional knowledge is generally defined as that knowledge which (1) is organized in abstract principles, (2) is continually revised or created by the professionals, (3) places strong emphasis upon the ability to manipulate ideas and symbols rather than physical objects and (4) requires a long enough term of specialized training so that the society views the professional as possessing skills which are beyond the reach of the untrained layman. William Goode has commented,

> Librarians themselves have found it extremely difficult to define their professional role and the knowledge on which it rests. To use a phrase like "specialization in generalism" is insufficient. . . . The repeated calls which librarians have made for a "philosophy of librarianship" essentially express the need to define what *is* the intellectual problem of the occupation.[59]

In short, the librarian does not know who he is. Is he a library mechanic, having to do with such clerical, technical work as cataloguing, shelf arrangement and signing-in-and-out management? Or is he an expert guide, with considerable training in knowledge retrieval and organization?

One point, at least, seems clear. Despite the expressed desire of librarians to become admired professionals whose expertise would make available the world of knowledge, the system of library education which developed in the nineteenth century was a form of schooling, in origin and by design, which merely produced good craftsmen, trained to perform jobs which were chiefly mechanical in nature. This relatively low level of training, which made a small intellectual demand on the student, did not evolve entirely because of the female majority in library schools. The rate of expansion in both size and numbers of libraries was the first influence. The demand for a rapid production of library workers encouraged library schools to grind out graduates after only a brief course of instruction in the fundamental skills of library economy. The older system of in-service training could not produce enough self-made librarians to satisfy the manpower needs of the country.

Carl White has outlined the second great influence on library education—the nineteenth-century development of technical education to fill the vacuum created by the breakdown of the classical curriculum and the medieval system of apprenticeship.[60] Library leaders were aware that a concentrated practical training had been demonstrated in other fields to produce the same results as learning by doing, but in less time and more systematically. Thus, detailed instruction in technical routines became the solid core of library training. Library education was in no sense designed to cultivate intellectual leadership, to produce trained high-level administrators, or to develop an abstract knowledge base for library science.

The predominance of women in library schools, on library-school faculties and in library work functioned as an unarticulated but inflexible framework into which "professional" education would have to be fitted. An emphasis upon the influence of women is not meant to downgrade the other elements which shaped library education or to deemphasize the other inherent weaknesses in the librarian's claim to professional status, nor is it meant to impose chauvinistic attitudes upon male library leaders. Nineteenth-century librarians, however, were men and women of their time, governed by traditional views of woman's role in society. They were faced with an unorthodox problem—how to devise "professional" training for young women. Their answer was caught between the upper and the nether millstones. The upper millstone was their hope that librarians would become indispensable educational leaders, with professional scope and value. The nether millstone was the reality of the library school student—a woman who most likely lacked scholarly ambitions or preparation, had no life-long vocational commitment and whose attitudes toward feminine sex roles led her to accept, and expect, administrative controls, low autonomy and subordination to clerical, routine tasks.[61]

No study of why library training developed as it did would be complete without a consideration of how it was influenced by the thought of Melvil Dewey. Dewey so molded library education that the whole period before 1923 is called the "Dewey period." Librarians, too, have their folk heroes; Dewey's whirlwind passage through library history is the source of much of librarianship's most colorful annals. The narrators who have given accounts of intimate contact with Dewey share a common characteristic—they are breathless, either with admiration or with rage.

Tall, powerfully built, astonishingly handsome, Melvin Dewey was priggishly devoted to the truth as he saw it. He had no use for the trivial frolics of life; wasted time was to him a moral issue. He even developed in his wife the habit of writing precise compilations of how each minute of the day had been spent. He was, above all, pragmatic, looking only for what was workable, then and there, to produce the desired results. Dewey has been called a "man-child," for his idealism, enthusiasm and impatience with any obstacle. Childish too was his simplistic assessment of the world and his mission in it. There is something maddeningly pretentious about a man who can decide, at seventeen, "to inaugurate a higher education for the masses,"[62] and who can write, at age seventy-six, in the same shallow prose,

> As I look back over the long years, I can recall no one I ever intentionally wronged, or of whom I should, now, ask forgiveness. . . . I have tried to do right, and so, if my race is run, I can go down into the last river serene, clear-eyed and unafraid.[63]

Yet burning zeal can carry one very far. Dewey's contributions to library development are unequaled, and his personal courage and unflinching faith in his mission will long be admired. It was Dewey who initiated library school education and aggressively promoted his standards of technical training in library mechanics.

A predominant characteristic of Dewey's, and important for its relationship to library education development, was his inordinate fondness for women. His male friends were few; his female friends appear to have been numerous. Throughout his life he preferred the company of women to men. He worked with them, played with them, and repeatedly got into trouble over them.

The trouble began as early as 1883 when Dewey hired six young women graduates of Wellesley to assist him in the organization of the Columbia University Library. At that time Columbia College was closed to women. Four years later Dewey again scandalized the campus by his insistence that women students be admitted to the first library school ever established. When the Trustees refused to allow Dewey classroom space because of the presence of women in the school, he furnished an unused storeroom on the campus and opened on schedule in defiance of the Trustees' orders. Shakily supported by President Frederick A. P. Barnard, the library school survived until 1889 when Dewey submitted his resignation to the Trustees shortly before his impending dismissal. During his time at Columbia, Dewey was sharply criticized for his open recruitment of women students and for his startling application form which included in it a request for height, weight, color of eyes, color of hair and a photograph.[64] Little tempered by time, Dewey's congenial intimacy with women set wagging in 1905 the "tongue of slander in sex matters," which even his eulogistic biographer concedes to have sent "stories sweeping like storms among the library leaders of the nation."[65] Dewey apparently had been guilty of some vaguely defined, but unorthodox, familiarities. The scandal prompted his wife to write scorching letters to the tale-bearers.

> Women who have keen intuitions know by instinct that they can trust Mr. Dewey implicitly. He has so many proofs of this and is so sure of his own self-control, that unconsciously his manner has grown more and more unconventional and familiar. . . . It is most unwise for any man to pass the bounds of convention, and he has been frequently warned of the danger. Knowing that I was absolutely free from jealousy and understood him perfectly, he has doubtless gone farther than with a wife who felt it necessary to watch her husband. . . . A wife who has lived more than a quarter of a century with her husband is surely the best judge as to whether he is pure minded. . . .[66]

Dewey's compatibility with women gave him insight which was unusual among men of his time. This remarkable statement was delivered before the Association of Collegiate Alumnae in 1886:

> Would a father say to his son, "My boy, your mother and I are lonely without you; you must stay at home, go out to afternoon teas with us, and keep us company in the big, empty house. I have enough for us all, so there is no need of your bothering your head about supporting yourself." Would he expect his son to be happy under such circumstances? Why, then, his daughter?[67]

Dewey had sincere respect for the intellect of women and successfully contended that Mary Cutler should be chairman of the library exhibit committee for the World's Columbian Exposition of 1893 because she was the most highly qualified candidate. He has often been praised because his defense of women's capabilities led him at times to suffer real personal sacrifice, as at Columbia. Any admiration for his support of women's rights, however, must be tempered by a recognition that Dewey had a strong personal desire for feminine company and an equally strong indifference to the presence of men. Indeed, his role as champion of women is a complex and intriguing one, for beneath it lies a grating note of paternalism. He did not call on women to assert themselves but instead set himself up as their valiant spokesman.

Dewey, with a progressive (as well as erotic) affinity for women, was obviously deflected by his sexist attitudes from his progressive design for a strong, highly intellectual new profession. The library school curriculum which Dewey devised at Columbia and later continued at the New York State Library School ruled out any "attempt to give general culture or to make up deficiencies of earlier education." Dewey, in a characteristically pragmatic decision, would reconcile the library needs of the country with the status of women in society by concentrating upon schooling which would teach the technical skills necessary to perform work on the lower rungs of the library ladder. The American Library Association's committee on the proposed library school at Columbia remarked that those who came to the school would probably wish to become administrators. Dewey quickly corrected them; the committee was told that "the plans all contemplate special facilities and inducements for cataloguers and assistants who do not expect or desire the first place."[68]

By 1905 library education had crystallized around Dewey's core of practical instruction of routine detail to a predominantly female force. Yet even though librarians had established library education as a system for non-professional training for library mechanics, they continued to wonder at the "appalling misconception" in the public mind of their "professional" qualifications and to bemoan the fact that the public had made them "the poorest paid professionals in the world."[69] In that year the American Library Association found an answer of sorts to the dilemma—the great librarians, it was agreed, were born, not made.

> Pooles and Winsors are not and never will be wholly produced by library schools. . . .
> Such eminent examples are born librarians. The born librarian will not need a school to teach him principles of classification . . . he will evolve systems of classifications and cataloging, and methods of administration without ever going near a school. . . .
> But there will never be many of him, and there will be thousands of library employees.[70]

It was for the low-level employee "that our schools are at present intended."[71] In the discussion that followed a consensus was reached by important library spokesmen like E. C. Richardson, Frederick M. Crunden, S. S. Green, Melvil Dewey and Herbert Putnam.[72] It was agreed that librarians of genius had no need of formal training. Unconsciously the national association had focused upon a central library truth. While females from the library schools became clerks and assistants and heads of small libraries, the most honored and well-paid librarians were men. The "best" librarians of the time were indeed not made, but born—born male.

The prevalence of women librarians also served to strengthen a non-professional bureaucratic system of control and low autonomy base for the library worker. In librarianship, as in teaching and social work, the dominance of women made more likely the development of an authoritative administrative structure with a stress on rules and generally established principles to control the activities of employees. In these feminized fields the highest success was secured through promotion to the administrative levels of the organization. This is in contrast to the pattern within established professions. In university teaching, for example, the productive practitioner is usually more honored within his profession than is the high level administrator of the university. Within librarianship and other feminized occupations, compliance to sex roles caused women to assume low levels of autonomy. Because sexist attitudes still prevail in the society, this basic situation has undergone little change since the nineteenth century.[73]

The changing image of librarianship graphically illustrates the many alterations which feminization brought to library work in the late nineteenth century. To call the public image of librarianship a stereotype does not make it an entirely erroneous concept, for the popular image of librarians is a by-product of deeper social realities. In the 1870s the popular concept of the librarian was that of a pre-occupied man in black—a collector and preserver who was never so happy as when all the volumes were safely on the shelf. He was thought to be ineffectual, grim and "bookish." Library literature of this period reflects the attempt of librarians to replace the image of the "old" librarian with a picture of the "new" librarian.

> The mechanical librarian is no more a finality than the acquisitive and conservative librarian. He is succeeded by . . . a type who is not content with removing the obstacles to circulation that his predecessors have built up, but tries actually to foster it; who leans more to the missionary and pastoral side of librarianship; who relies more on personal intercourse; who goes in for reference lists and annotated and interesting bulletins; who does not so much try to make it easy for an interested public to help itself among the books as to create an interested public.[74]

The popular image had shifted by 1905 to portray the librarian as a woman. The public's mental image of the librarian was consistently deprecatory. Meek, mousy and colorless had been added to the original "old" male librarian's traits of eccentricity, frustration, grouchiness and introversion. The public librarian came to be stereotyped as an inhibited, single middle-aged woman.[75] Librarian Harold Lancour quipped that he had heard so much about this lady that he was "growing rather fond of the old girl."[76] Howard Mumford Jones, musing on the caricature of the librarian, suggested that the image was "partly the product of limited budgets, and in part the product of genteel tradition. . . . This is not to say that all librarians are maiden ladies, but enough of them are to rank librarians with school teachers, Y.W.C.A. secretaries and social workers as persons less likely to go to night clubs than are receptionists or department-store buyers."[77] Unlike the librarians who had shaped public library standards, Jones understood well the chief reasons why professionalization continued to elude library workers: the training of librarians should include more about the insides of books and "less technical lore about what to do with the book as an object in space."

The feminization of public librarianship did much to shape and stunt the development of an important American cultural institution. The socially designated sexual roles which women acted out had a major influence upon the development of the library's "homey" atmosphere and its staff of "helpful" non-assertive hostesses. Increasingly librarians are seeking to change the traditional role of the public librarian. The hope is to establish librarianship on a scientifically-oriented, abstract-knowledge base, and to train the librarian as the indispensable expert in knowledge retrieval. The communication explosion has decidedly created a need for such a person; as the printed material grows to an unmanageable mass certainly someone, if not the public librarian, will move in to perform this vital function. However, until the librarian deals with the implications of feminization—with its varied inhibitory effects on intellectual excellence and leadership—progress toward professionalization will be limited. So long as sexist attitudes essentially govern the society, the basic situation which supported the service ideal and knowledge base of the nineteenth-century librarian seems unlikely to change.

NOTES

1 Cited in Robert W. Smuts, *Women and Work in America* (New York: Columbia University Press, 1959), p. 110.

2 Prepared by Charles Knolton Bolton, *The Athenaeum Centenary* (Boston: The Boston Athenaeum, 1907), p. 42. William Poole is generally credited with the hiring of the first woman librarian at the Boston Athenaeum in 1857. Poole's predecessor had barred women from the staff on the grounds that part of the library should be closed to impressionable female minds.

3 "The English Conference: Official Report on Proceedings," *Library Journal,* 2 (1878): 280. The *Library Journal,* organ of the American Library Association, is hereafter cited as LJ.

4 Joseph Adna Hill, *Women in Gainful Occupations, 1870-1920,* Census Monograph, No. 9 (Washington: Government Printing Office, 1929), p. 42. Librarianship has been termed a "profession" by the U.S. Census and is used in that sense here. Hill cites forty-three women library workers in 1870, 3,122 in 1900 and 8,621 in 1910. See Sharon B. Wells, "The Feminization of the American Library Profession, 1876-1923" (unpublished Master's Thesis, Library School, University of Chicago, 1967) for statistics on the number of women employed in library schools. Miss Wells counts 191 men and 18 women managing collections of over ten thousand volumes in 1875.

5 Melvil Dewey, "The Ideal Librarian," *LJ* 19 (1899): 14.

6 This analysis of the feminization of public librarianship rests upon a larger study of the socio-economic backgrounds and social and literary ideals of thirty-six library leaders in the period from 1876 to 1900. The selected librarians represent the profession's most influential spokesmen and are primarily the heads of urban libraries in the east, although important western library leaders are also included in the group.

7 U.S. Bureau of Education, *Public Libraries in the United States of America: Their History, Condition and Management,* Special Report, Part I (Washington: Government Printing Office, 1876), p. iii. Hereafter cited as "1876 Report."

8 Carl M. White, *The Origins of the American Library School* (New York: The Scarecrow Press, Inc., 1961), p. 14.

9 R. R. Bowker, "Libraries and the Century in America: Retrospect and Prospect," *LJ* 26 (1901): 5.

10 "1876 Report," p. 430. It is interesting to note that Perkins, who deserted his family to go West and to become the surly librarian at the San Francisco Public Library, left behind his young daughter, Charlotte Perkins Gilman, who later became a noted spokeswoman for women's rights.

11 "The English Conference. . . ."

12 The eight women among the selected thirty-six library leaders are: Mary Bean, Eliza G. Browning, Mary Cutler, Theresa Elmendorf, Caroline Hewins, Hannah James, Mary Plummer and Minerva Sanders.

13 Because librarians, at least until about 1885, were so vocal in their contempt for the low intellectual abilities of teachers in general, I deduce that most women librarians were better educated or of higher social standing than were most women teachers.

14 Mabel Newcomer, *A Century of Higher Education for American Women* (New York: Harper and Brothers, 1959), offers a good overview of the employment opportunities open to educated women in the late nineteenth century. The economic causes which she cites of the predominance of women teachers can also be applied to the feminization of librarianship. In 1870 three-fifths of all teachers were women. Also see: Robert E. Riegel, *American Women: A Story of Social Change* (Cranbury, New Jersey: Associated University Presses, Inc., 1970), pp. 132-200.

15 Aileen S. Kraditor, ed., *Up From the Pedestal* (Chicago: Quadrangle Books, 1968) and William L. O'Neill, *Everyone Was Brave* (Chicago: Quadrangle Books, 1969).

16 Richard le Gallienne, quoted in M. S. R. James, "Women Librarians," *LJ* 18 (1893): 148.

17 Linda A. Eastman, "Aims and Personal Attitude in Library Work," *LJ* 22 (1897): 80.

18 "Library Employment vs. the Library Profession," *Library Notes* 1 (1886): 50.

19 Ibid., p. 51.

20 Melvil Dewey, "Libraries as Related to the Educational Work of the State," *Library Notes* 3 (1888): 346.

21 Melvil Dewey, "The Attractions and Opportunities of Librarianship," *Library Notes* 1 (1886): 52. See also: Melvil Dewey, Address Before the Association of Collegiate Alumnae, March 13, 1886, *Lbrarianship as a Profession for College-Bred Women* (Boston: Library Bureau, 1886).

22 Lilian Denio, "How to Make the Most of a Small Library," *Library Notes* 3 (1889): 470.

23 Theresa H. West, "The Usefulness of Libraries in Small Towns," *LJ* 8 (1883): 229.

24 Mary Salome Cutler Fairchild, "Women in American Libraries," *LJ* 29 (1904): 162.

25 Idem.

26 Celia A. Hayward, "Woman as Cataloger," *Public Libraries* 3 (1898): 121-123; "Female Library Assistants," *LJ* 14 (1889): 128-129; John Dana, "Women in Library Work," *Independent* 71 (1911): 244.

27 Robert Wiebe, *The Search for Order, 1877-1920* (New York: Hill and Wang, 1967), pp. 122-123, discusses how sexual roles were expressed in this period by women social workers, lawyers and doctors in their service to children.

28 *LJ* 25 (1900): 123.

29 Idem.

30 Minerva Sanders, "Report on Reading for the Young," *LJ* 15 (1890): 59.

31 Annie Carroll Moore, "Special Training for Children's Librarians," *LJ* 23 (1898): 80.

32 E. M. Fairchild, "Methods of Children's Library Work as Determined by the Needs of the Children," *LJ* 22 (1897): 26.

33 Sophy H. Powell, *The Children's Library: A Dynamic Factor in Education* (New York: H. W. Wilson Co., 1917), pp. 1-7, 191-196, 255-271, is a careful study of the limited educational function of the children's section of the library. For a history of the development of library service to children see Harriet G. Long, *Public Library Service to Children: Foundation and Development* (Metuchen, New Jersey: The Scarecrow Press, Inc., 1969) and Effie L. Power, *Work With Children in Public Libraries* (Chicago: American Library Association, 1943).

34 For examples of women's mild tone see, Mary S. Cutler, "What a Woman Librarian Earns," *LJ* 17 (1892): 90; Mary E. Ahern, "The Business Side of a Woman's Career as a Librarian," *LJ* 24 (1899): 62; Martha B. Earle, "Women Librarians," *Independent* 49 (1897): 30.

35 "Woman's Meeting," *LJ* 27 (1892): 89-94.

36 "Proceedings," *LJ* 1 (1876): 90.

37 Caroline M. Hewins, "Library Work for Women," *LJ* 16 (1891): 273-274.

38 Cutler, p. 90.

39 Ibid., p. 91.

40 "Library Association of Central California," *LJ* 22 (1897): 308. Kelso later became a successful businesswoman in the field of publishing and remained an outspoken feminist.

41 Tessa L. Kelso, "Woman's Section of the A.L.A.," *LJ* 17 (1892): 444.

[42] Ahern, "The Business Side . . . ," pp. 60-62.

[43] Fairchild, "Women in American Libraries," pp. 153-162.

[44] Ibid., p. 162.

[45] Melvil Dewey, "The Profession," *LJ* 1 (1876): 5-6; Ernest C. Richardson, "Being a Librarian," *LJ* 15 (1890): 201-202.

[46] The first library school opened in 1887 at Columbia College. As a result of Williamson's critical survey of library schools in 1923, the curriculum standards in library education were revised and a national system of accreditation was established. Charles C. Williamson, *Training For Library Service: A Report Prepared by the Carnegie Corporation of New York* (Boston: The Merrymount Press, 1923); Sarah K. Vann, *The Williamson Reports: A Study* (Metuchen, New Jersey: The Scarecrow Press, Inc., 1971); C. Edward Carroll, *The Professionalization of Education for Librarianship* (Metuchen, New Jersey: The Scarecrow Press, Inc., 1970). For discussions of library professionalization see Philip H. Ennis, ed., *Seven Questions About the Profession of Librarianship* (Chicago: University of Chicago Press, 1961); Pierce Butler, "Librarianship as a Profession," *Library Quarterly* 21 (1951): 235-47; Robert D. Leigh, *The Public Library in the United States* (New York: Columbia University Press, 1969); Robert B. Downs, ed., *The Status of American College and University Librarians* (Chicago: American Library Association, 1958); William J. Goode, "The Theoretical Limits of Professionalization," *The Semi-Professions and their Organization: Teachers, Nurses, Social Workers*, ed. Amitai Etzioni (New York: The Free Press, 1969), pp. 266-313.

[47] White, *American Library School*, passim.

[48] Ennis, *Seven Questions*, p. 83.

[49] A. M. Carr-Saunders, *The Professions* (Oxford: Clarendon, 1933); T. A. Caplow, *The Sociology of Work* (Minneapolis: University of Minnesota, 1954); Ernest Greenwood, "The Attributes of a Profession," *Social Work* 2 (1957): 139-140; Howard M. Vollmer and Donald Mills eds., *Professionalization* (Englewood Cliffs, New Jersey: Prentice-Hall, 1966); Ronald M. Pavalko *Sociology of Occupations and Professions* (Itasca, Illinois: F. E. Peacock Publishers, Inc., 1971); Raymond M. Merritt, *Engineering in American Society* (Lexington, Kentucky: University Press of Kentucky, 1969); Daniel H. Calhoun, *Professional Lives in America* (Cambridge, Massachusetts: Harvard University Press, 1965); Kenneth S. Lynn, ed., *The Professions in America* (Boston: Houghton Mifflin Company, 1965).

[50] William F. Poole, "Buffalo Conference Proceedings," *LJ* 8 (1883): 281. See also, S. S. Green, *Libraries and Schools* (New York: F. Leypoldt, 1883), pp. 56-74; Max Cohen, "The Librarian as an Educator and Not a Cheap-John," *LJ* 8 (1883): 366-67; Melvil Dewey, "Public Libraries as Public Educators," *LJ* 9 (1886): 165.

[51] Charles Knowles Bolton, "The Librarian's Duty as a Citizen," *LJ* 21 (1896): 219-222; S. S. Green, "Personal Relations between Librarians and Readers," *LJ* 1 (1876): 74-81.

[52] Smuts, *Women and Work*, p. 36.

[53] For a thorough documentation of characteristic behavior of women workers see Richard L. and Ida Harper Simpson, "Women and Bureaucracy in the Semi-Professions," in Etzioni, pp. 196-265. The nineteenth-century woman would demonstrate even more strongly the traits which the Simpsons outline.

[54] Ennis, *Seven Questions*, pp. 7, 9. Marjorie Fiske, *Book Selection and Censorship* (Los Angeles: University of California Press, 1959), pp. 100-112.

[55] Sociologist Talcott Parsons has also noted the "tendency for women to gravitate into 'supportive' types of occupational role, where functions of 'helpfulness' to the incumbent of more assertive and ultimately, in the social function sense, more responsible roles, is a major keynote." Parsons points to sex composition as "both a symptom and partial determinant" of the pattern of "the 'quietness,' the rather passive character of the attributes of librarians as a group, wishing as it were to be unobtrusively 'helpful' but avoiding assertiveness." Talcott Parsons, "Implications of the Study," *The Climate of Book Selection*, ed. J. Periam Danton, (Berkeley: University of California, 1959), pp. 94-95.

[56] U.S. Bureau of Education, *Report of Commissioner of Education*, 1887-1888 (Washington: Government Printing Office), p. 1033.

[57] William Fletcher, *Public Libraries in America* (Boston: Roberts Brothers, 1894), pp. 32-33.

[58] My interviews with a leading university librarian and with several public librarians indicate a recent twentieth-century trend toward male homosexuals in library work. Their presence may be connected to the role-playing assumed by librarians in general. That is, to the extent that the homosexual male takes on the characteristics of femininity, he proves quite adaptable to playing a female service role. It may be, too, that male homosexuals, having been driven from most of the high status professions by prejudice, find women less hostile to their presence and thus feel more com-

fortable in a feminized working environment. On this point, note the formation of the Task Force on Gay Liberation during the 1970 American Library Association annual meeting.

59 William E. Goode, "The Librarian: From Occupation to Profession," Ennis, p. 13.

60 White, *American Library School*, pp. 32-33.

61 Normal schools were faced with similar problems during this period. A predominantly bureaucratic control is evident in school-teaching and librarianship. See Simpson and Simpson, pp. 196-221.

62 Fremont Rider, *Melvil Dewey* (Chicago: American Library Association, 1944), p. 8.

63 Grosvenor Dawe, *Melvil Dewey: Seer, Inspirer, Doer* (Albany, New York: J. B. Lyon Company, 1923), p. 76.

64 Ray Trautman, *A History of the School of Library Service* (New York: Columbia University Press, 1954), pp. 3-23.

65 Dawe, *Melvil Dewey*, p. 70.

66 Letter from Annie Godfrey Dewey, June 15, 1906, cited in Dawe, p. 70.

67 Dawe, *Melvil Dewey*, pp. 91-92.

68 "Report of the Committee on the Proposed School of Library Economy," *LJ* 10 (1885): 293.

69 Lutie E. Stearns, "The Question of Library Training," *LJ* 30 (1905): 68, 70.

70 "Fifth Session," *LJ* 30 (1905): 167-168.

71 Idem.

72 Ibid., pp. 164-176.

73 Simpson and Simpson, pp. 260-265. For current feminist protest see Anita R. Schiller, "The Widening Sex Gap," *LJ* 94 (1969): 1098-1100; Janet Freedman, "The Liberated Librarian," *LJ* 95 (1970): 1709-1711; Anita R. Schiller, "The Disadvantaged Majority: Women Employed in Libraries," *American Libraries* 4 (1970): 345-349.

74 "Editorial," *LJ* 17 (1892): 371. For discussions of the old and the new librarian see, "The New Librarians," *LJ* 15 (1890): 338; R.R. Bowker, "The Work of the Nineteenth-Century Librarian for the Librarian of the Twentieth," *LJ* 8 (1883): 247-250.

75 William H. Form, "Popular Images of Librarians,"*LJ* 71 (1946): 851-855; Robert Leigh and Kathryn W. Sweney, "The Popular Image of the Library and of Librarians," *LJ* 85 (1960): 2089-2091.

76 Ennis, *Seven Questions*, p. 74.

77 Howard Mumford Jones, "Reflections in a Library," *Saturday Review* 43 (1960): 34.

IMAGE AND REALITY:
THE MYTH OF THE IDLE VICTORIAN WOMAN

Patricia Branca

There is probably no other woman in history who has been as widely discussed as the Victorian woman. Nineteenth-century England produced some very eminent and quite controversial women, perhaps more than any other country at any previous period in history. Biographical studies on the lives of these pioneering women continue to have popular appeal. There is also a good deal of relevant information available in the literature on aspects of the women's movement.[1] However, these studies at most reflect individuals or groups who represent only a minority of Victorian women. What of the multitude of mute, inglorious females of whom no biography has ever been written, who, so far as we know, never did, nor said, nor thought a thing that would distinguish them from the mass of women of their day?

There is a growing number of historians who think they can tell us about the Victorian woman, and much of what they have said about her has been far from flattering. Indeed, she has become a cliché and a myth. She is often depicted as the "doll-like, bread-and-butter miss, swooning on a sofa," the frivolous, irrational, irresponsible creature of whim, the devotee of fashion, and of course, "the virgin-in-the-drawing-room," the strait-laced, thin-lipped prude, who blushed at such suggestive words as "legs."[2] The most pervasive image behind these characterizations is that of the idle Victorian woman—the "perfect lady"—the completely helpless and dependent female, whose only function in society was to inspire admiration and bear children.[3]

A rather more sophisticated version of the myth attempts to explain the origins of this paragon. It emphasizes that the Victorian woman was a new creature, the product of an increasingly wealthy industrializing society. The story so often retold goes as follows: In the early years of the century, the middle-class woman had been an active participant in the family, fulfilling vital tasks in the dairy, the confectionary, the store-room, the still-room, the poultry garden and the kitchen. She even assisted her husband with his business. She was truly the "helpmeet" of her husband. Her most important task was bearing children, and she was a loving and attentive mother. As the century progressed, a new prosperity brought about significant changes in the middle-class life style. The drive for social esteem became an obsession. Middle-class families wanted to show they had arrived by acquiring what has become known as the "paraphernalia of gentility"—large and expensive houses, elegant horses and carriages, and a retinue of servants—and the facilities for giving elaborate and lavish dinner parties. The "perfect lady" is said to have been an important element of the "paraphernalia of gentility," and this new striving for status is alleged to have brought about dramatic and direct changes in the life style of the middle-class woman.[4]

According to this view, middle-class parents, in their desire to imitate the upper classes, sent their daughters off to boarding schools where they were to acquire the elegant accomplishments necessary to becoming the "perfect lady:" a little French, some music, some dancing, the art of fancy needlework, and, of course, all the rules of proper etiquette. The middle-class woman no longer concerned herself with household affairs, for these were associated with those "lower" than she. Her domestic responsibilities were limited merely to supervising and complaining about her domestics.[5] She still maintained the important function of childbearing, but this also changed considerably. It appears that the "perfect lady" not only developed a disdain for household affairs but also for sex. Ideally, the "perfect lady" was to produce children by parthenogenesis; failing that, male impregnation was to take place in a dark bedroom into which the husband crept to create his offspring in silence while the wife endured the connection in a sort of coma.[6] After their births, the middle-class mother purportedly had little time for her children. They were given over to wet-nurses and nannies and governesses. A woman was considered to have done her duty to her children if she saw that they were fed, clothed and well supplied with toys.[7] The "perfect lady" was mother only at certain times of the day, and then only if it was convenient to her.

The Victorian wife is still considered the "helpmeet" of her husband in these interpretations, but the functions involved have necessarily changed. As the middle-class man achieved his position in the cruel, harsh, competitive outside world, he sought refuge in his home, which became his sanctuary. As "helpmeet," the Victorian woman was to provide the proper environment of respectability. She became the guardian of morality: righteous, gentle, sympathetic and most of all submissive.[8]

For the modern student, one of the most compelling features of this image of the Victorian woman, apart from its internal consistency, is the virtual unanimity with which historians have accepted and elaborated on it. The quality of the historians concerned varies greatly. Some are mere popularizers, seeking to capture that odd reader interest which delights in seeing Victorian women ridiculed, perhaps deriving some satisfaction in thinking what a long way we have come since, or, perhaps more Victorian than they think, finding discussion of sex respectable if phrased in terms of what nineteenth-century women were missing.[9] But more serious interpreters are involved as well. Feminists have found the image reasonable, however insulting it may be to Victorian women themselves, because it explains the source of the reaction that produced a large-scale feminist movement. Social historians such as J. A. Banks have advanced the level of discussion about such important matters as the causes and impact of birth control, while preserving most of the image intact.[10] However, we are now in a position to dispute major aspects of the conventional interpretation, partly because of the issues at least implicitly advanced in these earlier studies.

The purpose of this presentation is to see how the life of the idle Victorian woman in the image compares to several aspects of reality in the daily lives of married women in the central sector of the middle class—the largest group of women to whom the image is characteristically applied. The investigation centers on married women because the idle Victorian woman is generally depicted as married, and also because marriage provided the most typical role for the middle-class woman in the nineteenth century. Although this woman developed over at least a half-century, the discussion here centers on the mid-century decades, when the woman described above was supposedly in her heyday. Unquestionably the characteristics of middle-class women were taking shape during these decades, which came at the end of an extraordinary expansion of the class as a whole, whose rate of increase from 1803 to 1867, at 223 percent, was greater than the growth of the general population at 206 percent.

Before we can begin to compare image to reality, we must first examine one of the most difficult problems facing historians of women—the problem of sources. In spite of the great emphasis placed upon the role of the middle class in the nineteenth century, there is rarely any mention of women in the secondary treatments of the middle class. For example, Harold Perkin's book, *The Origins of Modern English Society 1780-1880,* deals with the impact of the middle class on nineteenth-century society at great length, but makes only passing reference to the women of the class.

The most significant gap in the primary sources is the lack of autobiographical data, which has led many investigators to rely heavily upon the fiction of the day.[11] The hazards here are obvious, and indeed an undiscriminating use of literature has contributed greatly to the formation of the image of the idle Victorian woman. For example, one might well assume from Austen's novels that most Victorian women had little to do but read poetry, relate local gossip and await the attention of gentlemen. Peter Laslett's caution against the use of the novel is worth repeating:

> ... it is indeed hazardous to infer an institution or a habit characteristic of a literary work and its story, from *Pamela,* for example, or from Elizabeth Bennett in *Pride and Prejudice* .... The outcome may be to make people believe that what was the entirely exceptional, was in fact the perfectly normal.[12]

This is indeed what has happened to the Victorian middle-class woman. The novel is not of course a completely useless source; it may, among other things, portray significant contemporary aspirations. Popular second-rate novels of the period can also be better utilized to get closer to reality. Nevertheless, the problems of interpretation are so great that it is difficult to contend that the historian should begin with novels or utilize them in the absence of elaborate supporting evidence.

The search for sources which are more representative of actual life is difficult and frustrating. There is an overwhelming amount of printed material available to the serious student of women in nineteenth-century England, including household manuals and women's magazines, all of which were written by and for the middle class. Professor Banks, in his study *Prosperity and Parenthood,* used this type of contemporary literature quite extensively for the first time, and his findings are cited regularly.[13] But Banks himself is the first to admit that his findings were tentative. What is needed now is a careful reevaluation of all this contemporary material not only for factual accuracy but also for the degree to which the ideas expressed are representative of wide public opinion.

To illustrate the difficult problem of evaluating contemporary sources, one needs only to look at two of the more popular works of the day—Mrs. Eliza Warren's book, *How I Managed My House on Two Hundred Pounds a Year*[14] and Mrs. Isabella Beeton's work, *The Book of Household Management.*[15] Among students of Victorian society, Beeton has become known as the mentor of the middle-class housewife. Her work is the one most often quoted as representative of middle-class life style.[16] From Beeton's advice to the English housewife, it does appear that the Victorian woman was much like her popular image. Her main duties were supervising the servants, seeing that the children were properly attended to by the nurse, making and receiving calls from her friends, and attending or giving lavish dinner parties. Warren, however, presented another version of the English housewife's life. According to her the average day of the mistress of the house was filled with housework, washing, cooking, crying children, shopping, quarreling with the maid, and managing financial problems. Both women claimed to be speaking to the middle-class housewife, but obviously they were not talking about the same woman. And here we get to the crux of the problem. Warren was quite specific about her reader, who lived on an income of £200 per year. Beeton's reader apparently lived on a considerably higher income.

Clearly we must come to terms with the material culture of the middle class before we can establish whether Warren or Beeton was more representative of the life style of the class. This is not, of course, the only way to approach the subject, for values and aspirations are significant in any full understanding of the middle-class woman in the nineteenth century. But a key flaw in contemporary and subsequent impressions about the middle class is that, except for often shaky Marxist characterizations, the middle class has been defined too exclusively in terms of values; the economic definition of the class has remained at best imprecise.[17] We need to determine how the Victorian woman actually lived, not how we think she should have lived nor, for the moment, how she thought she should live. Otherwise we cannot know if the values so often attributed to middle-class women applied to them all.

Admittedly, due to the insufficient data on incomes for the nineteenth century, it is almost impossible to specify exactly the economic situation of the average middle-class family. Recent studies have quoted £300 per annum, a sum considered to be minimal by J. A. Banks in his book, *Prosperity and Parenthood*.[18] However, we will contend that £300, far from being the minimum, was the maximum income level of most middle-class families in the nineteenth century. The £300 income level describes only a small proportion of the middle class, a distinctive upper-middle-class subgroup that had distinctive advantages—in education for example—which moved them close to the peripheries of the upper class. The number of people attaining this level comprised less than ten per cent of the middle class in the second half of the century and did not represent what we properly regard as middle class in terms of occupations and key values. Hence it is necessary to expand the income level downward to a range of £100-£300 to arrive at a figure typical of the annual middle-class income in nineteenth-century England.

This figure is based on two studies of income:[19] Patrick Colquhoun's *A Treatise on Indigence*,[20] which gives figures for 1803, and R. D. Baxter's *National Incomes*,[21] which reports on 1867. In different ways both studies allow a gross definition of the middle class in terms of occupations long accepted as typical, such as professionals, merchants, dealers, officers, agents, tradesmen and persons who buy and sell, foremen and clerks. These occupational groups can then be compared with income levels. Table 1 below gives the findings of both reports on the distribution of middle-class families according to income.

TABLE 1

Distribution of Middle-Class Families According to Income for the Years 1803 and 1867[22]

Income Per Year	Number of Families (1803)	Number of Families (1867)
Over £300	64,840	150,000
£100-£300	197,300	637,875
Under £100	32,000	757,250

Clearly the families who made over £300, although not negligible in terms of numbers, are not typical of the middle class. In 1867, they represented only 9.7 per cent of the total class, having grown more slowly than the other segments. The most significant change in terms of numbers was in the lower middle class, those who made less than £100 per year. Although by 1867 this group represented the largest segment of the middle class, the appropriateness of integrating it into a general definition of the class is limited by several factors. We know very little about the occupations of this group; above all, there appears to be considerable overlap in income level between them and the working class. For example, the highly skilled among the working class, according to Baxter, made between £50 and £73 per year.[23] The following discussion is limited to those who made between £100-£300 per year because their income level was clearly distinctive. It may be that further work will show significant connections between the life of the lower middle class and that of middle-class women but this will only amplify the contrast between the conventional image and economic reality. In the meanwhile the central segment of the middle class was both sizable and growing, constituting almost half the class in 1867.

Given the redefinition of income levels, it becomes clear that the middle class simply did not have the resources that would have been required to fit the popular image. This does not mean that knowledge of income provides definite conclusions about the substance of middle-class life, but it does open a variety of areas of inquiry.

Education is a case in point. We have readily accepted the notion, suggested by most of her contemporaries, that the middle-class girl was sent off to boarding school, where her mind was dulled by frivolous pastimes. Becky Sharp's schooling is often cited as being typical.[24] But this was not true for the majority of middle-class girls, who were in all probability educated in the home, usually by their mothers.[25] To be sure, we need more study of the education of middle-class girls in the nineteenth century, for again we are suggesting problems with existing interpretations rather than offering a detailed alternative.[26]

The main point here is that actual boarding-school costs were almost uniformly beyond the means of the majority of middle-class families. Frances Power Cobbe, for example, in her autobiography, quoted her bill for two years at a fashionable boarding school in Brighton in 1835 as £1000. The average price of a boarding school education has been cited as £130 per annum.[27] There were less expensive schools, such as St. Margaret's College, which advertised its ability to remedy the great deficiency in religious training and the neglect in the more solid parts of English education suffered by the young ladies attending most boarding schools. The financial arrangements were £60 per annum for girls under twelve, and £70 per annum for those above twelve. There was an additional entrance fee of £3. These fees included medical care and all other expenses except books and stationery.[28] There were schools that advertised costs as low as £25 to £30, according to a letter to *The Englishwoman's Domestic Magazine,* which seriously questioned the quality of education at such places.[29] These differences make it difficult to generalize about boarding-school education in the nineteenth century. But even the least expensive schools were well beyond the financial means of the bulk of middle-class families. Not many families could afford even £25 a year to send their daughter off to school, for this would amount to a yearly expenditure of 8 to 25 percent of the annual income for those families in the central segment of the middle class. Available composite budget projections suggest that 12 percent of the annual income was reserved normally for education plus servants' wages, charities, and incidental expenses.[30] Not until a family reached the £500-income level were there sufficient funds to educate even one child in one of the better boarding schools.[31] Given the limited means, even careful planning and saving for girls' education would not solve the problem except in unusual circumstances, for the average middle-class family had to provide for five children.

Another type of education defined as characteristically middle class was that provided by a governness.[32] The novel *Aurora Leigh* is often cited as best describing this system for the middle-class girl.[33] It is unlikely, however, that this type of education was at all common beneath the upper level of society. First, there simply were not enough governesses to serve the bulk of the middle class. According to the 1871 census there were only 55,000 governesses,[34] whereas four years before there were 150,000 families in the upper middle class alone (see Table 1). A family with the middle-class norm of five children, spaced two years apart, would require the service of a governness for ten years to take the education of even the eldest child well into the primary level. If we generously assume that two-thirds of the upper-middle-class families of 1867 had either passed or not yet reached their ten-year child-bearing period, the remaining segment would still have used up the entire corps of governesses by itself. As the aristocracy undoubtedly had first call on most available governesses, it is apparent that there were not enough to service the upper middle class alone. The cost of employing a governess explains why the tutorial system was so restricted. The wage of a governess ranged between £15- £100 per year, with the average centered in the £20- £45 range.[35] Again, this would require an expenditure of from 8 to 25 percent of a family's income, not economically feasible for any but the upper middle class.

Most middle-class girls spent the bulk of their time at home, taught by their mothers, for the obvious alternatives were uniformly too expensive. No doubt there were some who were fortunate enough to live near a day school and who could receive some type of formal education. Generally, these schools were few and far between and thus could service only a small proportion of the middle class, and rarely for more than a year of schooling. Most girls had to wait until a national system of education was established in the last quarter of the century.[36]

If we are ever to understand the middle-class woman of the nineteenth century, we must know what she did in the home, for this is where most middle-class women spent their entire lives—in their parents' home till they married (usually at the age of twenty-five) and then in their own home until their death. The conventional image properly notes this domestic focus, but there its utility ends. Reality for most middle-class women was that they spent all their days and many evenings in scrubbing, dusting, tending fires, for six to ten rooms in a three-to-four story home, in addition to the cooking, shopping, washing and sewing required for a family of seven. While the middle-class woman had assistance in her work, it did not save her from hard physical labor.

For another area in which the popular image has distorted the life style of the middle-class woman concerns servants. Census data alone correct this image, while confirming our conclusions about the limited economic circumstances of the housewives. Historians have delighted in discussing the relationship of servants to the middle class, but they rarely get beyond superficial data on values and attitudes. For example, the social historian J. F. C. Harrison suggests that employing domestic servants

> went to the very heart of the idea of class itself. The essence of middle classness was the experience of relating to other classes or orders in society. With one group, domestic servants, the middle class stood in a very special and intimate relationship; the one in fact played an essential part in defining the identity of the other.[37]

Conventionally, the domestic servant is viewed almost exclusively as a symbol that the family had arrived socially. It is common to hear that the main distinguishing characteristic separating a middle-class woman from those below her was an attitude of mind which demanded that she have at least one servant to wait upon her. In part this was true. However, historians have gone from one servant to many in defining the middle-class household in the nineteenth century. It is commonly assumed that the typical middle-class home was not complete until it had, at the very least, three domestics: a cook, a parlor-maid, and a nurse or housemaid.[38] This is a serious misrepresentation of the middle-class situation, for the typical home could not possibly have afforded to hire three domestics. In the majority of middle-class households employing domestics, there was only one servant, normally a maid-of-all-work, or to use the genteel term, general servant. Contemporaries agreed that the maid-of-all-work was the rule in England.[39] An analysis of the wages and the numbers and types of servants will confirm this. It also suggests that rather than merely representing status, the servant was essential to the middle-class woman if she was to meet the physical burdens of maintaining the household.

The average yearly wages of a cook and parlor-maid were both about £20, of a nurse-housemaid about £16. So the annual expenditure for the minimum number of domestics, as conventionally defined, amounted to £56.[40] Hence families earning £100- £300 per year would have had to expend anywhere from 20 to 50 percent of their incomes, and this was simply not economically feasible. In order to employ three domestics, a family had to have an annual income within the range of £400- £600, a range that would put them in the upper middle class. Almost all the contemporary sources agreed that at the £300 income level, only a maid-of-all-work, whose wage was between £9- £14 per year, could be employed, along with an occasional girl, and that on an income of under £300 only one servant could be afforded.[41]

The census data confirm further that the middle-class woman had to be content with a single servant. For example, the 1871 census listed 93,000 cooks.[42] If one allows a cook for every upper-class family, which according to Baxter numbered about 50,000,[43] that would leave only 43,000 cooks for the whole middle class. Since there were 150,000 families in the upper middle class alone, it is apparent that even within these ranks a cook was not always a part of the household. The only type of domestic servant that would begin to fill the needs of the more than

600,000 middle-class families who made between £100- £300 was the general servant (see Table 2).

TABLE 2

Female Domestic Servants 1851-1871[44]

Domestic Servant	1851	1861	1871	Per Cent Increase 1851-1871
General servant	575,162	644,271	780,040	35.6
Housemaid	49,885	102,462	110,505	121.5
Housekeeper	46,648	66,406	140,836	201.9
Cook	44,004	77,822	93,067	111.5
Nursemaid	35,937	67,785	75,491	101.1

The tremendous rate of increase during the twenty years after mid-century in the number of housemaids (121.1 percent), housekeepers (210.9 percent) and cooks (111.5 percent) has led some historians to conclude that these servants were becoming increasingly common in the middle-class home.[45] However, their numbers never approach even the number of middle-class families in the upper levels (see Table 1); and their increase simply reflected the growth in size and wealth of the upper class, which is significant but has no bearing on a study of the middle class. Indeed there is no guarantee that every household in the central segment of the middle class afforded a general servant, though most undoubtedly did, even in 1871, despite the fact that the rate of growth of this category had not kept pace with the expansion of the middle class. Since this was the only servant available to most middle-class homes, as confirmed both by their numbers and their cost, it is vital to know what she was like.

The idealized servant maid of Victorian literature, Mary, the housemaid of Mr. Nupkins of Ipswich, or Mary of the cherry-colored ribbons who took the heart of Sam Weller in Dickens' *Pickwick Papers,* was by no means the typical servant girl in the nineteenth century. The typical servant was, in fact, the coarsest of all domestic servants, certainly the least trained. She came from a background of extreme poverty, either from a laborer's cottage, where it was no longer possible to feed or clothe her, or from the wretched slums of the city. She had no experience with what the middle class considered to be the ordinary habits of civilized life, such as cleanliness, honesty and sobriety.[46] She was very young—in 1871 almost half of all general servants were under twenty years of age and more than a third were between the ages of 15-19.[47]

The typical general servant could not begin to provide a life of leisure for the middle-class mistress. By the end of the century it was felt that the problems associated with an untrained servant girl were greater than any help she could give.

The domestic-servant problem loomed as one of the most difficult responsibilities encountered by the middle-class housewife, as indicated by the extensive literature written on the subject and the number of letters asking for advice. Clearly, unfamiliarity accounted for some of the difficulties between mistress and maid, for during the nineteenth century many middle-class women came into contact with domestic servants for the first time and many were far from comfortable in their new role as employer. But this was only one aspect of the problem, for there were other factors endemic to the middle-class situation that must be examined.

The intimacy between the middle-class housewife and domestics accounted for many of their day-to-day difficulties. The middle-class woman, unlike her upper-class sister, had a direct, one-to-one relationship with her maid, and as a result she could easily become the object of much of the servant's displeasure. In contrast, the upper-class woman had a housekeeper to whom she gave all her orders, and the housekeeper in turn gave the orders to the various domestics. The upper-class woman rarely came into contact with the other servants, especially with one as low as the maid-of-all-work, and thus she did not encounter the many complaints and disciplinary problems. Because of the low wages and the extremely heavy work load, in a home that had the care of an average of five children, many young girls were constantly changing positions, rarely spending more than a year in one home. This frequent turnover created severe problems for the middle-class mistress. The housewife had to face the probability that by the time she worked out a suitable relationship with her servant, the servant would leave her for another position.

There are many other aspects of life, deriving at least in part from the economic reality, that need examination before we can begin to understand the middle-class Victorian woman. For example, one needs to know the condition of her physical health, given her heavy daily workload and the limited resources available for medical care. If the economic data dispose of the paraphernalia of gentility for most of the middle class, the question of the middle-class woman's role as consumer remains open. (If she could not afford the piano that has long been viewed as a standard feature of her home,[48] she did have some margin over subsistence that she could use to forge a more modestly novel life style, and this deserves serious attention.)

Motherhood is another topic for re-examination. As we have seen, most middle-class mothers could not afford the services of wet-nurses, nannies, and governesses. How did the changing concepts of childhood, with the related changes in child-rearing practices, affect the middle-class mother, with her still limited means? Did she continue to suffer the common tragedy of infant death? Was she herself often a victim of the vicissitudes of repeated childbirths, which brought thousands of deaths annually during the nineteenth century?[49] What was her role in family limitation, and how was this related to her economic circumstances? Given this reassessment of the economic position of the middle-class woman, we must re-examine her relationship with her husband, which the popular image depicts as based mainly on material considerations. Perhaps there was more mutual affection than we have assumed, and less seeking after status.

No doubt many women in the middle class did aspire to a more genteel life. A retinue of servants, a grand house and a piano must have been the dream of many young middle-class girls. However, with marriage many came to realize that they had to make do with the most economical and practical of luxuries. For the woman who had to make most of her clothing and that of her children, the sound of the sewing machine probably afforded as much delight as would a piano. The fact remains that no matter what her aspirations were, the reality was that she could not afford the life of the "perfect lady." Most middle-class women were probably far too absorbed in the affairs of the house and caring for their husbands and children to worry about an image they could not attain.

Thus it is obviously necessary to go beyond the stereotypes in assessing the middle-class woman of the nineteenth century. She was not a helpless or leisured woman, for she played a vital and active role in the Victorian family. The nineteenth century was a period of rapid transition, in which an urban, industrial society was being established. The conventional image of Victorian women has implicitly assumed that women recoiled from this new society or were held apart from it, and thus most social historians make only passing reference to the housewife. In fact, middle-class women were in the midst of the changes associated with modernization, for they managed resources above the subsistence level while lacking the funds to escape into a leisured existence.

There were women who did shape a new life style within the family, but only with considerable difficulty. They sought to improve their lot, but their level of income often held them back. Ultimately, they adopted such measures as birth control, that were basic to the more general modernization of women, but these decisions must be evaluated within the material framework of their lives. Birth control, for example, resulted not only from status seeking by middle-class males[50] but also from the effort of women to cope with the physical burdens of their lives. Some women, because of their responsibility for supervising a changing life style with restricted means, were afflicted with mounting anxieties. Not a few resorted to alcohol or drugs as a refuge—another topic that requires exploration as we move from image to reality. Successful adaptation to the new urban society was itself complex and difficult. Now that we are in a position to understand the material culture of middle-class women, we can move to a broader effort to assess both their successes and their failures and to place their study among the central concerns of social history.

I wish to thank Professor Peter N. Stearns for reading my essay. As always, his comments were thorough and to my advantage. And as the saying goes, any faults are my own.

[1] A good brief survey of the political struggle of women is William O'Neill, *The Woman Movement: Feminism in the United States and England* (Chicago: Quadrangle Books, 1969).

[2] Duncan Crow, *The Victorian Woman* (New York: Stein and Day, 1971), pp. 13, 26, 28.

[3] Harold Perkin, *The Origins of Modern English Society 1780-1880* (London: Routledge and Kegan Paul, 1964), p. 159.

[4] J. A. Banks and Olive Banks, *Feminism and Family Planning in Victorian England* (New York: Schocken, 1964), pp. 111-112.

[5] Crow, *The Victorian Woman*, p. 25.

[6] Banks and Banks, *Feminism*, p. 6.

[7] Martha Vicinus, ed., *Suffer and Be Still: Women in the Victorian Age* (Bloomington: Indiana University Press, 1972), pp. ix-x; Banks and Banks, *Feminism*, pp. 58-59; Crow, *The Victorian Woman*, pp. 45-52.

[8] Martha Vicinus, ed., *Suffer and Be Still: Women in the Victorian Age* (Bloomington, 1972), pp. ix-x; Banks and Banks, *Feminism*, pp. 58-59; Crow, *The Victorian Woman*, pp. 45-52.

[9] Crow, *The Victorian Woman;* see my review of Crow's book in *Journal of Social History* 6, no. 4 (Summer 1973): 513-515.

[10] J. A. Banks, *Prosperity and Parenthood* (London: Routledge and Kegan Paul, 1954).

[11] Patricia Thomson, *The Victorian Heroine, A Changing Ideal 1837-1873* (London: Oxford University Press, 1956).

[12] Peter Laslett, *The World We Have Lost* (New York: Scribners, 1960), p. 87.

[13] Geoffrey Best, *Mid-Victorian Britain 1851-1875* (London: Weidenfield and Nicolson, 1971); J. F. C. Harrison, *The Early Victorians 1832-1851* (London: Praeger Publishers, 1971).

[14] Eliza Warren, *How I Managed My House on Two Hundred Pounds a Year* (London, 1865).

[15] Isabella Beeton, *The Book of Household Management* (London: S. O. Beeton, 1861).

[16] Banks and Banks, *Feminism*, pp. 63-64.

[17] Roy Lewis and Edmund Upton Angus Maude, *The English Middle Classes* (London: Phoenix House, 1949); Charles Morazé, *The Triumph of the Middle Class: A Study of European Values in the Nineteenth Century* (Cleveland: World, 1966). In contrast to these studies is Adeline Daumard, *La Bourgeoisie Parisienne 1815-1848* (Paris: Ecole Pratique des Hautes Etudes, 1963) which is a good study that gets beyond values.

[18] Banks, *Prosperity and Parenthood*, p. 48; Best, *Mid-Victorian Britain*, p. 90; Janet Dunbar, *The Early Victorian Woman, Some Aspects of Her Life 1837-1857* (London: George G. H. Harrap, 1957), p. 66.

[19] Since this is a crucial point, the limited nature of the evidence is obviously unfortunate. Due to the many problems encountered in dealing with nineteenth-century statistics it is doubtful whether anything more precise can ever be established, save perhaps in local research using personal records. The two most obvious sources for the period are census returns and tax records, but the problems is that this material lacks class-specific data. There is no clear division of classes in major categories; for instance, under the industrial sector, of prime importance for the nineteenth century due to its tremendous growth rate, manufacturers and workers are listed together. The statistical accuracy of tax returns is thoroughly questionable due to the problems of widespread tax evasion and compilation which often resulted in counting individual tax payers more than once. Even though the studies of the nineteenth-century cannot match the statistical accuracy of a modern social survey, they at least offer a start toward a better interpretation of what was middle class.

[20] Patrick Colquhoun, *A Treatise on Indigence* (London: J. Hatchard, 1806). Colquhoun's findings reported in this study were based on the figures published in Perkin, *Origins of English Society*, pp. 20-21.

[21] R. D. Baxter, *National Income* (London: Macmillan, 1868). Baxter's findings have been used extensively by Perkin in *Origins of English Society*, pp. 419-421; and by Eric Hobsbawn in "The Labour Aristocracy in Nineteenth-Century Britain," in his work *Labouring Men* (New York: Anchor, 1967), pp. 321-370. This does not obviate the difficulties in the source, which may have been accepted too uncritically, but it does add some credibility, if only for want of anything better, to its use as a general guideline.

[22] Both Colquhoun's and Baxter's original findings were revised for this study in order to compensate for the elimination of occupational categories included by the authors which were not, strictly speaking, part of the middle class in the nineteenth century. For example, both works added

farmers as part of the middle class; but these were eliminated in this study which deals exclusively with the urban middle class. It should also be noted that the comparison of data from the two sources should be assessed in terms of changes in prices and rising incomes. Since it has been shown that there was very little increase in prices for most of the century, no adjustment was considered necessary for this factor. See George H. Wood, "Real Wages and the Standard of Comfort Since 1850," *Journal of the Royal Statistical Society* 72 (March 1909). There are no data available on whether incomes were rising within the middle class, and if so by how much, during the nineteenth century. However, Table 1 shows the largest increases in the middle class were in the two lower levels and not in the £300 plus sector; while this does not eliminate the possibility that within the central segment there was an increase in average income, it suggests that the principal trend was recruitment into the lower ranges rather than substantial enrichment. For a full discussion of this issue see Patricia Branca Uttrachi, "Health and Household: Material Culture of Middle-Class Women in Nineteenth-Century Britain" (unpublished doctoral dissertation, Rutgers University, 1973), Chapter 2.

23 Baxter, *National Income*, p. 64.

24 H. C. Barnard, *A History of English Education from 1760* (London: University of London Press, 1961), p. 22.

25 P. W. Musgrove, *Society and Education in England Since 1800* (London: Methuen and Co., 1968), p. 12.

26 The studies to date have tended only to emphasize the reform movements in education; for example, Josephine Kamm, *Hope Deferred: Girls' Education in English History* (London: Oxford University Press, 1965); but these changes were not significant until very late in the century.

27 Dunbar, *Early Victorian Women*, p. 136.

28 *The English Woman's Journal* (July 1859), advertisement.

29 *The Englishwoman's Domestic Magazine* (1868), p. 109.

30 John Walsh, *A Manual of Domestic Economy: Suited to Families Spending from £150 to £1500 A Year* (London: G. Routledge and Sons, 1874), p. 676.

31 *A New System of Practical Domestic Economy Founded on Modern Discoveries and the Private Communications of Persons of Experience*, 3rd ed. (London: H. Colborn, 1828), p. 407.

32 M. Jeanne Peterson, "The Victorian Governess: Status Incongruence in Family and Society," *Victorian Studies* 4, no. 1 (September 1970); also published in Vicinus, *Suffer and Be Still*.

33 Barnard, *English Education*, p. 155.

34 *Census of England and Wales, 1871*, Summary Tables, Table 14, p. xliv.

35 Peterson, "The Victorian Governess," pp. 11-12.

36 For a history of education in the nineteenth century see Barnard, *English Education;* Musgrove, *Society and Education;* and Brian Simon, *Studies in the History of Education 1780-1870* (London, 1960).

37 Harrison, *Early Victorians*, p. 110.

38 Banks, *Prosperity and Parenthood*, p. 76.

39 *The Englishwoman's Domestic Magazine* 9 (1864): 371.

40 Charles Booth, *Life and Labour of the People in London*, Vol. 8 (London: Macmillan and Co., 1896), p. 223.

41 Beeton, *Household Management*, p. 8.

42 *Census of England and Wales, 1871*, Summary Tables, Table 19, p. xliv.

43 Baxter, *National Income*, p. 36.

44 Banks, *Prosperity and Parenthood*, p. 83.

45 Ibid., p. 84.

46 Dunbar, *Early Victorian Woman*, pp. 49-50.

47 *Census of England and Wales, 1871*, Summary Tables, Table 19, p. xliv.

48 The cost of a new piano was too great for the average middle-class family budget. The price ranged between 20 and 100 guineas, as cited by Arthur Loesser, *Men, Women and Pianos: A Social History* (New York: Simon and Schuster, 1954), p. 259. Second-hand pianos were advertised in *The London Illustrated News* for £12 and up.

49 Three thousand women annually died in childbirth; see *Fifth Annual Report of the Registrar General of Births, Deaths and Marriages in England* (London, 1843), p. 380.

50 Banks and Banks, *Feminism*, passim; Banks, *Prosperity and Parenthood*, passim.

"WE ARE NOT BEASTS OF THE FIELD":
PROSTITUTION AND THE POOR IN PLYMOUTH AND
SOUTHAMPTON UNDER THE CONTAGIOUS DISEASES ACTS*

Judith R. Walkowitz
Daniel J. Walkowitz

Dr. J. C. Barr, examining surgeon at the Aldershot Lock Hospital, in a December 1867 letter to the War Office, described the nomadic life style of the prostitutes in Aldershot, a garrison town in Kent: "Several women have habituated themselves to a kind of gypsy mode of living, sleeping under horses in stables or large holes dug out of sandbanks." He deplored "the dehumanizing influence of the abominables places to which so many of the prostitutes are driven" and advocated a Lodging House Act designed especially for their district. Living in drains, sometimes even accompanied there by soldiers, the women assumed the excremental character of their surroundings: ". . . Their general condition was miserable in the extreme; dirty clad in unwomanly rags, some appearing half-starved covered with vermin, causing those near to them to shun them with aversion."[1]

William Acton's work on prostitution[2] popularized this view of the prostitutes residing in the garrison and dock towns of southern England. The prostitute as human residue comfortably fitted the conventional image of the utterly degraded and outcast woman. And it legitimized the kind of sanitary and penal measures by which the community might purge itself of a "material nuisance." In a society where "pollution" was the governing metaphor for the perils of social intercourse between the "Two Nations," the prostitute threatened morally and physically to contaminate respectable society.

Most attempts to describe the nineteenth-century lower-class prostitute have either accepted this indictment of these women or portrayed them as the silent

---

* We would like to thank the following people for their help with this project: Jean L'Esperance, Mary Sue Hartman, Raphael Samuels, the Ruskin College History Workshop, and the Rutgers history graduate students in Professors Hartman's and Daniel Walkowitz's seminars. The Rutgers Research Council generously assisted in the preparation of the manuscript.

victims of social injustice.[3] Not all of these women, however, conformed to this picture of the defenseless prostitute: during the 1870s and 1880s, in at least two South England dock towns, Plymouth and Southampton, women accused of being "common prostitutes" left a record of protest against the Contagious Diseases Acts—parliamentary legislation that sought to register and examine them for venereal disease. They were not dehumanized vagabonds, but rather poor working women trying to survive in bustling dock towns that offered them limited employment opportunities and that were hostile to young women who lived alone. They were very much a part of a lower-class community, and their general social and economic profile did not differ significantly from that of the rest of the poor in those districts. Their choice of prostitution was in no sense "deviant": it was in many ways a rational choice, given the set of unpleasant alternatives open to them. By and large, these women had multiple social identities: prostitution was for them a part-time or seasonal activity, or a stage in their lives that they would pass through. Hence, their "sexually deviant" behavior must be measured against their background and their expectations for the future, as well as against the general standard of lower-class sexual behavior. Nonetheless, by the mid-1880s, external forces, in particular the Acts themselves, may have helped to create a distinct professional class—it structured the choices open to these women and disrupted the pattern of their lives.

Several problems will direct our interest: who were the women accused of being prostitutes in these towns; how did they live; how did they respond to the web of social control set up by the Acts; what effects did the Acts have on their lives? A brief history of the Contagious Diseases Acts and their place in the tradition of repressive social legislation, as well as an historical sketch of the Plymouth and Southampton areas, provide a setting for the narrative of these women's social experience.

The Contagious Diseases Acts of 1864, 1866, and 1869 were instituted as a means of checking the spread of venereal disease among the unmarried soldiers and sailors stationed in various towns in Ireland and Southern England.[4] They established the apparatus by which women accused of being common prostitutes were registered, subjected to a periodical examination, and, if found suffering from a venereal disease, incarcerated in a certified lock hospital (a hospital containing venereal wards) for a period not to exceed nine months. The definition of "common prostitute" was vague, and consequently the Metropolitan police employed under the Acts had broad discretionary powers. When accosted by the police, a woman was expected to submit voluntarily to an examination or be brought before the local magistrates. At the trial, the burden was on the woman to prove she was virtuous—that she did not go with men, whether for money or not.

The War Office and the Admiralty were appointed to oversee the operation of the Acts, working in cooperation with local and central authorities. The plain-clothes Metropolitan police, who were stationed in subjected districts and assigned the task of identifying the women and enforcing their submission; the civil hospital authorities; and the local justices of the peace, all had very different sets of interests and styles of operation. The three successive bills of 1864,

1866, and 1869 extended both the territorial and legal jurisdiction of the delegated authorities to within a ten-mile radius of seventeen districts in England and Ireland.[5]

Certainly the desire of military authorities to safeguard a "healthy imperial race" contributed to the enactment of the Contagious Diseases Acts. But attention to military readiness and imperialist ventures abroad does not tell the whole story. In these Acts, one may perceive imperialist compulsions turned inward toward the domestic colonization of the poor. It is within the general atmosphere of social intolerance and institutionalized violence that the treatment of the lower-class prostitute becomes comprehensible. Criminal statutes against the common prostitute had their origins in the vagrancy laws, and the prostitute's legal status bore the taint of the outcast stripped of civil personality and constitutional rights. The vagrancy laws merely lumped her with beggars, thieves, and all "loose, idle and disorderly persons" who could not give a good account of themselves and their way of living.[6] They provided no statutory definition of a common prostitute, other than to designate her as female. Although they dealt with "street offences" they did not prohibit solicitation *per se:* only when her behavior represented a gross violation of public decency did the prostitute come under the purview of the law and become subject to police intervention.

Like the vagrancy laws the C. D. Acts were informed by a fear of contagion, and were part of the legal, institutional, and sanitary network that segregated and rationalized the treatment of the socially deviant. Supporters of the Acts readily found precedents for them in the provisions of the Poor Law, Common Lodging House Act and Vaccination Act, and the various police and judicial reforms of the mid-century designed to control street behavior and facilitate the efficient prosecution of disorderly persons and houses.[7]

The new clauses of the 1866 bill made clear the place of these Acts in the tradition of repressive social legislation. By requiring periodical examination, the 1866 Act extended police control over a much larger group of lower-class women, not simply diseased prostitutes but women suspected of promiscuous behavior. There had to be a corresponding change in the system of police intelligence. Previously, police had relied on reports from the men admitted to the military hospital. Now they were expected to go out to the community and maintain a tight surveillance over places where "public women" might congregate, principally the centers of working-class leisure activities and residential quarters—pubs, beershops, music halls, fairs, private lodgings and tramp common-lodging houses.

Although the Acts had been in force since 1864, it was not until 1870 that there was any sustained public outcry over them.[8] The Bill extended the Acts to a civilian population for the first time in Southampton. When a group of doctors also pressed for the extension of the Acts to the larger cities of the North, they touched off a counterattack by socially concerned Nonconformists. At the Social Science Congress at Bristol in 1869, a meeting of men was sponsored by prominent Wesleyans and Quakers to call attention to the Acts. This spurred the formation of the all-male National Association which first constituted itself as a group opposed to extension of the Acts to the North and subsequently expanded its goal to their repeal. The Ladies National Association organized shortly thereafter, and, under the leadership of Josephine Butler, promulgated its Women's Manifesto on December 31, 1869. The Manifesto denounced the Acts as blatant examples of the "double standard," depriving poor women of their constitutional rights. They also declared their moral objection to the official sanction of vice and expressed horror at the internal examination. The national campaign for repeal continued from 1870 to 1886, when the Acts, which had been suspended in 1883, were removed from the statute books. The campaign stimulated a series of parliamentary inquiries into the working of the Acts and provide a useful source of information on conditions in the subjected districts.[9]

The history of the national repeal campaign, a fascinating chapter in the history of Victorian reform and social feminism, will be told elsewhere.[10] This paper will explore the lives of the poor women who became the focus of public attention and debate. Do these women bear any resemblance to the tramps and social outcasts of Aldershot described by Dr. Barr in the opening quote? Aldershot, as Rev. Gledstone, a repeal agent touring the subjected towns in 1876 remarked, was a "town of yesterday," a town without history, which sprang up as a garrison camp in the early nineteenth century with inadequate accommodations and meager employment opportunities for a civilian population.[11] The Aldershot prostitutes characterized by Dr. Barr were camp followers, a large number coming from London and Ireland (20 percent from each)—wicked city women and degraded Irish whores. But men and women who moved into the docktowns of Southampton and Plymouth had predominantly come from the surrounding countryside and encountered a more complex and established community and economic life.

Plymouth and Southampton had a similar social and economic profile, but there were some significant differences that might begin to explain the varied course of the resistance movement in the two districts. Both districts were subjected to the Acts and placed under the supervision of the Admiralty. The repeal movement and the government both used Plymouth as the focus for their propaganda. The town was viewed as the model station where the success or failure of the C.D. Acts could be tested. Southampton, however, witnessed the greater legal resistance to the Acts. Plymouth had extensive government installations with large numbers of unmarried personnel, while Southampton was a commercial port. Government influence there was far less, and the repeal campaign enjoyed much larger indigenous middle-class support. Finally, both cities experienced considerable population and commercial growth in the mid-Victorian period, while offering the women who came in from the surrounding countryside very limited employment possibilities. Together, these cities present a comparative case study in reform agitation and the ability of women to resist.

Greater Plymouth, composed of Devonport, Stonehouse and Plymouth, and known as the Three Towns, constituted one station (Devonport district) and was first placed on the schedule in 1864. Located in the southwest corner of the country at the Devon and Cornwall border, Greater Plymouth became the "pattern station" of the C.D. Acts where the government allocated more resources and energy toward the effective operation of the Acts. As *The Shield*, the organ of the National Association, commented in 1870, it was the statistics from Plymouth "they always parade"[12] as evidence of the diminution of V.D. among the military and of the moral reclamation of the women brought under the Acts. The Admiralty subsidized the construction of the Royal Albert Hospital of Devonport in 1863, which nonetheless went under the guise of a civil hospital supported by voluntary contributions. The Royal Albert was operated during the 23-year period almost entirely at the Admiralty's expense, with the lock wards heavily subsidizing the civil side.[13] The repealers identified Devonport district as the important challenge, and repeatedly sent money and personnel there to stir up public indignation at the Acts.[14] Local supporters (a small band of socially concerned Quakers and Nonconformists), resident paid agents, and solicitors actively encouraged the women and "brothel keepers" of the Three Towns to elude the police and to resist the regulations of the Acts. Protest in these towns can be measured in many ways, but the refractory behavior of the poor women in the lock hospital wards and the resistance to the Acts in the courts clearly must be seen in the context of organized public opposition.

Southampton's history is somewhat different. With an entirely civilian population, it was not subjected to the Acts until 1870, largely because of the complaints of Portsmouth authorities (seventeen miles away) that diseased women from Southampton were coming into their town. Unlike the Three Towns, where well over a third of the men were in military service or employed in government installations, Southampton was a commercial port and consequently more independent of government policy.[15] The serious oppositon that greeted the Acts here came from within the community: from prominent Southampton religious and community leaders, and from a number of borough magistrates. The Admiralty was unable to provide hospital accomodations in Southampton for the women who had been found diseased, as the Royal Hants Infirmary whose managing committee was dominated by stalwart repealers adamantly refused to cooperate in the construction of lock wards.[16] And the attorney who defended the accused prostitutes, Robert Harfield, wielded considerable influence in the city. Certainly this public antagonism encouraged the women's resistance to the Acts and largely accounts for the great number in this district who refused to submit voluntarily to the Acts and to report for examination after an order had been made.[17] Lastly, the women had to leave Southampton to report to Portsea Hospital in Portsmouth, a notoriously inefficient and run-down establishment, a fact that would not encourage voluntary submission.

The social and economic conditions of the Southampton and Plymouth districts suggest something of the alternatives open to the laboring poor there and graphically illustrate familiar themes associated with the woman question: emigration, redundant women and limited job opportunities. While cut off from the industrial development of the North, both districts experienced a sizeable growth in the mid-Victorian period as a result of railway and dockyard expansion[18] (see Table). This expansion offered new employment opportunities

TABLE I

Population Statistics, 1851 and 1871

	Plymouth	Devonport	E. Stonehouse	Southampton
1851				
Total population	52,221	38,180	11,970	35,305
percent age 20 and over	59.0	60.1	59.2	57.0
percent female	54.4	57.2	60.3	54.6
1871				
Total population	68,758	49,449	14,585	53,741
percent age 20 and over	57.0		——	54.6
percent female	54.2		——	55.2
1851-1871				
Percent increase	31.7	29.5	21.8	52.2

and facilitated—by way of cheap rail travel—the movement of persons into the urban centers from the surrounding countryside. Plymouth's dock goes back to the time of William and Mary, but the creation of the Great Western Docks and the tie-up with the railroad network in the 1840s made it possible for the city to develop as an important commercial port and mail and emigration depot. As an older town, Plymouth always had a resident mercantile and professional middle class, and functioned as an important market town for Eastern Cornwall and Western Devon. Between 1851 and 1871 the populations of Plymouth, Devonport and East Stonehouse all increased by more than 20 percent. Southampton's growth was even more remarkable; its pace of expansion was almost double that of the Three Towns and comparable to that of the northern industrial cities. Between 1851 and 1871 Southampton's population increased 52.2 percent, from 35,305 in 1851 to 53,741 in 1871.[19]

These cities had markedly uneven sex ratios. Among adults, women predominated: in 1871, women over 20 constituted 55.2 percent and 54.2 percent of the population of Southampton and Plymouth-Devonport, respectively. But the figures for Greater Plymouth do not take into account the many men who lived in military quarters. In civilian sections, at least three out of every five adult residents were women.

Immigration to the cities was the prevailing demographic pattern in the early and mid-nineteenth century, and both districts reflect the localized character of that migration. Between 1841 and 1851, two-thirds of the rural parishes of Devon suffered a loss in population. But as W. G. Hoskins asserts, the migrants generally moved within a radius of 30 miles to Exeter, Devonport, Plymouth and the new seaside resorts. When men migrated out of the South, they tended to emigrate across the seas, rather than to the industrial North. This was dramatically indicated by the drastic population shift in Cornwall, another source of population for greater Plymouth.[20] After the financial collapse of the copper mining industry in 1867, there was a wholesale migration of the most skilled miners. They left behind twenty thousand dependents, women and children suffering from acute economic distress and the total destruction of community life. In this year real wages in the county fell 50 percent.[21] The closest large city and major railroad depot was Plymouth, a place to which these women resorted. According to the Town Clerk, a Mr. Phillips, the women from the Cornwall mining districts were an ever replenishing pool of prostitution. Careful, repressive measures were employed by Plymouth police to discourage their taking up residence: for example, young women apprehended fresh from the mining districts on a drunk-and-disorderly charge were not given the option of a fine. They were sent to prison to "give them the benefit of the chaplain's advice, and with instructions to the governor to pay their fare home if they will go."[22]

The census statistics reflect this movement from the rural districts into the cities. Emigrants were likely to be young and uneducated, with little or no industrial training. Males could find employment in the large casual labor force on the docks of Southampton or the Three Towns.[23] Young women, though, had severe disabilities: young single girls were increasingly closed out of field work, so that their previous employment would most likely have been as maids-of-all-work in a farmer's household. Cornish women may have done surface work on the now shut-down mines. Without further apprenticeship, that kind of previous industrial experience could fit them only for general domestic service, laundry work, or slopwork.[24]

With the new population came new slums. In both Southampton and the Three Towns, the first efforts to deal with urban problems were in the realm of sanitary engineering. The subsequent extension of municipal government in Southampton and greater Plymouth was largely a response to the need for efficient sanitary and law-enforcement agencies. Bye-laws to facilitate better control over the streets and "disorderly houses," as well as those that would regulate common lodging houses, were passed in the next ten years. Hence local civil authorities had identified the casual poor as a threat to public decency and health prior to the enactment of the C.D. Acts. Did the women brought under the Acts belong to the same general group? Statistical data obtained from hospital, police, and census records help to provide a social and economic profile of these women.

According to the 1871 census schedule, there were 77 adult female patients (three babies were listed as well) in the lock wards of the Royal Albert Hospital, Devonport. Almost nine out of every ten women (89.7 percent) were between the ages of 15 and 29, with the largest concentration between 15 and 24 (74.1 percent). Ninety-four and eight tenths percent were single, and 91.0 percent were born in Cornwall and Devon, with 42.9 percent born in the Three Towns. A statistical report of the Royal Albert lock register of 1868, enumerating all women sent to the hospital under the Acts for that year, produced similar results.[25] As to age, the two groups were virtually identical: 76 (91.6 percent) of the Portsea Hospital "prostitutes" were between the ages of 15 and 29, while the average woman's age was 21.2 years, compared to 21.8 years among the women at the Royal Albert.

If anything, these figures are slightly skewed toward the older age brackets (over 20), as the police and Admiralty authorities were anxious to demonstrate the "elimination" of juvenile prostitution as an important side benefit of the Acts.[26] As a consequence, young girls (under 15) were not included in the Metropolitan police statistics and were also unlikely to be sent to the lock hospital.

The statistics provided by the Metropolitan police of "known common women" in the subjected districts follow the pattern outlined above. These statistics have to be used with some caution. Local authorities hotly disputed the absolute numbers as well as complaining that young girls were underrepresented.[27] Nonetheless, this set of statistics provides a useful overview. Of the 2,411 "common women" listed in 1871 for all districts, 42.9 percent were in the 21-to 26-year age bracket, with 30.6 percent listed as under 21. Five hundred and three women were enumerated in the Devonport district: they were even more concentrated in the 21- to 26-year category (55.5 percent). Southampton listed a total of 160 women: 37.5 percent fell within the 21- to26-age range, while 38.1 percent were under 21. Hence, in 1871 the women of Southampton appear to be younger than either the women of the Three Towns or the overall average of the 17 subjected districts. The recent enforcement of the Acts (1870) there may account for this: there was insufficient time for the Acts to have a significant impact on the lives of the subjected women. In time the notoriety gained by the accused could prolong their career in prostitution and increase the proportion of women in the older age brackets. That proved to be the ultimate effect of the Acts by 1881.

But what of the women living on the streets: were they also young, single women mainly from the surrounding countryside? Two streets in Southampton, Cross (pop. 327), and Simnell Streets (pop. 288), and three streets in Plymouth, Central (pop. 135), Granby (pop. 212), and Summerland Streets (pop. 263), were chosen for study.[28] They were "notorious," "low" streets that numbered many residents prosecuted for brothel keeping. A statistical profile of these streets can tell us about these women's lives: their occupations, age, place of birth, and relationship to the heads of households. Moreover, since the 1871 census forms were to be filled out by the inhabitants, they can tell us how these people saw themselves.

These streets attracted much attention. They were repeatedly condemned in the local newspapers as infested with brothels and as sanitary abominations.[29] The connection between the physical condition of the streets and the behavior of the inhabitants was made clear in the Town Clerk's quip following the conviction of Maria Stevens, Granby Street, for brothel keeping in 1872: "The clerk jocosely remarked that the street was very unhealthy, its level being as low as the sea, and the inhabitants still lower."[30] In both Southampton and Plymouth these streets were the focus of repeal agitation: a Mrs. Kell of Southampton wrote a series of letters to *The Shield* in 1870, describing her attempt to obtain signatures for a petition against the Acts on Simnell Street. Making a "house to house visitation of the entire street," she spoke with "the poor girls who are brought under the influence of the Acts" as well as "poor but respectable neighbors" who "complained of the heartless way in which the girls were treated."[31] The conversion of Simnell Street to repeal became her personal mission: if these people could abhor the Acts, if the women could be offended by the whole examination process, and if they could be persuaded to resist, then the repeal movement had truly aroused popular indignation among those most directly affected. It had colonized Satan's Stronghold.[32] Indeed, the C. D. Acts were very much a reality of street life. On Cross Street, on Central Street and on Granby Streets, crowds would gather to witness women being dragged off to examination and were known to intervene in their behalf.[33]

Despite the difficulties of tracing women who frequently assumed other names, and despite the fragmentary character of the records available, it has been possible to locate women accused of being common prostitutes on these streets. On the three Plymouth Streets, 14 women between the ages of 15 and 29 had C. D. Acts records, and 27 in all had police records identifying them as prostitutes. Eight women on Granby Street alone were listed as prostitutes on the census manuscript. These 27 women constitute almost one out of four women in the 15-to 29-age category (22.7 percent) and more than two out of five of the young single women living alone in lodgings. On each of these Plymouth streets, one could also locate four to six couples or individuals who had previously been prosecuted or who would subsequently be prosecuted for keeping brothels. Most of them did not list themselves as prostitutes, as brothel keepers or even as lodging keepers. The historian must evaluate with care the census listings of these people and offer a qualitative judgment based upon supplementary evidence. Certain conclusions seem clear though: these people perceived and defined their lives in conventional terms; and decided economic pressures probably compelled them to assume multiple identities.

These streets do not provide a cross section of Southampton or Plymouth prostitutes. As police and hospital authorities noted, a social hierarchy of prostitutes existed to service clients of different classes.[34] The more prosperous women who were not street walkers, and who catered to a middle-class clientele, lived in "quieter" working-class residential areas. The women on these streets were the poor prostitutes who "went" with men of the working class and the soldiers and sailors of the town. For most of them, prostitution was not going to be a vehicle for social mobility out of their own class.[35] But even among "poor" prostitutes there were economic and social differences. The prostitutes on these streets were not as poor as prostitutes like Alice Smith, who lived with paupers and vagrants in the tramp lodging houses of Adelaide Street and Bragg's Alley, Devonport. They resided in private lodgings, rather than behind beershops and pubs as in Aldershot. Some could afford a room for themselves; some dressed better than others, like Mary Ann Avent of 4 Summerland Street, described as "gaudily dressed." Some lived a life of economic desperation and were in and out of the workhouse, while others would have enough money to try to bribe nurses to help them escape from the hospital.

The young single women enumerated on these streets, however, were not *all* prostitutes. But, given the "water police's" mode of operation, where they tended to register any young woman who moved into "disreputable" lodgings, any single woman residing alone on these streets would be suspect.[36] And it is important to examine this perception of deviance. It was on the basis of their being outlaws and deviants that the civil rights of prostitutes were entirely abrogated. But if they were social deviants, there should be something distinctive in their life experience. With the social data obtained from the census, we can begin to evaluate that assumption.

Was there any special character to these neighborhoods? Were they red-light districts or merely poor quarters? The most striking feature of these streets is how different they were from one another. Simnell Street contained common lodging houses inhabited by single dock laborers and families of hawkers. Cross Street, Southampton, while a "low" street and the scene of frequent drunken brawls, was the residence of skilled artisans living in nuclear families. Forty-five out of 70 households were nuclear (64.3 percent); including sub-families, 57 out of 77 (74.0 percent) families were two-parent headed. Yet both Simnell and Cross Streets had one or two houses characterized as brothels, where single women resided apart from their families. On the other hand, Plymouth's Granby and Central Streets, which opened into the Octagon, the pub and entertainment center of Plymouth,[37] had nuclear families living in single tenement rooms, yet almost two out of every three adults were women. However, Summerland Street, which was equally notorious, contained a preponderance of adult males. This was in large part due to the Italian musicians and travelers living in a caravan at the end of the street. Even within these streets, there was a tremendous social range: for example Police Constable John Brown and his family resided in a lodging house at 14 Summerland Street, next door to Thomas Kneebone, a well-known brothel keeper.[38]

The inhabitants of these streets tended to reflect the general immigration patterns of Southampton and Plymouth, and the women between 15-29 were no exception. On all three Plymouth streets, the majority of the inhabitants were born in Devon, Cornwall, and the Three Towns (61.7 percent on Granby Street, 91.1 percent on Central Street, and 84.7 percent on Summerland Street). Migrants into Plymouth had come overwhelmingly from Cornwall and the rest of Devon.[39] Likewise, 85.7 percent of the women aged 15 to 29, were born in the Three Towns, or in Devon and Cornwall counties: on Summerland Street every woman in that age group came from those areas. Southampton's two streets had a similar breakdown; 70.8 percent of the women aged 15 to 29 were born in the borough or in Hants.

With the exception of Simnell Street, which had a relatively low (36.5) percentage of women aged 15 to 29, the large majority of women in that age group were single, ranging from 63.2 percent (24 or 38) on Cross Street to 86.1 percent (31 of 36) on Central Street. All but one of the women aged 15 to 19 were single. The crucial age appears to have been between 20 and 24, the age of the women who outnumbered men on the streets, and who, in the case of the three Plymouth streets, constituted the largest concentration both of females and of single women. Furthermore, if we look at the women living alone in lodgings, a pattern seems to emerge: less than one-quarter of the single women aged 15 to 19 lived away from their families, while the proportions almost reverse themselves in the 20-to-24-year-old category (from 6 to 34 or 17.6 percent to 37 of 42 or 88.1 percent). On Central, Granby, and Summerland Streets, a woman between 20 and 29 was very much on her own. On these streets, women tended to live together in lodgings in groups of three of four throughout the whole street. And as we have noted, a sizable proportion (42.9 percent) had been identified as prostitutes.

Cross Street and Simnell Street look very different. Though they had almost the same total population as the three Plymouth Streets, there were only one-quarter as many single women between the ages of 15 and 29 residing there. In contrast to the Plymouth streets, where there were clusters of single women in lodgings throughout the streets, single women living alone on Cross and Simnell Streets resided in just one or two brothels. On Cross Street, most of the single women were daughters living in a nuclear artisan family; on Simnell Street, what few single women there were lived in the infamous Queen Charlotte Hotel. It was as if they had carved a profitable niche out for themselves as the center for commercial sex for the single male dock laborers in the lodging houses. On Cross Street, two of the nine single women residing outside their families lived in Mary Jeffries' "disorderly house," and another two in a similar establishment.

One hundred and three out of 134 single women, aged 15 to 29, were listed as needlewomen, dressmakers, milliners, servants or tailoresses, or as unemployed. Of the 33 unemployed, only nine were actually listed as prostitutes; most of the others lived with their families, and probably helped out at home. Some of the women, like Ellen Ponisi or Bella Fletcher, were too busy going in and out of the hospital or appearing in court to hold down a job with a respectable establishment. But for most of the women, these occupational listings probably represented what they might have done in the past, what they might be doing in the present, or what they might choose to go back to when they finished their present career. These *were* the employment possibilities open to women in Plymouth and Southampton in good times; not only was work seasonal and labor in surplus,[40] but the earnings of prostitution had to be measured against the salaries of domestic servants, needlewomen, and tailoresses. The latter three groups would earn no more than six to ten shillings a week (in the case of a maid-of-all-work considerably less) while a prostitute, even a "sailor's woman," could earn that in one day, at a shilling a "shot."[41]

Factors other than economic necessity may well have attracted young women to prostitution: independence from family control and a greater social and cultural freedom generally. The desire to break away from parental influence was evidently shared by other young people: Michael Anderson has indicated that a certain small percentage of single men and women with high wages in cotton towns would "desert" their families and go to live separately in lodgings.[42] Also, having pin money and access to the pub—the only facility in the working-class neighborhood that provided heat, light, cooked food, and sociability—certainly afforded the prostitute a degree of comfort shared by few other women in her community. It raised her living standard to that of men's.[43] Finally, certain forms of prostitution may not have represented a striking departure from accepted mores. Nineteenth-century commentators such as Francis Place described extensive sexual promiscuity among the lower classes.

While this may have entailed a rather structured form of premarital sex with steady boyfriends, it does indicate, at the very least, a separate working-class attitude toward female chastity. It is reasonable to assume, then, that women who moved into occasional prostitution had had previous sexual experiences and that for many the distinction between promiscuity and clandestine prostitution may have remained blurred.[44]

Sewing, dressmaking, millinery and domestic service were also the occupations identified by social investigators as the sources of women who moved into prostitution in the mid-Victorian period. However, the proportion of women listed as domestic servants (18.4 percent of all employed single women 15 to 29 years old) is considerably smaller than one would have expected. In the Rescue Society of London Reports, 90 percent of the women listed domestic service as their former occupation; Christopher Bulteel, secretary of the Plymouth Female Home, noted that most of the women entering that institution belonged to the lower class of domestic servants.[45] There are at least three possible reasons for this. First, most servants lived in the homes of their employers. The women on these streets were day workers, although a minority were servants employed in the lodging houses in which they resided. Since domestic servants were recruited from the social class of the laboring poor found on these streets, there should have been a large proportion of young women listed as such. That they had moved to middle-class streets might begin to explain why the proportion of women employed as domestic servants was below the city average. Secondly, rescue homes took in a preselected group; they admitted only younger women, particularly in the 15-to 19-age category, whom they saw as more amenable to reformation. Domestic service was a young girl's occupation; and these girls were not old enough to have moved into other trades. Finally, domestic servants may have sought out the rescue homes. Since rescue homes and penitentiaries specialized in making high-grade domestic servants out of low-grade ones (without recognizing the irony involved in such an effort), the homes may have been attractive to women who wanted better placements and character references.[46]

While highly visible, these women constituted only a minority of the people living on the streets. They were part of an ongoing community and were able to depend on their neighbors and kin for support. While a number of young women were apparently orphans, many others were able to call on female relatives for aid in times of crisis.[47] At their trials, aunts, mothers and married sisters who resided in town or in the neighboring countryside would often appear and testify on their behalf. In addition, the women brought under the Acts were often assisted by their neighbors: hidden when police came, lent money, or permitted to pay their rent later, when they had the money. This reflects the tradition of mutual aid among the poor, who understood much better than most middle-class reformers and philanthropists the character of seasonal and irregular employment and the hazards of poverty.

Among the other people who made up these poor communities were 384 children under 15 years old who lived on the streets. Of the men, approximately 20 percent were skilled workers; the rest were mainly dock laborers, pensioners and porters. There were always one to three publicans on a street, and a similar number of shopkeepers. Twenty men and women on Simnell Street described themselves as hawkers. Apart from the lodging-house keepers, laundresses, and hawkers, few married women were listed with an occupation.

The female lodging-house keepers, however, are a very important category for this study. With women greatly outnumbering men in the enterprise, it was one of the few occupations that made it possible for a woman to support a family. And quite a few of the women who let out lodgings on the streets, like Margaret Allen and Polly Turney of Central Street, and Mary Jeffries of Cross Street, were prosecuted as brothel keepers. Even if they had husbands in residence, the women clearly ran the houses.[48] Were they of a different class than the prostitutes residing in their houses? Were they the exploitative professionals generally associated with the term "brothel keeper?" Evidence would indicate that, while many were better off (they were able to pay a £5 fine and hire a solicitor at their trials),[49] others were poor women in the same financial straits as the prostitutes themselves. They did not own the houses; they ran them for male landlords. At least four women pleaded in court that they took in prostitutes "to keep the children from the parish."[50] Their marginal economic position is represented in the experience of Mary Charters. Described as a "middle-aged woman of dissolute appearance," on May 2, 1870, she was brought before the Plymouth Petty Sessions court on a drunk-and-disorderly charge. "She had formerly been in the workhouse which she left as she was made to wash, and she said she would rather go to prison than go there again." She was not given the option of choosing and was sent back to the drudgery of the workhouse. She appears on the 1871 Census at 9 Central Street, listed as head of household, married with no husband enumerated, 35 years old, born in Plymouth, occupation tailoress. She had five children, all under 15. Her married sister-in-law, a glovemaker, also resided at the address. Listed as boarders were Mary Ann Hitt, a 22-year-old out-of-work domestic with a police record, and Ellen Ponisi, a 23-year-old dressmaker born in Cornwall. Ponisi had been punished twice for refractory behavior in the Royal Albert during 1870, and had been sent to prison for 14 days for refusing to submit to examination. On August 8, 1870, George and Jane Vosper (8 Granby Street) were prosecuted for harboring her—a diseased prostitute. The Vospers' defense was paid for by the National Association, with Mrs. E. M. King, a "non-paid" agent from London, and Mr. Daniel Cooper, secretary of the Rescue Society of London, instructing the attorney at the trial. Hence we have a Central Street "brothel": a woman with children taking in two notorious young women in order to keep out of the workhouse.[51]

Exploitative relationships between brothel keepers and prostitutes *did* exist. Lodging-house keepers clearly made larger profits off prostitutes than other lodgers, charging them anywhere from 3s./6d. a week for a room to 13s. for room and board (which would be far more than a tailoress could earn in a week).[52] Brothel keepers brought to court on the complaint of repeal agents were sometimes exposed as spy agents for the police. This is well instanced in the case of John Tonkin of Dockwell Street, Plymouth. He was summoned for harboring a girl under 15 for nefarious purposes on the complaint of William Littleton, the Devonport tailor and registrar of marriages, who was the most active supporter of repeal in the Three Towns. The girl in question, Louisa Pearse of Torquay, Devon, had come to Stonehouse to visit her aunt. Her aunt had accused her of conducting herself improperly—she was keeping company with a sailor—and Louisa was "turned out of doors." John Marshall, the paid agent of the National Association, then found a position for her, where she remained for three weeks. On a Sunday afternoon at a beershop, she met a sailor, who took her to the Tonkins' residence where they stayed overnight, the sailor paying 1s. for the room. The next morning, Mrs. Tonkin (notice it was the woman) invited Louisa to stay. She testified that "the girl came to her house with a sailor and consented to stay there, and that when she did so, she (Mrs. Tonkin) went to Mr. Gale of the Metropolitan Special Police and told him that there was a strange girl in her house; and then added that she must do this, in order to live quiet."[53] In a similar case, the Metropolitan Police simply refused to give evidence against a brothel keeper who had been summoned by Marshall for harboring a 15-year-old "maid-of-all-work," an action that signified both official hostility toward the repealers and a willingness to shield brothel keepers who played along.[54]

The brothel-keeper-as-quack-abortionist figures largely in the Bessie Bunker case. Here a young girl petitioned to be released from examination. At her trial her mother claimed that when Bessie was sent to the Royal Albert Hospital she was not diseased, but simply weakened by "ill-usage": "The fact was the brothel keeper had given her some strong stuff to prevent her becoming *enceinte*, and this had made her ill."[55]

Both sides were vulnerable and could suffer at each other's hands. As today, most victims of crime were poor, and police columns of the newspapers frequently carried stories of women stealing blankets, sheets, and any other moveable item from their lodgings to be pawned. Harriet Smith of Southampton was the unfortunate victim of such a crime. Elizabeth Baker, a prostitute, had stolen a silk dress from her premises. Mrs. Smith let out rooms to Baker and two other women in order to support herself and her four children. "She made the women fine clothes," but this particular dress was stolen by Elizabeth Baker and pawned for 7s. Baker was sent to prison for one month, but Mrs. Smith was still required by the court to pay 7s. to the pawnbroker in return for the dress, as a way of penalizing her for her "life."[56]

Prostitutes and brothel keepers frequently engaged in brawls; but despite all this friction and self-seeking the brothel-lodging house was "home" to these women. In numerous instances women pleaded in court that they were no longer prostitutes, even though they were still residing in brothels; it was the only place they could go. Maria Barnett was one such case. On October 30, 1873, her landlady, Mrs. Ann Gunn, was charged with harboring a diseased prostitute. Barnett had been found to be diseased by Dr. Archer, the examining surgeon, and ordered to the hospital. Instead, she tried to hide out at Mrs. Gunn's. Inspector Anniss set a guard at both exits and sent in a constable to search the house for her; Barnett and a seaman who intended to marry her were found. Mrs. Gunn's case was dismissed on a technicality but this and the previous incidents reveal both the ambiguity in the prostitutes' relationship to her brothel-home, and the omnipresence of the police in her life.[57] The executive committee of the National Association considered pressing charges against Anniss for trespass. They were dissuaded, however, by the local Plymouth solicitor, a Mr. Vaughan, on the grounds that the house was indeed a brothel and no jury would convict the police.[58]

Social outcasts like Mrs. Gunn had no recourse against police trespass. Such people were under continual surveillance, and as Mrs. Tonkin remarked, they had to fall in line in order "to live quiet." Brothel keepers were prosecuted only when they grossly violated the understanding between themselves and the police. The local police would instigate a prosecution if thefts occurred, if young girls were sequestered there, or if the houses were too blatantly disorderly.[59] The Metropolitan Police concerned themselves with diseased prostitutes and juveniles.[60] While they had no legal power to enter and search dwellings, until 1877 they did so with impunity.[61] Perhaps their greatest weapon, in the case of the Plymouth area, was their power to inform against governmental employees and naval pensioners who let out rooms to prostitutes. If a pensioner proved uncooperative, his pension could be stopped, dock laborers and artisans could be dismissed, and pubs and beershops harboring diseased prostitutes could be placed "out of bounds" for the men in service.[62] Since Plymouth and Devonport (exclusive of Stonehouse) numbered 10,618 men, or 34.4 percent of the men over 20, who were in military service or worked in governmental installations, Anniss's power of intimidation was formidable.

In the same way, local and Metropolitan Police tolerated prostitutes as long as they adhered to an accepted norm of behavior. Numerous women identified as prostitutes were picked up on drunk-and-disorderly charges because the law did not prohibit solicitation: in fact, a drunk-and-disorderly charge was the usual means of getting an "immoral" woman off the streets.[63]

Police assumed that prostitutes were a separate and readily identifiable group: gaudily dressed, with heavy make-up and no bonnets. But that was not always the case. In January 1872, a soiree was held at St. George's Hall, Stonehouse, which many prostitutes attended. They later stopped at St. George's Tavern for a drink. The proprietor was subsequently charged with permitting persons of notoriously bad character to frequent his house. His defense, based on the argument that he could not tell they were unrespectable, was accepted and the case dismissed. Justice Liddell said in his decision:"Because the constable knew them to be prostitutes, that knowledge was not to be imputed to the defendant because of their being gaily-dressed. For it so happens nowadays there was such peculiarities in dressing, even by persons of good character that it would be difficult to draw the line."[64]

The Metropolitan police were supposed to be concerned exclusively with seeing that the women appeared for examination, and if diseased, went directly to the hospital. In reality, the ten special police in the Three Towns and the three men stationed in Southampton provided a supplementary force for street control. They knew the women much better than the local police. For example,

Inspector Anniss, who directed the Plymouth operations, resided above the examination room at Octagon and Flora Lane, around the corner from Granby and Central Streets. The neighborhood must have felt his presence twenty-four hours a day. Previous to 1864, he had distinguished himself in the apprehension of naval deserters, where he received a reward for each man brought in.[65] His bounty-hunter's appetite seems to have carried over to his new responsibilities. Over the years, the ubiquitous Anniss could be found testifying at affiliation cases, divorce cases, petty-theft trials where a woman's character had to be ascertained, white slavery cases and brothel prosecutions.

On and off the streets, the women were on the move. Between 1870 and 1886, many shifted from one institution to another—from the workhouse, to prison, to the hospital. The workhouse was traditionally the only place to which diseased prostitutes could resort. However, as hospital authorities remarked,[66] they were loath to do so unless physically incapacitated from carrying on their trade. The repressive regime of the workhouse was intended to make it unpalatable for any "ablebodied" person, or any one who could find a means of keeping out: it was a punishment for poverty. A woman with illegitimate children was not permitted outdoor relief; when forced inside, "females of dissolute and disorderly habits" were to be separated "from those of a better character."[67] "Promiscuous" women were deprived of visitation rights when ill, and of any outside communication.[68] Furthermore, Josephine Butler, who worked with Liverpool workhouse women, claimed that prostitutes in the workhouse were subjected to medical experimentation.[69]

The workhouse became a place of enforced confinement for social undesirables. In Southampton and Plymouth, women picked up for vagrancy or on drunk-and-disorderly charges were frequently given the option of prison or the workhouse, or of leaving town. They were not always paupers. Magistrates and workhouse officials worked cooperatively with C. D. Acts authorities. Pregnant women, who were not permitted to remain in the lock wards under the clauses of the Acts, were strongly "urged" to apply for a ticket to the workhouse. For example, Elizabeth Baker was brought before the Plymouth magistrates in 1873; she was told she could not remain at large, and must choose between prison and the workhouse.

The hospital and police authorities viewed workhouse women as part of the pool of women brought under the Acts. In 1870, Dr. Digan, then assigned to Southampton, went to the meeting of the Board of Guardians and requested the wholesale transferral of female patients in the workhouse lock ward to the Portsea Hospital. His message was clear: any poor woman with venereal disease (like any poor woman residing on certain streets) was a prostitute.[70] While the clerk warned against this "dangerous precedent," the Guardians were delighted to comply with Digan's request.[71]

Hence there existed a working relationship between law enforcement, the workhouse, and C. D. Acts authorities. The network of control and confinement was supplemented by local voluntary associations like the Mendicity Society and the rescue homes, penitentiaries, and orphanages that took in destitute and improvident girls and trained them to be domestic sevants. Public authorities and officials of voluntary associations did not just cooperate: they were often the same people. For, in these provincial towns, the economic and political elite involved a few individuals. For example, Christopher Bulteel, whose family owned the Naval Bank, was senior surgeon at the Royal Albert Hospital, treasurer of the Plymouth Female Home, and one of the Stonehouse Guardians. Likewise, Thomas Woollcombe was chairman of the South Devon railway, chairman of the managing committee of the Royal Albert, Town Clerk of Devonport, and a member of the executive board of the Barley House of Mercy. These were men who moved freely between the rhetoric of social control and public order and the ideals of sanitary and moral reform.

The resistance of the women of Southampton and Plymouth has to be measured against this formidable power bloc which loomed over the entire community of the unrespectable poor. Resistance to the Acts took many forms, most of which were "prepolitical." That is, protest was mainly personal, not collective, and directed against immediate threats to freedom rather than to the larger system of control and confinement. Over a period of time, however, the women did undergo some political education. Much of their resistance, such as community hostility toward the police and the riots in the hospitals were spontaneous lower-class responses to infringements on basic rights.

The closest thing to a political protest occurred in the courts. A number of court cases have already been cited; most involved women who refused to sign voluntary submissions, or refused to attend examination, or petitioned to be released from the hospital. The "Siege of Devonport," occurring during the spring and summer of 1870, was the most spectacular period of resistance in the Three Towns. Using almost exactly the same personnel and organization, Southampton experienced a similar period of resistance during the fall of 1870. In the Three Towns, middle-class reformers like Mrs. E. M. King and Mr. Daniel Cooper, and paid agents like John Marshall and Mrs. Lewis, handed out flysheets, visited the "low" streets, made contact with the brothel keepers, and went into workhouses and hospitals. Everywhere they sought to persuade women not to sign the voluntary submission. Everywhere they sought to persuade Plymouth and Devonport suffering under the C.D. Acts!" was a call to action. Decrying the internal examination as "the lowest and grossest insult," an affront to all women, she promised help for those who wished to escape this degradation.. "Many ladies have taken great trouble, have been put to great expense to come and speak to you. . . . Are you glad they are come? Are you grateful to them?" Then "Reform and Resist. Don't go willingly to the examination or to the Hospital, but let them *make you* go." At women's meetings throughout the spring and summer, working "women" mixed with "ladies" to hear condemnations of the Acts as class and sex legislation. Midnight missions were organized by Daniel Cooper. The press was generally antagonistic, denouncing the mixing of the sexes at the meetings as well as the presence of unrespectable women among respectable ones.[72]

The case of Harriet Hicks tells much about the character of the C D Acts resistance movement in Plymouth and the lives of the women caught up by the Acts. Harriet Hicks was the first woman to gain release from a lock hospital certified by the Acts after successfully petitioning the local magistrates. The trial proceedings, which were reprinted in the local newspaper, the *Devonport Independent,* under the heading, "Illegal Detention of a Woman at the Royal Albert Hospital, Devonport," were widely distributed as a flysheet by the repealers.[73] The testimonies of Harriet Hicks and Ebenezer Simmons, the man with whom she lived, detail her relationship with men and the "institution of marriage," and poignantly evidence both her incapacity to work through the bureaucratic machinery and her real difficulty in articulating her own feelings.

On July 13, 1870, at the Devonport Petty Sessions, Mr. Adams, a local solicitor employed by the repeal association, made an application on behalf of Harriet Hicks, declaring she was wrongfully held at the Royal Albert Hospital. Adams maintained she had never knowingly signed a voluntary submission form, and she was neither a prostitute nor suffering from venereal disease. Ebenezer Simmons, a butcher, testified first. He had been living with Harriet Hicks, a former prostitute, for six or seven years, and he had one child by her that had "died of miscarriage." In 1868 they had moved to Devonport from Falmouth, Cornwall, and taken a furnished room in a lodging house in Cornwall Street, one of the poor and, as police would later point out, "disreputable" streets in the borough. Shortly after her arrival, Hicks was placed on the police register,[74] and in 1869, was detained in the lock hospital for three months. The couple had subsequently moved to Plymouth, and for the past five or six months, had been living in a furnished room in a poor working-class district there. Ebenezer Simmons testified that seven weeks previous to this application, two of the "water police," (Metropolitan Dockyard police) Inspector Anniss and Constable Angear, "came into their room" and "demanded Hicks," saying "they had come for her and she must go with them as they had information she was diseased." "They did not say what the disease was." Hicks protested, "it was no such thing . . . she had not been with any one, not having occasion to, as he (witness) always brought her his weekly wages."

Mrs. Lewis, a home missionary from Birmingham, testified next. A professional rescue worker, she had been sent down by the local Birmingham Anti-Contagious Disease Acts committee to aid in the resistance cause.[75] She testified that she had gone to the Royal Albert Hospital on July 6 to see Hicks. Mrs. Lewis told her "she had heard from her husband (Simmons) that he sent her a message, and that he was keeping steady, not having been drinking as he had the last time she was here." As a consequence of their discussion, Mrs. Lewis contacted the solicitor and laid the application before the court.

Mr. Woollcombe, chairman of the managing committee of the Royal Albert and Town Clerk, objected.[76] There was no evidence that the "woman Hicks" had requested this hearing herself. Court was adjourned until the following day, at which time the principal protagonist of the courtroom drama, Harriet Hicks, was finally brought in. This was the first meeting she had had with her solicitor, Mr. Adams. She was clearly a passive participant who in no way had authorized the proceedings or requested release from the authorities. She was barraged with questions: Did she ever sign a voluntary submission? (No, she never made her mark on any paper before leaving the hospital.) Did the police have a warrant when they came to fetch her? (No.) Did she authorize Mr. Adams or Mrs. Lewis to make any application for her here yesterday? (No.) Did she ever complain to the doctors or nurses that there was nothing wrong with her? (No.) Only in the most tentative manner did she acknowledge asking Mrs. Lewis for help: "I told the lady who came to see me that I was detained, but I did not ask her to try and get me out. I told her I should like to go out. She did not say she would try and get me out but she would talk to the doctors when I was gone out of the room."

When she came to talk about her relationship with Simmons, she indicated a moral ambivalence about her situation. This may have been the consequence of a poverty of language, in which she was forced to resort to the moral and linguistic categories of the middle class.

> Q. You know the man who goes by the name of William Simmons, but whose name is Ebenezer Simmons? A. Yes. Q. Have you lived with him for some time? A. Yes, for six or seven years. Q. As his wife? A. Yes. Q. And you are not a prostitute? A. No; only to the one man. Q. Only to Simmons you mean? A. Yes.

> Mr. Ryder, another magistrate.[77] Q. You mean that you are not a prostitute, other than as living with one man without marriage? A. Yes, that's what I mean.

How did Ebenezer Simmons and Harriet Hicks articulate their feelings about each other? Their relationship was expressed in very concrete terms, as an exchange of money and services. As mentioned earlier, Hicks tried to prove she was faithful to Simmons, because she had no reason to be a prostitute "as he always brought her his weekly wages." Similarly, although Simmons acknowledged, "Before she lived with me she was a prostitute," he declared his trust in her:

> Q. But for five or six years so far as you know, she has kept herself strictly with you? A. You cannot answer for a woman being in all day long but she was home night times, and when I came home I always found my meals, and if I could not come home they were brought to me. Q. You had no fault to find with her? A. No, and I don't think anybody else has.

She had discharged her conjugal obligations in all other areas; there was no reason to question her fidelity in sexual matters.

Harriet Hicks' attorney tried to rest the case here. Through Simmons' testimony, he argued, he had shown reasonable proof of her character and that she was free of contagious disease. But Woollcombe objected and asked to bring medical evidence before the court that would justify her detention.

Mr. Moore, the resident medical officer, was called. He was asked about the disease Hicks was harboring:

> Q. Is it syphilitic? A. She has a disease which comes under the Acts. Q. What term do you enter it in your returns? A. . . . Under the head of syphilis.

Moore then explained that the sore was a vaginal ulcer and not "truly syphilitic." "It might not give syphilis, but it might produce gonorrhea or a like sore." He was asked by the magistrates and Hicks' solicitor to clarify his definition of venereal disease.

> A. All genital diseases, in man or woman, arising from excessive or impure sexual intercourse. Q. How did this sore arise, do you think. A. I believe it arose from excessive sexual intercourse. Q. But persons might be faithful to each other, and yet have

excessive intercourse, might such a sore arise from it. A. It might; but I should not think it probable.

The court ordered Harriet Hicks' discharge, and the decision was roundly applauded by the spectators in the courtroom.

The Harriet Hicks case affords a glimpse into the life of the unrespectable poor—an unmarried couple living together with a single room for a home—conditions familiar to the overwhelming majority of poor Plymouth families regardless of size. The woman was married to another man who had not supported her; she subsequently left him and went into prostitution. Separation was the working-class form of divorce. Simmons, a workman, was willing to acknowledge her previous history in court: she was a "fallen" woman who had "risen" again. And her status as a kept woman secured her freedom.[78] Marriage was a business matter—she provided the services and he supported her. This is not to say they didn't care for each other. Witness Hicks' concern over his intemperance, and *The Shield's* report of Simmons' periodic trips to the hospital with his wife's boots: "It is touching to read of Ebenezer Simmons going each time to the Hospital Gates with the woman he loves as his wife, enquiring from time to time if he could see her, and being refused at the Lodge, and, as one way of communicating with her bringing a pair of boots to leave for her."[79] The goals of their "marriage" were practical; they were tied to each other through the mundane, everyday necessity of making do.

The case also tells us much about the abuses committed under the Acts: of illiterate women forced to make their X's on documents they did not understand; of police barging into working-class residences at any time without warrants; of doctors grossly extending the limits of the Acts beyond the category of venereal disease as defined in the statutes—syphilis and gonorrhea. At a time when the symptoms and stages of syphilis were well-known and syphilis well-distinguished from gonorrhea, Moore's diagnosis was nothing short of pure medical quackery.[80] The C. D. Acts advocates had always scoffed at repealers as medieval in their belief that venereal disease was divine punishment for vice, but Moore's diagnosis of disease engendered by "excessive sexual intercourse" brought a theme of the witchcraft trials into a nineteenth-century context.[81]

But, for all its insight into the private life of a poor couple, the case of Harriet Hicks remains distinct from those of the pool of women accused of being common prostitutes. She was a newcomer to Plymouth, having arrived from a neighboring county within two years of her trial. But, unlike many Cornish women, she did not come alone; she was accompanied by a man. There is no evidence of any relationship with other people in the community. She had been married, and had resided with another man for six or seven years. At the time of her trial, she was probably in her early thirties or, at the very youngest, her late twenties. This would make her older than most of the women brought under the Acts. Also, her stable relationship was unusual. While a number of the women of Plymouth and Southampton had intermittent relationships with men, by and large, they were living by themselves or were involved with sailors who were not permanently in residence. This raises an important question concerning their relationships with men: was there any pimp system in operation? While Mayhew and, later, Booth detailed the existence of "bullies" and kept men in London, and similar evidence exists for Paris and New York,[82] the findings in Plymouth and Southampton are negative. That is, men do not appear on the census records of the streets where the women were living, and only with rare exceptions were they mentioned by police and hospital authorities. Acton's report on Aldershot in 1869 strengthens this view: he notes the "absence of any third party to make a tariff of their (the prostitutes') bodies and grow rich on the wages of their guilt."[83] Hence, the women appear to have been very much on their own, and free from at least one common form of exploitation.

Harriet Hicks left town shortly after her trial. Do all women's histories end like Hicks' with a return home? The statistics cited previously indicate that a sizable minority of these women were born in Southampton or Plymouth, and some continued to live with their families. The names of quite a few appeared subsequently in the police columns of newspapers, and a number of them can be traced moving in and out of institutions. Evidence would indicate that they remained in their community, and that their history was going to be affected by continued police surveillance.

The Harriet Hicks case provided the subjected women of Plymouth with an important political education and touched off an avalanche of legal resistance. Twenty-nine women summoned for non-attendance and non-submission (which was posted in the hospital as a violation of the law) were brought before magistrates in the summer months. Seven of them claimed they were no longer prostitutes but were living with seamen, who testified on their behalf. Some probably conformed to the picture drawn by Bracebridge Hemyng of "sailors' women," who maintained stable relations with a series of seamen and lived with them periodically when they came into port.[84] Others acknowledged that they were simply prostitutes, but, like Margaret Ward, objected to the examination procedure and to the unnecessary confinement in a hospital. The "Siege of Devonport" had for a short time brought voluntary submission to an end.

Meanwhile, even more intense resistance had begun in Southampton, resistance that was successfully sustained for seven years. During this period, there were 420 C. D. Acts cases brought before the magistrates, 133 for "non-submission" and 287 for refusal to appear for examination. In contrast, the Three Towns had only 118 such cases, 75 of them during 1870 and 1871.[85] Some Southampton women resisted as many as three, four and five times. Many factors contributed to the sustained Southampton resistance.[86] Southampton women generally received a more sympathetic hearing than those in Plymouth or Devonport. While a minority of cases were dismissed, many women were ordered to appear for fortnightly examinations for three to six months, rather than the maximum twelve customarily given when they signed the voluntary submission. An 1871 Admiralty report on the general working of the Acts in Southampton complained that the women never received a fair trial because of the "strong opposition shown by the Anti-C.D. Acts Society." The Society had an "office on High Street" with a "very influential committee of ministers of religion, ladies, and other persons who have thrown every obstacle in the way of the Acts being enforced. . . . Even some of our Borough Magistrates have been influenced by the opposition society."[87] Finally, the repeal organization's principal defense attorney, Robert Harfield, was a "highly respected solicitor."

In both districts, the repealers' legal defense efforts not only disarmed the authorities, but encouraged the women. The police and Admiralty had not expected to have to deal with women who were informed of their rights. As the Admiralty's chief inspector of hospitals, a Dr. Sloggett, remarked: "(who would) have foreseen that an association could exist of ladies who would employ men known for their skill in legal casuistry to explain to prostitutes all possible methods by which they could evade the provisions of the Acts?"[88]

Protest against the Acts also included physical resistance. When police constable Dyke tried to serve a summons on Jane Jeffries of 10 Cross Street to attend examination, she fled to the back of the house and called her mother. Mother and daughter returned, and Dyke began to read the summons. The mother, Mary Jeffries, quickly interrupted, "called him a black-looking bugger, and bloody sneak, at the same time caught hold of him with both hands, pinched him, and endeavored to force him out of the house." As he left, he saw her rip up the summons.[89] Mary Jeffries claimed that Dyke was reading the summons at length, and when she ordered him out of the house, he refused to go until he had finished reading. So she assaulted him. The local magistrates upheld her right to eject him forcibly under the circumstances.[90]

In Plymouth, middle-class repealers tangled with police on the streets, too, as sympathetic crowds gathered to support the protest. In July 1870, E. M. King and Daniel Cooper were brought up on charges of resisting the police outside the examination room and inciting Eliza Binney to do the same. A tremendous crowd had gathered to watch King struggle with the policemen. One of the witnesses for the defense was Samuel Dennaford, a beershop owner who lived a few houses down from Anniss. He indicated that he actively supported the repeal efforts and regularly distributed *The Shield* on the streets. In covering the trial, *The Shield,* with its large teetotaling readership, omitted mention of Dennaford's profession.[91] Cooper and King were each fined £5, which went into a police benevolent fund.[92]

When John Marshall was similarly charged in October 1870, he did not get off so lightly. A former dock laborer at the Millbay docks for ten years, who became the paid agent of the National Association, he was in a far more vulnerable position. He did not receive the option of a fine, but was sentenced to two months in prison. The Plymouth magistrates tried to impose a sentence with hard labor, but that was annulled.[93] Marshall, however, was not the only working-class person treated shabbily at the trial. When Sarah Mach, the woman he had allegedly incited to resist gave her testimony, Mr. Phillips, the Town Clerk, asked, "You have not received money to come here have you?" She defended her integrity: "I think we are allowed to know our own feelings: we are not beasts of the field."[94]

The obvious insults and discrimination did not win the authorities many friends among the laboring class. Popular hostility toward the Metropolitan police was one of the most persistent themes in the records of resistance. Much of the community intervention on behalf of the women had its origin in the intense dislike of interlopers like Inspector Anniss. Anniss was himself twice summoned, once for breaking and entering a woman's room, and once for assaulting a respectable working woman. In the first case, the complainant never proceeded beyond the summons. In the second case, which involved a chapel-going draper's assistant, the court decided it was a case of mistaken identity: someone had impersonated Anniss.[95] Anniss was acquitted, but the public sentiment against him was manifested in the courtroom disturbance:

> The decision was at first received with slight applause, which however was immediately followed by a violent and emphatic outburst of dissent from all parts of the Court. As the police did not make any effort at once to suppress this ebullition of feeling, in a very short time it increased to a perfect storm of indignation, and the Bench was literally hissed and howled at from all parts of the Court, and particularly from the crowded gallery. Men and women—indeed, the women seemed ten times more fierce than the men— stamped their feet, shook their fists and fairly grinned at the magistrates, and the Court ultimately broke up in confusion. Such a scene was never before seen or heard of in Plymouth Police Court, and it was surprising that no arrests were ordered. The excitement and disapproval soon spread to the vast mob outside, and on Anniss leaving the Court he was set upon by an excited crowd, and hissed and hooted at with all kinds of execrations and threats and even pelted with missiles.[96]

The excitement of the trials had their impact in the hospitals. Hospital authorities bitterly complained that every sensational trial or wave of agitation encouraged insubordination among the lockward patients. There is some direct evidence for this: on October 24, 1870, five women applied to be discharged from the Royal Albert on the grounds that they were not diseased. They were defended by a solicitor retained by the repealers. Three of them "spontaneously withdrew" their application. Another woman, Agnes Snowden, was discharged two days after her application, just prior to the trial. Mr. Ryder, one of the Devonport magistrates, remarked dryly that if the woman got well in two days, it was obviously not a "serious case."[97] The last applicant, Susan Edyr, had her request denied on the basis of testimony by Mr. Swain, the senior surgeon at the hospital who had examined her. Swain also happened to be sitting on the bench as one of the presiding magistrates. That evening, there was considerable disruption in the wards of the Royal Albert, and five women were placed in segregation wards for "bad language and disorderly conduct." Two of them, Margaret Ward and Susan Edyr, were among the women who had petitioned for release.[98]

Most protests in the hospitals related more directly to internal conditions and restrictions than to outside agitation against the C.D. Acts. These protests indicate the change in character and focus of resistance after 1872 in Plymouth and 1877 in Southampton. By then, money and support from middle-class reformers had substantially diminished, and the women subjected to the Acts were left to their own resources. Their behavior in the hospitals illustrates the degree to which they were able to maintain a degree of self-respect and independence under repressive conditions. In good part, their mode of resistance, in particular, the breaking of glass, was sterotyped behavior common to confinement situations. But the extent of the resistance, especially in Portsea Hospital, was noteworthy; it suggests that these women were particularly recalcitrant and resentful of infringements on their freedom.

Although the Portsea and the Royal Albert hospitals shared a similar function, they were very different institutions. Accordingly, women interned in their respective lock wards behaved quite differently. Portsea was quite literally, according to Dr. Sloggett, the "worst" lock hospital in England.[99] Sanitary conditions were appalling, and discipline arbitrary and ineffectual. The Royal Albert, on the other hand, was a model Victorian institution. Here control over the women was more consistent, more rationalized, and hence more insidious. The two hospitals thus present an interesting study in the nature of repression.

As early as 1868, there were periodic disturbances in both hospitals, but the Portsea experienced more frequent and extensive disturbances. Rioting occurred almost annually, and as late as 1882 women were jailed for breaking hospital windows. The 1873 "soup riot" suggests something of the dimensions of such disruptions and the conditions that spawned them. On January 1, 1873, a twenty-year-old patient named Julia Clark, "complaining of the quality of the soup and potatoes given for their dinner," began to throw the plates and tableware about. The resident matron admitted the soup was watery and managed to quiet the room. The next day, further disturbances broke out, and three more women were locked in the dark cells. But that night, the rioting broke out anew; when it had ended two days later, the police had arrested seven women and eight others had been locked into various confinement cells. On the eighth of January, Dr. Sloggett arrived at the hospital to investigate. He found Julia Clark sitting on a bed in a small room without light, with an untouched pile of bread and butter next to her. She had been in the room for five days, and Sloggett now described her as "contrite and submissive." She insisted she had no complaints, except in reference to the soup and potatoes, although she was visibly disappointed at not receiving her discharge. Sloggett then visited two other women in confinement cells. Laura Lewis, who had protested because she felt a letter she was expecting had been withheld, had been in the "dark room" for three consecutive days. And he discovered Violet Hill, who had complained of harsh treatment by the surgeon, in a room upstairs filled with broken glass. She had no clothes or furniture with her and had also been confined there three consecutive days. She was so battered by the experience (reacting with what Sloggett called such "obstinacy and false shame") that she asked to remain in the "room" rather than return to the ward.[100]

After further questioning, the meaning of the "soup riot" became clear. The resident medical officer had been "too readily disposed to adopt coercive measures in the repression of any acts of insubordination." Because he felt some of the women had been "saucy" with him, the doctor had refused to examine them the next week. Angry and disappointed, the women lashed out at the conditions most immediately intolerable: watery soup, restricted access to their mail, and generally harsh treatment. Fundamental, though, was a simple desire to get out.

The "soup riot" was not the last incident of violence at Portsea. When subsequent disturbances arose, confinement cells were repeatedly used, and one doctor even asked to be allowed to cut off the hair of any refractory patient as was done in the Vienna Lock Hospital.[101] The problem was not simply repression but the inconsistent manner in which it was administered; when Portsea tried to enact a correspondence rule restricting mail to patients that was exactly the same as a rule that had been in effect at the Royal Albert since 1866, another riot broke out. As Sloggett noted, the rule worked at the Royal Albert because the patients were used to it.[102] Anarchy reigned at Portsea, and the women had grown accustomed to the freedom and latitude that resulted. Thus, for the Admiralty, the problem of violent protest at Portsea was not rooted in the social conditions there, but in mismanagement. Sloggett lamented in 1879 that, since October 1878, 21 women had been jailed at Portsmouth and none at Devonport, and observed, "The frequent repetition of these offences at the Portsmouth Hospital is a very serious evil which reflects greatly with management. . . ."[103]

The success of the Royal Albert contrasted sharply with the dismal failure of the Portsea. Imbued with the reformist enthusiasm of the age, the Royal Albert, under Woollcombe's direction, dedicated itself from the first to the moral and physical rehabilitation of the women under its "care." The lock wards, which were intended as places of confinement for the women until their sores had disappeared, were to become the center of a new moral culture. The treatment was mainly purgative: the C.D. Acts were "necessary harsh measures to eradicate evils which are so engrained into the social habits of a large body of our people."[104] Authorities engaged in a colonizing effort; they sought to enforce "discipline based on personal kindness and affection."[105] Women who were previously "untouched by human sympathy" were now personally known to the hospital authorities and the police: they had "thus acquired a sense of individuality before unknown to them,"[106] and their behavior was more orderly in consequence.

The women could be thus transformed only if order was put into their lives and a strict regime enforced. Acton described in glowing terms the regime of the Aldershot Lock Hospital, and this vision of a sanitary utopia was also shared by the officials of the Royal Albert. The hospital was to provide a similar order of experience as the workhouse, subjecting the inmates to the rule of isolation, silence and constant observation. Entering the hospital, the patient was "fumigated" and had all her belongings removed. She was then molded into a standardized harmless nonentity: "appearing to great advantage in the hospital uniform . . . the demeanor of these women as we passed along, was most respectful; there was no noise, no bad language, no sullenness, no levity." In this patriarchal community of Mary Magdalenes the women were taught ordinary domestic duties, so that they might become needlewomen, washerwomen, and domestic servants. And it appeared that the older inmates had learned the lessons of the respectable poor: "I understand that perfect order is maintained among the older residents without much interference on the part of the surgeon, who has unbounded authority, though it requires great tact on his part to reduce newcomers to a proper state of submission and obedience."[107]

The patriarchal role played by the surgeon drew vociferous criticism from feminist repealers. Women like Caroline Nicholson, who had previously visited prostitutes in the workhouses, found themselves closed out of the Royal Albert and supplanted by a male chaplain. This was seen as part of a male conspiracy to divide women. The Acts, of course, were a creation of the "double standard," and the subjected women keenly sensed the misogynic character of the whole enterprise. One women complained bitterly to Josephine Butler:

> It is *men, men only men*, from the first to the last, that we have to do with! To please a man I did wrong at first, then I was flung about from man to man. Men police lay hands on us. By men we are examined, handled, doctored and messed on with. In the hospital it is a man again who makes prayers and reads the Bible for us. We are had up before magistrates who are men, and we never get out of the hands of men.[108]

Time and work discipline were brought into the women's lives. They were exposed to a prescribed routine of work, prayer, reading, sleeping, and eating. They were also taught the basic habits of cleanliness, and trained in the use of ablutions and lotions that were supposed to contain the spread of disease. But that routine could transform the women if only they were cut off from their past associations. Hence the frequent discussions in the Admiralty records over raising the walls ever higher, glazing in the windows, and limiting patients' correspondence.[109] The regime was constantly refined and elaborated, as hospital authorities found themselves dealing with recalcitrant patients who refused to be deferential. Some women not only had to be cut off from their past but from each other. Segregation wards were built in 1869 in order to isolate, yet keep refractory patients within the hospital.[110] And in the early 1870s the hospitals developed a strict classification system, separating the hardened old-timers from the impressionable young girls.

For those unwilling to endure the workhouse or prison, for those tired of police harassment and surveillance, and for those unwilling to submit to the repressive moral culture of the lock hospitals, there was another alternative: escape. Some just moved out of the district; for others there had existed in Plymouth since 1870 a kind of underground railroad that spirited women out of the district to rescue homes in London. A room had been fitted up in the National Association office as a haven for girls trying to elude the police.[111] Marshall and his wife resided there and oversaw the rescue operations, screening "unfortunates" for the Rescue Society of London. Constantly harassed by the police, who periodically stormed into his house, intimidated his wife, and even accosted him on the streets, Marshall became the male martyr figure of the campaign. With roots in the working-class community, he was able to establish an effective intelligence network among the poor. Like Inspector Anniss, he periodically cropped up in the police columns, appearing at trials unrelated to the C.D. Acts. His presence stood out in Plymouth courts. He was the only interested third party who supported indigent women in legal distress.[112] He was trusted by the poor and got their cooperation. In 1877 he indicated that two-thirds of the young women who applied for help had been found or brought there by poor women.[113] He often pacified irate landladies who were "put out on account of the police coming to the house" to badger a young girl.[114] But his success was not to last.

By 1875, Marshall seemed aware of the basic futility of his rescue efforts. Asked to explain the decrease in the number of women who applied to him for help, he stated, "The women become degraded by the examination and believe, so long as the law remains, they must submit."[115] He could offer them no alternative, outside of a stay in a rescue home in London and a future career as a domestic servant. The problems of poverty were much more than he could cope with; many of those who came to him were "women and children" coming for "warmth and food," not "common women" but simply friendless. For "financial reasons," the women were not assisted as much as "they or we desire" and they "were soon afterwards found walking the streets having all the appearance of 'registered' women. . . ."[116]

The Rescue Society in its *Reports* in the late 1870s and early 1880s expressed increasing dismay and concern over the hardened "professional" character of women sent from the subjected districts. In 1879 it remarked that "reformatory work (there) becomes more and more discouraging."[117] In 1880 the report from "our lock hospital" complained of the "bad moral influence of women from the Garrison towns" who accounted for most of the 16 percent who left before being restored to health.[118] In his testimony before the 1882 select committee, Daniel Cooper indicated that the Society would no longer accept women who had been subjected to the Acts because of their corrupting influence.[119]

By 1883, the C.D. Acts had been suspended. Control over the lives of accused prostitutes had not ended; it was merely transformed to new agencies. The takeover of Plymouth rescue activities by pro-C. D. Acts persons suggests the realignment of repressive social forces under which the prostitutes had to live after repeal. In 1879, Ellice Hopkins, the founder of the White Cross Army, came down to Plymouth to promote the establishment of an industrial school for girls. Meeting with "influential" community leaders, she discussed her pet project, which would be formulated in the Industrial School Amendment Act of 1881. The Act would enable police to remove children summarily from brothels and place them in industrial schools. Its intent was blackmail: according to Hopkins, working-class families had to be prevented from taking in prostitutes as a means of supporting themselves, on pain of losing their children. The effect would be to isolate further the unrespectable poor from the respectable poor. Hopkins noted the direct relevance of the proposed legislation to the Three Towns, where, she had been informed, 150 children were living in brothels. Her message was the same as that of the hospital authorities: social salvation necessitated the uprooting of old evil habits.[120]

The pro-C. D. Acts people—the guardians, hospital authorities, many of the magistrates—loved her. That was the kind of social-purity message they had been waiting for. They quickly banded together to form a rescue society of their own. Their Plymouth Friendless Girls Association later merged with the Social Purity Society and received the professional assistance of the Metropolitan police, who helped them track down juvenile girls on the brink of dissipation. The police had become the new missionaries. After the Acts were suspended in 1883, James Disberry, a former Metropolitan police constable, was actually hired as their rescue agent because of his intimate knowledge of the women.[121] The new rescue effort also won over almost all of the members of the Ladies Committee attached to Marshall's rescue home. Moral uplift was now divorced from questions of venereal disease and class legislation. In the face of this debacle, Marshall was instructed to close up the office. He and his wife left town, and he was ultimately sent on the repeal lecture circuit to speak at working-class gatherings.[122]

Ellice Hopkins, with her inadvertent appeal to middle-class male prurience, represented one of the strands of social purity that arrived on the scene in Plymouth. The Salvation Army was the other. It also set up a rescue home in Plymouth in 1886. It had been active there since 1882, and its open-air meetings and rowdy processions had excited much middle-class opposition. Alfred Balkwill, a socially concerned Quaker and one of the staunchest supporters of the repeal movement, welcomed them, and quickly came to their defense. For the Salvation Army had somehow penetrated the residium: "The complaint of the rough character of the crowd shows its success."[123] In its "vigorous disregard of form and convention,"[124] in the violence of its revivalist enthusiasm, it seemed to have reached the women emotionally in a way the repealers had failed to do.

By the time the C.D. Acts were suspended in 1883, something of the new social conditions under which the women had to live had become apparent. With repeal of the Acts imminent, military and local authorities scurried about looking for substitute legislation, arranging for the enforced detention of diseased prostitutes in the workhouse and lobbying for various Detention-in-Hospital Bills.[125] The Admiralty continued to pay for the confinement of prostitutes in civil hospitals, even after repeal.[126] New social-purity legislation, such as the Criminal Law Amendment Act of 1885 and the Industrial Schools Amendment Act of 1881, was adopted—repressive laws that gave the police additional arbitrary powers over women and children. These Acts tried to provide alternative penal arrangements for the prostitute, and new social-purity organizations offered moralistic goals in a non-controversial and non-political framework. Social and political questions had been separated out from moral concerns, and the feminist context of the repeal movement had been dissipated.

In summary, the picture that emerges of these women contrasts with the image of the voiceless victim that has dominated the literature on prostitution. These women were poor and led insecure lives, and it was a testimony to their conviction and self-esteem that they were able to protest against publicly humiliating procedures. Their resistance must be measured against the formidable network of control and confinement that loomed over the community of the unrespectable poor. It is not surprising that public resistance eventually dissipated in Plymouth and Southampton, or that the middle-class reformers agitating for the repeal of the Acts were unable to organize extensive working-class opposition in these towns, as they were in the North. For one thing, they were not dealing with an organized working class in Southampton and Plymouth. The resistance movement ultimately failed, but the amount of resistance that did exist under these circumstances was impressive.

Finally, what happened to these women by the time the Acts were repealed? Two pieces of evidence would suggest their subsequent history. As mentioned above, by the early 1880s, the Rescue Society of London refused to take women from the subjected districts into their homes, claiming they were a corrupting influence. Metropolitan police statistics further suggest the trend toward professionalization. The women subjected to the Acts were clearly getting older; many more were in the over-30 category. In the Devonport district, 106 out of 403 (26.3 percent) "known common women" were listed as being 31 years and older in 1881, while there had been only 54 women out of 557 (9.7 percent) in this age group in 1870. Southampton showed a similar trend: 4 out of 154 (2.6 percent) in 1870, as opposed to 20 out of 110 (18.2 percent) in 1881. Both repealers and C. D. Acts authorities agreed that the women were staying longer in prostitution, but, predictably, they differed on their explanations of this trend.[127] The change does suggest that prostitution had become more profitable; as a consequence of police surveillance, the amateur "dollymops" had been "deterred" and a streamlined, rationalized "work force" resulted. Also, as prostitutes became public figures through the registration process, it became harder for them to gain respectable employment and to move in and out of their various social identities. The history of prostitution in the later nineteenth century remains to be written, but one can begin to draw the outlines of that history: prostitutes were on their way to becoming the professional class of women, isolated from the general lower-class community, that exists in contemporary society.

NOTES

1 J. C. Barr to the War Office, Public Record Office (hereafter referred to as P.R.O.), W.O. 33 / 24, December 1867.

2 William Acton, *Prostitution,* Peter Fryer, ed. (New York: Praeger), pp. 56-58.

3 See Kellow Chesney, *The Anti-Society: An Account of the Victorian Underworld* (Boston: Gambit, 1970); Ronald Pearsall, *The Worm and the Bud: The World of Victorian Sexuality* (New York: Macmillan, 1969); Vernon Bullough, *The History of Prostitution* (New Hyde Park: University Books, 1964); Fernando Henriques, *Prostitution and Society, A Survey* (London: MacGibbon and Kee, 1968); and C.A. Pearl, *The Girl With the Swansdown Seat* (London: Bobbs Merrill, 1955).

4 An Act for the Prevention of Contagious Diseases at Certain Naval and Military Stations, 27 and 28 Vict. c. 85; An Act for the Better Prevention of Contagious Diseases at Certain Naval and Military Stations, 29 and 30 Vict. c. 96; and An Act to Amend the Contagious Diseases Acts, 1866, 32 and 33 Vict. c. 86. In part these Acts were the outcome of a series of parliamentary inquiries and Navy and Army Reports on the alarming rate of venereal disease among the military. And more generally, they reflected the growing concern over the sanitary, social, and moral state of enlisted men since the Crimean War, when the incredible mortality of troops in hospitals spurred attention to the inhumane living conditions of these men. See, E. M. Sigsworth and T. J. Wyke, "A Study of Victorian Prostitution and Venereal Disease," in *Suffer and Be Still: Women in the Victorian Age,* Martha Vicinus, ed. (Bloomington, Ind.: Indiana University Press, 1972), pp. 90-95.

5 The 1864 Bill, "An Act for the Prevention of Contagious Diseases at certain Naval and Military Stations," applied to eleven garrison and dock towns in England and Ireland — Plymouth, Portsmouth, Woolich, Chatham, Sheerness, Aldershot, Chichester, Shorncliffe, the Curragh, Cork, and Queenstown — and provided that a woman believed to be a common prostitute by a member of the special forces or a registered doctor, and suffering from a contagious disease would undergo medical examination, If found diseased, she could be detained in a hospital for up to three months. The accused could elect to submit voluntarily to the examination or be brought up before a local

magistrate (with all the publicity attendant to that event) and then be bound by his orders. Failure to attend examination or disobedience of hospital rules carried penalty of up to one month's imprisonment for the first offense and two months for the subsequent offense. The Contagious Diseases Acts of 1866 extended the Acts for three more years and added Windsor to the schedule. Finally, a parliamentary inquiry in 1868-1869 certified as to the beneficent effects of the Acts, extended them to five additional districts, including Southampton which was not a military depot, and to within a ten-mile radius of all districts subject to the Acts.

6 For example, Towns Police Clauses Act, 1847 (10 and 11 Vict. c. 89); Common Lodging Houses Act, 1851 (14 and 15 Vict. c. 28); Vaccination Act, 1867 (30 and 31 Vict. c. 84); Wine and Beerhouse Act, 1869-70 (32 and 33 Vict. c. 27, and 33 and 34 Vict. c. 29); Licensing Act, 1872 (35 and 36 Vict. c. 94); and, Summary Jurisdiction Act, 1879 (42 and 43 Vict. c. 49).

7 Leon Radzinowicz, *A History of English Law and its Administration from 1750*, 4 vols. (London: Stevens, 1948-1968), vol. 1, p. 19. The two vagrancy statutes relating to prostitutes were the Vagrancy Act of 1744 (17 Geo. c. 5) and the Vagrant Act of 1824 (5 Geo. 4. c. 83). For other acts related to the repression of "bawdy houses": see, 25 Geo. 2. c. 36; 28 Geo. 2. c. 18; and, 3 Geo. 3 c. 114.

8 N.A. "Women's Protest," reprinted in Benjamin Scott, *A State Iniquity; Its Rise, Extension, and Overthrow* (London: 1894), pp. 102-123.

9 "Report from the Royal Commission on the Contagious Diseases Acts (1871)," *Parliamentary Papers* (hereafter referred to as *P.P.), 1871 (c. 408-1), IX* "Report from the Select Committee on the Administration, Operation, and Effect of the Contagious Diseases Acts of 1866-69 (1879)," *P.P.,* 1878-79 (323), VIII; (1880), *P.P.,* 1880, (114), VIII; (1881), *P.P.,* 1881 (351), VIII; and, (1882), *P.P.,* 1882 (340), IX.

10 The national campaign to repeal the Contagious Diseases Acts will be discussed in Judith R. Walkowitz' Ph. D. dissertation on women, sexuality, and class and the Contagious Diseases Acts, 1869-1886, University of Rochester, to be presented, 1973-1974.

Over the years these parent organizations, organized along regional, religious, professional, and class lines, spawned an impressive array of special interest groups. But from the first, the important division was on the basis of sex; men and women formed their own separate organizations (although women were shortly admitted into the National Association in 1870) and began to define distinctive concerns and methods of agitation for their separate membership. Under the leadership of Josephine Butler, the Ladies National Association formulated a social feminist position that declared open hostility toward a series of male institutions and power centers (this is reflected in their resistance toward traditional methods of lobbying in Parliament), and an abiding concern over the welfare of the prostitute. It followed Josephine Butler's strong conviction in the socially redemptive power of personal evangelical philanthropy, which she saw as implicit to the peculiar mission of women.

The early organizers of both repeal organizations shared a set of social, political and religious commitments. By and large their party affiliation was Liberal, and they were part of the professional and commercial middle class. The early financial support for the National Association came from wealthy Quakers of Bristol and the North; in addition, most of the first signers of the Ladies Manifesto were members of the Society of Friends. Quite a number of the early members had previously ascended the public platform in support of the abolitionist crusade, the Anti-Corn law movement, and were presently involved in the temperance, educational and suffrage agitation. In addition to this organizational experience, many women had been involved in rescue work previous to the campaign. Hence, they had more than an abstract notion of the conditions and temptations of poor women, and they shared Josephine Butler's concern for personal missionary effort.

Finally, these organizations derived their greatest strength from the north, where middle-class reformers were able to forge effective alliances with self-respecting industrial working men. In 1875 the Ladies National Association encouraged working-class men to form themselves into a separate organization, the Working Men's National League.

11 Rev. Gledstone, *Shield* (London), April 14, 1877.

12 *Shield,* May 2, 1870.

13 See Inspector Sloggett's sketch, "History and Operations of the Contagious Diseases Acts in the Home Ports," P.R.O., Adm. 1 / 6418, Apr. 10, 1873; and Adm. 1 / 6835, August 14, 1886.

14 See E. M. King's plea for more money and persons to aid in the cause, *Shield,* August 15, 1870. The Minutes of the Executive Committee of the National Association, 1871-1886, vols. 2-6, Josephine Butler Collection, Fawcett Library, London, are filled with references to the sending of agents and monetary support down to Plymouth, in particular.

15 For a description of Southampton's commercial growth during the mid-Victorian period, see A. Temple Patterson, *A History of Southampton, 1700-1914* (Southampton: Southampton University Press, 1971), vol. 2, ch. 6.

[16] *Weekly Hampshire Independent* (hereafter referred to as *WHI*) (Southampton), February 26, 1870; and, the 1880 Report by Dr. Sloggett, Chief Inspector of Hospitals for the Admiralty, P.R.O., Adm. 1 / 6179, 1880.

[17] See the "Report on the General Working of the Contagious Diseases Acts in Southampton," P.R.O., Adm. 1 / 6206, January 31, 1871.

[18] See Patterson, *Southampton*, ch. VI, VII, and W. G. Hoskins, *Devon* (London: Collins 1964), 162-175. Growth statistics were taken from the 1851 Census. *P.P.*, 1852-1853 (LXXXVIII), pt. 1, and from the 1871 Census, *P.P.*, 1873 (LXXI), pt. 1.

[19] Patterson, *Southampton, p. 16*.

[20] Hoskins, *Devon*, 173; John Rowe, *Cornwall in the Age of the Industrial Revolution* (Liverpool: University Press 1953), pp. 311-322; and, Denys Barton, *Essays in Cornish Mining History* (Truro: Barton, 1968), vol. 2, pp. 48-55.

[21] Barton, *Essays*, p. 48.

[22] Testimony of Mr. Phillips, Town Clerk of Plymouth, before the Royal Commission of 1871, *P.P.*, 1871 (c. 408-1), IX: Minutes of Evidence, Q. 6398.

[23] "Second Report of the Commissioners on the Employment of Children, Young Persons, and Women in Agriculture," *P.P.*, 1868-1869 (4202), XIII: Mr. Portman's Report on Hants, Cornwall, and Devon, 106. In the 1871 Census, 1306 Southampton men, or 9.93 percent of all men over 20, and 2206 Plymouth and Devonport men, or 7.1 percent of all men over 20 in these two towns, were listed as general laborers. This latter figure does not include the dock laborers employed at government installations.

[24] See ibid., pp. 108, 135-137.

[25] P.R.O., Adm. 1 / 6122, February 3, 1869.

[26] See Inspector Anniss's testimony before the 1882 Select Committee, *P.P.*, 1882 (340): IX, Minutes of Evidence, Q. 3898-3900.

[27] In the Fall, 1871, the Devonport Town Council strongly objected to a speech by Home Secretary Bruce where, following Anniss's statistics, he claimed there had been 1,770 prostitutes in Devonport prior to the enforcement of the C.D. Acts. See *Shield*, October 14, 1870, and November 4, 1871. Also see the testimonies of Plymouth and Devonport police officials at the 1882 Select Committee, Q. 54, 481-483.

[28] Census (1871), *P.P.*, 1873, LXXI: pt. 1, x. Statistical data for the five streets discussed are based on the manuscript 1871 Census schedules, P.R.O., RG. 10 / 2120, RG. 10 / 1193, and RG. 10 / 1194.

[29] A.R.R. Preston to the editor, *Western Daily Mercury* (hereafter referred to as *WDM*) (Plymouth), June 24, 1870, identified Central Street and Summerland Street as "streets infamous for prostitutes."

[30] *WDM*, April 26, 1872.

[31] *Shield*, July 4, 1870, August 15, 1870, and September 3, 1870.

[32] This characterization of the atheistic, uncolonized urban residuum is taken from E. P. Thompson, *The Making of the English Working Class* (New York: Gollanz 1963), ch. 3.

[33] See the cases of Mary Jeffries, Cross Street, P.R.O., Adm. 1 / 6202, September 27, 1871; Sarah Jane Ferris, Granby Street, *WDM*, February 11, 1871; Elizabeth Trigger, Central Street, *WDM*, September 22, 1871.

[34] Inspector Anniss's testimony before the Royal Commission of 1871, *P.P.*, 1871 (c. 408-1), XIX: Minutes of Evidence, Q. 661,662.

[35] Susan Formage, 4 Central Street, was a notable exception: in 1873 she petitioned to be released from the requirements of the Acts as she was being kept by a gentlemen. *Shield*, September 20, 1873.

[36] See the testimony of Daniel Cooper, Secretary of the Rescue Society of London, before the Royal Commission of 1871, *P.P.*, 1871 (c. 408-1), XIX: Minutes of Evidence, Q. 1746.

[37] It was on the Octagon that the Mechanic's Institute was located, the prominent theatres, as well as the largest concentration of pubs.

[38] *WDM*, February 11, 1870, and November 22, 1870.

[39] The Irish on Granby Street, who constituted 16.5 percent of the street's population, were the notable exception.

[40] Portman reported a diminution in the pláces for a needlewoman in Plymouth as a result of the sewing machine. There was always a large turnover in positions for domestic servants; a sizeable proportion (estimated at 25 percent) were always in-between jobs. Moreover, much of the agitation took place during the period of economic depression after 1873, which hurt the seasonally employed.

[41] Acton, *Prostitution*, p. 57.

[42] Michael Anderson, *Family Life in Nineteenth-Century Lancashire* (London: Cambridge University Press, 1971), p. 124.

[43] Brian Harrison, *Drink and the Victorians* (London: Oxford University Press, 1971), p. 47.

[44] See, for instance, the letter from Francis Place to Richard Carlile, quoted in Marie Stopes, *Contraception: Its Theory, History and Practice* (London: John Bale, Sons and Danielson, Ltd., 1928), pp. 304-313. Conversations with E. P. Thompson, Gareth Stedman Jones and Raphael Samuels have confirmed this view of lower-class sexuality.

[45] See, Daniel Cooper's Testimony before the Royal Commission of 1871, *P.P.*, 1871 (c. 408-1), XIX: Minutes of Evidence. Also, *Reports of the Society for the Rescue of Women and Young Children, 1877-1882;* and *WDM,* June 10, 1870.

[46] For example, according to the 1871 Census, in the Southampton Home for Penitent Women 11 of the 18 girls were under 20, the average age being 18.56. See, Kathleen Heasman *Evangelicals in' Action* (London: Bles, 1962), ch. IX, "The Reform of the Prostitute;" and, Dr. Sloggett's "Report of Inspection of Several Female Penitentiaries," P.R.O., Adm 1 / 6179, August 29, 1870.

[47] See for example Anderson, *Family Life,* p. 147.

[48] This question is dicsussed at the trial of Bessie Kendle, who ran a brothel for her father. *Devonport Independent* (hereafter referred to as *DI*), October 22, 1883.

[49] See the cases of Mary Abb Bissett, *DI,* December 8, 1883; Joseph and Elizabeth Brooks. WDM, August 21, 1872; Mary Ann Carlle, WDM, Nov. 4, 1870; and, Elizabeth Allen, WDM, April 4, 1872.

[50] Elizabeth Hele, *WDM,* March 29, 1870.

[51] *WDM,* May 3, 1870; Royal Commission on the Contagious Diseases Acts, 1871, *P.P.,* 1871 (c. 408-1), XIX: Appendix C, 828; and, *WDM,* August 19. 1870.

[52] *WDM,* September 22, 1871; and, *DI,* September 19, 1874, and September 27, 1882.

[53] *DI,* September 19, 1874.

[54] See the case of Richard Dodge, *WDM,* August 7, 1871.

[55] *Shield,* July 1, 1871.

[56] *WHI,* November 18, 1874.

[57] It could be proved that Mrs. Gunn had knowledge of Barnett's presence as Emily had been let in by a friendly lodger. The aftermath in the Admiralty papers is most revealing. Since it was the first unsuccessful prosecuton of a brothel keeper under the Contagious Disease Acts, the Admiralty considered appealing the case. Dr. Digan, the Visiting Surgeon, objected that it would produce bad publicity. Moreover, Barnett was not really there for prostitution: the presence of a man in the house would be insufficient evidence, since "the fact that he was about to marry the girl would probably be accepted as extenuating circumstances." P.R.O., Adm. 1 / 6418, October 30, 1873, and November 5, 1873.

[58] Minutes of the National Association for the Repeal of the Contagious Diseases Acts, No. 1012, Nov. 10, 1873, and no. 1032, November 24, 1873.

[59] See the testimonies of Mr. Lynn, Chief Constable of Plymouth, and Mr. Wreford, Chief Constable of Devonport, before the 1882 Select Committee, *P.P.,* 1882 (340), IX: Minutes of Evidence, Q. 290-94, 316-22, 370.

[60] Anniss's testimony, ibid., Q. 11922-3.

[61] In 1877 the conviction of Charles Turner, a Stonehouse publican, for resisting police who were in search of a diseased prostitute, was overturned by the Queen's Bench on the grounds that the police had no proper warrant to enter the premises forcibly.

[62] See the 1882 Select Committee, App. 610.

[63] Testimony of Mr. Phillips before the Royal Commission of 1871, Q. 6470.

[64] *WDM,* January 27, 1872.

[65] P.R.O., Mepol. 1 / 58, January 25, 1860.

[66] Testimony of Dr. Sloggett before the Select Committee on the Contagious Diseases Acts, 1866-69, Q. 216-8.

[67] An 1842 Instructional Letter of the Poor Law Central Authority, quoted in Sidney and Beatrice Webb, *Poor Law Policy* (London: Longmans, Green, and Co., 1913), 65.

[68] See Emma Jones's letter to the Poor Law Board complaining of the mistreatment of her sick sister, a woman with illegitimate children: "I went to see her on Liberty Day and they would not let me see her as she has got three children in with her." P.R.O., M.H. 12 / 2434, June 26, 1870, and July 1, 1870.

[69] Josephine Butler, "An Appeal to the People of England on the Recognition and Superintendance of Prostitution by Governments," pamphlet in the Josephine Butler Collection, Fawcett Library, London.

[70] *Shield,* June 20, 1870; *WHI,* June 4, 1870.

71 Ibid.

72 *WDM,* June 8, 1870.

73 *Abolitionist Flysheets,* Josephine Butler Collection, Fawcett Library, London.

74 See Anniss' testimony before the 1882 Select Committee, Q. 10,627.

75 "Royal Commission on the Contagious Diseases Acts, 1871," Q. 12,573.

76 Thomas Woollcombe was the founder and guiding spirit of the Royal Albert Hospital. His role in the establishment of the Acts will be discussed in the Ph.D. dissertation by Judith R. Walkowitz mentioned above.

77 Mr. Ryder was one of the borough magistrates who was strongly critical of the hospital's policy of interning refractory patients in confinement cells rather than bringing them before the borough justices.

78 Thomas Woollcombe to Vernon Lushington, Under Secretary of the Admiralty, P.R.O., Adm. 1 / 6143, July 19, 1870.

79 *Shield,* August 1, 1870.

80 Theodore Rosebury, *Microbes and Morals: the Strange Story of Venereal Disease* (New York: Viking, 1971), 181.

81 The relationship between witchcraft accusations and an inadequate scientific understanding of causation of disease is discussed in Alan Macfarlane, *Witchcraft in Tudor and Stuart England: a Regional and Comparative Study* (New York: Harper and Row, 1970), and Keith Thomas, *Religion and the Decline of Magic: Studies in Popular Belief in Sixteenth and Seventeenth-Century England* (London: Scribner, 1970).

82 Bracebridge Hemyng, "Prostitution in London," *London Labour and the London Poor,* ed. Henry Mayhew (New York: Dover, 1968), vol. 4, pp. 250-252; Acton, *Prostitution,* p. 63; Charles Booth, *Charles Booth's London,* 9 vols., Albert Fried and Richard M. Elman, eds. (New York: Pantheon, 1968), p. 126; William Sanger, *History of Prostitution* (New York; Eugenics Publishing Co., 1939), p. 483; and, Abraham Flexner, *Prostitution in Europe* (New York: The Century Co., 1920), p. 32.

83 Acton, *Prostitution,* p. 56.

84 Bracebridge Hemyg, "Prostitution in London," pp.226-232.

85 "Report of the Assistant Commissioner of Police of Metropolis on operation of these Acts (1881)," *P.P.,* 1882 (29), LIII.

86 One of the most important factors in the Southampton resistance was the presence and effort of Reverand and Mrs. Kell. Mrs. Kell died in 1872 and Rev. Kell, a Unitarian minister and active social reformer, in 1874. After their deaths, the Southampton repeal campaign appeared to have lost an active center. Also, there is some evidence of a more autonomous and self-conscious working class, though the one attempt to organize a working men's repeal group seems to have failed. *(WHI,* May 27, 1871). Later in the decade, Admiral Maxse successfully organized an effort by seamen to win a wage increase.

87 P.R.O., Adm. 1 / 6206, January 31, 1871.

88 P.R.O., Adm. 1 / 6253, March 29, 1872.

89 P.R.O., Adm. 1 / 6202, September 23, 1871.

90 Ibid., September 9, 1871.

91 *Shield,* August 5, 1870.

92 P.R.O., Adm. 1 / 6180, August 4, 1870.

93 Speech of Sheldon Amos at a large public meeting at Stonehouse, *DI,* November 12, 1870.

94 *Shield,* October 28, 1870.

95 Police impersonators were a fairly frequent occurrence since the Metropolitan Police were plainclothesmen. The most sensational case of police impersonation took place in Portsmouth, where a man forced a girl "under the Contagious Diseases Acts to be examined by him, 'making' her take off all her clothing except her boots and stockings." He received seven years penal servitude. *Shield,* October 12, 1872.

96 The entire court proceedings were printed in the *DI,* October 7 and 14, 1876, and reprinted in the *Shield,* October 28, 1876.

97 *Shield,* November 5, 1870.

98 Royal Commission of 1871, App. C, 828.

99 P.R.O., Adm. 1 / 6236, September 16, 1872.

100 P.R.O., Adm. 1 / 6292, January 8, 1873.

101 P.R.O., Adm. 1 / 6292, July 12, 1873.

102 P.R.O., Adm. 1 / 6291, June 3, 1873.

103 P.R.O., Adm. 1 / 6498, January 16, 1879.

104 P.R.O., Adm. 1 / 6179, May 17, 1870.

105 P.R.O., Adm. 1 / 6418, February 6, 1875.

106 Ibid.

107 Acton, *Prostitution,* p. 95.

108 *Shield,* May 9, 1870.

109 P.R.O., Adm. 1 / 6122, January 16, 1869; Adm. 1 / 6123, March 1, 1869; Adm. 1 / 6418, September 26, 1872; and, Adm. 1 / 6417, March 15-16, 1876, and April 18, 1876.

110 P.R.O., Adm. 1 / 6123, April 5, 1869; Adm. 1 / 6418, September 26, 1872; and, Adm. 1 / 6418, June 15-17, 1873.

111 "Letter from the Right Hon. James Stansfield, M.P., to the Ladies National Association and the Other Repeal Associations Throughout the Kingdom, 1875," *Ladies National Association Reports,* 1870-86, Josephine Butler Collection, Fawcett Library.

112 "Value of a Rescue Society," *WDM,* January 12, 1872; ibid., October 26, 1872; and, *DI,* September 19, 1874.

113 *Shield,* February 10, 1877.

114 Ibid., June 9, 1877. This basic concern over public respectability recurs throughout the cases. What bothered "respectable" neighbors was not the "immorality" of a young woman but the notoreity gained by police visits.

115 John Marshall, quoted in a letter from James Stansfeld to the Ladies National Association, 1875, *op cit.*

116 *Shield,* January 20, 1877.

117 "Twenty-Seventh Annual Report of the London Society for the Rescue of Women and Children, 1879" *Rescue Society Reports,* Josephine Butler Collection, Fawcett Library.

118 "Twenty-Eighth Annual Report of the London Society for the Rescue of Women and Children, 1880," *Rescue Society Reports,* Josephine Butler Collection, Fawcett Library.

119 "Report of the 1882 Select Committee," Q. 3767-68.

120 "Proposed Industrial School for Girls," *Western Morning News* (Plymouth), November 25, 1879.

121 *WDM,* April 6, 1886.

122 *Minutes of the National Association for the Repeal of the Contagious Diseases Acts,* (IV, V) Josephine Butler Collection, Fawcett Library, nos. 2174 (December 8, 1879), 2201 (January 12, 1880), 2248 (February 23, 1880), 1908 (February 24, 1879), 4271 (January 12, 1885), 4411 (April 27, 1885), 4434 (May 11, 1885), 4566 (October 12, 1885), and 4751 (March 15, 1886).

123 "Is there not a cause?" Alfred Balkwill to the editor, *WDM,* June 22, 1883.

124 "Great Demonstrations," WDM, January 15, 1883.

125 P.R.O., Adm. 1 / 6278, May 8, 1883; Adm. 1 / 6287, 1884; Adm. 1 / 6718, September 15, 1884; "Deputation from Plymouth, Devonport, etc. to the Home Secretary," *DI,* May 26, 1883; and, editorial on Lord Hartington's Detention in Hospital Bill, *WDM,* July 9, 1883.

126 P.R.O., Adm. 1 / 6718, October 20, 1884; Adm. 1 / 6835, September 3, and 22, 1886, and April 4, 1887; Adm. 1 / 6287, April 30, 1888, and October 19, 1888; *Twenty-Sixth Annual Report of the Royal Albert Hospital, 1888-89,* Devonport Hospital, Devonport; and, *Twenty-Eighth Financial Report of the Royal Albert Hospital, 1890-91,* Devonport Hospital, Devonport.

127 Police officials tended to stress the improved health and longevity of prostitutes under the Acts; repealers emphasized the stigma attached to being a registered woman. The latter also acknowledged that the women who remained in the districts profited from the system and bragged about being "Queen's Women."

THE WELFARE OF WOMEN IN LABORING FAMILIES: ENGLAND, 1860-1950

Laura Oren

In the late 1880s, social investigators and statisticians in England unwittingly developed a new tool for analyzing the welfare of women in laboring families. In their effort to answer questions about "the condition of the people," they moved beyond a general study of prices and money wages to collect intensive data on the budgets of individual working-class families. Historians have generally followed the pattern established by these poverty surveys and have discussed the standard of living of the English working class in terms of household units.

But some of these budgets could also be used to refine our concept of welfare still further. Several of the budgets suggest, in fact, that the members of a single family did not necessarily share a single standard of living. Working-class women, at least those married to low-paid unskilled laborers, apparently claimed a disproportionately small share of the household's food, medical care, and leisure time. Money-handling customs in poor families sometimes may also have added to the privileged position of husbands and the sacrifice of wives.

The lessons of these late-nineteenth-century poverty surveys may be applied more widely. Broad economic and social changes reached working-class wives only after passing through the filter of the family's economy. In order to fully assess the impact of industrialization, urbanization, the social reforms of the nineteenth century, or the welfare state of the twentieth century on women's welfare, historians must cease to assume that "some members of a family cannot be rich while others are poor."[1]

The patterns revealed by the poverty surveys of the late 1880s may have originated before the industrial revolution. Evidence from other countries shows that cultural assumptions, rather than differences in physical size or type of work performed often determined the allocation of food between men and women. Professor Natalie Davis, for instance, found that the tradition of giving males more food was a very old one in England. It applied where both were working on the same site or field and did not seem "reasonably correlated" with energy needs or productivity.[2] Even before the industrial revolution, in the families of English agricultural laborers, food may have been distributed in similar customary proportions. Ivy Pinchbeck, for example, thought that the eighteenth-century agricultural laborer's wife was the most likely to suffer from any shortages of family earnings.[3] But industrialization probably imposed additional burdens on her. In the eighteenth century, working-class married women usually contributed either earnings or produce to the family budget. As a matter of fact, "public opinion . . . expected women and children to earn at least sufficient for their own maintenance, and men's wages were based on the assumption that they did so." Although "married women had never possessed a legal right to their own earnings, or their share of the family wage," it seems possible that their husbands did not feel free to divert those earnings from the household budget.[4] The eighteenth-century agricultural laborer's wife might keep a pig, hens, geese, or a cow or earn some cash from a bye-industry.[5] If income earned in these ways went straight to the wife, with no diversion through the husband's pocket, women would have been able to bolster their standard of living. Produce consumed by the family, although subject to the man's greater claim on food, at least went straight to the household table, without anything lost to tobacco or alcohol.

The industrial revolution, however, left married women stranded in the home, devoid of these bye-employments. Once it was assumed that men's wages ought to be enough to support the entire family,[6] income came to be more exclusively filtered through the husband's hands. In the nineteenth and twentieth centuries, married men of the laboring class generally withheld part of this income for their own personal use in the form of "pocket money." Under these circumstances, the bargain between husband and wife—the allocation of housekeeping and pocket money—became a key to the woman's standard of living.

Prior to the poverty surveys of the late 1880s, very few observers collected the detailed family budgets that we need to discuss with precision the distribution of welfare within the family. In the 1860s, however, Dr. Edward Smith, Medical Officer of the Privy Council, studied food consumption among both the agricultural and the urban laboring classes. He described the lot of rural women in this way:

> The wife, in very poor families, is probably the worst fed of the household. On Sundays she generally obtains a moderately good dinner, but on other days the food consists mainly of bread with a little butter or dripping, plain pudding and vegetables for dinner or supper, and weak tea. She may obtain a little bacon at dinner once, twice, or thrice a week; but more commonly she does not obtain it. In counties where milk is abundant she adds it more freely to her tea, but when othervise she drinks tea without milk, and during a part or the whole of the week without sugar also.

Smith felt that in towns,

> The wife fares relatively better, for as meat in some form is obtained more frequently than by the poorest families in the country, and the members of the family take their food together at home, she obtains her share . . . . In families where the pressure of

poverty is less felt the wife is better fed, but so long as much effort is required to obtain food for the children and the husband she remains generally the least fed.

The husband, on the other hand

... in the poorest agricultural families is certainly better fed than any other member of the family, for his labour being of the deepest importance to the family, the wife feels that he must be sufficiently fed if possible. . . .Hence he obtains nearly all the meat or bacon, where there is but little, and the week's supply, after the moderately good Sunday's dinner for all, is reserved. . . (for him). . . . He must also have a larger share of the bread, and in Dorsetshire, where cheap cheese in great part supplants bacon, the cheese also. The beer and cider, moreover, have some nutritive value, and they belong exclusively to him. . . .[7]

Although Smith felt that in towns the "food of the husband more nearly resembles that of the family," he still found that the man was entitled, "from his bodily wants," to a larger share.[8] In fact, in his 1863 study of the food of the laboring classes Smith reported that in towns, especially in London, the supper meal usually consisted of cheese and bread for the husband and cocoa, coffee, or tea with bread and fat for the rest of the family.[9]

In the nineteenth century the differences between the diets of men and women in the same family chiefly involved meat. John Burnett, the author of a social history of diet in England, concluded that from 1815 to 1914, in countryside and in town, husbands ate most of the meat in laboring families. He cited a butcher from Brigg who testified in 1843 that the women, on the other hand, "say they live on tea: they have tea three times a day, sop, bread and treacle, . . ."[10]

In the late 1880s, the poverty surveys pioneered by Charles Booth began to supply more complete evidence of the distribution of welfare in the family. It is from these inquiries and the sociological studies of the twentieth century that most of the evidence for this essay was drawn. Investigators collected data on household income and expenditure because they were trying to understand how poverty could persist in the midst of the tremendous progress and prosperity of industrial England. Some of these surveys not only illustrate the apportioning of food but also illuminate the way in which money was handled within the family. B. S. Rowntree,[11] for instance, developed a theory of "secondary poverty," which distinguished between those families in want because the absolute level of their income was inadequate to cover necessities and those in distress because they wasted or mismanaged their money. Rowntree and others, as a result, carefully recorded how much of the husband's earnings went directly into the housekeeping budget for family necessities, and how much was diverted through his pocket money for "wasteful" purposes. Other works written before World War I reveal something about the distribution of health and medical care within the family. In the early twentieth century the continuing high level of infant mortality rates inspired an infant welfare movement. Such studies as Magdalen Stuart Reeves' *Round About a Pound a Week* and the Women's Cooperative Guild's *Maternity: Letters from Working Women*[12] reflected both a concern about falling birth rates at a time when Britain's "national efficiency" and ability to compete industrially and imperially were being questioned, and a certain degree of conscious feminism. These surveys showed that women in the laboring class often received a disproportionately small share of health care and leisure time as well.

Historians have found that it is extremely difficult to obtain extensive and detailed evidence about food consumption in the English working class, even when calculating by household units. It is harder still to substantiate the differences between the diets of men and women within a family. As a result, in a recent article on "Working Class Diets in Late Nineteenth-Century Britain," O. J. Oddy used figures that reflected food consumption *per capita* within the family.[13] It is even more difficult, however, to properly evaluate in nutritional terms the evidence that is available. Inequalities in food consumption that simply reflected the average differences in physical size between men and women would in no way imply a special sacrifice on the part of wives. Without information about the body weights of the men and women studied it is impossible to determine what a particular division of food in a family meant in nutritional terms.

Given these limitations, it is nonetheless possible to give examples of the allotment of food in poorer families and to speculate on the significance of that distribution. Two influential poverty surveys, Reeves's *Round About a Pound a Week* and B. S. Rowntree and May Kendall's *How The Labourer Lives,*[14] reported family menus in sufficient detail to reveal the allocation of food by sex. Reeves investigated "respectable" South London laborers earning between 18s. and 30s. a week. Sample menus showed extra meat, extra fish, extra cakes, or a different quality of meat for the man. While the husband usually was entitled to "a rasher to his breakfast" and "a relish to his tea," the rest of the family might make both these meals from tea, bread, and margarine alone. Reeves estimated that the breadwinner consumed food worth 7d. / 8d. a day, while the rest of the family "had to live permanently on less than 3d. a day." In spite of this difference, she points out, "in no single instance did the man seem to be having more than enough or even enough."[15] There were traces of similar food-apportioning customs in other studies of town poverty as well.[16]

Rowntree and Kendall also found these patterns in their study of rural labor. Except for the shared Sunday meal, meat was usually reserved for the breadwinner. In all the sample diets they collected, "meat of some description figures . . . but, as already explained, it often represents a flavouring rather than substantial course. 'For the man only' is a remark found in many of the menus." A Leicestershire wife remarked rather ruefully, "I love meat . . . but I often go without. I've not touched it now for two days. I keep it for him; he *has* to have it." In rural Berkshire investigators were told that the women and children "eat the potatoes and look at the meat." Besides meat, including bacon, husbands sometimes ate extra vegetables, cheese, or eggs.[17] In the country an added tradition meant that the husband ate better than the wife: some laborers still got meals with their wages, or rations of beer or cider.[18] Valuing this extra food highly, a North Riding of Yorkshire man even refused his employer's offer of 16s. a week in place of the 9s. plus three meals a day he was then receiving. Fed at work, the laborer dined on bacon and tea for breakfast and beef or mutton for dinner, while his family at home appears to have had no meat at all.[19]

It is difficult to assess the significance of these sexual inequalities in diet. The families discussed in this essay were inadequately fed in general, and any deductions from a woman's diet, even if in proportion to her body weight, further undermined an already low nutritional standard. Since the disparity in diet usually took the form of reserving most or all of the meat for the man, there must have been a considerable protein deficiency in the woman's diet. During pregnancy, and especially lactation, she would have suffered even more. A modern estimate of daily energy requirements suggests that women who keep house and nurse their babies need as many calories a day as men who work as laborers. A working man burns 3100-3500 calories a day, while a pregnant woman should add an additonal 1000 calories to her usual 2300-2500.[20] Unfortunately, the woman's childbearing years, in the groups studied, usually coincided with one of the worst phases of the cycle of family poverty.[21] Few budgets contained the margin necessary to allow pregnant or suckling women the extra nourishment they required.[22] Instead, childbirth was a strain on the family's economy that was commonly met, like other extraordinary expenses, by curtailing the woman's diet.

In poor families there were few luxury or other unnecessary items to prune in time of need; food was the elastic item that had to absorb extra expenses. For example, Rowntree reported that York families who lived from "hand to mouth" met extraordinary expenses by cutting down on food. One woman explained that if there were boots to buy, "me and the children goes without dinner, or maybe only 'as a cup 'o tea and a bit o' bread; but Jim (her husband) ollers takes 'is dinner to work, and I give it 'im as usual; he never knows we go without an I never tells 'im."[23] Reeves found that when a family in South London borrowed from their neighbors to pay for a child's funeral, "for months afterwards the mother and remaining children will eat less in order to pay back the money borrowed. The father of the family cannot eat less. He is already eating as little as will enable him to earn the family wage. To starve him would be bad economy. He must fare as usual. The rest of the family can eat less without bothering anybody—and do."[24]

Childbirth and a growing family were two of the most common strains on the family budget. The Women's Cooperative Guild found that this meant, ironically, that at a time when the woman ought to be well fed, "she stints herself in order to save; for in a working-class home if there is saving to be done, it is not the husband and the children, but the mother who makes her meal off the scraps which remain over, or 'plays with meat-less bones.' "[25] Many of the working-class women who wrote the letters printed by the Guild complained of going without food during pregnancy in order to save for the coming confinement. Worse still, pregnancy must often have coincided with some other stress on the household's economy. One woman wrote that her husband was unemployed through most of her first pregnancy. During the second, he was ill, and her effort to care for the first child, take on laundry work, and save at the expense of her own necessities for both the confinement and her husband's doctors' fees nearly killed her.[26]

As the family grew, the woman once again met the extra expense out of her own standard of living. One would expect a father, cognizant of the extra children, to raise his contribution to the household budget at the expense of the pocket money he kept for his own personal use. But Reeves found that, instead, the husband "makes his wife the same allowance, and expects the same amount of food. She has more mouths to fill, and grows impatient because he does not understand that, though their first baby did not seem to make a difference, a boy of three, plus a baby, makes the problem into quite a new one." Reeves found that the part of the housekeeping money first set aside for the husband's dinners before there were any children, might remain constant even when there were six: "The unvarying amount paid for the bread-winner's necessary daily food becomes a greater proportion of the food bill, and leaves all the increasing deficit to be met out of the food of the mother and children. . . ."[27]

In his discussion of working-class women in the late nineteenth century, Peter Stearns identified still another extra burden that was met by economizing on the food of women and children. As prices began to rise again after 1900, Stearns suggested, many men "may have attempted to keep their wives on a fixed household budget."[28] Women had to stretch stable or only slowly growing housekeeping allowances to cover increasingly expensive family necessities. Once again, women could meet this pressure only by cutting their own nutritional standards.

Money-handling arrangements that kept a part of the breadwinner's earnings out of his wife's hands often widened the standard-of-living gap even further. In almost all poor families, and perhaps in the working class in general, money seems to have been divided into a portion for "housekeeping" and a portion for the breadwinner's "pocket money." There were two major ways of dividing income into these portions. In some cases the wife was in control: her husband handed all his earnings to her and received back a fixed sum for his pocket money. In mining villages this custom was called the "tip-up" and was sometimes performed before the front door so that the neighbors could witness and guarantee fair play. More commonly, the husband controlled the division of income. He would usually hand his wife a fixed sum out of his earnings each week. Most Victorian laborers earned irregularly to some extent. Some men fixed the housekeeping allowance around their average minimum earnings and reserved anything additional for their own pocket money.[29] Tips, bonuses, or overtime as well usually went into pocket money. Often a woman did not even know what her husband had actually earned that week and reported the housekeeping allowance alone to investigators of family income.[30]

Since the household necessities usually came out of housekeeping money, the way in which husband and wife divided income beween them became, as Michael Young has suggested, a key to the family standard of living.[31] The agreement determined what the housewife had available for rent, fuel, clothing and food. Rent being an unavoidable and a constant payment, food expenses were the main arena of the housewife's struggles with the limits of her weekly allowance. The proportion of the breadwinner's income allowed her could make this struggle easier or harder, and her own diet better or worse.

The available evidence permits only tentative generalizations about the usual division of a family's income. Ernest Phelps-Brown has estimated that, in the period 1906-1914, urban working-class men kept fully one-quarter of their earnings for pocket money.[32] In 55 budgets reported in eight poverty surveys, however, pocket money rarely amounted to as much as one quarter of the husband's wages. Rather, the proportion commonly ranged from a twentieth to a fifth, out of weekly wages usually running from 18s. to 26s. in towns, and a few shillings less in agriculture.[33] Since wives were often ignorant of their husbands' total earnings, and some men may have wished to conceal the amount of money they spent on alcohol, these figures may underestimate the actual ratio.

Pocket money was often used to pay for the husband's necessities. Frequently breadwinners provided their own clothes out of their part of the family income.[34] Although some husbands demanded an extra allowance from their wives for dinners eaten away from home, others covered the cost out of their pocket money.[35] Fares—like dinners out, usually a town expense—often came out of the man's allowance.[36] In the country, where the agricultural laborer seems to have taken less of the family income for his own private use, the husband might pay insurance or club money out of his pocket.[37] This happened in towns too, although Lady Bell cited one well-paid husband who insisted that his wife pay for his insurance, since she would be the one to benefit by it![38] Pocket money was sometimes used to buy the boys' shoes, or pay the installments due on the furniture, half the rent on an additional room for the family, or even part of the household expense of one child.[39] Maud Davies found an agricultural laborer who paid his club, firewood, coal and all outdoor expenses such as food for the pigs or fowls out of his 5s. a week (out of 15s.) pocket money. He also bought the family's clothing from profits on the garden and animals.[40]

Pocket money, however, was also a device for diverting part of the family income to use for the wage-earner's pleasures, chiefly smoking and drinking.[41] Some observers charged that up to a half of the intemperate man's wages went for beer, spirits, and tobacco, or a quarter in the case of a laborer who was never drunk.[42] They repeated heart-rending stories of men who wasted their families' sustenance on gambling and drinking.[43] Two temperance reformers, Joseph Rowntree and Arthur Sherwell, estimated that the average working-class family spent 6s. a week on alcohol.[44] Less biased, perhaps, is the estimate by a modern historian that judging from the *per capita* consumption of beer, "many families must have spent a third, and some even half or more, of all their income on drink."[45] Because a large pocket-money allowance could reduce the family budget from an adequate level to one that would not cover household necessities, this diversion of earnings could produce what Seebohm Rowntree called "secondary poverty," that is, poverty caused by inefficient expenditure rather than insufficient income. Indeed, Rowntree believed that drink was the predominant cause of secondary poverty.[46] Since women suffered disproportionately from any inadequacy in the family's budget, temperance appears, in fact, to have been a women's issue. Brian Harrison, in his study of *Drink and the Victorians,* recited the reproaches of reformers against male selfishness. They charged that "drinking places on pay days were besieged by wives desperately anxious to feed and clothe the family; many married couples fought over the wage-packet, and many wives were kept ignorant of its contents. . . . To make matters worse, drunken husbands were often stung by the wife's silent or open reproach into the wife-beating for which Englishmen were notorious abroad." Harrison essentially rejected these accusations, arguing that women had their own faults, and that even where "by modern standards—male selfishness did exist, there were good reasons for it."[47] But an appreciation of the vitality and importance of the male working-class culture associated with drink and drinkplaces does not alter the impact of money spent in this way on women's standard of living. Whatever nutritional and recreational benefits there were in alcohol went primarily to men. Rowntree and Sherwell, for instance, found that women did not drink, on the average, more than half the quantity of liquor consumed by men.[48] Whatever skimping was necessary to compensate for the lost income, on the other hand, was done primarily by women.

In addition to claiming the lion's share of the meat and drink, husbands in many cases also got most of the health care that was available. Throughout the nineteenth and early twentieth centuries the standard of medical care for the workingman himself, and for his family in particular, was low.[49] Working-class families could obtain medical help from a variety of institutions. The regularly employed or skilled man might belong to a friendly society which, in return for weekly contributions, usually gave sick pay, and paid for a doctor and hospital bed. But this covered only the member himself, not his wife and children. Family medicine was in the hands of medical clubs or contract practices run by local doctors. In return for a weekly subscription the whole family could be covered for medicine and the doctor's attendance. Provident dispensaries, operated by charitable institutions or private enterprise, also supplied general-practitioner care for either a weekly subscription or a fee per visit. Voluntary hospitals, a valuable resource for wage-earning families, were available in the larger towns. In some towns health visitors or public health authorities visited the women and children. The most widespread medical facility available to the laboring class was the poor-law infirmary. It provided decent care but stamped the whole family with a taint of pauperism, regardless of which member was helped.

Although the working-class family scrimped to insure even the smallest child for funeral benefits, men often monopolized sickness insurance. In one prosperous, unusually well-insured Somerset village in 1909, for instance, nearly every working-class householder and most of the young men were in a benefit society for medical care and sick pay. But their families were not nearly so well covered.[50] For the poorer families, sickness insurance was probably out of the question altogether, and one wonders whether a doctor's fee for anyone but the breadwinner could be spared out of such slender weekly budgets. The *Daily Herald's* observation about Britain before the coming of the National Health Service was probably as true of the nineteenth century as of the twentieth. They asked their readers "how many working mothers put up with a pain or a 'lump' for years for fear of costing her husband too dear—and died because urgent aid came too late?"[51]

Because they bore children, women also had special medical requirements. But the care that the wives of laborers received during pregnancy and childbirth was seriously deficient. Letters from working-class women to the Women's Cooperative Guild show that in a crisis a doctor was usually called but that many women waited too long before obtaining this aid, sometimes with fatal results. Repeated pregnancies meant routinely inadequate care. As a result the Guild found that in nearly two-thirds of the four hundred cases reported to them the conditions of maternity were neither normal nor healthy. Their women correspondants, who in general represented the better-paid strata of the working class, reported numerous pregnancy-related physical problems and a high incidence of miscarriages and stillbirths.[52] The wives of poorer laborers probably fared worse, even when they resorted to the medical services of the new Poor Law. In her study of the services,[53] Ruth Hodgkinson suggested that a large proportion of the half-million women confined each year had no medical attention except incompetent midwives. In 1842, Poor Law Guardians were ordered to allow medical orders for emergency outrelief to women in childbirth. But since the order involved extra fees of 10-20s. and an additional burden on the ratepayer, many unions were reluctant to grant them. Thus even women who tried to use the Poor Law were forced to fall back on the aid of midwives alone.[54]

This low standard of medical care in childbirth means that the birth rate may prove to have been the single most important variable affecting the health of women in the late nineteenth and early twentieth centuries. The distribution of welfare within the family in fact depends heavily on the number of its children. A small family means more than just fewer or safer pregnancies and better health. Like any other pressure on the family's economy, large numbers of children brought a disproportionate sacrifice of the mother's diet and other standards of living. Stearns did not overstate his case when he called the rapid decline in English family size that was evident for all classes after 1900 a "dramatic change" that reduced "the physical hardship and the responsibilities of the working-class wife." R. M. Titmuss was convinced that this decrease meant, "in terms of family economics, a rise in the standard-of-living of women which has probably been of more importance, by itself, than any change since 1900 in real earnings by manual workers."[55]

Part of the reason that childbirth made women ill was because they had no time to rest after confinement. As one woman wrote, "there is no peace for the wife at home. She is still the head and chancellor of the exchequer. If she were confined on Friday, she would still have to plan and lay out the Saturday money, and if it did not stretch far enough, she would be the one to go short or do the worrying."[56] This and other evidence suggest that holidays, or even leisure itself, like meat, were marked for men only.'[57] A vicar of a city parish told Charles Booth that "the men . . . have a good time compared to the women, who lead fearfully hard and almost slavish lives."[58] A study of the ways in which a wife's ordinary day differed from her husband's could undoubtedly reveal even more about the distribution of welfare in the family.

At the beginning of the twentieth century the British state began to intervene more actively to guarantee the welfare of its people. The form that intervention took at first offered less to women than to men. Part I of the National Insurance Act of 1911, "Lloyd George's Ambulance Wagon," with one exception excluded dependent wives. The workingman received unlimited general practitoner medical care and 10s. a week to maintain his family while he was sick. The wife of an insured man, however, did not receive any medical care under the Act, although she was entitled to a 30s. lump-sum payment at childbirth. One of the architects of the 1911 bill, William J. Braithwaite, admitted that insurance was almost entirely meant for the world of adult male wage earners.[59] In fact, even working women had a tenuous place in the scheme. Excessive medical claims by insured women before World War I led an investigating committee to conclude that married women malingered, and others to insist that a woman's illness was not an insurable risk. By 1932 public furor over the resulting strain on the participating friendly societies' funds led to a new law. Women's statutory benefits were drastically reduced, but the friendly societies were still not satisfied. They wanted to see all working women, upon marriage, "required to requalify for national health insurance as if they were new entrants paying 26 weekly contributions and being excluded from the maternity benefit for a year, and from disability benefit for two years." The government, bearing in mind the newly enfranchised women over thirty, rejected this amendment.[60] National Insurance was not built to accomodate women, rather it was designed to protect the efficiency of male workers.

Legislation was slow to affect the customary allocation of welfare in the family. Nor did the generally higher living standards of the twentieth century abolish the differences in standards of living between husbands and wives. Even in 1957, Richard Hoggart noted that "the old habits of looking well after the wage-earners, particularly in food, is still alive; . . ."[61] Hard times still meant more sacrifice for wives than husbands. The Pilgrim Trust's famous 1938 study of *Men Without Work* found that "the wives bear the brunt of unemployment in these large families." The wives of unemployed men displayed "obvious signs of malnutrition" and habitually gave their husbands and children the "extra nourishment" provided by the Unemployment Assistance Board for their own use.[62] Following the precedent established by the Women's Cooperative Guild's study, *Maternity,* in 1939 a Women's Health Inquiry Committee collected data on 1,250 married working-class women. Almost twenty-five years later they found that women continued to absorb the extra burdens that additional children or any special need placed on the family's budget.[63] In the 1950s, in the prosperous coal-mining areas, the bitter habits of the hungry thirties still persisted: middle-aged and older women served "a heavy meal for their families" and "a mere snack for themselves."[64]

Like their predecessors, twentieth-century workingmen rarely handed over the whole of their weekly wage packet to their wives. Charles Madge's 1943 study of the *War-Time Pattern of Saving and Spending* examined the question of pocket money in great detail.[65] He found that the proportion of men who gave all their earnings to their wives varied from 5-15 percent in most of industrial England, to 24-49 percent in Lancashire cotton towns. Madge believed that the higher figures showed that "women are the dominant personalities of Lancashire.[66] Ferdynand Zweig later interpreted the tradition of giving the whole wage packet to the wife in the same way. Indeed, he felt that the prevalence of the custom revealed a "matriarchal" strain in Lancashire.[67] In mining villages in the twentieth century, however, the practice of the "tip-up" gradually died out. Although Rhys Davies, M.P. and ex-miner, insisted that when he worked in the pit "every collier I knew placed the whole of his wages on the table at the weekend. . . ," investigations in 1949 and 1956 told a different story. By mid-century miners, too, followed the custom of the housekeeping allowance, or "wages for the missus."[68]

Wives in this century, like their mothers and grandmothers before them, often did not even know how much their husbands actually earned.[69] "Fixed and pretty rigid, 'wages for the missus' " were usually based on regular earnings and excluded overtime or extras.[70] As earlier, husbands gave up some of their pocket money to the needs of a growing family, although their share of the family income did not fall in proportion to the cost of maintaining the extra children. Young remarked that the financial burden of an extra child fell especially upon the mother and other children. Some husbands, in fact, "behaved like employers. They did not increase their wives' wages as the size of the family increased."[71]

Slow to adjust their pocket money downward in time of need, twentieth-century workingmen seemed quick to augment it when times were flush. Higher wages apparently allowed the breadwinner to devote a larger proportion of them to his personal use.[72] Wages for the missus, in fact, generally lagged behind any advances in men's earnings.[73] Men seemed reluctant to change the housekeeping allowance because "it is easier to raise household expenses than compress them afterwards if something goes wrong."[74] Under these circumstances inflation, even with workingmen's wages rising rapidly, ate into the housewife's standard of living. Young observed that during inflation:

> Unorganized workers, in common with all groups with relatively fixed incomes, do less well. Since wives have no unions, each has to reach her own individual arrangement, or bargain, with her husband. Like other unorganized workers, their money income may not advance as fast as prices.[75]

As a result, he concluded, the level of prices might be more important to the standard of comfort of wives and children than the fluctuation of their breadwinners' wages.

Higher wages and greater prosperity in this century, then, did not eliminate the uneven distribution of income between husbands and wives. On the contrary, if Madge was correct in estimating that the average husband kept roughly a quarter of his earnings as pocket money in 1943, the disparity was at least equivalent, if not greater.[76] But in the modern welfare state services are as important as income. Particularly with respect to health, women gained significantly from the government's intervention in the welfare of the family. Margery Spring-Rice's report on *Working Class Wives: Their Health and Conditions* revealed that in 1939 ill-health and inadequate medical care was still common for women. But when the National Health Service replaced national insurance in 1948, medical care became equally available to the men and women of the working class. Other services, like food and milk supplements, also contributed directly to the welfare of women.

Although the inequalities persisted in the twentieth century, it became harder to ignore the effect of family organization on the allocation of individual welfare. The revelations of surveys and the battles of women like Eleanor Rathbone finally bore some modest fruit in 1945. In that year the Labour government introduced a family allowances bill that provided money grants for each child after the first. As drafted, the law gave the father legal right to the allowance, although either parent could cash the check. There was little disagreement about the substance of the bill, but this clause raised a furor within Parliament. Eleanor Rathbone, M.P. for the English Universities, swore that she would vote against a measure she had formulated and championed for the last twenty-five years if the clause was not changed. She warned that women's organizations were incensed, and she viewed the government's draft as an attack on the status of women. Although some male members of Parliament defended the workingman who was impugned for drinking away his family's sustenance, even they supported the change.[77] The government accepted an amendment and paid family allowances directly to the mother.

Looking back on the changes since 1948, Young concluded in 1952 that "all in all, the Welfare State has undoubtedly been an agency for transferring income from men to women and children." Indeed, many welfare services had been financed at least partly out of the higher taxes on tobacco and alcohol, which were consumed primarily by men. But, he warned, the benefit had already begun to diminish. Given the customary division of income between housekeeping and pocket money, the inflation that seemed equally characteristic of the welfare state had begun to put economic pressure on working-class wives. Only some of them were able to compensate by going to work themselves.[78] Even the welfare state has not eliminated the role of family arrangements in distributing welfare.

Any simple picture of a single standard of living for an entire family is inadequate. Industrialization and the growth of state intervention in welfare had, in fact, different impacts on women and men. Throughout these experiences, the family's economy mediated between the family and its economic environment. It is important to understand the nature of that mediation because the uneven allocation of welfare between men and women has long been deeply embedded in English culture. The pattern was followed in both the town and the country, and in both the nineteenth and the twentieth centuries. The man's claim to pocket money, for instance, was so strong that in 1905 the Central (Unemployed) Body found that London wives even sent some of the supposedly minimal cash allowances for families to their husbands who were away on unemployed relief works.[79] Indeed, unemployed men, as desperate as they were, commonly refused colony relief work because they objected to receiving only 6d. a week pocket money.[80] Some who accepted these terms complained bitterly at "not being treated as men owing to their not being able to handle the money. . . ."[81]

The division of income into housekeeping and pocket money lasted, as well, despite evidence of at least some resistance from wives. For example, some working-class wives seemed to think that men who allowed a larger proportion of their earnings to the housekeeping were better husbands. Bell reported that among steelworkers' families in Middlesbrough, "the criterion of whether a man is a 'good' husband or not is often . . . the proportion of his wages which he gives to his wife."[82] According to Reeves, South London wives:

> . . . seemed to expect judgement to be passed on the absent man according to the amount he allowed them. Many were the anxious explanations when the sum was less than 20s. (for men earning from 18-30s. a week)—that it was "All 'e got," or that " 'e only keeps one and six, an' 'e buys 'is cloes 'isself, and 'e's teetotler an' dont' 'ardly smoke at all." The idea among them, roughly speaking, seemed to be that if he allowed them less than 20s. explanations were required; if 20s., nothing need be said beyond "It ain't much, but you can't grumble." If over 20s., it was rather splendid, and deserved a word of notice about once in six weeks.[83]

What explains the strength of these arrangements in the family's economy? Helen Bosanquet once called the Victorian family a kind of "mutual benefit society with extended benefits."[84] Since most of the extended benefits appear to have accrued to husbands, it seems strange that wives cooperated in the enterprise. We must remember, however, that by the mid-nineteenth century women were peculiarly dependent on their husbands. Bereft of the bye-employments of pre-industrial England, married women had to rely chiefly on the earnings of their husbands. Women who worked often earned barely enough to keep themselves, let alone to support their children. Home work, favored by married women, was the lowest-paid and most sweated labor of nineteenth-century England. A husband's sickness meant work and income lost; his death brought even greater calamity. The only alternative to poorly paid women's work was the Poor Law. The wife deferred to the breadwinner because without him her own situation would have been even worse.[85]

The efficiency and health of the chief breadwinner was essential to the welfare of the entire family. Thus, Reeves wrote, the wife often decided "to feed him sufficiently and to make what is over do for herself and the children. This is not considered and thought-out self-sacrifice on her part. It is the pressure of circumstances. The wage-earner must be fed."[86] The wife also often accepted the diversion of family income to her husband's pocket money out of necessity. The part of a man's pocket money that went to his trade union or friendly society subscription should be considered in the same light as extra food. Both protected his industrial efficiency, and thus, his capacity as a wage-earner.

But what about the pocket money that men "wasted" on alcohol or tobacco? Why didn't women challenge this apparent selfishness? A Berkshire laborer once explained to his wife that if he did not get his weekly ounce of tobacco, "I should want more food,"[87] but it seems unlikely that the equation was always that simple. Stearns has suggested that women in poor families needed to keep their husbands not only healthy, but "if possible happy." As a result they concealed from their husbands the sacrifices they made to cope with the family's poverty.[88] The extra share of welfare protected men's psychological, as well as physical health. A man's pocket money may have functioned as his sweetener, his incentive to keep on working, or, as Rowntree and Kendall said of the tobacco that agricultural laborers consumed each week, his "solace."[89] Women and men in the laboring class shared a hard life. But wives were more locked into it than their husbands. With so few opportunities for them to support themselves, women had to rely on the good faith of the breadwinner, on his willingness to keep on working to earn enough to support the family and not just himself. A man's right to his small pleasures, to a part of his wages freely spent, to a proportion of any raises he might achieve, could bolster his incentive to keep going. When asked why their husbands kept their usual pocket allowance after more children came along, the women explained to Madge in 1943 that "You can't expect them to work for nothing."[90]

Perhaps pocket money encouraged men to work by giving them the illusion of independence. Vulnerable and sometimes even helpless in the economic market where he sold his labor, the working husband demanded to feel like a "man" in his own family. The control of money somehow conveyed independence. For example, inmates of Poplar's poor-law labor colony received no spending allowance. Because they were paupers they had forfeited their right to independence, symbolized by pocket money.[91] Evidence from the twentieth century suggests that in order to retain their self-respect many English working-class husbands had to feel independent of their wives, or even superior. As Hoggart put it: "A man can't be without money in 'is pocket'; he would then feel less than a man, feel 'tied to' his wife and inferior to her, and such a situation is against nature."[92]

In the twentieth century this psychological protection may have become more important than any physical benefits. Earlier, under conditions of extreme poverty, the husband's extras may have guaranteed primarily the health and efficiency of the breadwinner. But the greater prosperity of the twentieth century has not eliminated the unbalanced distribution of income within the family. Stearns found that as early as 1908, men took the bulk of the gain from any advance in wages as their families moved out of the subsistence category.[93] Later in the twentieth century, investigators found that there was a tendency for men in higher wage brackets to allocate a smaller proportion of their earnings to housekeeping than men who earned less.[94] A study of coal mining in 1956 revealed that "the young married men today do not as a rule give the greater part of their share in the industry's comparative prosperity to their families.[95] By 1943 male consumption of tobacco and alcohol probably had little nutritional significance. Instead, Madge reported, it was associated with "male gregariousness" and social prestige, it had the narcotic effect of deadening other frustrations, and it even gratified the husband's psychological propensity to spend.[96] Prosperity did not destroy the traditional family economy. Rather, it emphasized the psychological benefits of the husband's special place in the family.

In 1914 Reeves defended married men against those who accused them of wasting their families' sustenance on their own pleasure. She argued that in laboring families the amount of self sacrifice required of a man, "if he be at all tender-hearted towards his family, is outrageous." But the poorly paid man should not be expected to be superior to the middle-class man in the matter of self-denial and self-control. She found it understandable that a "hard-working, steady, sober man" might spend 2d. a day on beer, 1d. on tobacco, and 2d. on tram fares "without being a monster of selfishness, or wishing to deprive his children of their food."[97] That was obviously true. Nonetheless, it was the structure of the family's economy that allowed husbands to indulge themselves, however modestly, while wives could not. When wages rose later in the century, moreover, pocket money became less essential to the maintenance of the efficiency of the breadwinner. Indeed, in some households, "an undercurrent of rivalry between the demands of the family's well-being and the demands of the husband's pleasure" became clear.[98]

It is easier to understand the role the family played in the English economy of the nineteenth than in the twentieth century. In order to reduce the pressures, both physical and mental, on the husband's standard of living, the rest of the family had to take second place. Through the medium of the family's economy the wife served as a buffer for her husband. She absorbed the blows of an insecure existence and provided the necessary margin for continuation of family life out of her own, and the children's standard of living. The uneven distribution of welfare between husbands and wives in part represented an active effort by laboring people to defend themselves against the economic system without abandoning family life. Although the form that defense took was not inevitable, it was understandable in a society where men were supposed to be the bread-winners and heads of families. The wife's elastic standard of living served as a buffer for the larger economic system as well. Unskilled laborers in the nineteenth century commonly received wages that were inadequate to supply a moderate-sized family with bare physical needs.[99] Without the wife's willingness to absorb a disproportionate share of that insufficiency, the husband would have been a less efficient industrial worker.[100] This was especially true during a period in which the State largely refused responsibility for alleviating poverty.

In the twentieth century the broader functions of the working-class family's economy are less evident. But the consequences for the welfare of women are quite apparent. Social historians who want to understand the allocation of individual welfare in modern England must not stop at households. We need to know more about those arrangements within the family that distributed benefits so unevenly to the men, women and children who lived together.

1 Michael Young, "The Distribution of Income Within the Family," *British Journal of Sociology* 3 (1952): 305-321.

2 From a private communication to the author, November 15, 1972. Professor Davis found these allotments indicated in wage-lists either with or without food salaries.

3 Ivy Pinchbeck, *Women Workers and the Industrial Revolution, 1750-1850* (New York: Augustus M. Kelley, 1969), p. 104. See Alice Clark, *The Working Life of Women in the Seventeeth Century* (London: G. Routledge and Sons, 1919), pp. 79, 86 for a similar point.

4 Pinchbeck, Women Workers, pp. 1, 312; and Clark, *Working Life of Women*, p. 54.

5 Dorothy Marshall, *The English People in the Eighteenth Century* (London: Longmans, 1956), p. 174.

6 Pinchbeck pointed out that few married women worked in factories, even in cotton textile areas, *Women Workers*, pp. 197-199, 313.

7 Dr. Edward Smith, *Practical Dietary for Families, Schools, and the Labouring Classes* (London: Walton and Maberly, 1864), pp. 199-201.

8 Smith, *Practical Dietary*, p. 201.

9 Dr. Edward Smith, "Report to the Privy Council on the Food of the Poorer Labouring Classes," *Parliamentary Papers* 1864, xxviii, p. 223. See also his earlier report "On the Nourishment of the Distressed Operatives," *Parliamentary Papers*, 1863, xxv, p. 320.

10 John Burnett, *Plenty and Want* (Harmondsworth, Middlesex: Penguin, 1966), p. 45. See also pp. 161, 168, 175, 185.

11 B. S. Rowntree, *Poverty: A Study of Town Life* (London: Longmans, Green and Co., 1922).

12 Magdalen Stuart Reeves, *Round About a Pound a Week* (London: G. Bell and Sons, 1914); Women's Cooperative Guild, *Maternity: Letters From Working Women* (London: G. Bell and Sons, 1915).

13 O. J. Oddy, "Working Class Diets in Late Nineteenth-Century Britain," *Economic History Review*, 2nd series, vol. 23 (August 1970), p. 317.

14 Reeves, *Round About a Pound;* B.S. Rowntree and May Kendall, *How the Labourer Lives: A Study of the Rural Labour Problem* (London: Thomas Nelson and Sons, 1913).

15 Reeves, *Round About a Pound*, pp. 103, 117, 120; p. 149; for example, pp. 115, 122, 127; pp. 142-143.

16 For example, Rowntree, *Poverty*, pp. 273, 311, 332; Charles Booth, *Life and Labour of the People in London* (1902-1904; reprint ed., New York: AMS Press, 1970), Poverty Series, vol. 1, p. 145; Women's Cooperative Guild, *Maternity*, pp. 58-59, 151; *cf.* Oddy, "Working Class Diets in Late Nineteenth-Century Britain," pp. 320-321.

17 Rowntree and Kendall, *How the Labourer Lives*, p. 308-309, 213, 246; see also, pp. 63, 68, 112, 125, 254, 291, 293.

18 Rowntree and Kendall, *How the Labourer Lives*, p. 196. John Burnett claims that tea had become the staple drink of women and children in rural England after 1850, while husbands continued to receive their beer or cider allowance, *Plenty and Want*, p. 162.

19 Rowntree and Kendall, *How the Labourer Lives*, pp. 142, 149. Maud Davies reported that agricultural laborers received beer or ale daily, and sometimes milk or meals, *Life in An English Village* (London: T. Fisher Unwin, 1909), p. 115.

20 I am assuming that housekeeping falls in the category of "work done standing or walking" and that laborers did "work developong muscular strength," see Clara M. Taylor and Orrea F. Pye, *Foundations of Nutrition* (New York: Macmillan, 1966), p. 52.

21 According to Rowntree, an individual was poorest during infancy, when he or she started a family, and during old age, *Poverty*, p. 171.

22 For example of one budget which did see Women's Cooperative Guild, *Maternity*, p. 25.

23 Rowntree, *Poverty*, p. 84; see also Reeves, *Round About a Pound*, p. 137.

24 Reeves, *Round About a Pound*, p. 68.

25 Women's Cooperative Guild, *Maternity*, p. 5.

26 Women's Cooperative Guild, *Maternity*, p. 23; for examples of women going without food to save for confinement see pp. 18, 58, 133.

27 Reeves, *Round About a Pound*, pp. 155, 157.

28 Peter Stearns, "Working Class Women in Britain, 1890-1914," in *Suffer and Be Still: Women in the Victorian Age,* ed. Martha Vicinus (Bloomington, Indiana: Indiana University Press, 1972), p. 116.

29 For example, Eleanor Rathbone, *Report on the Results of a Special Inquiry into the Conditions of Labour at the Liverpool Docks* (Liverpool: Liverpol Economic and Statistical Society, 1903), p. 54, or H.A. Mess, *Casual Labour at the Docks* (London: G. Bell and Sons, 1916), p. 43.

[30] Lady Florence Bell, *At the Works: A Study of a Manufacturing Town* (London: Edward Arnold, 1907), p. 78, reported that in over one-third of the houses she investigated the women did not know what their husband's wages were. See also Davies, *Life in an English Village*, p. 101 and A. L. Bowley and A.R. Burnett-Hurst, *Livelihood and Poverty: A Study in the Economic Conditions of Working-Class Households in Northampton, Warrington, Stanley and Reading* (London: Ratan Tata Foundation, 1915), p. 66; for the division between housekeeping and pocket money see Ernest Phelps-Brown, *The Growth of British Industrial Relations* (London: Macmillan, 1965), p. 21.

[31] Young, "The Distribution of Income Within the Family," p. 309.

[32] Phelps-Brown, *Growth*, p. 21. He assumed an average of the equivalent of 1½ adult male wageearners who earned a total of 45s. for a full week's work in each family.

[33] The budgets were taken from Booth, Rowntree and Kendall, Rowntree, Bell, Kowley and Burnett-Hurst, Reeves, Davies, and Enquiry by the Lord Mayor into the Unemployed Question in Liverpool, *Full Report of the Evidence Before the Commission* (Liverpool: n.p., 1894). E. Phelps-Brown thought that agricultural laborers earning 12-14s. a week kept as little as 6d., *Growth*, p. 21. Rowntree and Kendall show a minimum for agricultural laborers of enough pocket money to cover one or two ounces of tobacco a week, *How the Labourer Lives*, p. 185.

[34] For example, see Reeves, *Round About a Pound*, p. 9; Rowntree and Kendall, *How the Labourer Lives*, p. 87; Booth, *Life and Labour*, Poverty Series, vol. 1, p. 144.

[35] Reeves, *Round About a Pound*, pp. 114, 122; Charles Booth, *Life and Labour in London* (London: Macmillan, 1904), "Notes on Social Influences and Conclusion," p. 87; Booth, *Life and Labour*, Poverty Series, vol. 1, p. 145.

[36] Reeves, *Round About a Pound*, pp. 9, 75, 87.

[37] Davies, *Life in an English Village*, p. 102; for examples of paying for necessities out of pocket meney see pp. 210, 214, 235, or Rowntree and Kendall, *How the Labourer Lives*, pp. 87, 179, 190.

[38] Bell, *At the Works*, p. 80. For townmen paying for necessities see Reeves, *Round About a Pound*, pp. 124, 147, 174.

[39] Booth, *Life and Labour*, Poverty Series, vol. 1, p. 146; Reeves, *Round About a Pound*, p. 109.

[40] Davies, *Life in an Enblish Village*, p. 214.

[41] For example, Reeves, *Round About a Pound*, p. 9; Bell, *At the Works*, p. 79; Rowntree and Kendall, *How the Labourer Lives*, p. 75; C. Violet Butler, *Social Conditions in Oxford* (London: Sidgwick and Jackson, 1912), p. 220.

[42] Joseph Rowntree and Arthur Sherwell, *The Temperance Problem and Social Reform* (New York: Hanson, 1900), p. 12; Booth, *Life and Labour*, Notes, p. 70.

[43] For example, Bell, *At the Works*, pp. 244, 247 and Butler, *Social Conditions*, p. 220.

[44] Rowntree and Sherwell, *The Temperance Problem*, p. 20.

[45] Burnett, *Plenty and Want*, p. 199.

[46] Rowntree, *Poverty*, p. 176.

[47] Brian Harrison, *Drink and the Victorians: The Temperance Question in England 1815-1872* (Pittsburgh: University of Pittsburgh Press, 1971), pp. 46-47.

[48] Rowntree and Sherwell, *The Temperance Problem*, p. 6; See also n.a., *The Heart of the Empire* (London: T. Fisher Unwin, 1902), p. 27.

[49] Bentley B. Gilbert, *The Evolution of National Insurance in Great Britain* (London: Joseph 1966), p. 312; See p. 304 and Phelps-Brown, *Growth*, p. 36 for description of the medical facilities available.

[50] Davies, *Life in an English Village*, pp. 250, 254.

[51] Almost Lindsey, *Socialized Medicine in England and Wales, The National Health Service, 1948-1961* (Chapel Hill: University of North Carolina Press, 1962), p. 473.

[52] See Women's Cooperative Guild, *Maternity*, for discussion of inadequate care and p. 194 for its results; for examples of waiting to call medical aid, see pp. 36-37, 39.

[53] Ruth Hodgkinson, *The Origins of the National Health Service: The Medical Services of the New Poor Law 1834-1871* (Berkeley: University of California Press, 1967).

[54] Hodgkinson, *Origins*, pp. 3134.

[55] Stearns, "Working Class Women in Britain, 1890-1914," p. 102; Richard M. Titmuss, *Essays on the 'Welfare State'* (London: Unwin University Books, 1963), pp. 94-95.

[56] Women's Cooperative Guild, *Maternity*, p. 89.

[57] For example in Reeves, *Round About a Pound*, p. 192; Pinchbeck, *Women Workers*, p. 280; and Margaret Hewitt, *Wives and Mothers in Victorian Industry* (London: Rockliff, 1958), p. 67.

[58] Booth, *Life and Labour*, Notes, p. 86.

[59] William J. Braithwaite, *Lloyd George's Ambulance Wagon* (London: Metheun, 1957), p. 55.

[60] See Gilbert, *Evolution*, pp. 434-435 and Bentley B. Gilbert, *British Social Policy 1914-1939* (Ithaca: Cornell University Press, 1970), p. 299.

61 Richard Hoggart, *The Uses of Literacy* (New York: Oxford University Press, 1970), p. 41; see also, p. 112.

62 Pilgrim Trust, *Men Without Work* (Cambridge: The University Press, 1938), p. 139.

63 Margery Spring-Rice, *Working Class Wives: Their Health and Conditions* (Harmondsworth, Middlesex: Penguin, 1939), for example, pp. 57, 189. See also Lucile A. Shaw, "Impressions of Family Life in a London Suburb," *Sociological Review* 2 (July 1954): 181.

64 Norman Dennis, Fernando Henriques, and Clifford Slaughter, *Coal is Our Life: An Analysis of a Yorkshire Mining Community* (London: Eyre and Spottiswoode, 1956), p. 243.

65 Charles Madge, *War-Time Pattern of Saving and Spending* (National Institute of Economic and Social Research, Occasional Papers iv) (Cambridge: Cambridge University Press), 1943.

66 Madge, *War-Time Pattern,*, p. 53.

67 Ferdynand Zweig, *Women's Life and Labour* (London: Victor Gollancz, 1949), p. 49.

68 Zweig, *Men in the Pits* (London: Victor Gollancz, 1949) and Dennis *et al., Coal;* for Rhys Davies, see *Parliamentary Debates, (Hansard) Official Report* (London: H.M. Stationary Office, 1945) 1944-1945, vol. 408, col., 2354.

69 Hoggart, *Uses,* p. 49; Young, "The Distribution of Income Within the Family," p. 307 citing B.S. Rowntree, *Poverty and Progress* (London: Longmans, 1921).

70 Zweig, *Women's Life,* p. 51; see also Madge, *War-Time Pattern,* p. 54 and Zweig, *Labour, Life and Poverty* (London: Victor Gollancz, 1949), p. 14.

71 Young, "The Distribution of Income Within the Family," pp. 311-312. See Madge, *War-Time Pattern,* pp. 59-60.

72 See Dennis *et al., Coal,* p. 138 or Zweig, *Labour, Life and Poverty,* p. 14.

73 See Dennis *et al., Coal,* p. 191 or Zweig, *Men in the Pits,* p. 96. See Young, "The Distribution of Income Within the Family," p. 313.

74 Zweig, *Women's Life,* p. 51. See also Zweig, *Men in the Pits,* p. 96.

75 Young, "The Distribution of Income Within the Family," p. 317.

76 Madge, *War-Time Pattern,* p. 2. He found the proportion was 25 per cent in Glasgow, but only 16 per cent in Leeds, p. 53. Other sources show approximately one-third of income kept, Zweig, *Women's Life,* p. 50; Shaw, "Impressions of Family Life in a London Suburb," p. 181; and Zweig, *Labour, Life and Poverty,* p. 14.

77 *Parliamentary Debates,* cols. 2283, 2275, 2282, 2322, 2337.

78 Young, "The Distribution of Income Within the Family," pp. 317-319.

79 N.a., *Last Year's Unemployed* (London: Charity Organisation Society, 1906), p. 6.

80 Bermondsey Distress Committee, "Report for 1905-1906" (Bermondsey, London: 1905-1906), p. 6.

81 Central (Unemployed) Body, "Minutes of the Working Colonies Committee," (London: n.d.) vol. 2, p. 84.

82 Bell, *At the Works,* p. 78.

83 Reeves, *Round About a Pound,* p. 17. See also Hoggart, *Uses,* p. 48; Madelaine Kerr, *The People of Ship Street* (London: Routledge & Kegan Paul, 1958), p. 48; Women's Cooperative Guild, *Maternity,* p. 18. Madge, *War-Time Pattern,* found evidence of "revolt against the whole system" in Glasgow, p. 54. For other examples of twentieth century complaints or resistance see Norman Dennis *et al., Coal,* p. 211 and Geoffrey Gorer, *Exploring English Character* (London: Cresset Press, 1955), p. 132.

84 Helen Dendy Bosanquet, *The Family* (London: Macmillan, 1906), p. 223.

85 The editors of *Maternity* were struck by their correspondants' consciousness of the subordinate position of women. Without economic independence they found themselves in the power of their husbands, Women's Cooperative Guild, *Maternity,* pp. 7-8.

86 Reeves, *Round About a Pound,* p. 156. See also Rowntree, *Poverty,* p. 169; Rowntree and Kendall, *How the Labourer Lives,* p. 309; Spring-Rice, *Working-Class Wives,* p. 106; and Women's Cooperative Guild, *Maternity,* p. 20.

87 Rowntree and Kendall, *How the Labourer Lives,* p. 75.

88 Stearns, "Working Class Women in Britain, 1890-1914," p. 106. For examples of concealment see Reeves, *Round About a Pound,* p. 172 and Women's Cooperative Guild, *Maternity,* pp. 151, 159.

89 Rowntree and Kendall, *How the Labourer Lives* p. 312.

90 Cited in Young, "The Distribution of Income Within the Family," p. 314.

91 Poplar Board of Guardians, "Minutes of the Farms Visiting Committee" (Poplar: June 9, 1905), vol. 1, pp. 38-39.

92 Hoggart, *Uses,* p. 50. London women said that a man would feel like his wife's slave if she took all his money, Zweig, *Women's Life,* p. 48.

93 Stearns, "Working Class Women in Britain, 1890-1914," p. 116.

94 Zweig, *Women's Life,* p. 51.
95 Norman Dennis *et al., Coal,* p. 191.
96 Madge, *War-Time Pattern,* p. 73.
97 Reeves, *Round About a Pound,* pp. 152-153.
98 Norman Dennis *et al., Coal* p. 189.
99 Even by B. S. Rowntree's low standards, *Poverty,* pp. 166-167.
100 Married women also served as an industrial reserve in the family. The wives of casually employed laborers, for instance, often went to work only when their husbands were idle.

A CASE STUDY OF TECHNOLOGICAL AND SOCIAL CHANGE: THE WASHING MACHINE AND THE WORKING WIFE

Ruth Schwartz Cowan

The family does not have as many functions as once it did—or so conventional historical wisdom tells us. Before the industrial revolution, the family was the focus of production. Households were large because many hands were needed to do the work. They were also self-sufficient, or more or less so; producing and processing almost everything that was needed for their own support. Children were socialized at home and by their parents; the world they were socialized into was the world encompassed by their own four walls. Tensions were managed at home, authority was found at home, protection was sought at home, and charity began at home. On top of all this, if the family produced for the marketplace, the goods it produced were all produced at home and by joint effort of the members of the household.

With the advent of the industrial revolution all this has changed. The family is no longer the focus of production. Households are smaller, and so are the nuclear families that form their core. Hands are no longer needed to do the work; there is no work to be done; food, clothing and shelter are produced and almost completely procesed outside the home; consumption is the only function that remains intact, and that function is expanding continuously to fill the vacuum created by the disappearance of all the others. Children are socialized in schools and by teachers; the world they are socialized into is bounded not by the four walls of their homes, but by the limits of our galaxy. Tensions are managed by psychiatrists; authority is found in Washington or on television; protection is provided by governments; and charity begins with Aid for Dependent Children and the United Fund. The household no longer produces for the marketplace; goods are produced by factories and not by families. Consequently, the economic tie that once bound so tightly, the mutual financial dependency that once kept so many husbands, wives and children at home, has come undone; divorce rates go up; children leave home earlier and marry earlier; women go out to work; and the authority of the husband diminishes accordingly. The family, like the Marxist state, seems doomed to wither and die.[1]

Such is the conventional wisdom. There may indeed be much truth here: who can deny, for example, that the number of children per family has decreased, or that more children spend more years in school than they used to, or that the forms of production have changed radically, or that the rural household is no longer the norm, or that husbands and fathers no longer have the authority, by law and by custom, that they once had over their wives and children? Surely no one can question these conclusions, reached after generations of painstaking historical, sociological and economic research. But there are certain corollaries of this conventional wisdom, particularly certain assumptions about what has happened to the "distaff side" of these vestigial families, which need to be examined carefully, especially in the light of the "new consciousness"—the sense that women have today that so much of what they have been taught to believe about themselves and about their history is merely myth, a fantasy created by scholarship done by generations of men.

We tend to assume, for example, that as the functions performed by families have shrunk or disappeared, the functions performed by women—adult women—within these families have similarly diminished. If the family is not producing, either for the marketplace or for its own consumption, and if there are fewer children to be borne and raised and if those few children are educated outside the home, then there must be less for women to do. Furthermore, if one result of the new technology has been the accessibility of labor-saving devices in the home, then what is left for women to do must take less time and less effort than it once did. The net result of these convergent trends—the loss of family function and the introduction of machine technology—is the liberation of women from their homes. Wives and mothers can enter the labor force because their homes and families demand less of their time and energy.

Coincidentally (or perhaps not so coincidentally) at just the moment when women were freed to enter the labor force, the labor force was prepared to accept them; this was the result of the same two convergent trends. When production moved out of the household and into the factory, jobs were created outside the home. The steady growth of machine technology meant that some of those jobs could just as well be performed by delicate, nimble women as by strong, brawny men. In fact women may have fitted better into the burgeoning capitalistic industrial system than men because their labor was cheaper; cheap labor was just what the economic system needed. The labor market was not only prepared to accept women, it positively demanded them, and this demand helped to stimulate the supply.

Furthermore, as the capitalistic industrial system expanded, more and more jobs were created in the service sector of the economy, just the sort of jobs that could be filled by middle-class women without loss of social status. The typewriter and the telephone made it possible for women to find gainful employment outside their homes without a conflict of roles. The typist and the telephone operator were performing service functions for the primary producers, just as they had been in their homes. Their skills could be developed and utilized without extensive training and investment, making it possible for them to enter and leave the labor force at will, to return to their homes whenever the occasion or the situation demanded that they do so.

Thus the growth of machine technology liberated women in four separate ways: by causing the shift from household to factory production, by making factory work easier, by creating labor-saving devices for the home, and by developing machines (and concomitant social roles) that permitted middle-class women to adapt themselves to the labor market, and thereby to become more independent. Small wonder then that according to conventional wisdom, technology has been the principal cause of all the gains that women have made in the past 150 years. If women have acquired economic and political rights that they never had before they can thank the industrial revolution (a revolution made by men) for granting them. If women have been liberated by those rights, if now they are able to chart their own courses to fulfillment as separate individuals, they can do so only by the grace of the washing machine, the supermarket delivery system, the textile mill and the typewriter.

If the "new consciousness" has taught us nothing else, it has taught us to look this particular gift-horse squarely in the mouth and to recognize the grace of the new technology as a dubious grace at best. The washing machine, the supermarket delivery system, the textile mill and the typewriter may have been the source, not of liberation, but of another bondage, a bondage somewhat subtler but no less strong, than that of rural women in days of yore. If the washing machine made household laundry simpler, it may also have made it more demanding by raising standards of cleanliness; at the turn of the century very few farmers expected to have a clean suit of underwear every day. If the supermarket delivery system means that a wider variety of foods are available, highly processed and ready to be consumed with very little time spent in cooking, it also means endless hours spent parading up and down the aisles and standing in the lines, packing up the cars and unpacking them at home. If the textile mill put cash in the pockets of young New England females, it also may have made them doubly grateful for any suitor who promised an acceptable way out of the mills, cash in their pockets or not. And if the typewriter drew millions of women into the labor force, it also helped to confirm their vision of themselves as subservient, replaceable and relatively passive workers.

Thus the growth of machine technology may well have been a double-edged sword for women. We do not know for certain—very few of the hypotheses that I have just mentioned have been subjected to careful scrutiny. Having assumed, in accordance with conventional historical wisdom, that the washing machine freed women from an onerous chore, no one has bothered to ask whether the chore itself may not have been changed profoundly by the machine. By the same token, we have not asked who was doing the washing, thereby neglecting the possibility that the washing machine may have transferred the responsibility of laundering from a paid employee (the laundress) to the housewife, thus increasing the demands upon her time. Similarly, we do not know whether the time spent in buying all the food required for a household is not as much or more than the time that was once spent in more extensive food preparation. The textile mill, the typewriter and any number of other innovations that appear on the surface to have benefitted women may, in reality, have simply changed the terms of their bondage.

Accepting the possibility that advanced technology may not be a total blessing for women, we are in a position to scrutinize some of the conventional assumptions. Starting from the top and working down: Is it really true that the functions performed by adult women have diminished as the functions performed by families have disappeared? It is, after all, equally possible that the few functions that are left to the family, particularly the chores attached to consumption, were formerly shared by many members of the household but have now almost completely devolved upon the adult women, thereby increasing, not diminishing, their tasks. It is also possible that from the point of view of a woman's *time,* the functions have not disappeared at all; the suburban mother does not have to teach her children to read and to write, to spin and to sew, but she does have to drive them back and forth to all the schools, extra-curricular classes, lessons and social engagements that modern socialization requires, which may be just as time-consuming and less personally rewarding. It is also possible that as the functions performed by families have shrunk, social expectations about a woman's role have actually increased—that women are now expected to keep their families better clothed, better housed, better fed and better adjusted—and that these increased expectations have placed new demands on a woman's time by increasing the number of functions that she is expected to perform—from nutritionist, to comparison shopper, to electrical repairwoman, to semi-professional psychiatrist. Once again, we do not know whether any of these hypotheses are true, but we do have certain pieces of information that suggest that the conventional postulates are wrong. A time study of rural and urban housewives in 1930 revealed almost no difference in hours spent on housework (61.0 hours on the farm, 63.2 hours in towns and cities) but the distribution of time was quite different: farm women spent more time on meal preparation than their city cousins (44.3 hours compared to 37.6 hours) but city women devoted more hours to the care of family members than farm women did (12.5 hours compared to 7.3). [2] Two decades later, in 1947, the comparison had changed profoundly; farm women still reported that they spent about 60 hours per week on household chores (60.55, to be exact) but women in cities under 100,000 population reported a total of 78.35 hours, and women in larger cities were logging in an astounding 80.57.[3] If the conventional wisdom is sound, the results of these two surveys should have been quite different; farm women should have spent more time on chores in 1930 (presumably, their homes were less modernized than city homes) and there should have been an overall decrease in hours spent in housework by 1947 (as electrical appliances were, by that time, quite widespread). These odd results confirmed a study of rural housewives in the 1920s which revealed that those without electrification spent only 2 percent more of their time on household chores than women whose homes were electrified and who had the benefit of many labor-saving devices.[4] Clearly something is wrong with the conventional wisdom, but as yet we do not have enough information to know precisely what it is.

Even if we were to discover that the three surveys cited above are wrong and that, on this point, the conventional wisdom is valid—that is that modern technology has in fact resulted in substantial time-saving at home—it would not necessarily follow that married women rushed into the labor force as a result of the time saved. In all the literature on women's labor-force participation (and it is substantial) I am aware of only two attempts to correlate the advent of labor-saving devices in the home with the flight of married women into the labor market, and both attempts are, by the authors' own estimation, failures. Clarence D. Long, a labor economist, tried various techniques to estimate the saving in household labor since the turn of the century and found that he was unable to do so with any degree of reliability.[5] Valerie Kincade Oppenheimer, a sociologist, tried to correlate the rise in the number of household appliances over time with the rise in married women's labor force participation over time and found an interval of at least twenty years between the two trends.[6] As Long put it,

> In combination, developments in "technology for the home" could have released a substantial amount of female labor for gainful employment. However, there was only the crudest information as to their extent or the ultimate effect of the saving in labor, which would just as likely have gone to a higher standard of housekeeping or more leisure for the housewife as into the labor force.[7]

Thus the information that we have available to us at present does not indicate that the conventional wisdom is wrong, nor does it indicate that it is right. My own research suggests that Long's guess is correct, that—at least initially—housewives used labor-saving devices to raise their standard of household care, thereby maintaining or even increasing the burden of their chores. The editors of the *Ladies' home Journal* summarized the early ideology of household technology quite succinctly in an editorial in 1928:

> The fact is that the American home was never a more satisfying place than it is today. Science and invention have outfitted it with a great range of conveniences and comforts. . . . For the first time in the world's history it is possible for a nation's women in general to have or to be able to look forward to having homes and the means of furnishing them in keeping with their instinctive longings. The women of America are to be congratulated, not only in the opportunity, but because of the manner in which they are responding to it. When the record is finally written this may stand as their greatest contribution.[8]

If Long's guess (and mine) is true, then Oppenheimer's twenty-year gap becomes understandable: two generations of American women used their electrical appliances to create more "satisfying" homes, and it was only in the third generation that women began to suspect that the satisfaction was a ruse. More research will be needed to prove whether this hypothesis, or any other (including the conventional one), is correct.

More research will also be needed to verify several other facets of the conventional picture. While it is doubtless true that no particular physical strength was required to fill most of the occupational slots created by the industrial revolution, is it also true that this led to a greater demand for female labor, or that this demand existed because female labor was cheaper, or that it stimulated the supply of women who were willing and able to enter the work force? Long, for example, has concluded that, "There is no convincing evidence that the higher female participation rate in some areas results from greater employment opportunities—at least as measured by unemployment of males."[9] Furthermore it seems clear that if women do replace men in particular industries or in particular occupational slots, they do so for only very short periods of time, either at the very earliest stages of industrialization in that industry or when the men are away at war.[10] We do not see women on the assembly lines in Detroit or in the cutting rooms on Seventh Avenue, and this leads us to suppose that men and women in the labor force are not quite as interchangeable as the conventional model suggests. Jobs are sex-typed, and this creates two separate labor markets, one for men and one for women, and any model of the relationship between technology and social change that does not take this fact into account is bound to need revising.[11]

Finally, though it is true that married women have been entering the labor force in greater and greater numbers, and that the vast majority of these women have entered in the service occupations, is it also true that the fact of their employment outside the home necessarily leads to independence from the authority of their husbands and the demands of their children? Since women enter the work force in jobs in which they are subservient, passive and often temporary employees, it is difficult to see how their work could encourage a spirit of independence. Since the vast majority of these women also insist that they work primarily to supplement their husbands' wages and to provide a better standard of living for their families, they can hardly be said to have emancipated themselves from the familial context.[12] Time studies that compared the daily schedules of married French women who worked with those who did not revealed, when the results were standardized for social class, these significant differences: the women who did not work got more sleep and spent more time in home entertainment and leisure; they also did more sewing and mending. Otherwise the time expenditures for both groups were almost identical, hardly an indication that entrance into the labor force signals release from familial obligations, at least in France.[13]

Thus it is evident that in certain crucial respects we do not fully understand the impact of technology on women; conversely, we know even less about the impact of women on technological growth, but that is another matter. We have been blinded, in part, by the dictates of conventional wisdom; we do not understand the impact of technological growth on women simply because we once thought we did understand it, and failed to ask what now appear to be relatively obvious questions. The study that I am undertaking, and of which this article is a preliminary report, is designed to ask just those kinds of questions—particularly the questions that deal with the growth of household technology (as the questions that deal with industrial technology would require a separate study, to answer).

When did various labor-saving devices come on the market and to whom were they designed to appeal? Is there a cause-and-effect relationship between the diffusion of those devices and the disappearance of domestic servants? If so, which is cause and which effect? Did the appliances actually result in time-saving, or did they lead rather swiftly to drastic changes in standards? Is there a cause-and-effect relationship between the growth of household technology and various indicators of social change—entrance into the labor force, divorce rates, birth rates, etc.? If there is, again, which is cause and which effect?

As the methodological problems involved in such an inquiry are enormous, it seemed best to begin by framing a tentative hypothesis and devising ways to test it. In order to frame that hypothesis, it also seemed best to isolate a population, as the relationship between the household technology and social change is bound to be different for different social classes. Partly because of the availability of primary source materials, and partly because they are an important population, I chose middle-class women, the sort of women who entered the labor force in white-collar work, who had enough income to be able to afford either domestic servants or household appliances, and enough education to enter professional or semi-professional careers, if they had wished to or been able to. One type of source material that is particularly useful in providing information about these women is the "ladies" magazine—the journals that have been specifically directed to this audience and concerned with its needs.

My preliminary reading of these journals, primarily *The Ladies' Home Journal* (1886 to present), has led me to frame the following working hypothesis: The initial effect of the diffusion of household technology among middle-class women was to raise standards of household care and to transfer several functions that had previously been performed outside the home or by paid employees to the purview of the housewife. Concurrently, time-priorities changed for housewives; whatever time they saved—let us say in cooking—they were expected to transfer to other tasks, primarily child care. Consequently there appears to be no immediate relationship between the growth of household technology and the indicator of social change with which it is ordinarily thought to be associated—that is, the entrance of married women into the labor force.

The truth or falsity of this hypothesis can be demonstrated in various ways, all of which will be used in this study, as I am convinced that there is no single method that is uniquely useful in research of this kind. Statistical indicators of technological growth (homes electrified, numbers of homes with various appliances, cost of appliances) are available, as are similar indicators of social change; the problem of combining these data through the techniques of regression and correlation analysis is difficult, but not insoluble. Content analysis of articles in ladies' magazines, both fiction and non-fiction, can yield valuable information about changes in expectations, if there were any, and this information can be supplemented by the less precise but more traditional materials of social history, materials garnered from careful reading of sources for insights into patterns of change. Cookbooks, particularly successive editions of the same text, government publications for housewives and mothers, private diaries, etiquette manuals—these all contain materials that can be assessed quantitatively and qualitatively.

My hypothesis would be dismaying if it turns out to be true because it suggests that social change cannot be produced by technological innovation, or at least that such change cannot be produced quite as easily as we once assumed. Our thoughts about domestic and foreign planning have been predicated on this assumption for many years; if you want to curb poverty in India, introduce modern agriculture and birth control; if you want to teach underprivileged children how to manage in the modern world, bring television sets and reading machines and computerized teaching into their classrooms. Perhaps these programs have failed precisely because we placed so much faith in technology, in which case it is well for us to learn the source of our error. On the other hand, once having learned the source of our error we must face the fact that social planning and social reorganization will be much more difficult than we had assumed, that, for example (and to use an example that is pointedly close to home) the relationship between the sexes is not likely to be transformed simply by the introduction of a male contraceptive or a bigger and better vacuum cleaner.

NOTES

[1] W. F. Ogburn and M. F. Nimkoff, *Technology and the Changing Family* (Cambridge, Massachusetts: Houghton Mifflin, 1955) presents a classic and more detailed statement of the conventional wisdom epitomized here. For another example see Viola Klein, *Britain's Married Women Workers* (London: Routledge & Kegan Paul, 1965), Ch. 1, "Industrialization and the Changing Role of Women."

[2] Hazel Kryk, *Economic Problems of the Family* (New York: Harper & Row, 1933), p. 51. These are the results of a survey of 288 farm and 154 town and city families in Oregon. A similar study of 559 farm and 155 town and city families in a number of states gave almost identical results.

[3] Ethel Goldwater, "Women's Place," *Commentary,* 4 (December, 1947), pp. 578-585.

[4] Ogburn and Nimkoff, *Technology,* p. 152.

[5] Clarence D. Long, *The Labor Force Under Changing Income and Employment* (Princeton, New Jersey: Princeton University Press, 1958), pp. 120-123.

[6] Valerie Kincade Oppenheimer, *The Female Labor Force in the United States,* Institute of International Studies, Population Monograph Series, No. 5 (Berkeley: University of California Press, 1970), pp. 29-39.

[7] Long, *Labor Force,* p. 10.

[8] "Homebuilders," *Ladies' Home Journal* (February 1928), 32.

[9] Long, *Labor Force,* p. 8.

[10] See for example Neil J. Smelser, *Social Change in the Industrial Revolution: An Application of Theory to the British Cotton Industry* (Chicago: University of Chicago Press, 1959). Smelser shows

that the number of women in the cotton mills increased between 1820 and 1850 but then fell off as economic conditions eased for the families of operatives.

11 Oppenheimer, *Female Labor Force,* pp. 64-140.

12 See for example Lois W. Hoffman, "The Decision to Work," in *The Employed Mother in America,* eds. F. Ivan Nye and Lois W. Hoffman (Chicago: Rand McNally, 1963), pp. 18-39; and Klein, *Britain's Married Women Workers,* pp. 34-47.

13 Alain Girard, "Working Hours and Time Schedules: The Time Budget of Married Women in Urban Centers (France)," in *Employment of Women,* International Seminars 1968, No. 2 (Paris: OECD, 1970), pp. 185-214.

NOTES ON CONTRIBUTORS

Lois W. Banner is Assistant Professor of History at Douglass College, Rutgers University. Her recent publications include: "On Writing Women's History," *Journal of Interdisciplinary History* 2 (Autumn 1971); "Religion and Reform in the Early Republic: The Role of Youth," *American Quarterly* 23 (December 1971); and "Religious Benevolence as Social Control: A Critique of an Interpretation," *Journal of American History* 60 (June 1973). Her book, *Women in Modern America, 1890-1974* is to be published by Harcourt, Brace, Jovanovich in 1974.

Patricia Branca, Assistant Professor of History at the University of Cincinnati, is co-author (with Peter N. Stearns) of *New Roles and Old: The Impact of Modernization on Women* (Forum Press 1973), and "Saints and Sinners Again: Victorian Sexual Attitudes," in *Becoming Visible: Women in European History,* eds. Renate Bridenthal and Claudia Koontz (Houghton Mifflin 1974).

Ruth Schwartz Cowan is Assistant Professor of History at the State University of New York at Stony Brook. She is completing a study of the impact of technology on social change, particularly with regard to domestic technology.

Elizabeth Fee is an instructor in the history of science at SUNY / Binghamton, where she has been involved in initiating a women's studies program. She is presently completing a dissertation on "Science and Feminism in England, 1860-1900."

Dee Garrison is a member of the history department of Livingston College, Rutgers University.

Linda Gordon is a member of the History Department at the University of Massachusetts, Boston. She is currently completing a study of the birth control movement in America, and is compiling an anthology on the subject of women's work in America to be published in the fall of 1974.

Mary S. Hartman, Assistant Professor of Douglass College, Rutgers University, teaches modern European history. She has published articles in the *Journal of Modern History* and *Victorian Studies,* and is currently completing a study of middle-class women and crime in nineteenth-century France and England.

Jo Ann McNamara is an Assistant Professor of History at Hunter College of the City University of New York. She is the author of *Gilles Aycelin: The Servant of Two Masters* (Syracuse University Press, 1973), and is presently at work with Suzanne Wemple on a study on Carolingian women.

Regina Markell Morantz has taught at Queens College and C. W. Post College. She is currently at work on a book on pioneer female physicians.

Laura Oren, Assistant Professor of History, University of Rochester, is currently completing a dissertation on "Attitudes and Policies Toward the Casually Employed in England, 1889-1914."

Catherine Bodard Silver, an Assistant Professor of Sociology at Brooklyn College, is the author of *Black Teachers in Urban Schools* (Praeger 1973), and is currently completing a study of Frederic LePlay.

Daniel Scott Smith is Assistant Professor of History at the University of Connecticut, on leave for the 1973-1974 academic year as Visiting Research Fellow at the Office of Population Research, Princeton University. His publications include, "The Demographic History of Colonial New England," *Journal of Economic History* 32 (March 1972), and "Cyclical, Secular, and Structural Change in American Elite Composition," *Perspectives in American History* 4 (1970).

Carroll Smith-Rosenberg is Assistant Professor in the Departments of History and Psychiatry, University of Pennsylvania. She is presently working on a book concerning women's role change and social stress in nineteenth-century America and on a study of gender role socialization in America, 1785-1895. Her recent publications include "The Hysterical Woman: Sex Roles and Role Conflict in Nineteenth-Century America," *Social Research* 39 (1972), and "Beauty, the Beast and the Militant Woman: Sex Roles and Social Stress in Jacksonian America," *American Quarterly* 22 (1971).

Daniel J. Walkowitz is an Assistant Professor of History at University College, Rutgers University. He is editor (with Peter N. Stearns) of a book of essays on workers in the industrial revolution, published by Transaction Press, 1973. He is completing a book on class, culture, and working-class life in mid-nineteenth-century America.

Judith R. Walkowitz, is an instructor in history at University College, Rutgers University. She is currently completing her dissertation on prostitution, social control, and the Contagious Diseases Acts.

Barbara Welter is Associate Professor and director of the graduate program in history at Hunter College, CUNY. She is the author of numerous articles, including "The Cult of True Womanhood: 1820-1860," *American Quarterly* 18 (Summer 1966), and the editor of *The Woman Question in American History* (Dryden Press 1973). Her textbook on women's historical role in the United States is to be published next year, and a film on the history of American feminism, for which she did the research and dialogue, will be released shortly.

Suzanne Wemple is an Associate Professor of History at Barnard College. Her study, *Atto of Vercelli: Church, State, and Society in Tenth-Century Italy,* is to be published later this year. She is presently at work with Jo Ann McNamara on a study of Carolingian women.

Ann Douglas Wood is Assistant Professor of English at Princeton, where she teaches a course on Women in America, 1820-1920. She has written extensively on nineteenth-century social and cultural history, and is now completing a book on sexual and religious changes in nineteenth-century America, *The Sentimental Sabotage*.